The Workforce Investment Act

MW00492005

The Workforce Investment Act

Implementation Experiences and Evaluation Findings

Douglas J. Besharov
Phoebe H. Cottingham
Editors

2011

W.E. Upjohn Institute for Employment Research
Kalamazoo, Michigan

Library of Congress Cataloging-in-Publication Data

The Workforce Investment Act : implementation experiences and evaluation findings / Douglas J. Besharov, Phoebe H. Cottingham, editors.
p. cm.
Includes bibliographical references and index.
ISBN-13: 978-0-88099-370-8 (pbk. : alk. paper)
ISBN-10: 0-88099-370-7 (pbk. : alk. paper)
ISBN-13: 978-0-88099-371-5 (hardcover : alk. paper)
ISBN-10: 0-88099-371-5 (hardcover : alk. paper)
1. Occupational training—Government policy—United States. 2. Occupational training—Government policy—United States—Evaluation. 3. Occupational training—Law and legislation—United States. 4. Employees—Training of—Law and legislation—United States. 5. Vocational guidance—Law and legislation—United States. 6. United States. Workforce Investment Act of 1998. I. Besharov, Douglas J. II. Cottingham, Phoebe H.

HD5715.2.W666 2011
370.1130973—dc22

2011010981

Cover design by Alcorn Publication Design.
Index prepared by Diane Worden.
Printed in the United States of America.
Printed on recycled paper.

Contents

List of Abbreviations

ACF	Administration for Children and Families
ADARE	Administrative Data Research and Evaluation
AEFLA	Adult Education and Family Literacy Act
AFDC	Aid to Families with Dependent Children
ALMP	Active labor market program
APPAM	Association for Public Policy and Management
AR	Autoregressive
ATE	Average treatment effect
CAA	Career advancement account
CBTI	Community-based training initiative
CETA	Comprehensive Employment and Training Act
CPS	Current Population Survey
CRC	Consumer report card
DHHS	Department of Health and Human Services
EDWAA	Economic Dislocation and Worker Adjustment Assistance
ESF	European Social Fund
ETA	Employment and Training Administration
ETPL	Eligible training provider list
FERPA	Family Educational Rights and Privacy Act
FETPIP	Florida Education and Training Placement Information Program
FNS	Food and Nutrition Service
FSET	Food Stamp Employment and Training Program
FSP	Food Stamp Program
FY	Fiscal year
GAO	Government Accountability Office
GPRA	Government Performance Results Act
HGTI	High growth training initiative
HPB	High performance bonus
IES	Institute of Education Sciences
IT	Intent to treat
ITA	Individual training account
JSA	Job search assistance
JTPA	Job Training Partnership Act

LATE	Local average treatment effect
LMI	Labor market information
MDTA	Manpower Development and Training Act
MTE	Marginal treatment effect
NDNH	National Directory of New Hires
NFJP	National Farmworker Jobs Program
NJS	National JTPA Study
OIG	Office of the Inspector General
OMB	Office of Management and Budget
PRA	Personal reemployment account
PRWORA	Personal Responsibility and Work Opportunity Reconciliation Act
PY	Program year
SCHIP	State Children's Health Insurance Program
SCSEP	Senior Community Service Employment Program
SDA	Service delivery area
SED	Sectoral Employment Demonstration
SEI	Sectoral Employment Initiative
SIPP	Survey of Income and Program Participation
SNAP	Supplemental Nutrition Assistance Program
SSP	Separate State Program
SWA	State workforce agency
TAA	Trade Adjustment Assistance
TANF	Temporary Assistance for Needy Families
TT	Treatment on the treated
USDOL	U.S. Department of Labor
VR	Vocational rehabilitation
WASC	Work Advancement and Support Center
WIA	Workforce Investment Act
WIB	Workforce Investment Board
WIN	Work Incentive Program
WIRED	Workforce Innovation in Regional Economic Development
WPRS	Worker Profiling Reemployment Services
WRIS	Wage record interchange system
YEDPA	Youth Employment Demonstration Program

Acknowledgments

Many people worked on this volume, and it is not possible to mention them all here. A few, however, deserve special thanks.

Ines Hartwig, Dirk Reyntjens, and their colleagues at the European Commission's Directorate-General for Employment, Social Affairs, and Inclusion, first suggested the project and provided funding to bring paper authors and other expert discussants together. They also asked the authors probing questions and gave them incisive comments that helped shape the final papers that are published in this volume.

Phoebe H. Cottingham, formerly commissioner of the National Center for Education Evaluation and Regional Assistance, within the U.S. Department of Education's Institute of Education Sciences (IES), helped structure and organize the entire project. She helped select the authors, guided them through the process of writing and rewriting their papers, and then brought all their good work together in this volume. In short, her broad knowledge, wisdom, and enthusiasm infuse this volume.

Patrick Tiedemann of the University of Maryland's Center for International Policy Exchanges organized the Washington, D.C., conference at which first drafts of the papers in this volume were presented, and assisted in their finalization for this volume. Teyanna Munyan ably assumed his responsibilities when she joined the staff.

Finally, but most important, this volume is the product of the joint efforts of more than 30 individuals. Each of them cooperated in shaping their individual contributions so that the end result would be one interconnected whole.

1
Introduction

Phoebe H. Cottingham
U.S. Department of Education (retired)

Douglas J. Besharov
University of Maryland School of Public Policy

Over a decade ago, Congress initiated a major shift in federal work-force policy through the Workforce Investment Act (WIA) of 1998. WIA aimed to consolidate and modernize disparate workforce programs, and to assure that job seekers and employers benefited from a more open and effective utilization of federal funds. No single study has examined all aspects of the act. There are many studies of its program features, as well as efforts to estimate the economic outcomes for those receiving WIA services.

This volume examines WIA's objectives and the evidence on program performance and impact. The chapters originally were commissioned for a meeting held with staff of the European Commission for a discussion of WIA lessons and the implications for future workforce programming in the United States as well as Europe.[1] The chapters are organized into five general areas:

1) understanding WIA,

2) program implementation,

3) performance management,

4) impact evaluations, and

5) future evaluation choices.

The 2009 congressional appropriation for WIA was over $15.9 billion, including $3.3 billion for three WIA employment and training programs that replaced prior Job Training Partnership Act (JTPA) programs.[2] WIA funds are allocated to states based on five-year plans. States are responsible for using the funds for services operated under local entities. The European Social Fund of the European Commission (EC) allocates approximately $70 billion across seven-year cycles (roughly equivalent to the annual WIA appropriation) to EC member states for workforce services, of which occupational training is a major component.

The chapters in this volume focus exclusively on the U.S. experience, framed to help the European Commission staff in its deliberations on workforce programming to understand how the WIA performance management systems function, as well as the role of evaluations assessing workforce programs.

UNDERSTANDING WIA

WIA's main purpose, as set forth in the 1998 legislation, was broad: "*to consolidate, coordinate, and improve employment, training, literacy, and vocational rehabilitation programs in the United States.*" Indeed, WIA introduced extensive changes in the nation's publicly funded workforce programming. As summarized by Dianne Blank, Laura Heald, and Cynthia Fagnoni in Chapter 2, "An Overview of WIA," public workforce programs had become "fragmented"—an "uncoordinated patchwork of programs and agencies" suffering from "inefficiency, duplication of effort, and confusion for the job seeker."

The solution in the 1998 WIA legislation, Blank, Heald, and Fagnoni note, was to decrease the previous focus on income eligibility as the only basis for accessing services (as well as the focus on job training as the primary means for getting a job) and increase the focus on assessment and marketing existing skills. These changes placed more emphasis on personal responsibility, self-service, and consumer awareness in choosing options. The consolidation of services was to take place locally, through a new system of WIA One-Stop centers, guided by state and local entities to assure service coordination and customer access as required by WIA.

Whether WIA indeed produced the efficient streamlining of funds into open access systems as intended is a question that Blank, Heald, and Fagnoni believe is not fully answered. There are 25 reports by the U.S. Government Accountability Office (GAO) over the decade responding to questions raised by members of Congress about WIA (see Chapter 2). (*Editor's note: The Government Accountability Office changed its name from the General Accounting Office in 2004. For readers' ease and consistency, we use the current name in the text and references throughout the book.*)

By being made available at the local level through one entry point—the One-Stop centers—the 16 different federal programs (see Table 2.1) would no longer require potential applicants to go to different offices to apply for services. For fiscal year 2009, Congress appropriated over $15.9 billion for the 16 mandatory programs, including $3.3 billion for three new WIA programs (Adults, Dislocated Workers, and Youth) replacing prior JTPA programs.[3] The federal program offices were expected to work with the U.S. Department of Labor (USDOL), as the department was given overall responsibility for administering the provisions of WIA.[4]

WIA also initiated major changes in how funding for training services is distributed, by mandating that training funds be sent through individual training accounts (ITAs) to the training providers chosen by the WIA participants eligible for training services. Under JTPA and the Comprehensive Employment and Training Act (CETA), training funds went directly from the governmental entity at the state or local level for training service contracts with providers who were also responsible for recruiting trainees, typically from other local agencies. A second change under WIA required a process for establishing eligibility of WIA training providers. The training providers who are to receive ITA funds for training services to WIA participants need an established track record of positive outcomes that meet or exceed each state's performance criteria. WIA required states to establish eligible training provider lists (ETPLs) of providers and approved training course offerings that have met and continue to meet the state's performance criteria.

Blank, Heald, and Fagnoni point out that in 2001, the GAO found the requirements on training providers to be overly burdensome because so few people were referred under WIA. Subsequently, the USDOL began to provide waivers of the ETPL requirements, and 40 states obtained such waivers (see Chapter 6 for more on ETPLs).

In terms of governance, WIA required state governors to set up a state Workforce Investment Board (WIB) to oversee WIA implementation at state and local levels, with local WIBs organized to oversee the One-Stop center operations. Governors decide how many members will serve on the WIBs, and they are required to assure that a private sector representative is named to chair each board, and that those representatives make up the majority of board members. Blank, Heald, and Fagnoni report that WIBs average 40–60 members, and that in 2007 there were 1,850 One-Stop centers, under the jurisdiction of a WIB (a regional WIB can be given several centers in its jurisdiction).

A key question in many GAO reports on WIA is whether the new performance management was being established. GAO reports repeatedly urge the USDOL to move more quickly to establish the requirements in clear, unambiguous terms. In particular, WIA mandated that the USDOL establish performance measures on five outcomes to be used by all states, and that the USDOL negotiate with each state on their minimal performance levels for each measure. (States may add measures or set higher levels for particular jurisdictions.) Central in the WIA performance system is the congressional requirement that states use Unemployment Insurance (UI) records for three of the five WIA performance measures—job placement, retention, earnings—with other sources for measuring skill attainment and customer satisfaction.[5]

The early years of WIA showed how challenging it was for states to develop new performance systems based on the UI records. Blank, Heald, and Fagnoni note that overall, the use of UI records for timely analysis and reporting at the operations level in WIA has proved less successful than hoped for time-sensitive management functions. In response, the USDOL has allowed states to use "supplemental data" to fill gaps in the UI wage records and collect job placement outcome information from sources other than UI records, or the "supplemental data sources." In 2004, over 75 percent of local areas reported that "they directly follow up with participants after they leave the program . . . to help fill gaps until the data are available from the UI wage records." In some cases the supplemental data are viewed as interim indicators to manage WIA programs or predict WIA performance outcomes. Blank, Heald, and Fagnoni believe the GAO recommendation to allow continued use of supplemental data is sensible.

Ultimately, WIA did advance the linking of WIA and UI record systems to record the placement and earnings results, but states, USDOL, and researchers use these files more for monitoring overall progress. The USDOL operates a nationwide, computerized WIA Standardized

Record Data (WIASRD) system for states to input data on aggregated counts or averages, based on what states collect from the One-Stop centers, providers, and employers.

The central and more difficult part of the performance management challenge emanating from WIA was the required establishment of definitions of participant status to be used across the state-run WIA system to measure performance at the local and state levels. In 2005, the U.S. Office of Management and Budget called for common measures—the harmonization of performance measures across a larger swath of federal workforce and training assistance programs managed not only by the USDOL but other federal agencies, according to Blank, Heald, and Fagnoni. In general, progress was slow, although USDOL eventually made advances to improve the accuracy of performance data and settle performance measures, beginning in 2005.[6]

The WIA performance management system was further complicated by Congress asking that the performance goals be set through negotiations between individual states and the USDOL. Blank, Heald, and Fagnoni summarize the criticism of negotiation without a standardized and uniform procedure for establishing what are reasonable performance goals. Also, many expressed concerns that without adjustment procedures, the system discourages One-Stop centers from providing services to those who appear less likely to get and keep a job. Most recently the USDOL has used a regression model to set national performance goals, based on data on job seekers in local labor markets, using the WIA database and other data.[7] Another concern the authors describe is that only a small proportion of job seekers who receive services at One-Stops are actually reflected in WIA outcome data. In the 2004 GAO study, only about 5 percent of job seekers who walked into a One-Stop center were registered for WIA and tracked for outcomes. The self-service customers, those seeking information on their own, are actually the largest group served under WIA. Blank, Heald, and Fagnoni point out that the GAO has recommended that the USDOL consider ways for states to track all job seekers coming into One-Stop services, but this presents problems when self-served customer results are combined with other WIA customers who obtain more intensive services, especially training.

Blank, Heald, and Fagnoni conclude that there still is not a uniform national practice for tracking registrants in WIA, undermining accuracy of performance data and the ability to compare states equitably. They also note the inherent tensions between local entities, state entities, and the federal government.

PROGRAM IMPLEMENTATION

Many of the WIA issues noted by Blank, Heald, and Fagnoni are explored in depth in other contributions to this volume. All draw on federal studies of WIA's implementation, especially during the first half of the 2000–2009 decade, when attention focused heavily on the new role of One-Stop centers, the performance management system, and what features appeared to be more successfully implemented than others.

In Chapter 3, "The Use of Market Mechanisms," Christopher T. King and Burt S. Barnow summarize the early implementation challenges in eight states in 2003–2005. They draw conclusions similar to those of Blank, Heald, and Fagnoni concerning the central importance of a potentially stronger performance management system in WIA than existed under JTPA. Under JTPA, the federal government did not attempt to set performance standards at all, leaving it to local service delivery areas (SDAs) to set their own performance standards with approval by the lead state office. Under WIA, the top level of the performance management structure is now at the federal–state level, after the startup phase when states had less performance system direction from the federal level.

King and Barnow conclude that there was considerable tension associated with the implementation of the new WIA performance management system. Having local and state layers of government adjust to operating with a set of standards derived from a higher level brought resistance from some at the local level. The focus was on state WIA leaders first "negotiating" standards with federal officials and then translating them to local areas, often with differing rules according to state policy. The principal complaint about this approach centers on states having to apply the negotiated state performance standards for all One-Stop centers within their state. King and Barnow find that in the eight states studied, there was considerable variation across the states in their performance standards under WIA. Both state and local staff disliked WIA performance measures and standards, believing JTPA performance management worked better. According to King and Barnow, performance standards are seen as arbitrary numeric goals, with no allowance or adjustments for serving more distressed areas (as many claimed the JTPA adjustment allowances provided).

Another concern arising during the transition from JTPA to WIA was who collected the data to measure program outcomes and how accessible it was for program operators. JTPA performance measures of program outcomes relied on job placement reporting by providers who would conduct their own follow-up contacts with program participants. WIA deliberately sought to shift the reporting responsibility to state entities, requiring the utilization of Unemployment Insurance administrative records to document who was employed. The plan was that state entities first collect participant information from One-Stop center providers and then match the individual participant records with reports submitted by employers to the state Unemployment Insurance office.

King and Barnow describe the extent to which this intended change in who collected outcome data brought extensive deliberations and contentions over how program entry and exit status would be defined in the WIA performance management systems. One-Stop center operators understood that who counts as a WIA participant would form the base count for establishing their performance record for judging how many of the WIA participants succeeded in finding jobs. Naturally, program operators want to include as WIA participants those most likely to succeed in finding jobs, and exclude those who are likely to fail in achieving the outcome. After considerable negotiation at the federal level, it was finally agreed to exclude job seekers who do not utilize the core WIA services, focusing on those using the second and third service tiers, called "intensive" and "training." This shifted attention to defining what were core services. Similar disputes arose over defining when a WIA participant has exited WIA, and thus is countable as a successful job placement or not.

In response, the USDOL established a reporting system to be used by states and One-Stop centers, containing a standardized set of definitions, extensive documentation, and technical explanations. More recently, the USDOL commissioned work on how to introduce adjustments to performance standards to take account of state and local economic conditions and job seeker characteristics (see Chapter 9).

Another key change in workforce programming under WIA was the requirement that there be universal access at entry to the One-Stop centers, meaning no barriers on entry to core services of the job search and information assistance. Users of One-Stop centers do not have to pass eligibility requirements that in the past limited core services to low-income persons or the long-term unemployed. This was a major change from most of the JTPA job training programs that had requirements to keep training just for the economically disadvantaged or long-term unemployed.[8]

Some believe that disadvantaged populations have had less access to job training under WIA than under JTPA because of the open access and no low-income eligibility requirement. In their state case studies conducted during the early phase of WIA, King and Barnow find tension over spreading WIA funds in a way that may not be for those who would gain the most, the disadvantaged. Studies looking at very large samples of WIA participants in training do not necessarily support the presumption that disadvantaged populations have lost out on access to training through WIA due to open access policies. (See Chapter 13 for a summary of an extensive study of WIA participants.) It appears that disadvantaged populations are the beneficiaries of WIA adult training and the youth programs. While the total number of disadvantaged people in WIA training may be less than was true under JTPA, the most recent study, across 12 states, finds that adults in WIA training are, on average, disadvantaged in prior earnings, employment, and education. Dislocated workers receiving WIA services, as was true during the JTPA decade, overall have less disadvantaged backgrounds, and reflect the general population in terms of education, work experience, and prior earnings.

Another major change under WIA is the funneling of job training funds through ITAs, essentially vouchers tied to the job seeker, not job training providers. States and localities have some flexibility in setting the dollar value of ITAs, and within a One-Stop center can tailor the value to fit with individual customer choices. The main purpose of ITAs is to provide job seekers who need and/or want training with many choices among eligible providers and training courses, rather than be limited to just a few training options or slots determined by contracts with a few providers to provide training for groups of job seekers.

King and Barnow find that ITAs have been well received and appear to be working because there is flexibility in ITA values, as determined by states and localities. They report that in most centers, policies allowed ITAs to be adjusted by center staff based on the job seeker's needs.

During the JTPA and CETA program years, many focused on the seemingly ineffective job preparation programs for the disadvantaged. In Chapter 4, "Customized Training," David A. Long explains why traditional job training was unpopular with many employers, noting the trade-off that companies see between retraining their own employees for new skills needed in the business versus finding new employees trained by others, especially training paid for by government as a way to reduce unemployment or help the disadvantaged. Long explores why customized training may be more effective than the training focused exclusively on raising general skills of the unemployed or disadvantaged, typically for jobs at the lower end of the job market. As the economy changed, traditional job training became disconnected from job-specific skills needed by employers in high-growth, new markets. Long defines customized training as "the provision of particular employee skills needed by specific firms in their current and new workers."

Customized training is done outside the firm, by intermediaries who take on the role of recruiting and screening applicants for customized training when partner employers are looking to hire new skilled workers, which Long notes also allows programs to give priority to low-income and disadvantaged groups. He believes customized training should also be distinguished from "off the shelf" training provided by vocational education. Customized training is responsive to the needs of specific local employers in filling particular skilled work positions, with a commitment by the employer to employ some or all successful completers of the training (or continue employing incumbent workers) and share the costs of the training.

Long also examines research on incumbent worker training, that is, in-house training of employees by employers. Several nonexperimental studies used large 1990s data sets to look for a difference between the productivity (wage growth, performance ratings, and career advancement) of employees who reported receiving in-house training provided by employers and the productivity of employees who did not have the training. The three studies produced varying estimates of the average rate of return (from 17 to 50 percent) to the firms from in-house training, but it is not clear how well these studies controlled for selection biases.

Long recalls early efforts under WIA and by private foundations to fund demonstration projects or partnerships that engaged business and training entities to align WIA-sponsored job training with private sector employers, with a focus on sector training. He summarizes why the idea of customized training is even more popular under WIA, and reports on a recent study that rigorously examines customized training impacts in three sites in a foundation-supported project. He says that participants earned 18 percent (about $4,500) more than controls during two years from baseline during the 2004–2008 period (Maguire et al. 2009). The three sites were located in urban areas with trainees who appeared little different from WIA training program entrants and therefore may be relevant for WIA efforts to develop customized training.

Studies limited to a few sites where a particularly impressive program has been established, while useful to learning if something quite unusual actually is making the differences claimed, need further testing through replication. This is where the news can go sour, as rigorous replication studies often fail to find the same effects as in the original program site where strong vision and commitment may produce a charged-up staff with specific synergy with customers and businesses. Some believe original sites may have built fortuitous partnerships with particular employers that are most difficult to replicate in new sites. Long recalls how the USDOL replication study of the San Jose CET (customized) model training program, which was very successful in the 1990s, could not find similar net impacts. Where moderate impacts appeared, they were in replication sites that seemed to have more "faithfully implemented" the original training program. This indicates how difficult it is to turn highly promising, even effective training programs into large-scale franchises or regular program practice. Similar problems are present in education, where rarely if ever have successful particular program models been "scaled up" into major service systems that reproduce effects anywhere near those found in an original small-scale study. Moreover, the costs are great to introduce change by extensive scaling up, as opposed to testing changes in practice within the existing system where the change may be more doable, or more gradual expansion of a program started in one site.

Looking to the future of customized training, Long notes that there are several issues. One is the matter of curriculum, and how to know that customized training meets the needs of both employer and potential worker. He cautions that some customized training initiatives tend to build from past training curriculums, which presents problems if new business sectors are being targeted or when new skills are needed. Another issue is the effort that training providers or intermediaries have to put forth to prescreen potential trainees to make good career matches, as well as provide ongoing support.

Input from the private sector and active engagement is an important WIA objective. The WIBs are considered the key entity that brings in private sector perspectives to One-Stop centers. There are also state WIBs, whose key responsibility is advising on the state's performance standards and the policies governing eligible provider lists. The WIBs are supposed to bring input in from employers, business groups, and other stakeholders on policies and operational plans for local One-Stop centers as well as the state. Reports are spotty and generally are not very convincing that WIBs have brought the strong private sector engagement intended. Some conclude that the WIBs have too many stakeholders, and that many of them are conflicted or compromised by WIB member associations with WIA, either as major training providers or contractors to WIA.

David Heaney considers the role of the private sector in managing One-Stop centers in Chapter 5, "One-Stop Management and the Private Sector." He notes that WIA intended private sector engagement to be welcomed in operating the centers, not just on the WIBs. WIA placed "a high premium on employer-driven strategies and integrated service delivery through colocating key providers under one roof . . . to effectively leverage the strengths of [a] diverse set of partner organizations operating side by side." Business and employers should determine the content of programs for preparing the workforce.

Heaney offers a critical perspective, however, on whether the private sector is engaged in WIA. He believes that active participation of the private sector has been stymied in One-Stop center operations. He argues that the history so far has been progressively less employer-business input as WIA implementation progressed. Heaney notes that at first those serving as One-Stop center operators included a healthy distribution across private for-profit, nonprofit, and public sector managers. Over time, the procurement process appears to have narrowed the distribution, with far fewer for-profits or business entities. In fact, fewer entities now compete for the One-Stop center operating contracts.

Without more effective private employer input, Heaney is concerned that job seeker selections made through customer choice may be out of sync with the realities of the existing market, or a true employer-driven service delivery system. Training providers do not necessarily adapt effectively to market realities. Heaney urges consideration of policies that would attract a greater number and more diverse set of qualified bidders from all sectors for One-Stop center management, including allowing risk/reward tolerance levels in the pricing and design of contracts. He believes operators should have flexibility to refine and change practices much as takes place in typical company staffing operations, rather than be restricted to overly prescriptive practices that have unknown effectiveness (for example, caps on administration costs and profits discourage private sector involvement in WIA).

Heaney agrees with the widespread criticism of WIB representation requirements that seem to burden these important advisory groups with too many interested parties and decrease WIB effectiveness. He sees a parallel burden or inefficiency in One-Stop centers because center staff attempt to handle too many interested agencies and customer calls. He favors giving center managers more authority to make decisions on performance, quality, and corrective actions. He also urges that more evaluation should be done, however, before attempting to change the performance management system.

The overarching watchword of the WIA system is accountability: accountability for results but also assuring that data is fully used so those involved in the WIA system know what is going on, and how the various responsible parties are performing. In addition to the new performance management system established at the federal-state level, information that helps the clients and staff in the system make wise choices is essential. WIA managers also are accountable for how the public funds are spent on training opportunities, to assure that the most effective training opportunities are identified and funding goes to the effective trainers. This requires management review of performance records of training providers, and designation, based on performance standards, of who is eligible to receive WIA training funds through the ITAs. Public access to the performance records is an essential part of an accountability system to assure that providers of training services make available performance records so customers can see the potential payoff in a job and earnings by previous trainees.

In Chapter 6, "Eligible Training Provider Lists and Consumer Report Cards," Carl E. Van Horn and Aaron Fichtner report on their study of four states' progress in developing performance records and publicly available information. They find evidence that the new accountability system requirements under WIA for the provision of training services have been implemented to some degree, thereby demonstrating that accountability systems that meet the 1998 WIA vision are possible. Therefore, they point out, what is most important is not the more limited training that some find being funded under WIA—it is the WIA requirement that states set up new workforce systems for deciding who needs, receives, and provides training. Those eligible for training are required to have the opportunity to review and select from lists of training courses rather than be assigned to a training course by program administrators. The lists of training courses and providers appear on the state lists of eligible training providers—those who have verifiable records of results based on previous trainees that have been deemed by states as meeting state performance standards. The information is translated into state consumer report systems to disseminate the performance training outcomes for each provider and program, so that ITA holders and others can view the training options meeting the standards.

As Van Horn and Fichtner point out, under JTPA, training services were typically procured directly by local government agencies that selected the occupational concentrations and the service providers. Basically, an annual plan would select providers who would offer what was thought to be suitable occupational training for local populations. The government administrators would procure set numbers of training slots to be filled during the year, and then use up the slots by various entity referrals. This system could not assure that those who would benefit most got training, or that the training provided was necessarily effective in helping the job seeker secure a new job. It was convenient for government administrators, but likely led to waste or inappropriate or ineffective training purchases. Job seekers were simply placed in particular training slots because the slots were already committed under the contract. Some believed that better outcomes were possible if job seekers were provided much better information on the labor market in general, on the occupations (and their requirements) most likely to be in demand, and to have some understanding of the employment results that others had achieved by taking a particular provider and occupational training track.

Van Horn and Richtner conclude that the UI records as mandated by WIA are being used to varying degrees to build statewide listings of eligible training providers and customer report cards that give summaries of provider performance records. The delayed availability of UI records noted by others has not prevented the creation and updating of eligible training provider lists in some states.

Based on their research conducting interviews in four states during 2009, Van Horn and Richtner find progress in recent years. In the four states, there are provider lists and performance measures called for under WIA that have surprisingly deep repositories of in-depth information. In the four states examined—Florida, New Jersey, Texas, and Washington State—these efforts actually began before WIA and were funded by the USDOL as part of their pilot initiatives prior to WIA. It took years of work to reach the data accumulation now available. All states now have online performance reporting systems in use, which is an achievement. These efforts required pulling together data from the state entities managing WIA, UI, and education and training organizations, and calculating average performance levels. The information also encourages the training institutions to provide explicit details on the particular training or career certification courses available and the placement results obtained by their course takers.

For New Jersey, as an example, Van Horn and Fichtner report that the online eligible training provider list contains more than 600 education and training providers, offering more than 3,000 training programs. Performance data are not yet available on all courses, as only one-third of the provider files contain performance averages that are outputted to consumer report cards on every course and/or provider. The report cards have to be based on WIA-supported students, and for some courses there are too few WIA course takers to produce an average (in these cases the placement information is averaged across all courses sponsored by a training provider).

It is important to note that, in contrast to much earlier reports by others finding inability or ineffectual use of UI records by states, state capability has grown and the picture may be different. At least in the four states reported on by Van Horn and Fichtner, and relying on their recent interviews, all now have state-run, fully developed ETPL systems with consumer report card systems, and all utilize UI records to calculate outcomes.

Van Horn and Fichtner also report that the ITA system has stimulated the large providers, such as postsecondary education institutions, to help WIA trainees secure other public funding sources for which they may be eligible, thereby adding to the ITA funding. It is quite likely that training choices are influenced not only by the ITA voucher value, but the potential to tap other sources of support for trainees that training institutions can provide.

PERFORMANCE MEASUREMENT

Accountability for using public funds to achieve the public objectives is widely expected. In workforce programming, being able to assure accountability by measuring performance appears to be a straightforward process, because the end result, a job and increased earnings, should be easily measured. Under WIA, establishing the benchmarks for measuring performance, with allowance for state negotiation to reflect economic conditions, brought two advances over the past: 1) a common set of definitions was established, permitting national assessment of overall achievements and comparisons of state and local assessments; and 2) full computerization of administrative records allowed more timely reporting of results.

In Chapter 7, "The Challenges of Measuring Performance," William S. Borden recommends establishing standardized definitions before a program is initiated to assure comparability across geographical and function units. Borden looks at WIA performance measurement issues as a case example of the complexities inherent in creating, maintaining, and using performance systems for management. He speaks from his experience in helping government agencies design and implement performance management and data validation systems, not only for WIA but other programs in the USDOL and the Department of Health and Human Services. These performance systems are clearly necessary, says Borden, because "tracking and measuring customer flow, services, and outcomes is inherently desirable and even necessary to managing any modern organization. Therefore, the question is not whether we should track customer flow and services and measure performance, but whether and how we should use the data to determine funding, incentives, and sanctions."

Many mistakenly believe performance can be monitored through relatively simple systems that capture seemingly obvious goals and processes. Alas, as Borden notes, there are "challenges that are little known except to the state and federal staff managing the performance systems, and that are often not clearly understood. There is very little that is easy and straightforward about measuring program performances. Seemingly simple concepts . . . are actually very complex . . ." The many conceptual and operational issues raise significant questions about motivation, state–federal political power sharing, and the management of government programs.

Borden makes clear that he agrees with others who believe that program evaluation and performance management derive from different sources and motives and that keeping them as separate functions is warranted. WIA, he notes, "has shown that it is difficult to measure performance well, and that using inaccurate performance data to drive policy and incentives leads to misallocated resources." Administrative data are needed to accomplish both functions: to understand and monitor program operations, and to carry rigorous evaluations using randomization of applicants.

Standardized definitions, according to Borden, are critical and must be established before developing system software and validation checks that provide information essential for program managers to keep on top of the complex systems. In short, definitions must be agreed to by those engaged in various levels of operations, enforceable, and support consistency checks so essential for building the performance system. Arriving at standardized definitions challenges programs with shared governance structures. Those working within the structures develop stakeholder interests, and are typically more concerned about meeting their goals than improving their results. Consequently, Borden notes, they tend to have "somewhat exaggerated reaction to the burdens imposed by performance systems." He points out that in WIA, a diverse system, "forces of fragmentation and inconsistent data are so great that only a very strong and standardized performance management system can overcome or at least neutralize" the stakeholder pressures. Despite the progress made in WIA in developing measurement definitions and performance systems, there remain the inherent tendencies by some program operators to resist any seemingly externally determined system that may challenge their perceptions of performance. Borden suggests a number of ways to get "buy in" from program operators to a system. It is very important, he says, to focus initially on building strong data capacity through effective performance management tools and methods rather than on the punitive aspects of performance management.

Borden sees wide variation among states, grantees, and local program operators in their level of sophistication and case management data they collect. Many, he says, collect far more detailed performance data than anything imposed by the USDOL. Federal efforts should focus on the key data validation component, to raise every state and grantee to a minimum acceptable level of data management and data reliability.

On the issue of the impact of performance management on customer selection, Borden finds a conundrum because barriers to success tend to be subjective and unreliable, and consequently very difficult to measure. He suggests that computing performance separately for different classes of customers based on barriers still provides the clearest information to program operators. If performance is adjusted after the fact using regression models, results should be similar. The problem with using negotiation under WIA to obtain flexibility and avoid the complexity of regression-based adjustments is the overall absence of systematic and consistent performance goals across states.

An effective management system does have costs to establish, but there are also considerable costs to allowing states to administer their own programs and make their own rules—no usable national data can come from this type of devolution. In the case of WIA, where Congress tried to confront an overall system that was highly fragmented and turn it into the One-Stop system, with seamless access for the customer, there are obvious challenges to building a successful reporting process. For example, there are still fragmented funding streams coming into the One-Stops, with requirements for data collection and reporting to many programs and agencies with varying and even conflicting definitions of customer characteristics. The challenge is to acknowledge that specialized programs may be more effective in serving difficult populations, but there is still a need for reliable and consistent data across all the states and local areas to improve the entire performance process.

Even more important, if program operators see performance as a game, not a management tool, they are tempted to manipulate reporting their outcomes. Borden reviews the ways outcomes are distorted in WIA, such as who is actually enrolled and how services are defined, and of course manipulating exit dates. He concludes with this summary: "Do not attempt to measure something you cannot define or validate, and make sure the calculations are reliable and well tested."

Borden's main concern, echoed in other chapters as well, is that the accuracy of management system data is likely to be compromised if the performance data is used for funding decisions, and for assigning financial rewards or sanctions or incentives in general.[9] Incentives encourage program staff to pick those considered most likely to succeed and recruit them for services ("creaming"), a selection bias at odds with the program goal to get the most net benefit for costs. Distorted data provide inaccurate counts. Borden believes most data systems simply do not have the accuracy required for discerning true performance differences. He recommends that performance management systems be kept out of incentive systems, and operate as they are intended: to assist managers in watching how their systems are operating.

A similar view to Borden's is presented by Burt S. Barnow in Chapter 8, "Lessons from the WIA Performance Measures." Barnow appraises the role of performance management measures as contrasted with measures from impact evaluations. He notes that evaluators see performance management as a kind of offshoot of their process or implementation studies. "Process studies document what happened while the program is implemented, impact evaluations assess what difference in outcome measures was due to the intervention, and cost-benefit analyses assess whether the benefits of a program exceed the costs." Barnow believes the key differences between performance management and evaluation activities are "matters of depth of analysis and causality." Performance management relies on "easy to collect data on inputs, activities, and outputs." Functions important to impact evaluations are not included and would be too expensive and even irrelevant in any event within a performance measurement system. This includes evaluation functions such as tracking long-term outcomes, and of course establishing and tracking a control group created out of the applicant pool.

Hence, performance management systems typically utilize some judgment about what a program should or could accomplish in job placements and earnings of participants—the program performance standards. These judgments at the local level are inferred from the placement and/or earnings of the last cycle of participants, or averaged performance records for what seem to be similar programs and participants. These performance judgments can be reasonable or unreasonable, but they are not impact evaluations.

Another purpose of performance management systems is to establish a feedback process that gives signals back to those who are responsible—accountable—for obtaining results, and that applies rewards and sanctions on work units or individuals involved. Government performance management systems typically build on the bureaucratic system, or the bureaucratic process pipeline, as the production process in a program. Systems establish measures of what should be accomplished at various points in the pipeline, such as success rates in recruiting customers, proportion eligible for services who were offered them, response patterns of customers, retaining customers for the desired time period, and status at exit. Evaluations, however, view such pipeline checkpoints as implementation variables whose purpose is to describe what the program looks like. Evaluators direct their attention primarily on whether program completers or exiters succeeded in some externally determined outcome (e.g., a job) relative to what they might have accomplished without the program.

Barnow concludes there are three central issues in the debate over performance management and evaluation in the workforce area:

1) Does performance management influence, indeed negatively distort, the service system itself in ways not intended by the program designers? Barnow believes there is evidence of too much distortion, and it is negative rather than positive.

2) Does attaching incentive systems to performance systems bring the results intended? Barnow believes there should not be large rewards and/or sanctions, as there is not evidence that these have markedly changed management practices, consistent with conclusions in Wandner and Wiseman, as well as in Borden.

3) Can adjustments reduce distortions created by the performance management system? Barnow favors adjustments more for im-

parting "fairness" and psychologically reducing the tendencies to distort measures or game the system than for overall effectiveness, but cites no particular studies on the question.

Theories or explanations are plentiful regarding why one should expect that performance management systems can and do distort the behavior of agencies subject to the performance measures. Program operators, Barnow notes, respond to performance management systems by spending resources "trying to look good rather than doing good." This includes modifying the timing of entry and/or exit, or "more pernicious effects, as when programs engage in 'cream skimming' and serve those less in need to receive better performance scores."

Studies find that such service changes are identifiable as direct responses to the performance management system rather than responses to the clients. Barnow reviews the reasons why this happens, why managers display "selection biases" in choosing or helping the customers. He notes that studies comparing the characteristics of WIA enrollees versus JTPA enrollees find that WIA enrollees shifted upward toward individuals with few barriers to employment. WIA also had reduced levels of enrollment, and researchers concluded that selective registration was the reason.

Barnow further points out that studies comparing estimates of short- and long-term program impacts obtained in rigorous evaluations with the measured outcomes on the same program units as captured in the performance management system clearly show there is very little relationship between the two. Either the correlations are nonexistent or very weak. Thus, Barnow concludes that performance management system results are by design short term, and do not capture very strongly program impacts.

Barnow also concludes that performance management systems should not deploy large rewards and/or sanctions, as these efforts are very weakly related—if at all—to program impacts and encourage data distortions. Program management, in short, is not nearly as important as sound evaluation in guiding overall policy directions, and has limited support as an assurance that a program is achieving the central objectives of the policymakers.

Given that performance management systems risk distortions in who is served away from program purposes, does adjusting performance standards reduce incentives to torque the program service and customer mix? Here there is another debate. Those who look at the wide differences between local populations and economic conditions confronting program managers argue that programs should not be penalized for performance outcomes in more difficult conditions. Thus, adjustments to performance standards are a reasonable approach to level the playing field. Those opposed to adjusting performance standards argue that setting lower expectations for some programs than others perpetuates inequities. Barnow approves of adjusting performance standards to take account of particular program goals, participant characteristics, and environmental conditions, and thus, to judge different programs in different circumstances appropriately.

Arguments in favor of adjustments to WIA performance standards regained momentum during the 2000–2009 decade. The GAO and others recommended that the USDOL develop procedures that could be used by states and localities for making adjustments for local economic conditions and client characteristics. Until such adjustments are implemented, it is difficult to say whether the gaming and resulting shifts in populations served are reduced when adjustments in performance standards are introduced.

A set of adjustment techniques for WIA developed by Randall W. Eberts is presented in Chapter 9, "Recent Advances in Performance Measurement." Eberts created the adjustment system for the USDOL, so his chapter is designed to help one understand what can be done in the WIA context, using the much richer data sources now available than under JTPA. Eberts's objective is to develop procedures that can be used to adjust state and local WIA performance targets for factors that affect performance outcomes but are outside the control of state and local administrators. The intent is to level the playing field by making the targets neutral with respect to the observed characteristics of WIA participants and of the local labor market conditions in which they seek employment.

As noted earlier, the lack of adjustments in setting performance outcomes has been a major complaint about WIA, especially since the predecessor program, JTPA, had allowed particular statistical adjustments (derived from regression estimates) to be employed by SDAs in setting their performance standards with the states. WIA, in contrast, called for performance outcomes or standards to be set through negotiated standards between federal and state offices, with no allowance for particular adjustments.

Eberts's techniques require two adjustment procedures to reach a general adjustment model: first, national performance targets are adjusted for changes in the unemployment rate using regression estimates, and second, state and local performance targets are adjusted for differences in local market conditions and personal characteristics of WIA participants. This results in adjusting each state's targets according to the extent a state's participant and local labor market characteristics differ from those at the national level.

The weights used to adjust the values are estimated by using data on outcomes of individual participants of workforce programs from the WIASRD rather than the aggregated local data used under JTPA adjustment formulas. Thus, this adjustment procedure for WIA relies on direct estimates of the effects of unemployment rates on performance measures for various programs at the local level using the data on individuals in the three programs within WIA: Adults, Dislocated Workers, and Youth. Further, the adjustment framework assures the targets for local workforce areas and state targets add up to the national target.

The tables in Chapter 9 provide the estimating models and results. They present the variation in unemployment rates at the local (county) level nationally from January 2000 to November 2008, as well as the estimated relationships between participant characteristics and the five WIA performance measures (entered employment, retention, average earnings, credential, and employment).

Eberts also demonstrates how the adjustments from the statistical model compare, for each state, with negotiated performance levels and actual performance levels, with a wider spread observed for the statistical model. The results using data from 2006 (Table 9.6) reveal that adjusting the performance standard for a state (e.g., percent entering employment) could increase the difference between actual performance levels and the adjusted performance standard versus the prior difference between the actual and the negotiated standard. These increases go in different directions. For some states, the procedure brings the adjusted standard closer to the actual; for other states, the adjusted standard moves even higher than the unadjusted (negotiated) standard. The impact may not be favorable for all states; some do better without the adjustment of their negotiated standard.

Even with adjustment procedures, a performance management system still has to incorporate how the results will be used. Will the results be linked to incentives or rewards in support of meeting or exceeding goals, as well as penalties of some kind? In Chapter 10, "Financial Performance Incentives," Stephen A. Wandner and Michael Wiseman review the use of incentive awards, called high performance bonuses (HPBs), in three major federal social programs: 1) WIA, 2) Temporary Assistance to Needy Families (TANF), and 3) Food Stamps. Overall, they urge caution on attempting to manage through incentives, finding that generally field operations operate with the immediacy of decision making on matters that are poorly reflected in performance measures and goals. In the three major federal social programs, Wandner and Wiseman find no evidence that incentive (or bonus) schemes in public sector social programming matter in the ultimate public policy outcome because there are counterfactuals that provide a comparison. Since all administrative units (e.g., states) are placed under the same HPB, there are no counterfactuals. The authors therefore deploy case study methods to draw conclusions.

Wandner and Wiseman describe the patterns of WIA HPB grants awarded from 1999 to 2004 (funding for these grants was dropped beginning in 2005). They point out that these HPB awards were based on the negotiated agreements between states and the regional offices of the USDOL that set performance levels to encourage state and local setting of performance levels that fit with local conditions. Wandner and Wiseman observe that federal negotiators had to measure and weigh local factors on their own without uniform methodology that assured equitable treatment among states and regions. They conclude that the patterns of HPBs vary widely by state and region. Overall, during the nine years of WIA incentive funds, five states received 31 awards, or 25 percent of all awards, and nine states received no awards. "The variation is so great," observe Wandner and Wiseman, "that it appears that USDOL has been, in part, rewarding behaviors that attempt to game the system . . ." and that "whole regions of states garner[ed] a significant number of awards." In addition, the WIA monetary incentives were very small, so one would not expect a strong relationship between WIA incentives and WIA programs. Indeed, state plans on intended uses of incentive grants show that states used the funds for new programs or increases in services rather than individuals involved in frontline service—there has been no incentive for staff to provide more effective services.

TANF provides another example, say Wandner and Wiseman, of "no evidence" that an HPB in a federal program affected state policy or program effectiveness. The size of TANF HPBs was small, averaging overall $200 million per year, or less than 1 percent of total outlays, they report. Also, in contrast to WIA, the program was voluntary for states (yet, most states participate in the competition), and capped at 5 percent of a state's TANF block grant.

Wandner and Wiseman offer several observations on the TANF experience with HPBs. Since the TANF HPB program was based on information not available to state- and local-level program managers, it could not provide any real feedback to program operators. Further, the Department of Health and Human Services did not link or publicize possible best practice lessons that might have been discernable among states winning the top awards. Wandner and Wiseman also note that, as with WIA, the TANF HPB system did not allow one to decipher what particular performance areas drove higher rewards (too many indicators were part of the process). While top state managers may have welcomed the public recognition of the bonus awards, they used the funds for special projects rather than individual staff recognition. The TANF HPB operated from 1998 through 2004, ceasing in 2005 in the TANF reauthorization.

The third case study on financial incentive results in federal programs focuses on the Supplemental Nutrition Assistance Program (SNAP), formerly called the Food Stamp Program, administered by the Food and Nutrition Service of the U.S. Department of Agriculture and operated locally by state governments or by county governments with state supervision. The HPB for SNAP, conclude Wandner and Wiseman, is better designed and operated, but the program's small size and universal availability make its impact difficult to assess.

Wandner and Wiseman point out that the HPB application to the Food Stamp Program operates in a different program environment. Most important, the SNAP benefit is delivered by electronic benefits transfer into a special credit card for recipients to use to purchase food, with eligibility determination monthly. While this federal program has much larger outlays ($37.7 billion in the 2008 fiscal year) than either TANF ($25 billion) or WIA ($16 billion), it is an entitlement and has clear eligibility rules. The policymaker issues tend to be assuring that those eligible are reached and that error rates are kept to some tolerable levels. The authors note how much attention went into quality control of the benefit errors prior to the 2002 initiation of performance measures and HPB payments, thereby clearly establishing the measures.

While the HPB awards paid out under SNAP are small ($48 million in 2008), Wandner and Wiseman find that nationally SNAP had increasing averages on performance measures. It is impossible to conclude that this would be due to the HPB, but it is consistent with the intended effect. Wandner and Wiseman believe that HPB may be working in SNAP to improve performance because the HPB is based on the direct connection with what is done and what should be monitored at the ground level. Not only is the HPB directly tied to local operations, it can be audited and has very good statistical inference, meaning the precision of the estimates is calculable, with confidence intervals around the point estimates. Finally, the Food and Nutrition Service has made efforts to link the HPB results with promising practices.

Wandner and Wiseman also report on other studies on performance pay within differing agency environments and conclude that the same finding is repeated in each study: agency staff react by selective reporting; frontline staff tend to cream skim. They also point to significant difficulties encountered by federal agencies in managing federal–state performance bonus systems. Wandner and Wiseman sum it up: "High-performance bonuses in government programs [are] an inefficient use of federal resources."

IMPACT EVALUATIONS

Impact evaluations of federal programs are now regularly mandated in Congressional authorizations and appropriations. In Chapter 11, "Ten Years of WIA Research," Paul T. Decker summarizes the most influential evaluation research on workforce programming, and relates it to the state of evaluation knowledge that has been available so far on WIA.

Decker first looks at findings from implementation studies of WIA during the early WIA years, through 2006. He examines whether the seven key principles of WIA were fulfilled. Overall, he finds that most implementation studies are in agreement on which WIA program principles seem to have worked relatively well, and which are more mixed. This reflects the particular new WIA operational features a study was designed to address. None of the implementation studies were able to look at what was going on across all the states; most were designed to look at WIA principles expected to produce problems in the early part of the decade within selected states.

For service coordination, a key change sought by Congress, Decker finds that it generally succeeded through local One-Stop service centers, but that there have been challenges, including the fact that WIA's mandatory partners have made only limited financial contributions, and that conflicting goals impede partnerships. Decker also cites the lack of common data systems. On prioritizing customer choice, Decker concludes that ". . . local workforce investment agencies have enthusiastically embraced customer choice by offering a wide range of core and intensive services and establishing ITAs to facilitate customer choice of training," but there are weaknesses due to incomplete cooperation by training providers in providing information to meet the ETPL requirements.

Decker notes that strong positive responses are apparent over the decade to the universal access principle of WIA, and he marks it as an area of great progress. However, tensions exist between core and intensive services for a wide range of customers with a smaller group getting the more extensive training. The emphasis on performance management as a driving force for effective service delivery is marked by mixed success. The 17 performance goals were too numerous and complex, the data used to measure performance were of uncertain reliability and received too late by agencies to use in managing the program, and local agencies tended to focus on managing the performance system to make the numbers. Decker finds that progress was made by the USDOL in 2005, in response to demands for common measures.

The WIA principle of close connections to and with the private sector is another area with mixed results. Decker points to the substantial local variation in how much state and local WIA agencies have connected with the private sector. WIA remains a public policy area with examples of success and examples of disappointment in connecting with the private sector. Decker says that while youth programs have been implemented, it is still challenging to find eligible providers, find and retain at-risk out-of-school youth, and establish WIA eligibility.

Setting the stage for considering WIA evaluations, Decker briefly recalls the results from large-scale evaluation studies of federal employment training programs prior to 1995. He believes that the national study of JTPA, the predecessor to WIA, was "a critical turning point in the creation of evidence." Not only did the study use random assignment of applicants to a treatment group offered JTPA services or to a control group denied access to JTPA, but by design the study sought to obtain a nationally representative study sample—a first for an experimental study in employment training program evaluations. The JTPA study found that overall, men and women obtained equivalent net benefits per enrollee. Subsequent longer-term follow-up analyses conducted by the GAO (using Social Security earnings records) looked at impacts five to six years later, finding sustained earnings gains among both men and women.

Decker summarizes as well two experiments testing dislocated worker interventions that were conducted during the JTPA period. These tests of changes in dislocated worker programming focused on similar populations but had different program conditions. The conclusions from both interventions were comparable and had considerable impact on policy. It was shown that by using job search assistance only treatments with dislocated workers, the workers speeded up in the timing of their reemployment and had increased earnings versus the dislocated workers who had no job search assistance offered or required. Although the impacts were short lived, the benefits outweighed the program costs, so taxpayer funds invested in this strategy had a payoff. Also, in both demonstrations, those that offered training on top of the job search assistance had no greater outcomes than those in the job-search-only group. The findings stimulated changes in state UI programs, specifically, the use of statistical recipient profiling to identify UI recipients likely to face long unemployment spells, and to direct UI recipients to mandatory reemployment services as a condition of continued benefit payments.

Further studies of mandatory job search assistance for profiled UI recipients in the 1990s confirmed the earlier findings from the Texas and New Jersey demonstrations. Decker notes: "In contrast to the substantial body of evidence on JSA's effects for dislocated workers, the effects of more intensive classroom training or of job training have not been fully tested for dislocated workers using an experimental design."

WIA replaced JTPA in 1998. The first USDOL experimental study of WIA impacts, now in field operations, is comparable to the JTPA study in design and focus, and uses a nationally representative sample design. Decker reports that the study uses random assignment of applicants to a group that has access to all WIA services that will be compared to one or more groups with limited or no access, again seeking a nationally representative sample. Decker explains that the only random assignment study of WIA prior to the new national study focused on a program implementaton issue that arose early in WIA's history. This was the question of how best to provide ITAs, the vehicle for funding training under WIA. Due to the changes made under WIA in how training opportunities were accessed, it was decided to determine if it mattered how WIA center staff offered the ITA vouchers. The study compared three alternative methods of administering ITAs: guided customer choice, structured customer choice, and maximum customer choice. Decker concludes that the ITA experiment "supports the widespread use of the 'guided choice' model by local agencies in the current [WIA] environment." The study is now in a long-term follow-up phase, tracking outcomes six to seven years.

Decker notes that a sequel to the ITA experiment—the personal reemployment account (PRA)— extends the training voucher question to the dislocated workers. It was designed to test vouchers offered to UI recipients as an alternative to participation in WIA. It took place in seven states in 2004. Findings echoed the ITA experiment reports. Finally, a third USDOL study on training vouchers began in 2006 and is ongoing. Career advancement accounts (CAAs) rigorously test how best to structure training vouchers, and test this new type of ITA by offering it to spouses of military personnel in 18 military installations in eight states.

These three studies—ITA, PRA, and CAA—are all rigorous, in-depth investigations of what happens if public sector funds are funneled through voucher programs under WIA into support for adults seeking training to find a new or better job. The results will undoubtedly be useful for the next decade, as the expansion of WIA as an entry point to not only jobs but education and training raises issues about the most cost-effective strategies to accelerate preparation for skill-specific needs in the economy and competitive positioning. Decker summarizes the findings from two nonexperimental studies of WIA (see Chapters 12 and 13) and compares them with the earlier JTPA and dislocated worker study findings, adjusting all earnings estimates into 2005 dollar equivalents for ease in comparisons.

Kevin Hollenbeck reports on nonexperimental estimates of WIA impacts in Chapter 12, "Short-Term Net Impact Estimates and Rates of Return." Hollenbeck utilized data from studies conducted independently of each other in response to issues within particular states, so the WIA study samples were determined by particular programs or services that were each study's foci. As noted by Hollenbeck, the studies used the entire universe of program exiters in selected years in three states with varied time periods. Further, each study examined a slightly different set of workforce development programs covering different time periods, and thus each study selected slightly different population groups drawn to the particular workforce programs of interest for the studies. In most cases, the program service population for the WIA adult and WIA dislocated worker groups could be identified within the state study, and thus the findings across states for these groups could be combined. The results focus on the programs offered under WIA for job training in order to compare with JTPA impacts.

Hollenbeck examines the earnings and employment impacts and hours of work and wage rate impacts from participation in WIA Adult, Dislocated Worker, and Youth programs, including how these key outcomes changed over time post program. Hollenbeck also estimates the benefits and costs, incorporating estimates of impacts on fringe benefits, tax payments, and income-conditioned transfers, to arrive at rates of return from the programs for the public and society as a whole, or the rates of return for individuals served by the programs, for state taxpayers, and for society as a whole.

Hollenbeck combines the program administrative data in the WIASRD system with state UI records and state Employment Service (ES) records. Comparison groups were constructed using propensity scoring to statistically match individuals who had not participated in WIA within each state to the WIA participants in the state. The matching relied on the administrative records available through WIA, ES, and UI systems.

The study states covered in Hollenbeck's analysis were Washington State (two studies, one very early, 1998–2000, and the other later, during 2002–2004); Virginia (2004–2005); and Indiana (2005–2006). The state study samples were constrained in Washington State, as WIA records did not include the date of entry, only the date of exit. Therefore Hollenbeck conducted his impact estimations across all the study states using quarter of the date of exit from WIA as the starting point for the follow-up analysis. Hollenbeck assembled administration data at the individual level for the treatment and comparison group samples receipt of transfer income from UI benefits, Food Stamps, Medicaid, TANF benefits, and fringe benefits and taxes on earnings, as well as the employment and earnings outcomes. These allowed estimating not only employment and earnings during the preprogram and postprogram outcome time periods but the ways WIA participants might have received both positive and negative benefits by participating in WIA, the benefits or costs to taxpayers, and the overall social benefit-cost estimates that combine both the program participant gains or losses and the taxpayers' benefits or costs.

Hollenbeck concludes there were strong and positive results on the post-WIA earnings for adult WIA populations in that all appear to have statistically significant earnings and employment impacts from participating in WIA although of varying magnitudes and trends over time depending on the state study. The point estimates of average quarterly earnings for the WIA Adult program show gains in earnings on average, beginning in the short-term time period (two to three full quarters after program exit) of $146–$711 per quarter. The WIA Adult earnings gains during the long-term follow-up time period (from 4 quarters to 12 quarters after program exit) average $455–$463 per quarter.

The results for youth in WIA are less positive. Hollenbeck estimates that short-term earnings gains among youth in WIA are near zero and not significant. The long-term average earnings gain among WIA youth was mixed—in one state study it was significant at $325, but in another state it remained not significant and near zero. It should be recalled that under JTPA, estimates of youth earnings gains from training were negative and statistically significant in the short term, and near zero and not significant in the long term.

For two of the state studies, Hollenbeck was also able to decompose the net impacts into employment, wage, and hours impacts, finding positive net impacts and returns on investment for virtually all of the programs. He also finds very strong and positive, statistically significant impacts on earnings for the dislocated workers who participated in WIA in the short term and the long term, varying between $410–$784 and $310–$771, respectively. Because of the baseline for the studies at program exit, the opportunity costs or forgone earnings experienced by dislocated workers from entry into WIA are not incorporated in the short- and long-run earnings and employment estimates.

Hollenbeck's benefit-cost analysis estimates that the discounted net benefits to participants over the first 10 quarters after exit range between $3,500 and $5,000 over all three groups. There are important differences between the groups. The costs to dislocated workers of participating in WIA (the forgone earnings) are so large that the net benefit return for dislocated workers is consistently negative. Hollenbeck estimates the losses to those entering WIA by tracking through ES and UI files the preprogram earnings and employment. He also projects from the estimates for the first 2.5 years after exit from WIA, all the private and public benefits and costs over the first 25 years after program exit, and over the working lifetime.

These projections show that for dislocated workers and youth in the states studied, the private and public benefits and costs from their participation in WIA produced overall negative rates of return. In the case of dislocated workers, the main explanation of the negative rate of return is the loss of earnings they experience, on average, by participating in WIA, and essentially delaying reemployment and the earnings benefits obtained that the comparison group obtains. In addition, the public costs for training of dislocated workers outweigh the public benefits obtained in Hollenbeck's estimates. However, employment gains still exist and are strong enough so that Hollenbeck suggests considering policies, such as a stipend, for dislocated workers in the training programs to offset the forgone earnings.

The youth population also has a negative social return that outweighs the marginal economic gains in Hollenbeck's benefit-cost analysis. The earnings gains for youth were essentially zero, so the program costs easily exceeded the benefits of WIA serving youth, at least in the one state study undertaken in Washington State by Hollenbeck and Huang (2003). The earnings and employment gains estimated for the first 2.5 years after the adult population exited WIA training were enough to outweigh forgone earnings, and allow Hollenbeck to conclude that the overall social benefits were greater than the social costs.

A national nonexperimental study of WIA impacts was undertaken by a team led by Carolyn J. Heinrich with Peter R. Mueser, Kenneth R. Troske, Kyung-Seong Jeon, and Daver C. Kahvecioglu. The study is summarized in Chapter 13, "A Nonexperimental Evaluation of WIA Programs." The objective was to reach the national WIA participant population in a study for the USDOL, but Heinrich and colleagues caution that they could not obtain a truly representative national sample. Heinrich and colleagues use the point of program entry to begin the study observation period. The study evaluates two WIA programs: the Adult program, serving largely disadvantaged individuals, and the Dislocated Worker program, serving those who have lost jobs.

Heinrich et al. draw a number of conclusions regarding the most immediate or short-term (immediately after WIA entry) earnings impacts WIA participants obtain, contrasted with their longer-run patterns of gains (up to fours years after WIA entry); differences by gender; differences between the Adult WIA program participant gains and the Dislocated Worker WIA program participant gains; and possible interactions of earnings gain patterns with various selection bias considerations, such as measured differences (and the unobservable differences) between the participant and comparison study samples at baseline and preprogram and the variance in participation patterns in WIA.

In discussing the conclusions on short- and long-term impacts, Heinrich and colleagues emphasize how different the results are for the Adult versus the Dislocated Worker programs. They also stress that by examining the likely long-term benefits of training—the benefits estimated for the last 11–16 quarters (generally the fourth year after program entry)—one obtains some gauge on whether the WIA programs pass a benefit-cost standard.

Earnings for men and women in the WIA Adult program increased during quarters 11–16 after WIA entry that average annualized earnings gains of 26 percent for women ($2,363) and of 15 percent for men ($1,676). The employment rate increments estimated are 12 percent for both men and women, or employment rates rising by about 6.5 percentage points. The WIA Dislocated Worker program estimate by Heinrich and colleagues presents annualized earnings gains in quarters 11–16 after program exit that are very small and not significant. Employment rates, however, appear to increase by 4–5 percentage points, or 7–8 percent gains, and are statistically significant. They point out that dislocated worker populations are, on average, those who have strong work histories and higher wages so their entry into services such as training or extensive career counseling remove them from the successful job finding process evident in control groups in experimental studies of dislocated workers. There are diminished earnings and employment for dislocated workers during program participation, with about four years needed to recoup and return to the "normal" pattern, and eventually show some earnings gains.

For the Dislocated Worker program, the earnings impacts would need to be long lived to exceed costs, and earnings gains for dislocated workers who are men are basically not discernable, meaning benefits do not exceed costs. The study estimates that the WIA Adult program clearly satisfies a benefit-cost standard for both men and women if the earnings impacts continue for a period of just two or three years. For the Dislocated Worker program, the evidence is much less clear.

Heinrich and colleagues describe the latitude in WIA that states have used to structure the One-Stop system to reflect local preferences, under direction of the local agency, the WIB, stressing that there are wide variations across localities. They note that the sequential service mandate may cause "negative selection into training" because one must have been unsuccessful in obtaining employment through core and intensive service sequences to be eligible for training. On the other hand, they also note that it has been found in most sites that "as many as a third of those who participate in WIA have a particular training goal prior to program entry (they are often referred to WIA by the training provider), and, in general, WIA staff make an effort to accommodate them." It is also expected that the performance measures encourage positive selection of those perceived to be most successful in the labor market for WIA services.

The authors point out how there is no simple picture of what services a customer receives under WIA. For example, a recent study finds that nationwide, about one in five WIA participants received only core services, and about two in five were coded as receiving training services (Social Policy Research Associates 2006). Of those receiving training, up to 10 percent received on-the-job training and another 5 percent received basic skills training, with the remainder receiving occupational and other training. It is also interesting that half of all training recorded was funded by ITAs, with two-thirds of those in training receiving some kind of credential. Somewhere between a half and a third of WIA participants exited the program in less than 26 weeks, the balance remaining in WIA and then exiting were in the program for at least a year. The impact estimates in the study could not consider how all these different service patterns might shift the overall average earnings and employment estimates per participant in the Adult or Dislocated Worker programs, but there is considerable study discussion of how these patterns could be theorized to influence such estimates.

Overall, the main conclusions are the consistent and significant gains obtained by women and men in the WIA Adult program, in contrast to the lack of such gains, in general, among those in the WIA Dislocated Worker program, and that conclusions regarding program effectiveness should not be based on the very short-term recorded earnings and employment within the first year after program exit. To ignore the more significant gains for Adult program participants, which emerge by years three and four, misses a potential public sector investment payoff rarely found through solid, rigorous evaluations. Heinrich and colleagues urge investing random assignment studies that can offer findings that are more confirmatory. Some of the study findings appear consistent with the earlier random assignment study of JTPA, especially in the ineffectiveness of providing training as the main service for the Dislocated Worker population. The Heinrich team could not replicate the important studies of the effectiveness of incentives that encourage swifter reattachment to jobs, but they note that these strategies appear to be a more efficient approach. The Adult program findings, on the other hand, support those who believe job search assistance and training services are effective when dedicated to those with weak employment experience or attachment to the mainstream economy.

FUTURE EVALUATION CHOICES

The term *evaluation* encompasses many different efforts to assess the effects of a policy, program, or particular practice. Whatever the focus, central to evaluation standards is how well the counterfactual produces reliable impact estimates. The next set of papers reviews the conditions that need to exist to implement particular evaluation designs, noting which conditions reduce or increase reliability.

In Chapter 14, "Nonexperimental Impact Evaluations," Haeil Jung and Maureen A. Pirog review the history of employment and training program evaluations, focusing on the Manpower Development and Training Act (MDTA), which began in 1962, and CETA, which began in 1973. Evaluations of CETA were nonexperimental and drew samples of participants from a longitudinal manpower survey that tracked participants to compare with those not in CETA, drawn from the Current Population Survey. Jung and Pirog recall that these evaluations produced widely varying findings that drew serious examination of why the findings varied, and stimulated beginning efforts to use experimental designs, which had begun to test other employability programs outside of the CETA system. Evaluation specialists began to compare findings from experiments with efforts to replicate the experiment using comparison groups such as one would draw from the Current Population Survey and other sources.

Jung and Pirog describe the outgrowth of the replication studies, an ongoing methodological concern with what data conditions and which nonexperimental methods might be the second-best fits to what would be obtained if an experimental study could have been undertaken. Accompanying this were efforts to define and measure the types of selection bias that produced estimates from nonexperimental studies that did not get close to experimental estimates. They point out that, although there may be logistical difficulties encountered in implementing a random assignment experiment, these difficulties must be weighted against the likelihood of giving bad advice to policymakers, the likely result of applying nonexperimental techniques in many situations without taking account of the assumptions.

Jung and Pirog aim their discussion to those who, it is assumed, are not able to use experimental methods given the constraints from program operations such as mandatory participation and thus must choose among nonexperimental methods. They first observe the various types of questions that experimental methods address, and then discuss the sources of selection bias that an econometric estimator might correct for. Jung and Pirog point out that there are different types of selection bias in training programs, and the challenge is to understand how the sources of the selection biases might operate in particular training program contexts.

Four key conditions that nonexperimental evaluations need to have in order to reduce the measurable sources of bias, according to Jung and Pirog, are 1) comparison groups drawn from the same local labor markets as the programs studied, 2) the same instrumentation used to collect data from the treatment and comparison groups, 3) the same range of values for the observed characteristics of the comparison group's members as for treatment group's members, and 4) the same distributions of the values across the ranges of the treatment and comparison group.

Jung and Pirog also advise caution in specifying the policy question, noting that the policy question addressed in intent to treat evaluations is different from the question addressed in treatment on treatment evaluations. The former includes the applicants assigned to the program who may drop out after baseline and thus addresses whether the program overall had a desirable impact on the eligible population. Evaluations that focus on those who received the treatment are aimed at the effects for a subgroup of those eligible. Thus, these evaluations cannot capture the overall policy effectiveness of expenditures on treatments offered to a much larger group of eligible people. The authors review the modeling methods used to work on estimates for groups who somehow do get treatment (the subset of the intent to treat population), relying on the observables captured in data sets. These techniques include difference-in-differences extensions on matching, regression discontinuity design, and the marginal treatment effect using local instrumental variables, and are summarized along with earlier modeling methods such as regression estimators, propensity score matching, and difference-in-differences.

In Chapter 15, "Designing Reliable Impact Evaluations," Larry L. Orr, Stephen H. Bell, and Jacob A. Klerman give an overview of the directions taken in evaluation science over the 40 years of efforts to evaluate job training programs, pointing out how over time the standards become more certain and focused on experimental designs. Orr, Bell, and Klerman note that for the first job training studies of MDTA during the 1960s, evaluations started out with simple before-after methods looking at whether postprogram earnings improved over preprogram earnings.

Important work by economists pointed out that preprogram earnings are simply a marker of the reason why one comes for job training:

one has lost a job so earnings are nil; then one finds a job, whether through a job training program or other strategies. Rebounding from a job loss naturally leads to most eventually finding another job. This Ashenfelter dip, the natural drop of earnings due to job loss–job recovery before one needs the services of a job training program, means one has to have some comparison of similar people who are also going through the job loss–job gain cycle. During the 1970s, evaluations focused on using data about people who looked similar in that they too had suffered loss of a job.

By the 1980s, economists analyzed how well methods using such data sources (typically national longitudinal data) could replicate the findings from some of the first national experimental studies of workforce programs, such as the Supported Work evaluation by Manpower Demonstration Research Corporation. Recognition that past, nonexperimental studies could not produce scientifically valid program impact estimates brought congressional requirements for more rigorous evaluations. A prime example was the serious investment in the National JTPA Study, using experimental methods to assign over 20,000 applicants to job training or control groups in sixteen local programs and study the outcomes for an extended period. Other workforce programs received rigorous evaluations as well.

Orr and his colleagues stress that experimental methods (using random assignment to allocate applicants to the program or to a control group) are not only scientifically accurate, but they avoid the methodological debates that accompany presentations of nonexperimental results. The lack of comparability between nonexperimental evaluation methods versus the experimental method is the fact that by randomly assigning eligible applicants for a training program into two groups—the treatment group allowed to enter the program and the control group that is not allowed to enter the program—the two samples, due to random assignment, have by chance the same set of background factors represented in them. Most important, they have the same set of unobservable characteristics, motivations, and experiences that are unknown. If, for example, one were to select a comparison group of nonparticipants as the counterfactual, one cannot ever be assured that the factors are taken into account that turned them from potential application and participation into a nonparticipant.

The authors review efforts to improve nonexperimental methods to bring them closer in credibility as experimental studies. This question stimulated many methods studies, testing how close the results from these methodological developments are to those from a study done with experimental methods. They note that it is particularly the case in workforce program evaluations that the nonexperimental methods are "not well-suited" to econometric modeling of job loss–job gain and the accompanying loss of earnings. Those who have come the closest have the benefit of data sets of large numbers of individuals that have extensive longitudinal data on the employment and earnings on the individuals.

Orr, Bell, and Klerman also emphasize that a major problem with using nonexperimental methods is that, before a program evaluation is put into the field, one has no really viable rule that specifies what will produce the estimate closest to the estimate obtained in an experimental evaluation. Thus, while after an experimental study is completed, one may check out which nonexperimental method applied to the experimental data appears to come closest, before the study one has no way of judging this. Design parameters are critical for estimating study costs, and are more indeterminant if a nonexperimental method is used. With an experiment, there are much stronger estimates possible of what will be required to conduct the study, so both the costs and the likelihood that the study will find significant effects if they exist are firmer and provide more assurance to policymakers that funds are being wisely applied.

Advances have been made using experimental methods, as Orr and his colleagues explain. They should be recognized and their use encouraged, for they demonstrate that it is possible to apply experimental methods to a variety of program conditions. The authors provide examples, including spreading control groups over many sites, decreasing the allocation percentage, as well as allowing program operators to increase the odds of assignment to treatment for preferred applicants or testing greater levels of intervention versus the standard services, and using administrative data instead of surveys.

The latest plans for a national random assignment study of WIA are discussed in Chapter 16, titled "Neither Easy Nor Cheap," by Sheena McConnell, Peter Schochet, and Alberto Martini, who are leading the new WIA experimental study. The authors remind us of the ways evaluations have affected policy and programmatic decisions, new demands on experimental studies, and how future evaluations may need to be tailored.

The first evaluation of the Job Corps (which actually was nonexperimental in design) found it cost-effective. This was the first time policymakers had a major, national longitudinal study assessing a job program, and the findings led them to increase the funding and sustain the program. Job Corps has remained popular, with the longest "life" next to Head Start. When the JTPA evaluation findings for youth were released much later showing there was no significant earnings gain, and even hints of negative impacts for some subgroups, the response was major programmatic changes and reduced funding as well. One experimental test of reemployment services for jobless people on UI led to changes in UI services, requiring worker profiling and reemployment services for recipients likely to exhaust benefits before finding employment, basically requiring those recipients to receive services much as welfare benefits are conditioned on participation. Another experimental study led to the creation of the Self-Employment Assistance program for those on unemployment compensation, to help the unemployed start their own small business.

McConnell, Schochet, and Martini urge planners of future evaluation to pay attention to lessons learned from over 30 years of experiments in workforce programs. First on their list of key lessons is the careful development of the evaluation questions a study will take on. (A rigorous study can only accommodate a few questions.) The question dilemma first arises by confronting whether to evaluate the whole program or which components of a program are effective. The authors believe the second strategy is advantageous in workforce program evaluations. Whole programs these days have too much complexity, too many moving parts. One may learn more by focusing on particular program areas aimed to help identified target groups. Target groups, however, need to be clearly identified in the evaluation plan, as they are typically broken into subgroups. One is constrained by evaluation costs to a limited number of subgroups. Trying to collect a lot of demographic variables and then fishing around later, testing out different subgroups, is considered "milking," and reviewers will ask what the original plan was for testing the key hypotheses driving the program design and the subgroup characteristics specified *a priori*. McConnell and her colleagues also remind evaluation planners that the procedures and data to be used to draw the counterfactual are also critical to assuring that one can obtain the sample(s) needed for the questions.

On the question of evaluation design, in situations where a "no service offered" control group cannot be established within the existing program, the authors urge trying an experimental design that uses "randomized encouragement," in which all the eligible participants are assigned to services, but the random assignment sets up a lottery assigning an encouragement to some participants to voluntarily use more services. This incorporates random assignment into program operations, with the assignment being to the encouraged group or to the regular service menu.

McConnell, Schochet, and Martini also provide a summary of nonexperimental designs, noting the difficulties involved. They strongly recommend that the regression discontinuity or propensity score methods be used rather than less credible methods. They conclude that the regression discontinuity approach has the most promise when experimental methods are not viable. The selection rule for receiving the treatment is fully known under the regression discontinuity approach. The propensity score approach has to rely on modeling using observable baseline data, so one cannot know for sure whether the unobservables are introducing substantial bias into the findings.

The authors note the methodological efforts to use propensity score methods that match program participants to a comparison sample and appraise how successful these methods are at getting estimates that are stable and similar to experimental results. McConnell and colleagues conclude that while some estimation techniques appear more successful than others in replication studies focused on particular experimental data sets, they believe that it is the data available that can be used for the comparison group that determines the validity of the estimate, rather than the nonexperimental technique. In other words, the things that matter are whether the data contains an extensive and good set of matching variables for modeling the participation decision, such as extensive preprogram earnings histories, samples possible from the same geographic areas as the experimental study group, and same follow-up data sources available for treatment and comparison groups.

McConnell and colleagues also summarize the issues that arise when using administrative records, especially the state UI data that studies on WIA have used. They point out how important it is to have data on service receipt among program participants and the control group. Typically the latter requires special surveys. Having data regularly collected in administrative systems has been a great advantage in studying programs (for both experiments and nonexperimental studies). And, they argue, an experimental design will pay back dividends. The costs of conducting experiments are not nearly so high as once believed, with the availability of systems tracking employment and earnings that can be linked to the program records, and by doing the assignment within the workforce system, comparing different alternatives for important populations, policymakers have very credible estimates about whether more costly alternatives matter, as well as the realities of who is attracted to these programs, who stays, and who seems to obtain real benefits.

Turning to lessons from evaluations of U.S. workforce programs to the evaluation of Active Labor Market Programs (ALMPs) in the European context, Jeffrey Smith in Chapter 17, "Improving Impact Evaluation in Europe," draws on the North American experience and contrasts it with European practices. He makes the case for three particular features in the North American context that he believes would improve policymaking in the European context: 1) greater use of random assignment methods, 2) recognition and adoption of serious cost-benefit analysis, and 3) greater attention to developing and using evaluation industry entities such as takes place in North America. Smith points out that there are European practices that could or should be considered as improvements within the North American context, including the rich, well-maintained, and accessible administrative data and specific data elements (e.g., caseworker ratings of clients, the emphasis on documenting sanction regimes for benefit recipients). Further, he notes that European countries vary greater in their research and evaluation capacities being applied to ALMPs.

In support of investing in experimental studies, Smith notes that the "key advantage [is] that their simple design makes them easy to explain and hard to argue with . . . giving them a policy-influencing power not enjoyed by even the cleanest nonexperimental designs." Further, the high-quality data produced yield substantive advances in understanding labor markets. Smith acknowledges that there are limitations, including the questions that cannot be addressed through experimental methods. Some have difficulty understanding what use can be made of experimental results, noting the treatment dropouts and crossovers from control groups, and the limitation on external validity, or generalization to people or areas that were not represented in the experiment. Social experiments that aim for "national representation" cost a great deal, because compliance of the scientifically drawn sample may require extra resources, but they satisfy those who want the most general assessment.

There are also policymakers and program administrators who will express ethical objections to random assignment. Smith comments, "In my experience, these objections nearly always represent a cover for simply not wanting to know the answer." While it is empirically the case that "many, maybe most, programs fail when subjected to serious evaluation," Smith counters that this may indicate that indeed it is "important constituencies, such as workers and agencies or firms that provide the treatments" who have an interest in a program's existence in the first place. He notes that these constituencies also have an interest in low-quality evaluations or misleading performance measures in place of experimental evidence that compels others to challenge the program's existence.

In response to those who express concerns about service denial, it is quite possible, where resources are not constrained, to design random assignment so that all receive some type of service, with multiple treatment arms. In cases where a program can only serve a portion of the presumed beneficiaries, the experimental design is an equitable way to allocate the scarce resources. There are also randomized encouragement designs, with the assignment being to an incentive to participate, where no one is excluded, and the incentive provides an exogenous variation in treatment status. Another type of design is "randomization at the margin," where the group selected for randomization are those at the end of the list deemed most critically in need of services.

All in all, notes Smith, the experimental evaluations of workforce programming conducted in the United States have often led to policy changes, as he recalls a number of examples where shifts in policies and program funding were the results of an experimental study. He also explains why cost-benefit analysis is the most important contribution to arriving at "a direct policy conclusion." The message is clear about the value of a program to the taxpayers who fund it. An important example is the cost-benefit analysis associated with the U.S. National Job Corps Study that has brought rethinking of a long-standing program.

Smith observes that "the modal European ALMP evaluation . . . contains no cost-benefit analysis at all." While it is true that Europeans stress employment as the key outcome in workforce programming rather than earnings (one needs earnings to have a monetary benefit in cost-benefit analysis), he believes that recognition that employment impacts typically are negative or zero, discourages serious consideration of benefit-cost analysis. Smith also notes that the public sector in Europe does not believe it so important to cost out public services. Nevertheless, knowing the duration of program impacts is important as well, and a part of cost-benefit analysis.

Finally, Smith considers why there are such marked differences in the quantity and quality of workforce evaluations across countries. He observes how robust the evaluation sector is in the United States, the variety of entities engaged, and the very large size of the evaluation sector. In contrast to the European patterns, Smith believes the centering of the research market, the research activity, outside of government is critical in that it encourages and supports independent, objective appraisals of government programs. He recommends European governments consider how they might consolidate funds for evaluations, to increase the size of the European evaluation market, and open the market to a variety of research entities, both within Europe and from outside.

Smith notes that parallel with the U.S. growth in the research sector was the broad agreement that it is best for government not to undertake directly the evaluation of programs it funds and manages. He concludes by noting the imprint of neoclassical economics as possibly influencing the agreement regarding the role of independent research, as well as other broader and deeper differences across countries in individualism, deference to authority, the importance of social class, and average education.

CONCLUSIONS FROM THE CONFERENCE

WIA brought changes in the workforce training system because it shifted responsibilities between layers of government. States became principal actors in WIA, as they were given responsibility for determining the funding to local entities responsible for outreach and coordination and making decisions about system operations and performance standards. This shifted these decisions away from the federal offices to local and state control.

Performance management became the central focus of the USDOL's management of WIA, and for states as well. WIA offers an excellent example of the kinds of changes that can accompany stronger accountability requirements in federally funded social and educational programs. The act's performance management mandates occurred at a time of extensive computerization of administrative records throughout government, and was able to take advantage of the new systems and efforts to link records across systems. Despite the expectations regarding easy transfer of performance systems into government, however, the systems may not be operating with the incentives expected, due to confusion and manipulations possible within the systems. It is unclear, as well, whether the investments in closer tracking of the users or beneficiaries of federal programs for the purposes of performance management actually helped job seekers gain faster access to jobs and achieve higher earnings. More likely, as these data files are made available to researchers, more will be learned about how the program works and what services are provided.

Implementation of WIA took time. Most states obtained waivers from the USDOL in the early years of the act to set up performance standards for the One-Stop centers, providers, and settled on the data requirements without operating fully the new accountability structures. States had to invest in large and comprehensive databases to create lists of effective providers deemed eligible to serve WIA applicants. New and better labor market and local economy information repositories were also created under WIA. One-Stop centers focused on encouraging individual "shopping" of WIA services and training options, with both staff and customers of One-Stop centers welcoming the shared responsibility.

Nonexperimental evaluations of WIA (at least the programs aimed at unemployed adults and at dislocated workers) have had mixed findings. Two studies find significant positive effects for adult job seekers who use WIA as opposed to those who do not. The findings are very different for dislocated workers. Here the two studies find no positive effects for dislocated workers. Comparison groups appear to move more quickly into jobs and thus dislocated workers in WIA suffer lost wages while in WIA services. Whether dislocated workers eventually overtake the earnings obtained by their counterparts in the comparison group seems to depend on the length of follow-up. Estimates of the average longer-term net earnings gain among the dislocated workers appear to be less than the average social cost estimates of the WIA program for this group.

All of the evidence on WIA program effects on employment and earnings is suggestive, rather than confirmatory. Studies that produce confirmatory evidence need experimental designs to establish participant and control groups. The suggestive findings are based on methods that are careful and clear about the limitations of the impact estimates. It is fortunate that the effects of WIA, as it is now operating some 12 years after its creation, are finally being examined in new federal studies under way using randomized designs, but it will be several years before early results are known.

Notes

1. The meeting was a cross-national policy dialogue organized by the Center for International Policy Exchanges at the University of Maryland's School of Public Policy. This dialogue, one of a series with different entities (including the Association for Public Policy Analysis and Management), was organized by the University of Maryland Center and was held on November 7, 2009, in Washington DC. The topic, "Evaluation and Performance Management of Job Training Programs: What Can the European Social Fund Learn from the WIA Experience?" was developed in response to inquiries from the staff of the European Commission concerned with commission workforce programming. Patrick Tiedemann, research associate at the Center for International Policy Exchanges, assisted in organizing the meeting.
2. Nearly $3 billion was added to the Adult, Dislocated Worker, and Youth programs under WIA in the American Recovery and Reinvestment Act of 2009 as a one-time increase to be spent by December 31, 2010.
3. If a job seeker doesn't get a job at tier 1, they move into tier 2, and then, again if no job, to tier 3.
4. Four federal agencies retained responsibility for distributing funds under each program to states, in most cases retaining existing formulas for distribution to the states, and other requirements and regulations from prior legislation, with amendments in WIA to accommodate the coordinated access to services entry points.
5. Blank, Heald, and Fagnoni report that their June 2004 GAO study report "estimated the cost of doing participant surveys, as was done under JTPA, at approximately

$13.25 per participant compared with the cost of automated record matching to UI wage records, which costs less than $0.05 per participant."

6. At the same time, the USDOL is working on an enhanced data reporting system called the Workforce Investment Streamlined Performance Reporting system, to consolidate reporting requirements across several other USDOL programs, and lead to a single reporting structure that can track an individual's progress through the One-Stop system.

7. See Chapter 9 for a description of how adjustments to the WIA performance levels can be carried out.

8. The WIA training program for youth, however, is targeted for the out-of-school youth.

9. See especially Chapters 3, 8, and 10.

References

Hollenbeck, Kevin M., and Wei-Jang Huang. 2003. *Net Impact and Benefit-Cost Estimates of the Workforce Development System in Washington State.* Technical Report No. TR03-018. Kalamazoo, MI: W.E. Upjohn Institute for Employment Research.

Maquire, Sheila, Joshua Freely, Carol Clymer, and Maureen Conway. 2009. *Job Training That Works: Findings from the Sectoral Impact Study.* Philadelphia, PA: Public/Private Ventures.

Social Policy Research Associates. 2006. *2004 WIASRD Data Book.* Report prepared for the U.S. Department of Labor. Oakland, CA: Social Policy Research Associates.

Part 1

Understanding WIA

2
An Overview of WIA

Dianne Blank
Laura Heald
Cynthia Fagnoni
U.S. Government Accountability Office

Over time the U.S. workforce development system has seen incremental changes in its structure, its services, and the role that federal, state, and local officials play in decision making. Beginning with MDTA of 1962 and continuing with CETA of 1973 and JTPA of 1982, services were largely focused on training for low-income individuals or those on public assistance. The array of job training programs operated in an uncoordinated patchwork of programs and agencies that served this population, often resulting in inefficiency, duplication of effort, and confusion for the job seeker. But, with the passage of WIA in 1998, the workforce development system has undergone a fundamental shift in the way employment and training services are provided. Comparing the structure of WIA to its predecessor programs, we see several key themes emerge in the progression of employment and training policy in the United States. These include

- a decreasing focus on income eligibility as the only basis for accessing services;
- a decreasing focus on job training as the primary means for getting a job—assessing and marketing existing skills becomes the service of choice;
- an increasing focus on personal responsibility through self-service and consumer awareness, for example, in choosing training options;
- a greater focus on reducing duplication of effort—but through consolidating services, not programs;
- an increasing role for the private sector in guiding policy and a focus on the employer as customer; and
- a greater focus on both state and local decision making.

Since 2000, the GAO has issued more than 25 separate reports on WIA alone, many of which included recommendations regarding various aspects of WIA. This chapter draws on GAO work conducted between 2000 and 2009 in which the GAO examined the nature of the challenges confronting officials at all levels—federal, state, and local—in implementing the Workforce Investment System, what has been done to address them, and the challenges that remain. The first two sections of this chapter cover the consolidation of services in One-Stop systems and the structure of the three programs authorized under WIA. The third section focuses more explicitly on the performance accountability provisions for the three WIA-funded programs.

KEY ELEMENTS OF WIA'S APPROACH AND HOW THEY WORK

WIA made several important changes to the existing employment and training system, but two are key: 1) it consolidated services for most federally funded employment and training programs for adults and youth; and 2) it redesigned services under the largest employment and training program, JTPA, when it created three new funding streams— WIA Adult, Dislocated Workers, and Youth. States were required to implement these changes by July 1, 2000.

Consolidating Services in the One-Stop System

To create a more comprehensive workforce investment system, WIA required states and localities to bring together the services of most federally funded employment and training programs into a single system, called the One-Stop system. Prior to WIA, services to job seekers were often provided through a patchwork of agencies and offices. While many of the programs shared similar goals, their services were rarely coordinated, creating an environment of confusion and frustration and hampering efforts to help job seekers get and keep a job. For about a decade before WIA was passed, states and localities had been experimenting with integrating some of their employment and training services, but none had gone so far as to include the full range required under WIA.

The USDOL has overall responsibility for administering the provisions of WIA. Sixteen federally funded workforce development programs administered by four separate federal agencies, including the USDOL, are required to provide their services through the One-Stop system. In fiscal year 2009, Congress appropriated over $15.9 billion for the 16 mandatory programs, including about $3.3 billion for WIA. In addition, several of these programs, including all of the WIA-funded programs, received additional funding under the American Recovery and Reinvestment Act of 2009. The three WIA-funded programs in particular received a total of $3.2 billion in additional funding. Even without the additional funding, these three WIA-funded programs combined currently constitute the largest federally funded employment and training program in the United States. (See Table 2.1.)

Each state must have one or more designated local workforce investment areas, and each local area must have at least one comprehensive One-Stop center where core services for all mandatory programs are accessible. WIA allows flexibility in the way these mandatory partners provide services through the One-Stop system, allowing colocation, electronic linkages, or referrals to off-site partner programs. While WIA requires these mandatory partners to participate, it does not provide additional funds to support the One-Stop system infrastructure, such as facilities or data systems. As a result, mandatory partners are expected to share the costs of developing and operating One-Stop centers. In addition to mandatory partners, One-Stop centers have the flexibility to include other partners in the One-Stop system to better meet specific state and local workforce development needs. Services may also be provided at affiliated sites, defined as designated locations that provide access to at least one employment and training program.

While officials at all levels have generally considered the changes to be moving the system in the right direction, creating these One-Stop centers where services were consolidated across a broad range of programs was a daunting task and states and local areas encountered some challenges along the way.

Table 2.1 WIA's Mandatory Programs and Services and Fiscal Year 2009 Appropriation

Federal agency and mandatory program	Fiscal year 2009 appropriation ($, millions)	Services provided and target population
Department of Labor		
WIA Adult	862	Assessment, counseling, job readiness skills, and occupational skills training to individuals age 18 or older. Priority for intensive services and training is given to low-income individuals and public assistance recipients.
WIA Dislocated Worker	1,467	Assessment, counseling, job readiness skills, and occupational skills training to workers age 18 or older who have lost their jobs due to plant closures or layoffs.
WIA Youth	924	Assistance for youth ages 14–21 to complete an education program or to secure and hold employment. 30% of funds used on out-of-school youth.
Employment Service (Wagner-Peyser)	704	Assessment, counseling, job readiness and placement to any individual seeking employment who is legally authorized to work in the United States.
Trade Adjustment Assistance	958	Assistance to workers who lose their jobs due to international trade. Benefits include training, income support while in training, job search, relocation assistance, assistance with health insurance, and wage insurance for certain older workers.
Veterans' employment and training programs	239	Counseling and placement services to veterans, including those with service-connected disabilities; connections to other programs that can fund training.
Unemployment Insurance	2,833	Income support to individuals eligible under state law, who have become unemployed through no fault of their own and are looking for work.
Job Corps	1,684	A residential program that provides job training and job-readiness skills to disadvantaged at-risk youth ages 16 to 24.

Program		Description
Senior Community Service Employment Program	572	Assessment, counseling, placement assistance, occupational skills training, and part-time community service employment for low-income persons age 55 and over.
Employment and training for migrant and seasonal farm workers	83	Assessment, counseling, placement assistance, occupational skills training, and other supportive services for economically disadvantaged migrant and seasonally employed farm workers.
Employment and training for Native Americans	53	Assessment, counseling, placement assistance, occupational skills training, and other supportive services for Indian, Alaskan Native, and Native Hawaiian individuals.
Department of Education		
Vocational Rehabilitation Program	2,975	Assessment, counseling, placement assistance, occupational skills training, and other rehabilitative services to individuals with disabilities; priority is given to those with the most significant disabilities.
Adult Education and Literacy	567	Assessment and basic skills and literacy training to adults over the age of 16, not enrolled in school, who lack a high school diploma or the basic skills to function effectively in the workplace and in their daily lives.
Vocational Education (Perkins Act)	1,272	Improvement of vocational and technical education programs through curriculum and professional development, purchase of equipment, services to members of special populations, and other activities.
Department of Health and Human Services		
Community Services Block Grant	700	A wide array of assistance, including, but not limited to, employment or training to low-income families and their communities.
Department of Housing and Urban Development		
HUD-administered employment and training	n/a	A wide range of employment- and training-related services to residents of public and assisted housing and other low-income persons, including the Community Development Block Grants.

SOURCE: Departments of Labor, Education, HHS, and HUD.

Governance of the One-Stop system

WIA called for the development of workforce investment boards to oversee WIA implementation at the state and local levels. At the state level, WIA requires, among other things, that the Workforce Investment Board (often called the "WIB") assist the governor in helping to set up the system, establish procedures and processes for ensuring accountability, and designate local workforce investment areas. WIA also requires that boards be established within each of the local workforce investment areas to carry out the formal agreements developed between the boards and each partner, and to oversee One-Stop operations. The WIBs have no control over the funds for most of the mandatory partner programs and have only limited authority over a portion of the WIA funds designated for adult and youth activities.

WIA specifies the categories of members that should participate on the workforce investment boards, but does not prescribe a minimum or maximum number of members. It allows governors to select representatives for the board from various segments of the workforce investment community, including business, education, labor, and other organizations. The specifics for local board membership are similar to those for the state. Private-sector leadership and involvement on these boards has been seen as crucial to shaping the direction of the workforce investment system. In that respect, WIA requires that private-sector representatives chair the boards and make up the majority of board members.

WIA's statutory requirements for the WIBs created some challenges for states and localities, at least initially. As a result of the board membership requirements, boards became rather large and unwieldy. In a 2001 report, we noted that the average number of members on state workforce boards often exceeded 40 and sometimes reached as high as 64. Local boards were just as large. By comparison, major private-sector corporate boards often have around 12 members. Officials reported that the size of the boards made it difficult to recruit the necessary private-sector board members and made it difficult to set up and conduct meetings. Some local areas experimented with different approaches to reduce the size of boards, including developing extensive committee structures (GAO 2001). Currently, the USDOL reports that the state and local WIBs are about the same size as they were at WIA's inception. However, the department notes that well-functioning boards have found that dividing into subcommittees has allowed them to function more efficiently.

One-Stop infrastructure

In 2007, we reported that WIA's service delivery infrastructure was still evolving, and between 2001 and 2007, the number of One-Stop centers nationwide—both comprehensive and affiliated sites—had declined somewhat, a fact that states most often attributed to a decrease in funding. At last count, there were 1,850 comprehensive One-Stops across the country. Services for mandatory programs were increasingly available through the One-Stop system in 2007, though not always on site. States continued to have services for two key programs—WIA Adult and Dislocated Workers—available on site at the majority of the One-Stop centers. The on site availability of some other programs— such as Job Corps, Migrant and Seasonal Farm Workers, Senior Community Service and Employment Program, and Adult Education and Literacy—had declined slightly between 2001 and 2007. However, the overall availability of these programs' services increased, largely because of substantial increases in access through electronic linkages and referrals. Despite the increased availability of some programs at One-Stop centers, in some local areas the linkages between key programs never really developed. In 2007, we reported that several states had not fully integrated all of their Wagner-Peyser-funded Employment Service (ES) activities into the system. Six states reported in our 2007 survey that they operated stand-alone ES offices, all completely outside the One-Stop system. Another four states reported having at least some stand-alone offices outside the system (GAO 2007a). At that time, we recommended that the USDOL step up action to require all ES offices to be part of the One-Stop system. Labor Department officials tell us they remain committed to a fully integrated system and are providing technical assistance to state and local officials and to system partners to promote better integration.

Lacking a dedicated source of funding to support infrastructure, most states and local areas rely heavily on one or two programs to support One-Stop costs, although some states disperse the costs among numerous programs. WIA and the ES were the two programs most often identified in our 2007 survey as funding sources used for infrastructure—the nonpersonnel costs of operating comprehensive One-Stop centers. Of the 48 states that were able to report on infrastructure funding for comprehensive One-Stop centers, 23 states identified WIA as the top funding source and 19 states reported that Employment Service funds were the largest funding source. In a 2003 report on promising One-Stop practices, we noted that some local One-Stops were finding other ways to creatively increase One-Stop funds through fee-based services, grants, or contributions from partner programs and state or local governments. Managers said these additional funds allowed them to cover operational costs and expand services despite limited WIA funding to support One-Stop infrastructure and restrictions on the use of program funds. For example, One-Stop operators in one local area reported that they raised $750,000 in one fiscal year through a combination of fee-based business consulting, drug testing, and drivers' education services (GAO 2003a).

Coordinating services across programs

WIA sought to reduce the confusion and redundancy that existed in workforce development programs. It did so by requiring that programs coordinate services—it did not consolidate the programs. To facilitate this coordination, WIA provided the flexibility to states and local areas to develop approaches for serving job seekers and employers that best meet local needs. This local flexibility has allowed innovation in streamlining services across the array of programs in the One-Stops. In our 2003 study, we report that states and localities found creative new ways to serve job seekers. In particular, a group of 14 One-Stops, identified as exemplary by government officials and workforce development experts, used at least one of several different approaches to streamline services—they took steps to ensure that job seekers could readily access needed services, they cross-trained program staff on all of the One-Stop programs, or they consolidated case management and intake procedures. For example, to ensure that job seekers could readily access needed services, One-Stops we visited allocated staff to help them navigate the One-Stop system, provided support to customers with transportation barriers, and expanded services for One-Stop customers. They consolidated case management and intake procedures across programs through the use of shared service plans for customers and shared computer networks.

Focus on the employer as customer

WIA requires that the One-Stop system engage the employer as customer by helping employers identify and recruit skilled workers. Engaging employers is seen as critical to successfully connecting job seekers with available jobs. In our 2003 promising One-Stop practices study, officials at the exemplary One-Stops we visited told us they engaged and served employers using at least three different methods. Most of the One-Stops had specialized staff who conducted outreach to individual employers or to industry clusters and served as their primary point of contact for accessing One-Stop services. In addition to dedicating specialized staff, all of the One-Stops we visited worked with intermediaries to engage and serve employers. Intermediaries, such as a local Chamber of Commerce or an economic development entity, served as liaisons between employers and the One-Stop system, helping One-Stops to assess the workforce needs of employers while connecting employers with One-Stop services. Finally, these One-Stops also tailored their services to meet employers' specific workforce needs by offering an array of job placement and training assistance designed for each employer. These services included specialized recruiting, pre-screening, and customized training programs (GAO 2003a).

Despite the efforts of the One-Stop centers to engage employers, the extent to which the One-Stop center is actually positioned to serve their needs has been a concern to many. In 2004 and again in 2006, we surveyed randomly selected small, medium, and large employers to determine the extent to which they were aware of, used, and were satisfied with the One-Stop system. We found that employers mostly used One-Stop centers to fill their needs for low-skilled workers. Most medium and large employers were aware of and used the system and were satisfied with its services (see Figure 2.1). Regardless of size, just over 70 percent of employers responding to our 2006 survey reported that they hired a small percentage of their employees—about 9 percent—through One-Stops. Two-thirds of the workers they hired were low-skilled workers, in part because they thought the labor available from the One-Stops was mostly low-skilled. Employers told us they would hire more job seekers from the One-Stop labor pools if the job seekers had the skills they were seeking. Most employers used the centers' job posting service, fewer made use of the One-Stops' physical

Figure 2.1   Percentage of Business Establishments Aware of, Using, and Satisfied with One-Stops

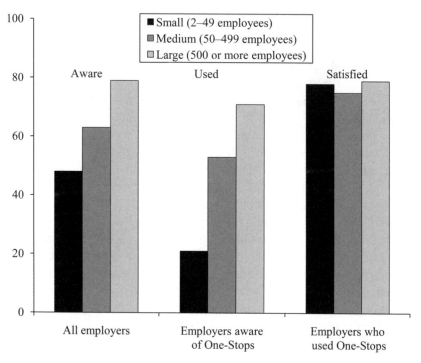

SOURCE: GAO (2005a).

space or job applicant screening services. Still, when employers did take advantage of services, they generally reported that they were satisfied with the services and found them useful because they produced positive results and saved them time and money. When employers did not use a particular One-Stop service, in most cases they said that they either were not aware that the One-Stop provided the service, said they obtained it elsewhere, or said that they carried through on their own (GAO 2005a, 2006).

The Structure of the Adult, Dislocated Worker, and Youth Programs

Program services provided under the three new WIA funding streams represented a marked change from those provided under JTPA.

WIA combined JTPA's year-round and summer youth programs into a single year-round youth program, with summer work experience as one component. WIA's two adult programs provided for a broader range of services to the general public, no longer using income to determine eligibility for all program services.[1] The newly authorized WIA programs no longer focused exclusively on training but provided for three tiers, or levels, of service for adults and dislocated workers: core, intensive, and training. Beyond redesigning services and eligibility, WIA also mandated major changes in the way these programs measured success. The changes to the Adult and Dislocated Worker programs had a greater impact on the overall service structure than those made to the Youth program. This paper will, therefore, focus on the two adult components of WIA—Adults and Dislocated Workers.

WIA-funded services to adults and dislocated workers

WIA provided for three tiers, or levels, of service for adults and dislocated workers: core, intensive, and training. Core services include basic services such as job searches and labor market information. These activities may be self-service or require some staff assistance. Intensive services include such activities as comprehensive assessment and case management, as well as classes in literacy, conflict resolution, work skills, and those leading to a high school diploma or equivalent—activities that generally require greater staff involvement. Training services include such activities as occupational skills or on-the-job training. These tiers of WIA-funded services were to be provided sequentially, at least initially. That is, in order to receive intensive services, job seekers had to first access core services and demonstrate that those services alone would not lead to getting a job that would provide self-sufficiency. Similarly, to receive training services, a job seeker had to show that core and intensive services would not lead to such a job. Over time this requirement has been relaxed, and the USDOL no longer requires that job seekers access each level of service. But, through their work experience and assessments, job seekers must be able to show that core (or intensive) services would not lead to getting a job.

Unlike prior systems, WIA requires that individuals eligible for training under the adult and dislocated worker programs receive vouchers—called individual training accounts—which they can use for the training provider and course offering of their choice, within certain limitations. Because past systems were criticized for lacking outcome data on their training programs, WIA limits participants' use of the vouchers to those training providers who have a track record of positive outcomes. Authorized training providers and their approved course offerings must appear on an eligible training provider list (ETPL). To be on the list, the providers are required to collect and report data, including completion rates, job placement rates, and wages at placement on all the students enrolled in that course. This procedure has to be repeated for any new course offering that training providers may want to place on the ETPL. To stay on the list, training providers must meet or exceed performance criteria established by the state.

In our 2001 report on early implementation issues, we reported that training providers found these requirements overly burdensome (GAO 2001). They questioned whether it was worthwhile to assume this burden because so few individuals were being referred to them under WIA, especially when compared to the number of students they served overall. Providers began limiting the number of courses they offered to WIA-funded students, and some providers dropped out completely. To help alleviate these concerns, the USDOL began issuing waivers of the ETPL requirement. Currently, 40 states have waivers that allow them to forgo this requirement.

Despite early concerns about the amount of training under WIA, in a 2005 report, we found that substantial WIA funds were being used to fund training. Local boards used about 40 percent of the approximately $2.4 billion in WIA funds they had available in program year 2003 to provide training services to an estimated 416,000 WIA participants, primarily in occupational skills.[2] However, the vast majority of job seekers receive self-assisted core services, not training. Not everyone needs or wants additional training. And even when they do, they need help deciding what type of training would best match their skill level while at the same time meeting local labor market needs—help that includes information on job openings, comprehensive assessments, individual counseling, and supportive services, such as transportation and child care. Of the funds available in program year 2003, 60 percent was used to pay for these other program costs, as well as to cover the cost of administering the program.

WIA's funding structure

WIA's funding structure and process are complex. Once Congress appropriates WIA funds, the amount of money that flows to states and local areas depends on a specific statutory formula that takes into account such factors as the unemployment rate, the number of long-term unemployed, and the number of low-income adults and youth in the population. The USDOL allots 100 percent of the Adult funds and 80 percent of the Dislocated Worker funds to states. The Secretary of Labor retains 20 percent of the Dislocated Worker funds in a national reserve account to be used for National Emergency Grants, demonstrations, and technical assistance, and allots the remaining funds to each of the 50 states, the District of Columbia, and Puerto Rico.[3] Upon receiving its allotments, each state can set aside no more than 15 percent to support statewide activities. These may include a variety of activities that benefit adults, youths, and dislocated workers statewide, such as providing assistance in the establishment and operation of One-Stop centers, developing or operating state or local management information systems, and disseminating lists of organizations that can provide training. In addition, each state can set aside no more than 25 percent of its dislocated worker funds to provide rapid response services to workers affected by layoffs and plant closings. The funds set aside by the states to provide rapid response services are intended to help dislocated workers transition quickly to new employment. After states set aside funds for rapid response and for other statewide activities, they allocate the remainder of the funds—at least 60 percent—to their local workforce areas (see Figure 2.2).

The formulas for distributing the funds to the states for the three WIA programs were left largely unchanged from those used to distribute funds under the predecessor program, JTPA. However, these formulas do not reflect the current program structure, and, as states and localities have implemented WIA, they have been hampered by funding issues. States' funding levels are not always consistent with the actual demand for services, and in previous work, we identified several issues associated with the current funding formulas (GAO 2003b). First, formula factors used to allocate funds are not aligned with the target populations for these programs. For example, while long-term unemployed individuals are no longer automatically eligible for the Dislocated Worker

Figure 2.2 WIA Funding Streams for Adults, Youth, and Dislocated Workers

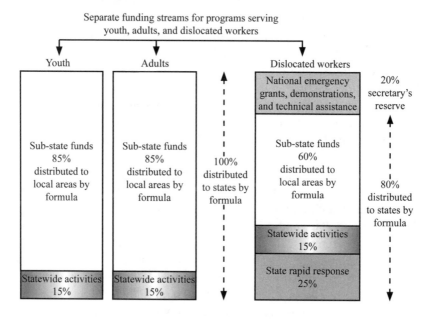

NOTE: A maximum of 10 percent of local funds may be used for local administration.
SOURCE: Employment and Training Administration.

program as they were under JTPA, this factor continues to be used. Second, allocations may not reflect current labor market conditions because there are time lags between when the data are collected and when the allocations become available to states. Third, the formula for the Dislocated Worker program is especially problematic, because it causes funding levels to suffer from excessive and unwarranted volatility unrelated to a state's actual layoff activity. Several aspects of the Dislocated Worker formula contribute to funding volatility and to the seeming lack of consistency between dislocation and funding. The excess unemployment factor has a threshold effect—states may or may not qualify for the one-third of funds allocated under this factor in a given year, based on whether or not they meet the threshold condition of having at least 4.5 percent unemployment statewide. In a study we conducted in 2003, we compared dislocation activity and funding levels for several states.

In one example, funding decreased in one year while dislocation activity increased by over 40 percent (see Figure 2.3). This volatility could be mitigated by provisions such as "hold harmless" and "stop gain" constraints that limit changes in funding to within a particular range of each state's prior year allocation. The Adult formula includes such constraints, setting the hold harmless at 90 percent and the stop gain at 130 percent.

In our 2007 testimony before Congress we highlighted funding stability as one of the key areas for focusing legislative action. We suggested that if Congress wished to make broader funding formula changes, reducing the volatility in the Dislocated Worker allocation by requiring the use of hold harmless and stop gain provisions in the formula would help stabilize funding and better foster sound financial practices (GAO 2007b).

Figure 2.3 An Example of the Mismatch between Dislocated Worker Funding Allocation and Dislocation Activity—Massachusetts

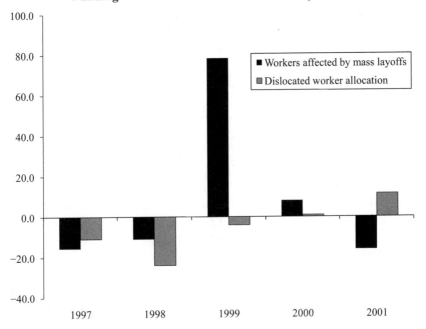

SOURCE: U.S. Department of Labor, Bureau of Labor Statistics, and Employment and Training Administration.

WIA's Performance Accountability Provisions

WIA was designed to provide for greater accountability than its predecessor program by establishing new performance measures, a new requirement to use UI wage data to track and report on outcomes, and a requirement for the USDOL to conduct at least one multisite control group evaluation. In general, WIA's performance measurement system captures some useful information, but it suffers from shortcomings that may limit its usefulness in understanding the full reach of the system and may lead to disincentives to serve those who may most need services. Moreover, despite WIA's efforts to improve accountability, little is known about what the system is achieving.

WIA established new measures, new data source, and some state flexibility

WIA was designed to promote greater accountability in federal workforce programs by establishing new performance measures for the three WIA-funded programs—the Adult, Dislocated Worker, and Youth programs. In its guidance during early implementation, the USDOL defined 17 performance measures for these programs. (See Table 2.1 for a complete list of the WIA performance measures.) Most of the measures that relate to adults, dislocated workers, and older youth are similar to those used under JTPA, including job placement, job retention, and wage gains or replacement. New under WIA, however, are measures for the attainment of a credential (a degree or certification of skills or training completed) and the "customer satisfaction" of both job seekers and employers (see Table 2.2).[4]

In addition, WIA sought to improve the comparability of data by requiring that most of the WIA performance measures rely on UI wage records as the primary data source for tracking employment outcomes. This contrasts with JTPA, which obtained data on participant outcomes by following up and surveying participants. The UI wage records provide a common yardstick for long-term comparisons across states because they contain wage and employment information on about 94 percent of the working population in the United States, and all states collect and retain these data. In addition, researchers have found that wage record data are more objective and cost-effective than traditional

Table 2.2 Statutory Performance Measures for the Three WIA-Funded Programs as Defined by the USDOL at Time of Implementation

WIA funding stream	Performance measure
Adult	Entered employment rate Employment retention at 6 months Average earnings change in 6 months Entered employment and credential rate[a]
Dislocated Worker	Entered employment rate Employment retention at 6 months Earnings replacement rate in 6 months Entered employment and credential rate[a]
Older Youth (age 19–21)	Entered employment rate Employment retention at 6 months Average earnings change in 6 months Entered employment/education/training and credential rate[a]
Younger Youth (age 14–18)	Skill attainment rate Diploma or equivalent attainment Placement and retention rate
Customer satisfaction	Customer satisfaction for participants[a] Customer satisfaction for employers[a]

[a]Indicates measures new under WIA.
SOURCE: USDOL.

survey information. For example, in our 2004 study, we estimated that the cost of doing participant surveys, as was done under JTPA, was approximately $13.25 per participant compared with the cost of automated record matching to UI wage records, which costs less than $0.05 per participant (GAO 2004). Furthermore, the UI wage records make it easier to track longer-term outcomes, such as the earnings change, earnings replacement, and employment retention six months after participants leave the program. Without UI wage records, tracking these outcomes would require contacting or surveying former participants, perhaps many times after leaving the program.

WIA is similar to JTPA in holding states accountable to performance goals by making incentive awards or imposing sanctions. However, unlike JTPA, under which the USDOL established performance goals using a computer model, WIA affords states some flexibility by allowing them to negotiate their performance goals with the department. States, in turn, negotiate performance goals with each local area. The law requires that these negotiations take into account differences in economic conditions, participant characteristics, and services provided. To establish equitable performance goals, the Labor Department and the states have primarily relied on historical data to develop their estimates of expected performance. These performance estimates are the starting point for negotiations. States that meet their performance goals under WIA are eligible to receive incentive grants that generally range from $750,000 to $3 million. States that do not meet at least 80 percent of their WIA performance goals are subject to sanctions. If a state fails to meet its performance goals for one year, the USDOL provides technical assistance, if requested. If a state fails to meet its performance goals for two consecutive years, the state may receive a 5 percent reduction in its annual WIA formula grant.

Performance goals can act as a deterrent to service

A long-standing challenge in assessing the performance of job training programs has been how to reward successful outcomes without creating an incentive for program managers to help only the most promising customers. With regard to WIA, as well, our 2002 study reported that many states were citing performance goals as a factor in local staff decisions about who would receive services (GAO 2002a). In states we visited, moreover, some officials told us that local areas were not registering many people, largely due to their concerns about meeting performance goals in serving job seekers who may be less likely to get and keep a job. One state official described how local areas were carefully screening potential participants and holding meetings to decide whether to register them. As a result, individuals who were eligible for and might have benefited from WIA-funded services may not have received them.

Measuring performance based on changes in participant earnings for some adults and earnings replacement for dislocated workers can also be a deterrent to service. In our 2002 study, state officials reported that local staff were reluctant to register two types of customers: already-employed adults and dislocated workers (GAO 2002a). State and local officials explained that it would be hard to increase the earnings of employed adults and to entirely replace the wages of dislocated workers who are laid off from high-paying, low-skilled jobs or from jobs requiring skills that are now obsolete. Similarly, in several local areas we visited for our study of older worker services, officials said they considered performance measures a barrier to enrolling older workers who are seeking part-time jobs because such placements could amount to lower earnings and lowered program performance as measured by client earnings (GAO 2003c).

Performance data has not always reflected all customers served at One-Stops

Under WIA, job seekers who only receive self-service and informational services are not included in the performance measures; therefore, only a small proportion of job seekers who receive services at One-Stops are actually reflected in WIA outcome data. Since self-service customers are estimated to be the largest portion of those served under WIA programs, it is difficult to know what the overall program is achieving. In a 2004 study, we reported that some estimates show only about 5 percent of the job seekers who walked into a One-Stop were registered for WIA and tracked for outcomes (GAO 2004). Furthermore, with regard to employers, the WIA measure only collects general information on employers' satisfaction and the data are not generally useful at the state and local level.[5] This makes it difficult to know how well individual One-Stops are working with and serving their employer communities.

GAO's recommendation: In 2005, the GAO recommended that the USDOL work with states and consider ways to track all job seekers who use any of the One-Stop services, including self-services. Since then, the Labor Department has begun to require states to collect and report a count on all WIA participants who have used the One-Stop system. The department has also taken steps to increase the information it has about employers who use the system. Currently, it only measures employer satisfaction, but it has secured approval from the Office of Management and Budget (OMB) to collect more extensive information (GAO 2009).

Lack of clarity in federal guidance has affected comparability of data

The USDOL's guidance to states at the time of implementation lacked clarity in key terms and contributed to inconsistency in the way that data have been collected and reported. Because WIA does not require outcome measures for all job seekers, the Labor Department provided written guidance to states on who should be registered for WIA services and included in the performance measures. However, the guidance was open to interpretation. For example, it told states to register and track outcomes for all adults and dislocated workers who receive core services that require significant staff assistance, which left states to decide what constituted significant staff assistance. As a result, states and local areas have differed on whom they track and for how long—some starting when participants receive core services, and others not tracking until they receive more intensive services. In a 2005 study, most states reported that they provided their own guidance to help local areas determine which jobseekers should be registered and tracked under the WIA performance measures (GAO 2005b). For example, one state developed a list of staff-assisted services that would trigger registration under WIA.

In addition, the lack of a definition for a credential led to performance data that are not comparable across states for the credential measure. The USDOL allowed states and local areas to determine what constituted a credential and to develop a statewide list of approved credentials with input from employers. As a result, some states limit "credentials" to diplomas from accredited institutions, while other states may, for example, consider a credential completion of formal training as defined by education partners (GAO 2002a). Still other states may have expanded their criteria to include completion of job readiness training, on-the-job experience, and or just one workshop. In our study of WIA youth services, we also found that the USDOL's guidance on defining skill attainment for youth was unclear and open to interpretation (GAO 2002b). Given the broad range of definitions states and localities employ, performance assessment based on the outcomes on the credential and skill attainment measures may be of limited value, even within a single state.

GAO's recommendations: To help ensure that the WIA performance measures result in more accurate and comparable data across states, we recommended that the USDOL establish a standard point at which to register participants and that it monitor states to ensure that they adhere to this policy. We also asked Congress to consider requiring that information be collected and reported for all WIA participants, including those who only receive self-service and informational services. In 2005, the USDOL issued new guidance that sought to better distinguish between self-service and informational activities that would not require participants to be registered and One-Stop services that require significant staff assistance and would require registration. Even with this additional guidance, we continue to be concerned that there will not be a uniform national practice for tracking registrants, which undermines the accuracy of performance data.

We also recommended that the USDOL issue guidance with a clear definition for what constitutes a credential and skill attainment. In its 2005 guidance, the Labor Department clearly defined credential to be a degree or certificate and stated that work readiness certificates will not be accepted. In addition, the department replaced the skill attainment measure with a literacy and numeracy gains measure that clearly specifies the level of improvement needed and types of assessments that can be used.

UI wage records have data gaps and time delays

While UI wage records provide a more objective means to measure outcomes over time, these data also have some shortcomings. State wage record databases only include wage information on job seekers within their state; they do not track job seekers who find jobs in other states. To help states gain access to wage information when their clients move to other states, the USDOL established the Wage Record Interchange System (WRIS)—a clearinghouse that makes UI wage records available to states seeking employment and wage information on their WIA participants. In 2006, Labor assumed responsibility for administering WRIS. Initially, when the department took the system over from a nonprofit organization, many states withdrew because of a perceived conflict between the department's federal enforcement role and states' responsibility for protecting data confidentiality. The USDOL developed a data sharing agreement to address confidentiality. All but one state now participates in WRIS (GAO 2009).

Another shortcoming is that UI wage records do not contain information on about 6 percent of workers, such as self-employed persons, most independent contractors, military personnel, federal government workers, and postal workers. To compensate, the Labor Department allows states to collect data to determine employment outcomes in other ways, such as contacting participants after they leave the program. In a 2004 study, 23 states reported that they would not have been able to show that they met minimum performance levels on at least one performance measure without supplemental data (GAO 2004). At that time, the department was considering whether to discontinue the use of supplemental data for filling gaps in the UI wage records, citing data quality concerns.

GAO's recommendation: We recommended that the USDOL continue to allow the use of supplemental data for reporting outcomes, but develop more stringent guidance and monitoring of these data. The Labor Department agreed with our recommendation and has continued to allow the use of supplemental data.

The ability to measure employment and earnings outcomes is significantly delayed, given the time lapse from when an individual gets a job to when it appears in the UI wage records. State procedures for collecting and compiling wage information from employers can be slow and time-consuming. Data are collected from employers only once every quarter and employers in most states have 30 days after the quarter ends to report the data to the state. After the state receives the wage report, the data must be processed, which can delay the availability of the wage record data for reporting on outcomes for several months. The time lags in receiving wage data affect when outcomes are reported and limit the data's usefulness for gauging current performance.

States and localities have supplemented WIA measures with their own

While UI wage records are useful for tracking outcomes over time, we found that this information alone does little for real-time program management. In a 2004 study, state and local officials reported that they collected their own data to assess whether they are likely to meet their federally required performance levels and manage their programs on a real-time basis (GAO 2004). States have taken an active role in helping local areas monitor their progress toward meeting their performance goals. Almost all states developed information technology systems to help local areas organize, track, and report WIA performance data for program management. At the same time, about three-fourths of local areas collect outcome information from other sources to help them assess whether they are meeting their WIA performance levels and to help them manage their programs. According to our 2004 study, over 75 percent of local areas reported that they directly follow up with participants after they leave the program, collecting job placement or earnings information to help fill gaps until the data are available from the UI wage records. In addition, nearly all of the local areas reported that they track other types of interim indicators to manage their WIA programs. These are most often the number of registered WIA participants, services provided to participants, the number of participants who completed training, and the number of WIA exiters. In some cases, these interim indicators can help local areas predict their WIA performance outcomes. For example, one local official told us that knowing the number of participants who complete training helps predict the number of participants who will find a job.

In addition to the WIA performance measures, states and localities also reported that they use their own indicators to gauge overall One-Stop performance (GAO 2004). We identified four basic types of indicators: 1) job seeker measures, 2) employer measures, 3) program partnership measures, and 4) family and community indicators. (See Figure 2.4.)

Job seeker measures. Even without a federal requirement to do so, our survey showed that almost 90 percent of local areas gather information on One-Stop job seekers, even if they are not registered and participating in any particular federal program. Most often local areas reported that they require the One-Stop centers to track and report the number of job seekers who visit the One-Stop in a single time period, usually through a paper and pencil or computer log. In addition, we found that local areas are tracking additional information on these job seekers such as how many program referrals they receive, how satisfied they are with services, and what types of outcome they achieve.[5]

Figure 2.4   Four Types of Indicators That States and Local Areas Use to Assess Performance of One-Stops

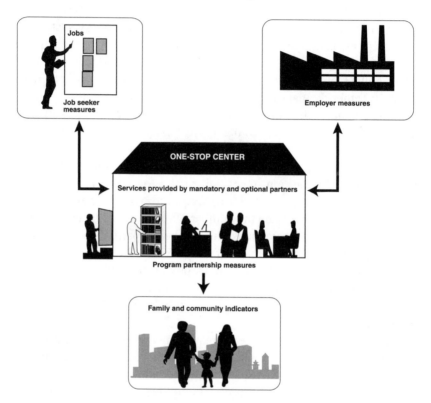

Source: GAO analysis.

Employer measures. Many local areas also track information on employers' use of One-Stops to improve services to employers. About 70 percent of local areas nationwide reported that they require One-Stop centers to track some type of employer measure, such as the number of employers that use One-Stop services, how many hire One-Stop customers, and the type of services that employers use. For example, a One-Stop center we visited tracks employers that repeatedly use One-Stop services and those who have not. It uses this information to reach out to employers who have not returned for services to encourage them to use the One-Stop again.

Program partnership measures. Most of the programs that provide services through the One-Stop system have their own performance measures, but as we have reported in the past, these outcomes cannot be readily summed to obtain an overall measure of One-Stop performance. However, one-third of the local areas told us that they combine in one report some of the outcomes under the key federal measures—including wages at employment or other earning indicators—and use this report to assess the One-Stop system as a whole. In addition to tracking outcomes for the various One-Stop partners, some local areas measure the level of coordination among One-Stop partners, and also the range and quality of services they provide.

Family and community indicators. A few local areas look beyond One-Stop services to individuals to assess how well One-Stops are meeting the needs of the family and the community. In their written comments to our survey, several local areas told us that they consider some type of community indicator, such as changes in the local unemployment rate or increases in the average household income in the local area, to be the best way to determine the overall effectiveness of their One-Stop system.

The USDOL uses WIA performance data for negotiations of performance goals and awarding incentives or imposing sanctions

The USDOL compiles states' reported performance data annually to develop national performance goals under the Government Performance and Results Act.[6] In addition, these national goals are used as a starting place to negotiate performance goals with states. While WIA requires that the annual negotiations for performance goals take into account differences in economic conditions, participant characteristics, and services provided, these factors may not be adequately considered by all states or the labor department in the negotiations. In our 2004 study, we found that state and local officials we interviewed thought their performance levels were set too high for economic conditions at that time (GAO 2004). For example, some local officials said that their negotiated performance goals for changes to or replacement of earnings were based on a stronger economy and did not reflect recent increases in the unemployment rate. Under JTPA, the USDOL used an adjustment model to account for factors beyond the control of local programs, such as high unemployment. Under WIA, some states have used their own adjustment model or other methods in the negotiation process, but until recently, the department did not take steps to assure that all appropriate factors are taken into account and treated in the same way in negotiations and that, as a result, there is consistent assessment across states.

The GAO's recommendation: We recommended that the USDOL develop an adjustment model or other systematic method to consistently account for different populations and local economic conditions when negotiating performance levels. In recent guidance for negotiating program year 2009 performance goals, the Labor Department used a regression model to set national performance goals. The department said that the goals were based on estimates developed from administrative and economic data on job seekers within their local labor markets that it has compiled from its WIA database or other data systems (USDOL 2009).

The Labor Department has expanded uniform reporting for all its workforce programs

In 2005, the USDOL began requiring states to implement a common set of performance measures for all employment and training programs under its purview, including the WIA-funded programs. This was at the impetus of the OMB, which in 2002 requested that all federal agencies with job training programs develop some common performance measure. In responding to the OMB initiative, the USDOL has substituted some of its new common measure definitions for counterpart measures as previously defined when first implementing WIA. These changes have included such measures as the entered employment rate, employment retention rate, and average earnings measure. While many federal job training programs require performance measures that track similar outcomes, they have varied in their terminology and in the way their measures are calculated. For example, the Wagner-Peyser-funded Employment Service uses a different time period than the WIA adult program to assess whether a participant got a job. With the common measures, both programs use the same time period to report this measure.

The USDOL has also made efforts to streamline and integrate the performance reporting structures of all the federal programs under its purview, but realization of this goal has been delayed. In 2004, the department had proposed a single, streamlined reporting structure that would have replaced reporting structures for most of its employment and training programs. In a 2005 study, we found that the department developed the concept in limited consultation with key stakeholders, and as a result, it underestimated the magnitude and type of changes required (GAO 2005c). We recommended that it consider alternative approaches to implementing such a structure. In response, the department substantially modified the design and is now working toward implementing an enhanced data reporting system called the Workforce Investment Streamlined Performance Reporting (WISPR) system. If implemented, the new reporting structure would consolidate reporting requirements across several other Labor Department programs in the One-Stops and ultimately replace their existing reporting systems with a single reporting structure. Its integrated design would, for the first time, allow the Labor Department and states to track an individual's progress through the One-Stop system. For the time being, the USDOL has delayed its implementation to focus on new reporting for the American Reinvestment and Recovery Act funding.

CONCLUDING OBSERVATIONS ON REAUTHORIZATION

WIA was due to be reauthorized in 2003, but efforts thus far have stalled, most often due to competing demands requiring the attention of the authorizing committees. When bills have been forwarded, competing philosophies regarding governance and service delivery strategies have kept them from being passed.

Reauthorizing WIA has never been more urgent than it is today. Workforce trends and the economic downturn have placed greater demands on the workforce investment system than ever before. At present, the system is stretched thin. If we as a nation are to maintain our competitiveness for the higher-skilled jobs, we must place more emphasis on training workers to keep their skills current—before they are threatened with layoff. We must develop better linkages between education and employment, and we need greater involvement of employers in federal, state, and local workforce development efforts.

Increasing labor force participation will require improving basic skills levels, including language skills, and greater involvement of employers and unions in designing education and training opportunities. But all of this comes at great financial cost. Large and growing federal deficits are constraining government spending, just as state and local budgets are already struggling to meet the growing needs with less revenue. In light of these concerns, and in the process of reauthorizing WIA, some key questions need to be answered.

- How can we ensure that policymakers have the information they need—about what works and what doesn't—to make critical decisions about where to place their scarce resources?

- How might the key players in this system at all levels—federal, state, local, and the private sector—be brought to the table to participate as stakeholders and investors?

- How can we balance flexibility and accountability without unintended consequences in who gets served?

- How can we learn more about what the overall One-Stop system is achieving when only a small portion of One-Stop customers are registered and tracked in the performance measures?

- What can be done to make the system more nimble and able to adapt to changing economic and budgetary conditions?

Notes

1. Participants are not required to meet income eligibility requirements to receive services; however, when funds are limited, priority for intensive services and training under the adult program is given to low-income individuals and public assistance recipients.

2. Note that the percentage of job seekers who received training in that year may be somewhat lower than 40 percent due to the cost of training relative to other services. The estimate of WIA participants may include some participants more than once, because some individuals may have received more than one type of training.

3. For additional information on National Emergency Grants, see GAO (2004).

4. Guidance from the USDOL defines a credential as a nationally recognized degree or certificate or a recognized state/locally defined credential.

5. While WIA requires that all states track job seeker customer satisfaction, Labor does not require a sufficient sample size to be useful to each local area.

6. The Government Performance and Results Act is intended to focus government decision making, management, and accountability on the results and outcomes achieved by federal programs.

References

Government Accountability Office (GAO). 2001. *Workforce Investment Act: Better Guidance Needed to Address Concerns over New Requirements.* GAO-02-72. Washington, DC: GAO.

————. 2002a. *Workforce Investment Act: Improvements Needed in Performance Measures to Provide a More Accurate Picture of WIA's Effectiveness.* GAO-02-275. Washington, DC: GAO.

————. 2002b. *Workforce Investment Act: Youth Provisions Promote New Service Strategies, but Additional Guidance Would Enhance Program Development.* GAO-02-413. Washington, DC: GAO.

————. 2003a. *Workforce Investment Act: One-Stop Centers Implemented Strategies to Strengthen Services and Partnerships, but More Research and Information Sharing Is Needed.* GAO-03-725. Washington, DC: GAO.

————. 2003b. *Workforce Investment Act: Issues Related to Allocation Formulas for Youth, Adults, and Dislocated Workers.* GAO-03-636. Washington, DC: GAO.

————. 2003c. *Older Workers: Employment Assistance Focuses on Subsidized Jobs and Job Search, but Revised Performance Measures Could Improve Access to Other Services.* GAO-03-350. Washington, DC: GAO.

————. 2004. *Workforce Investment Act: States and Local Areas Have Developed Strategies to Assess Performance, but Labor Could Do More to Help.* GAO-04-657. Washington, DC: GAO.

————. 2005a. *Workforce Investment Act: Employers Are Aware of, Using, and Satisfied with One-Stop Services, but More Data Could Help Labor Better Address Employers' Needs.* GAO-05-259. Washington, DC: GAO.

————. 2005b. *Workforce Investment Act: Labor and States Have Taken Actions to Improve Data Quality, but Additional Steps Are Needed.* GAO-06-82. Washington, DC: GAO.

————. 2005c. *Workforce Investment Act: Labor Should Consider Alternative Approaches to Implement New Performance and Reporting Requirements.* GAO-05-539. Washington, DC: GAO.

————. 2006. *Workforce Investment Act: Employers Found One-Stop Centers*

Useful in Hiring Low-Skilled Workers; Performance Information Could Help Gauge Employer Involvement. GAO-07-167. Washington, DC: GAO.

————. 2007a. *Workforce Investment Act: One-Stop System Infrastructure Continues to Evolve, but Labor Should Take Action to Require That All Employment Service Offices Are Part of the System.* GAO-07-1096. Washington, DC: GAO.

————. 2007b. *Workforce Investment Act: Additional Actions Would Further Improve the Workforce System.* GAO-07-1051T. Washington, DC: GAO.

————. 2009. *Workforce Investment Act: Labor Has Made Progress in Addressing Areas of Concern, but More Focus Needed on Understanding What Works and What Doesn't.* GAO-09-396T. Washington, DC: GAO.

U.S. Department of Labor, Employment and Training Administration (USDOL). 2009. "Training and Employment Guidance Letter No. 09-08, Change 1." Washington, DC: USDOL/ETA.

Part 2

Program Implementation

3
The Use of Market Mechanisms

Christopher T. King
University of Texas at Austin

Burt S. Barnow
George Washington University

This chapter is based in part on a larger study of the implementation of WIA conducted with colleagues in eight states and 16 localities from 2003 to 2005.[1] After presenting background on WIA and the study, we present key results concerning one of the more important and controversial aspects of the act: increased emphasis on market and market-like mechanisms in the delivery of workforce services in the United States. We then discuss these findings and wrap up with a series of conclusions and recommendations, both for informing the WIA reauthorization process, which is now under way, and for providing guidance to the European Social Fund.

BACKGROUND

WIA has been described as a "major overhaul" of the nation's approach to employment and training, as a "fundamental departure" from previous programs, and as "the first significant attempt to retool" these programs in two decades (Barnow and King 2003). The act institutionalized changes in workforce policies and practices that began to surface as a handful of early-implementing states (e.g., Florida, Indiana, Kentucky, Louisiana, Pennsylvania, Texas, Utah, Vermont, and Wisconsin) operationalized the act's provisions beginning in July 1999. These and other states had developed and implemented One-Stop Career Centers prior to the 1998 enactment of WIA legislation, some of them, such as

Wisconsin and Pennsylvania, as early as the mid-1980s. Major changes authorized under Title I of WIA included

- fostering more coordinated, longer-term planning for workforce development programs;
- institutionalizing One-Stop Career Centers as the cornerstones of the local workforce delivery system;
- sequencing job seekers' services from core to intensive to training services;
- implementing universal eligibility for core services via One-Stop Career Centers; and
- increasing reliance on market mechanisms.

The last set of changes, market mechanisms, is the main focus of this chapter.

THE WIA STUDY

The WIA study was conducted using the field network methodology developed over several decades for use in understanding program implementation.[2] In each of the participating study states, a spectrum of workforce system actors was interviewed. Using a structured interview guide, elected officials (e.g., legislators), policymakers, agency officials, program directors, community and technical college administrators, business and chamber of commerce leaders, state and local Workforce Investment Board (WIB) directors and staff, One-Stop Career Center directors and staff, advocates, and workers in community-based organizations were interviewed. In addition, leaders and staff of workforce development, education, and related programs were engaged in discussions to obtain a broad perspective of workforce development activities.

A number of researchers have examined WIA, most focusing on early WIA implementation experiences across a broad range of issues. Employment and Training Administration staff began conducting internal implementation studies of WIA in 1998 and 1999. The Employment and Training Administration (ETA) also funded a two-track national WIA implementation study by Social Policy Research (SPR) Associates that featured visits to 16 states and numerous localities and One-Stop

Career Centers between 1999 and 2001 (D'Amico et al. 2001), as well as assisting the ETA with consolidating WIA implementation data for all 54 states and territories. Buck (2002) of Public/Private Ventures also studied early WIA implementation in five cities, focusing largely on how new market mechanisms (e.g., individual training accounts [ITAs], performance measures) and One-Stop requirements affected workforce programs and participants. Frank et al. (2003) of the Center for Law and Social Policy analyzed national data for the 2000–2001 period, comparing early participation, demographics, and services under WIA with similar data for the final year of JTPA.

The ETA also funded Administrative Data Research and Evaluation (ADARE) project researchers from several universities and private, nonprofit research institutions who examined early participation and service patterns, and WIA performance measures (Mueser et al. 2003; Stevens 2003) and estimated quasi-experimental net impacts from WIA participation on employment and earnings (Hollenbeck et al. 2005).

Finally, O'Shea and King (2001) explored early experiences with WIA and related programs in three states (Tennessee, Texas, and Washington) and at least two local workforce investment areas in each as a pilot for the eight-state WIA study. They focused on problems and opportunities experienced by these states while implementing new WIA features (e.g., eligible training provider lists [ETPLs], service sequencing) and also explored ways in which states and local areas addressed expanded authority under WIA in their own particular context.

These studies, together with policy interest from the ongoing WIA reauthorization debate and ETA discussions, helped shape the focus of the eight-state WIA study, which addressed the following topics, among others:

- leadership and governance, including issues regarding the decentralization of authority and responsibility;
- One-Stop organization and operations;
- services and participation;
- market mechanisms, their use and effects, including labor market information, performance standards, and training provider certification; and
- the use of information technologies.

The study examined the experiences of eight states, 16 local workforce investment areas, and more than 30 One-Stop centers with the administration and delivery of employment and training services under WIA and closely related programs. Table 3.1 lists the study states and areas, and the field researchers. Study sites were selected using a purposive selection strategy focusing on region, urban/rural populations, the organizational approach of One-Stop systems, and WIA early implementation status.

As part of the selection process, field researchers considered organizational structure, service delivery practices, implementation obstacles, population statistics, urban/rural mix, number of One-Stops, and size. Field researchers also obtained recommendations and supporting information from state officials, regional ETA staff, and the National Governors Association. The sample—which included small

Table 3.1 States and Local Workforce Areas Studied

Florida	First Coast (Region 8), Citrus, Levy, and Marion Counties (Region 10) Researchers: Burt Barnow, Amy Buck
Indiana	Ft. Wayne (Northeast), Indianapolis/Marion County Researchers: Patricia Billen, Richard Nathan
Maryland	Baltimore City, Frederick County Researchers: Burt Barnow, Amy Buck
Michigan	Lansing (Capital Area), Traverse City (Northwest) Researchers: Christopher King, Daniel O'Shea
Missouri	Kansas City and vicinity, Central Region Researchers: Peter Meuser, Deanna Sharpe
Oregon	Marion, Polk, and Yamhill Counties (Region 3) The Oregon Consortium/Oregon Workforce Alliance (TOC/OWA) Researchers: Laura Leete, Neil Bania
Texas	Austin (Capitol Area), Houston (Gulf Coast) Researchers: Christopher King, Daniel O'Shea
Utah	Salt Lake City (Central), Moab/Price (Southeast) Researchers: Christopher King, Daniel O'Shea

NOTE: Utah is organized as a single, statewide workforce investment area. This is unusual but not unique. Other states with single workforce areas include South Dakota, Vermont, and Wyoming. Under prior workforce training programs (e.g., CETA), states such as South Carolina also were organized as single-program states.

and large states, and urban and rural areas with a range of organizational structures and service delivery approaches—was weighted to "leading-edge" workforce development states (e.g., Florida, Michigan, Texas, Utah). As a group, these states had less difficulty with some of WIA's new features, since they had either already begun to implement them on their own or, given their long-standing experience with workforce reform, would be expected to have an easier time doing so. The study's findings were based on WIA policies and service delivery experiences observed during the summer and fall of 2002, when field researchers conducted site visits and interviewed state and local actors, as well as on changes that occurred subsequently.

USE OF MARKET MECHANISMS: KEY FINDINGS

WIA continued the trend of moving toward a market-based system that is results driven and determined more by customer choice. Four key market-based mechanisms are discussed: labor market information (LMI), provider certification, ITAs, and performance management systems.[3]

Labor Market Information

While not a market mechanism per se, labor market information (LMI) provides customers with information about employment opportunities and promotes and facilitates the workings of the labor market. All states have LMI units that provide information for the state as a whole and for individual labor markets. In addition to producing information about the current status of the labor market, states also produce labor market projections that include 10-year occupational employment projections. A unit in the state Employment Service usually operates LMI programs. LMI funding comes from several sources, including the Bureau of Labor Statistics (BLS) in the USDOL, which is responsible for producing and coordinating employment statistics at the national level. Both state and national LMI is available at One-Stop Career Centers via the Internet.

Generally, states have made strides toward improving the quality and presentation of their LMI in recent years. In several study states, some of the WIBs expressed dissatisfaction with aspects of the state's LMI program and purchased supplementary information from private vendors. These complaints often reflect a desire for more detailed vacancy data that the state cannot produce because of budgetary constraints. This study did not cover the states' labor market information systems in sufficient depth to judge their scope and quality. However, it appears that state labor market information programs are aware of the concerns from local workforce investment areas and are trying to meet their needs. The transition to the Standard Occupational Code (SOC) system for all federal programs producing information on occupations and the emergence of ETA's O*NET, the Occupational Information Network, also should enhance the value of labor market information. O*NET provides occupational skills and aptitude requirement information and identifies occupations requiring similar skills.

Provider Certification

Under JTPA, the federal employment and training program that preceded WIA (1982–1998), vendors did not have to meet performance criteria to be eligible to provide training to participants. To improve accountability and enable customers to make more informed choices, WIA established the ETPL, giving the responsibility to states for establishing the ETPL application procedures. Providers on the list, whose eligibility is reviewed every 12–18 months, are required to furnish performance information to the state's workforce agencies for WIA customers and for all enrollees (whether a WIA customer or not) for each occupational training program on the list.

Experience to date raises questions about whether, under its current structure, the ETPL provides sufficient valid information to justify its costs and inconvenience. The experiences of the study states varied, and while a few states found the ETPL to be useful and a minimal burden, in most states the providers, the state, or both complained that gathering the data was expensive and not worth the effort. Because results must be provided for each individual occupational training program rather than for the provider as a whole, the reports frequently covered such a small number of participants, particularly the results for only WIA participants, that there were too few enrollees to provide statistically meaningful results. Combining data for various occupations would resolve the small sample problem in some instances, but by combining data across offerings, prospective students would not be able to assess the provider's performance for specific offerings.

Among the states covered in this project, Florida experienced the fewest problems with the ETPL requirements. Florida had already established the Florida Education and Training Placement Information Program (FETPIP) prior to WIA to track education and training vendor performance. Administered by the Florida Department of Education, FETPIP collects, maintains, and disseminates placement and follow-up information on Florida education and training program participants by relying on linkages to UI wage and other employment and earnings records.

Utah also did not experience major difficulties with these requirements. The state has modified its program since it was initially established in early 1999. However, obtaining providers for its list caused some problems because the state then lacked a fully developed system of community and technical colleges.

Texas experienced some problems with its ETPL process. The initial 1999 system was paper based and viewed as cumbersome, though improvements to the system have eased the problems. Difficulty accessing outcome data remains a challenge for institutions and the state. Some state officials speculated that a number of providers had let their listing lapse so they could reenter the system using the more lenient standards for new listings.

Maryland staff at the state and local level indicated that the ETPL created significant problems. Local officials in the two Maryland areas reported that the process of getting a provider on the list was time consuming and confusing. Providers were hesitant about putting programs on the list, and many programs had too few participants to yield reliable performance data. A state official noted, however, that the ETPL process helped the state weed out education and training institutions that were operating illegally.

Michigan did not report major problems with the ETPL system, but state officials noted that instituting ETPL appeared to have reduced WIA participation of community colleges and technical schools in the state. Community colleges in the state now apply for certification only for those programs for which they expect to get substantial numbers of training referrals.

Missouri had to modify its data collection system to accommodate the ETPL requirements. The Department of Elementary and Secondary Education maintained a list of providers prior to WIA, and has established a system to remove most of the burden of data collection from vendors. At the time of the study, state officials recognized that data matching requirements would increase as the WIA program matured, but the state and local areas reported only minimal problems with the ETPL.

ETPL requirements presented some challenges in Oregon, but state officials worked hard to assure that WIA did not discourage the use of community colleges as training providers. The state adopted policies to assure that nondegree sequences would count as a "program" for WIA ETPL purposes and assumed all responsibility for reporting training provider results. The state expedites the ETPL approval process when a participant wishes to enroll in an unlisted program, and the process can be completed in one week.

Indiana officials characterized the ETPL approval process as an administrative burden, but not prohibitively so. State officials indicated that training providers are reluctant to collect the required performance information because of the small number of expected WIA enrollees.

The best strategy at this time may be to relax the ETPL requirements to allow states and local areas time to develop more economical tracking systems and strategies to address programs with few WIA enrollees. Performance-based contracting offers one approach to holding providers accountable for placing participants, but its track record is mixed.[4] Other possibilities include combining data for several years for judging outcomes and waiving ETPL requirements for small programs.

Individual Training Accounts

In addition to mandating the use of One-Stops, another significant change instituted under WIA was the establishment of ITAs. In an effort to provide more customer choice, WIA mandated that under most circumstances adults and dislocated workers who were to receive training services must be provided with ITAs that let them select their own training provider and occupational program (subject to local workforce investment agency restrictions). Exceptions to the ITA rule were made for customized and on-the-job training (OJT), where participant provider selection would make little sense, and when there was a training program of demonstrated effectiveness offered by a community-based or other organization in the area to serve special participant populations facing multiple employment barriers.

ITAs are essentially vouchers, though not in their purest form (see Barnow and King [1996]). Prior to WIA there had been only limited experience with the use of vouchers in workforce development programs (see Barnow [2000, 2009], and Trutko and Barnow [1999]). Vouchers give WIA participants the freedom to select the program they believe would best meet their needs, but the evidence on the effectiveness of vouchers for disadvantaged populations has been mixed, with some studies showing that this group frequently overreached in selecting programs.

There were other potential problems with ITAs. Local WIBs might have argued that it made little sense to hold vendors and programs accountable for participants' performance if participants were making the selection. This potential pitfall was avoided by permitting local programs to exercise latitude in limiting ITA use to programs in which participants were qualified and for in-demand occupations. In addition, the ETPL is intended to screen out programs that are ineffectual in placing participants in suitable jobs. The remaining concern is that the use of ITAs would provide uncertainty to providers on how many participants they might serve in a given year, making it difficult for them to plan and staff their offerings.

Overall, ITAs appear to be a somewhat successful feature of WIA. They are popular with participants and accepted by the local WIBs as a useful program feature. An important aspect of this success is that local boards have the flexibility to set limits on the programs' time and costs, and to have a "guided choice" approach to ITA use. Under the guided-choice approach, local WIA programs provide strong guidance or restrict ITA use to programs they believe correspond to the participant's aptitudes and abilities. The ETA conducted an experiment operated by Mathematica Policy Research to determine the advantages and disadvantages of three levels of consumer choice for ITAs (see D'Amico et al. [2002] and McConnell et al. [2006]). This experiment concluded that the three approaches to balancing consumer and WIB choice did not yield strong findings favoring any one of the approaches over the alternatives.[5]

The site visits did not provide much information on the three exceptions to the use of ITAs, but other evidence suggests that customized training and OJT are among the most effective training strategies.[6] The exception for special populations permits local boards to make use of particular exemplary programs when warranted. This exception was not observed in the field visits, and no other evidence on this provision was identified, so it would be useful for the ETA to conduct research on the use of this provision. The ability of local WIBs to set time and dollar limits on the ITAs is useful because it permits local boards to determine the balance between the number of participants served and the cost per participant. Some local boards require that participants use the lowest cost provider when there are alternatives, but others do not. A case could be made for requiring the lowest cost provider for a particular program, but it can also be argued that local boards are in a better position to determine if the programs offered are truly equivalent.

States in the study sample often left decisions on implementing ITAs to the local boards, which usually used a guided-choice approach for customer choice. The local boards commonly established time and cost limits, but there were many variations. Study results indicated that choice was limited either because many providers did not list their programs on the ETPL or there were a limited number of providers in the state.

In Maryland, customer choice was limited by the reluctance of providers to sign up for the ETPL. Both local areas visited for the study used a guided-choice approach. Local programs used alternatives to ITAs. Baltimore, for example, had several customized training programs and wanted to expand their use, as they commonly had high placement and wage rates.

Michigan had already implemented a consumer-oriented voucher system for work-related education and training programs prior to WIA, so adaptation to the WIA requirements was not difficult for the state's WIBs. Michigan's ITA cap was determined locally, and generally ranged between $1,000 and $3,000 for individuals whose income was less than 70 percent of the lower living standard income level and who met certain other requirements. Staff reported that some training providers had established fees for their programs at the ITA cap for their local board. This phenomenon, where the ceiling becomes the floor, is a potential abuse in areas where there is insufficient competition among providers.

Missouri's local boards generally limited the reimbursement available through their ITAs, although the state specified that training allocations had to be made on a case-by-case basis. In interviews, Missouri staff stressed the importance of matching participants with programs where they were likely to experience labor market success. Staff of the local boards used aptitudes and interests to guide participants into appropriate choices.

In Florida, local boards had the option of setting dollar and time limits for ITAs. Local boards almost always used a guided choice approach to the ITAs. Local officials in Florida expressed concern that when they permitted participants to enroll in long-term training programs, some of their training funds were committed but not spent. Thus, it sometimes appeared that they were underspending even though the funds were fully allocated. These officials wanted the system modified so that they could fund programs expected to last more than one year by placing funds for the out years in an escrow account to assure continuous funding for participants.

Texas started slowly in its use of ITAs, in part because the state initially interpreted WIA more as a work-first program. When the state shifted to a business-oriented, demand-driven system, interest in training and ITAs increased.[7] Local workforce investment areas could establish their own ITA caps, which varied substantially, ranging from $3,500 in one local workforce investment area to $10,000 in another. As in Michigan, some Texas officials reported that vendors sometimes priced their programs at the local ITA cap.

Utah used a guided choice approach for its ITAs. State officials reported that their major challenge in the use of ITAs was a lack of sufficient numbers of training providers.

Performance Standards and Incentives

Performance management has been an important aspect of workforce development programs for many years. CETA (1973–1982) included a limited performance management system in its later years (1980–1982), and JTPA featured a comprehensive performance management system by the mid-1980s. WIA modified JTPA's performance

management system in several important ways. Under JTPA, only local areas were subject to performance standards, but under WIA the
states have standards as well. Under JTPA, local standards were adjusted by a statistically based regression equation to hold local areas
harmless for local economic conditions and the characteristics of participants served, but under WIA state standards are determined through
negotiations, and adjustments are only possible if an appeal is filed and
approved.[8] Finally, under JTPA, performance was initially measured at
the time of termination and 13 weeks after termination, but under WIA
performance is measured, based on UI wage records, 26 weeks after
termination from the program.

There were a total of 17 core performance measures for WIA in
the early to mid-2000s. For adults, dislocated workers, and youth ages
19–21, the core measures were the entered employment rate; employment retention six months after entry into employment; earnings change
from the six months prior to entry to the six months after exit; and the
obtained credential rate for participants who enter unsubsidized employment or, in the case of older youth, enter postsecondary education,
advanced training, or unsubsidized employment. For youth between the
ages of 14 and 18, the core performance measures were attainment of
basic skills and, as appropriate, work readiness or occupational skills;
attainment of a high school diploma or its equivalent; and placement
and retention in postsecondary education and training, employment, or
military service. There were also customer satisfaction measures for
both participants and employers.

All states and local areas in the study sample expressed concerns
about the performance management system under WIA. Most officials
interviewed indicated that the WIA system was a step backward from
the approach used under JTPA. They decried the absence of a procedure
to adjust for characteristics of participants served and local economic
conditions; state and local officials stated that failing to adjust for differences in these factors means that states and local areas are not placed
on a level playing field.[9]

State officials expressed concern that the ETA regional office officials did not enter into real negotiations with state officials; they all
indicated that the federal officials did not negotiate on what the state
standards should be, citing pressure from the federal government to
meet its standards. They also said they were dissatisfied with the defi-

nitions of who was considered a covered system participant and when participants were terminated, which they considered vague. This ambiguity made it possible for the local workforce investment areas to engage in strategic decision making about whom they enrolled and when they considered someone an exiter in order to enhance their measured performance. Officials also expressed concern that WIA had too many performance measures, with 17 for adults, dislocated workers, and youth.

Interestingly, more than half the states in the study sample—Florida, Indiana, Oregon, Texas, and Utah—actually *added* more performance measures to the mandated federal ones, which made the assertion that there were too many performance measures somewhat questionable. Often, however, these added measures were to provide state and local staff with either more systematic measurement of workforce performance or more immediate information for managers regarding how participants were faring with program participation (O'Shea, Looney, and King 2003a,b).

WIA reauthorization could provide an opportunity to improve the performance management system for the program.[10] Lessons can be learned from the states' criticisms of the current system, as well as the actions they have taken to enhance the WIA performance management system. In the interest of fairness and to avoid incentives for creaming, where they serve eligible individuals more likely to do well on the performance measures instead of those with greater labor market barriers, an adjustment mechanism should be added to the system. The regression-based adjustment approach used under JTPA is one possibility, but even the subjectively established adjustment procedure that the ETA subsequently implemented in 2006 was an improvement.[11] Moreover, the concept of using negotiations to set standards should not be precluded when an adjustment model is used. The adjustment model could be used to develop a starting point, followed by negotiations to determine the final standard. For the negotiations to be meaningful, however, a more systematic approach should be used so that both sides believe the system is fair.[12]

The definitions of WIA entry and exit, as well as the boundaries of the different service categories, are currently too vague to form the basis of a nationally uniform performance management system. Several states in the research sample have begun developing "system measures," which capture performance for entire labor market areas rather than for a specific program such as WIA. A few have explored developing measures that reflect return on investment (ROI) as well. Texas, through its state workforce board association, has estimated ROI for a broad array of workforce funding streams at the state and local levels from participant, taxpayer, and societal perspectives (King et al. 2008). Although incorporating costs into performance management is important, work should proceed with caution because limits on follow-up data and imperfect information can cause such measures to provide misleading signals.

The appropriate follow-up period for performance measures should also receive renewed attention. The 26-week follow-up period in WIA permits the performance management system to do a better job of capturing longer-term program effects, but this is at the expense of information timeliness. Reliance on UI wage record data results in information delays of up to nine months. Thought should be given to ways to accelerate data collection and/or using shorter-term measures in addition to or instead of the longer-term measures so that more timely feedback can be provided.

Evidence of strategic behavior or "gaming" to improve measured performance was found in a majority of the states in the study sample.[13] This does not mean that these states were doing anything contrary to the WIA law or regulations, only that they were modifying their behavior to improve measured performance. Some local areas indicated that in response to the performance management system they took steps to improve their measured performance. Local areas employ creaming and strategic behavior when recording individuals' enrollment and/or program termination.

Maryland's state board was concerned that the current system of measuring performance for individual programs did not permit the state to gauge performance for the state as a whole. To deal with this issue, the state developed a "system report card" with nine measures that applied to an entire labor market area rather than a specific program: 1) the credential rate, 2) the high school dropout rate, 3) the college readiness rate, 4) investment per participant, 5) the self-sufficiency rate, 6) the One-Stop Career Center usage rate, 7) customer satisfaction, 8) job openings by occupation, and board effectiveness.

Florida has long been a leader in exceeding performance requirements of federal programs. Legislation enacted in 1996 required the state to develop a three-tier performance management system for its programs. Tier three focuses on federally mandated measures; tier two measures are grouped by program and target group and provide measures appropriate for specific population subgroups. Tier one measures are broad economic measures applicable to almost all workforce development programs. The state also developed a "Red and Green Report" that compared regions on a number of short-term performance indicators based on administrative data; regions in the top quarter on a measure are shown in green, and regions in the bottom quarter are marked in red.[14]

Texas is another state with a strong history of performance management. When the eight-state study was completed the state had instituted 35 performance measures for its workforce development programs. Texas measures performance on a monthly basis, and the Texas Workforce Commission has a committee that meets monthly to address performance problems. As the eight-state WIA report was prepared, Texas was considering implementing a tiered performance management system.

Oregon was in the process of implementing a set of uniform, systemwide performance measures for its workforce development system. These 13 measures will apply to all state agencies that are partners in the system. Oregon officials view the state systemwide measures as important for building an integrated system. As the study was being conducted, the state was requesting a waiver from the USDOL to use the state measures for reporting under WIA.

Indiana uses three systemwide measures to award WIA incentive funds: customer satisfaction, earnings gains, and credentials acquired. Similar to Oregon, Indiana submitted a waiver request to the USDOL to use its systemwide measures in place of the WIA performance measures; the request was denied.

Since fieldwork was completed for the eight-state WIA study, most study states continued work on WIA's market mechanisms and related features. Four study states—Florida, Michigan, Oregon, and Texas—participated in the Integrated Performance Improvement (IPI) project led by Washington State and convened by the National Governors Association (see Saunders and Wilson [2003] and Wilson [2005]). This project, which sought to develop *system-level performance measures* for state workforce development systems, produced a draft "blueprint" of measures that was rolled out in a series of meetings for states. IPI's blueprint has served as an alternative to the Office of Management and Budget (OMB) Common Measures. Florida's efforts are showcased in the blueprint. Additional state updates include the following:

- *Indiana* continued an incentive award system for local WIBs that began in October 2002. Each WIB was awarded $1,000 for each of the 17 WIA performance measures that it met each year. Incentive awards were also being used in vocational and technical education areas.

- *Maryland* put previous system standards on hold in 2005, as officials believed they might not be adequate measures of system performance. The administration formed a new unit to focus on performance.

- *Michigan* continued to be actively involved in developing regression models for adjusting performance levels for its local WIBs, relying on consultants from the W.E. Upjohn Institute for Employment Research in Kalamazoo, and the Corporation for a Skilled Workforce in Ann Arbor. They developed the Value-Added Performance-Adjustment System model (see Bartik, Eberts, and Kline [2009]).

- *Missouri's* Division of Workforce Development (DWD) evaluates clients using a Self-Sufficiency Standard that's updated annually and designed to indicate the level of income necessary to meet basic living expenses. It serves as an important tool in evaluating program success. In addition, DWD also began using the Performance ScoreCard, a comprehensive system of measures for evaluating Missouri's workforce development system. The Performance ScoreCard is composed of 10 measures, including market share, client satisfaction, employment, and earnings.

- *Texas* in 2002 suspended the initial regression models used for WIA performance modeling due to perceived data anomalies. The model had relied on JTPA data for the state, but was producing counterintuitive results as WIA data were utilized.

Additionally, as part of the effort to move from program-driven services to employer-driven services, the Texas Workforce Commission instituted a series of employer-based measures for local boards. Texas also was one of the first states to implement the OMB "common measures" for its workforce programs.

CONCLUSIONS

Market mechanisms now play a far more important role in U.S. workforce development programs than ever before. While they are likely here to stay and have been largely accepted by policymakers and program officials at all levels, issues regarding their appropriateness as well as their effectiveness should be acknowledged.

Economists generally agree that more and better information on both opportunities and outcomes for customers and providers improves the functioning of markets. However, it remains to be seen whether what WIA mandates and states and local WIBS have implemented is the best way to accomplish this given the context within which the programs operate, i.e., federalism. Increased LMI, the ETPL certification lists, and performance standards are designed to help consumers make good choices in terms of selecting the right employment and training strategy to meet their needs. ITAs are the preferred mechanism for consumers to exercise their choice for occupational skills training. But, there are conceptual and practical problems to consider.

First, information is typically incomplete and may not be sufficiently accurate. LMI's shortcomings are well known. It is based largely on past trends that often do not support reliable projections of labor market opportunities 10 or even a few years into the future. In addition, there is a growing body of research that demonstrates that near-term outcomes from employment and training programs tend to be poor proxies for longer-term impacts. Numerous researchers have documented problems with WIA data collection and reporting systems for participation and performance in addition to the authors. It isn't clear that providing more information to consumers actually assists them with making good choices unless the quality and timeliness of that information can be greatly improved. After a big push to enhance LMI and its accessibility in the 1990s, with dwindling budgets, far fewer resources have been invested in recent years. At the same time, emerging evidence suggests that finding the right job with the right employer in the right industry sector makes a real difference in workers' employment and earnings success (see Andersson, Holzer, and Lane [2005] and Brown, Halti-wanger, and Lane [2006]). Being able to access and use good LMI is clearly necessary.

Second, as in many markets, information for job training programs tends to be highly imbalanced or asymmetric, such that training providers are far better informed than prospective participants. When "sellers" are much better informed than "buyers," unless added steps are taken to protect them, economic theory suggests that inferior goods may crowd out superior ones over time (the so-called lemons problem). This too is cause for concern.

Third, as Barnow (2000, 2009) and Barnow and King (1996) have pointed out in other work, economically disadvantaged participants with low literacy skills and more limited knowledge of labor market opportunities may be ill-suited to taking full advantage of ITAs even with the provision of more information.

It is worth noting that the combined effect of several factors led to minimal usage of ITAs under WIA. First, stronger emphasis on "work-first" or labor force attachment strategies under WIA served to deemphasize training as an option for participants. Second, the cumbersome and costly nature, real or perceived, of the ETPL requirements initially created reluctance on the part of community colleges to offer training via ITAs for the WIA system. Third, substantial WIA budget reductions in recent years have cut the amount of funding available for training.

Conclusions from the WIA study relevant to the use of market mechanisms include the following:

States and localities in the study sample have embraced newly devolved authority and responsibility for workforce investment under WIA, giving rise to an increasingly varied workforce development system across the country. As with welfare, health, education, and other policy areas, states and local areas—led by governors, mayors, and county executives, as well as legislators and state and local workforce administrators—have served as "laboratories of democracy," experimenting with new ways of doing business in workforce investment. A number of the study states had been in the vanguard of workforce policy reform, some of them pioneering market-oriented mechanisms and other changes well before WIA introduced and encouraged such changes nationally. Among the study states, efforts in Florida, Michigan, Texas, and Utah stand out.

The current approach to measuring and managing performance under WIA does not fit well with the intergovernmental approach to U.S. workforce policy that has evolved in recent decades. State and local officials and One-Stop center staff were nearly unanimous in expressing displeasure with performance measurement and management under WIA, often harking back to what was done under earlier workforce programs like JTPA for more promising practices. The predominant view was that prior to WIA, program participation and outcome data were of higher quality, performance standards negotiations processes were more balanced between the federal and state governments and between the states and local WIBs, and there was more emphasis on managing programs for improved results as opposed to the achievement of what tended to be viewed as arbitrary numeric goals.

One concern stems from the absence of consistent approaches to deciding when a customer becomes a participant or a former participant (exiter). Another has to do with the absence of a performance adjustment process to hold states and areas harmless for serving harder-to-serve populations and operating in economically distressed areas; for example, the JTPA regression adjustment model that was used for much of the 1980s and 1990s was perceived by most state and local officials interviewed as a good strategy to discourage creaming and to level the playing field between areas with different economic conditions. Most state and local officials also complained that relying on UI wage record data to capture labor market outcomes leads to delays in measuring results and to having data that are not useful for day-to-day management. A number of states in the sample—including Florida, Oregon, Texas, and Utah—are recognized leaders in the design and use of measures that gauge the performance of the workforce system as a whole, as well as more comprehensive performance management approaches.[15] Three of these states—Florida, Oregon, and Texas—were active participants in the IPI initiative led by Washington State, working with the National Governors Association to develop workforce system measures. Improvements to WIA's data collection and reporting mechanisms and its approach to performance measurement and management are needed. Under the intergovernmental system that has evolved for workforce investment, tightening up the accountability system goes hand in hand with granting governors and WIBs discretion and flexibility to design their own programs. Policymakers can be "loose" in allowing states and localities to shape their service strategies to meet what they perceive as the needs of their particular labor markets and target populations, but they should be "tight" in terms of specifying the measures and assuring that the measures capture performance in an accurate and timely manner. This approach is in accord with best practice in both the public and the private sector, as characterized by Osborne and Gaebler (1992) and Peters and Waterman (1982).

A number of new market mechanisms introduced by WIA, including ITAs and, to a lesser extent, provider certification processes, appear to be working better than expected. Despite early difficulties with implementing the ITA and eligible provider certification processes, for the most part the states and local areas studied have now incorporated these features into their policy frameworks and day-to-day operations for adult and dislocated worker programs. In part, this may reflect low demands for training services since WIA was implemented, but it may also reflect the experience that some of the sample states had with similar approaches before WIA. Based on the field research, leaders of many local boards and One-Stop centers appear to be pursuing a "guided choice" approach to ITAs. More variation was found among the states in how well the eligible provider list requirements function. There is support for the concept, but the requirements for its operation were seen as overly rigid.

When WIA is ultimately reauthorized, this research suggests that the system needs to deal with a number of challenges related to the implementation and use of market mechanisms. Some of these are highlighted below.

Balancing accountability and flexibility under a broad-based federal grant-in-aid program such as WIA. In a system that is federally funded and state and locally administered, states and local areas are granted the flexibility to operate the programs as they see fit to meet their own goals and objectives. At the same time, the federal government retains the responsibility for making the lower levels of government accountable for their actions. The challenge is finding the right mix of flexibility and accountability so that an accountability system tailored to achieve federal goals does not thwart state and local governments from addressing what they see as their own needs.

Maintaining cooperative federal-state-local relationships on an ongoing basis for monitoring and overseeing local WIB and One-Stop activities. Under WIA, most of the funds flow from the federal government to the states to the local workforce investment areas to the One-Stops and finally to the service providers. There are a number of advantages to giving the states and localities more authority over the funds, but the current system requires that each level of government have specific authority and oversight responsibilities. The challenge is to find the right balance among the federal, state, and local levels of government to assure that the federally financed system is appropriately overseen.

Assuring that reporting and performance requirements do not adversely affect customer selection, services provided, and outcomes. Performance management has helped align the interests of state and local programs with those of the federal government, which has funded the programs, and enabled identification and improvement of low performers. Unfortunately, research indicates that performance management systems sometimes inadvertently lead to creaming (denying services to hard-to-place groups), undue emphasis on short-term services, and strategic behavior by government agencies and other organizations. An ongoing challenge is to strike the right balance in the performance management system so that good behavior is identified and rewarded while inappropriate or ineffective behavior is discouraged. In addition, performance management requires that timely and accurate data be collected. A further challenge is to balance the burden of data collection, timeliness, and accuracy in measuring the outcomes.

Developing ROI measures as an important component of workforce evaluation systems. Since JTPA referred to workforce programs as investments, there have been efforts to treat them as an investment and measure the return on support for the programs. Although this is a straightforward concept, implementing ROI, even at the national level, is quite difficult for a number of reasons. ROI calculations require estimates of the impact of the program on outcomes of interest, particularly earnings. This, in turn, not only requires obtaining earnings information for five or more years after program participation, but also estimates of what earnings would have been in the absence of participation. It is well established that the best way to obtain such information is through a classical experiment where eligible individuals are randomly assigned to receive the service or denied access. Classical experiments have been used successfully for evaluations of the Job Corps and JTPA, but they are time consuming and expensive. Texas and other states (e.g., Washington State) have pursued ROI estimation using a quasi-experimental method for capturing the impacts on employment, earnings, and other outcomes (Hollenbeck and Huang 2006; and King et al. 2008). ROI should be viewed as a longer-term evaluative measure of program performance rather than a near-term performance indicator.

Another complication is, ironically, that recent efforts to better coordinate and integrate programs have made it difficult to identify program costs associated with a participant. Some of the resources provided to customers at One-Stop centers are likely to have been paid for by other customers, and in some cases individuals are coenrolled in other programs. Currently, WIA does not require states and local programs to track costs at the individual level, and doing so would be difficult or impossible without arbitrary assumptions. At the state and local levels, the problems are magnified. It is not clear that states and localities can afford to undertake random assignment experiments locally or measure costs in the detail required for a cost-benefit analysis. Thus, proxy measures based on national estimates and procedures might have to be used.

RECOMMENDATIONS

In this section, we propose recommendations for WIA reauthorization as well as issues for the European Social Fund to consider as it develops and institutes more comprehensive performance measurement and management featuring greater use of market mechanisms.

WIA Reauthorization

The following recommendations related to the use of market mechanisms are offered for policymakers to consider in the WIA reauthorization process:

WIA should improve and substantially tighten data collection and reporting by states and local workforce boards systemwide. In the private sector that is often held up as the model for public programs to emulate, it is axiomatic that, if a result is important, it must be tightly measured. Despite the rhetoric in WIA (and related programs), this has not been the case. In addition to collecting more accurate data on participation and services, outcomes should be better measured. UI wage records, which serve as the primary data source for measuring employment and earnings outcomes, could be enhanced to include fields for starting date, hours worked, and even occupation (the latter to facilitate gauging whether placements are training related). The Wage Record Interchange System that supports the WIA (and ES) performance measurement could also be improved and made available for research uses to support better understanding of the outcomes and impacts from workforce services. In addition, the currently dormant effort to develop a systemwide management information system that would collect data for customers across a wide range of programs would provide an opportunity to link outcomes to the entire investment made for an individual.

WIA should return to funding, developing, and fostering the use of better LMI and LMI-related tools for use by local workforce boards, employers, and participants, as well as state planners. If WIA and related services are to be delivered in a market-oriented mode, the entire system requires much better information, improved access to the information, and tools for using it. A number of states (e.g., Florida, Oregon, Texas, Utah) are well-established leaders in the LMI arena and, through their national organizations, could assist in developing plans and tools for such an effort.

WIA should also do more to encourage and support the provision of skills training in growth sectors of the economy, whether through the use of ITAs or other means. OJT and customized training are proven strategies for training, as has been noted. ITAs may be a useful approach if implemented well (i.e., with a guided-choice model) in many workforce areas, but may not be appropriate in others, for example, in more rural areas where few provider choices are available. Overreliance on ITAs should be avoided until processes such as the ETPL are better developed.

Congress should broaden the ETPL process for provider certification beyond WIA to ensure that it is more balanced and comprehensive, not just coming from WIA. Some of the difficulties that surfaced with the ETPL process, including resistance from community and technical colleges, may be avoided if the process encompasses workforce and education programs on a more systemwide basis. To make good choices, consumers—both workers and employers—need systematic knowledge about the performance of all such programs, not just those funded by WIA. In addition, flexibility should be added so that states can properly balance the paperwork required with the information that is provided. Recent initiatives funded by the U.S. Department of Education and the USDOL to support development and implementation of linked longitudinal data systems in many states should make such effects much easier.[16]

Congress should establish a mechanism in WIA and related workforce and education legislation for carefully reviewing the "common measures." To date, the OMB "common measures" have mainly been embraced by the USDOL for its program offerings. Moreover, the IPI measures that were developed and vetted by a number of leading states and their local programs appear to offer somewhat better measures than the ones that were initially promulgated by the OMB and the USDOL in a mainly top-down process. If these measures are to truly be "common," they require such a review and likely a better process. Moreover, the interest in developing common measures should not be pursued to the point that programs are forced to measure success only by how well they perform on the common measures. For some education programs, for example, learning may be as important an outcome as earning. Even in some labor programs, such as the Senior Community Service Employment Program, postprogram employment and earnings may not be as important as in a more traditional training program.

WIA should explicitly provide for and support the development and use of performance adjustment models or other less complex but effective approaches to ensure that services to harder-to-serve groups are encouraged rather than discouraged. The ETA has done much more in the last few years along these lines, but including such provisions within the act would be an important statement of policy for the workforce system. As noted earlier, regression modeling is often useful for objectively taking account of differences in participant characteristics and economic conditions, but other approaches, including negotiation, can be used to take account of factors that cannot be incorporated well into regression models.[17]

WIA should also provide for more systematic capacity building across the system to foster best practices and professional development in performance management and related areas. Market-based systems tend to function best when they are supported by knowledgeable professionals and have access to accurate information and related assistance. It has been more than a quarter century since the regional network of institutional grantees—competitively procured university-based centers that provided professional talent development, research and evaluation, and technical assistance to the workforce system—were eliminated from the federal budget. Congress and ETA should restart this important effort.

WIA should continue to support evaluations using random assignment to treatment status in conjunction with research on less expensive, less intrusive quasi-or nonexperimental impact estimation. Classical experiments are generally perceived as expensive and time consuming, but they offer the most irrefutable evidence of program impacts. Nonexperimental evaluations can be performed more quickly and at lower cost (Hollenbeck et al. 2005; Smith, King, and Schroeder 2008), but they generally rely on very strong assumptions that cannot be tested, e.g., the absence of unobserved variables that affect the outcomes of interest. There is currently vigorous debate about when nonexperimental approaches are adequate, but the only way the debate can be resolved is to conduct studies that combine the approaches. Indeed, much of the most important recent work on nonexperimental estimation techniques was built on the experimental evaluations of JTPA and the National Supported Work Experiment.

European Social Fund

Making detailed recommendations on the use of market mechanisms for the European Social Fund is premature at this point. However, some issues that it should consider as it proceeds with its work along these lines include the following:

Context is all-important. One-size-fits-all solutions involving such market mechanisms are unlikely to work well. Europe's institutions and traditions—including especially relationships between employers, labor, and government regarding workforce development programs—are dramatically different from those in the U.S. Tripartite, collaborative relationships, a stronger role for government in many aspects of society and the economy, and mediation of market forces are an integral part of Europe's fabric, even if recent trends suggest movement more toward market approaches. Instituting a stronger role for market mechanisms will likely take more time and thought as to how the European context can and should be addressed.

Overreliance on market mechanisms should be avoided unless and until labor market information and outcomes data are far more robust and its major consumers—both job seekers and employers—and governments have ready access and are able to make effective use of it. LMI and reliable outcomes data are essential for the other market mechanisms to perform well. As indicated above, relying on market forces to guide market choices and outcomes in the absence of such information is likely to produce poor results and do so inefficiently. Consumers and governments also require tools to properly access and use such information.

Notes

1. Barnow and King (2005) authored the final project report. All reports from the project, including a series of eight state case studies, can be found both on the Rockefeller Institute and USDOL/ETA Web sites: See http://www.doleta.gov/reports/searcheta/occ/ or http://www.rockinst.org/quick_tour/federalism/wia.html.
2. See Lurie (2003) for a description of the field network methodology and its features.

3. More detail on this and other topics is available in the individual state reports published by the USDOL and the Rockefeller Institute (Rockefeller Institute of Government 2004a,b).

4. Spaulding (2001) finds that performance-based contracting was associated with better participant placement and wage outcomes in 1998 when JTPA was in effect, but the ETA identified a number of abuses of performance-based contracting in the 1980s and discouraged its use.

5. Barnow (2009) interprets the evidence on vouchers from a number of studies a bit differently, concluding that vouchers with more agency control may produce greater impacts for customers.

6. See Barnow (2004) and King (2004, 2008) for a review of the evidence on the effectiveness of alternative training strategies. Isbell, Trutko, and Barnow (2000) review the evidence on customized training.

7. This experience is borne out by unpublished figures from the Texas Workforce Commission and independent analysis conducted by Hollenbeck, King, and Schroeder (2003) for the ADARE Project.

8. States determine how local standards are set. Most states follow the federal approach and set local standards through negotiations.

9. Lack of adjustment for participant characteristics may increase incentives for workforce investment areas serving difficult populations to engage in "creaming," where they serve eligible individuals more likely to do well on the performance measures instead of those with greater labor market barriers.

10. Refinement of performance measures will need to take account of the common measures developed by the OMB for job training and employment programs.

11. More recent ETA Training and Employment Guidance Letters on this topic are discussed in King (2006).

12. John Baj at Northern Illinois University's Center for Governmental Studies devised a simpler alternative to regression-adjustment models based on comparisons to similar states to assist states and localities in conducting negotiations as part of the ongoing ADARE Project. For more information see http://www.fred-info.org.

13. ADARE project reports by Mueser and Sharpe (2006) and Stevens and Stack (2006) discuss this issue and provide insights into its motivating factors and effects.

14. Florida no longer uses the color-coded reports, but the state still produces tables comparing performance across local areas.

15. See reports prepared for the National Governors Association and the ETA by O'Shea et al. (2003a,b).

16. For more information on these initiatives, see http://nces.ed.gov/programs/slds and http://www.doleta.gov/pdf/.

17. See Barnow and Heinrich (2010) and King (2006) for a discussion of alternative approaches to adjusting performance standards.

References

Andersson, Frederik, Harry J. Holzer, and Julia I. Lane. 2005. *Moving Up or Moving On: Who Advances in the Low-Wage Labor Market?* New York: Russell Sage Foundation.

Barnow, Burt S. 2000. "Vouchers for Federal Targeted Training Programs." In *Vouchers and Related Delivery Mechanisms: Consumer Choice in the Provision of Public Services*, Eugene Steurele, Van Doorn Ooms, George Peterson, and Robert Reischauer, eds. Washington, DC: Brookings Institution Press, pp. 224–250.

———. 2004. "An Overview of United States Employment and Training Programs and Their Effectiveness." In *Meeting the Needs of Business and Workers in the 21st Century: Proceedings of a Joint United States and European Union Seminar*, U.S. Department of Labor, Bureau of International Affairs, ed. Washington, DC: U.S. Department of Labor, Bureau of International Affairs, pp. 1–49.

———. 2009. "Vouchers in U.S. Vocational Training Programs: An Overview of What We Have Learned." *Journal for Labour Market Research* 42(1): 71–84.

Barnow, Burt S., and Carolyn Heinrich. 2010. "One Standard Fits All? The Pros and Cons of Performance Standard Adjustments." *Public Administration Review* (70)1: 60–71.

Barnow, Burt S., and Christopher T. King. 1996. "The Baby and the Bath Water: Lessons for the Next Employment and Training Program." In *Of the Heart and Mind: Social Policy Essays in Honor of Sar Levitan*, Garth Mangum and Stephen Mangum, eds. Kalamazoo, MI: W.E. Upjohn Institute for Employment Research, pp. 255–282.

———. 2003. "The Workforce Investment Act in Eight States: Overview of Findings from a Field Network Study." ETA Occasional Paper 2003-03. Washington, DC: U.S. Department of Labor, Employment and Training Administration.

———. 2005. "The Workforce Investment Act in Eight States." ETA Occasional Paper 2005-01. Washington, DC: US Department of Labor, Employment and Training Administration.

———, eds. 2000. *Improving the Odds: Increasing the Effectiveness of Publicly Funded Training*. Washington, DC: Urban Institute Press.

Bartik, Timothy J., Randall W. Eberts, and Ken Kline. 2009. "Estimating a Performance Standards Adjustment Model for Workforce Programs That Provides Timely Feedback and Uses Data from Only One State." Upjohn Institute Staff Working Paper No. 09-144. Kalamazoo, MI: W.E. Upjohn

Institute for Employment Research, January 28 (revised version of the 2004 working paper).

Brown, Claire, John Haltiwanger, and Julia Lane. 2006. *Economic Turbulence: Is a Volatile Economy Good for America?* Chicago: University of Chicago Press.

Buck, Maria L. 2002. *Charting New Territory: Early Implementation of the Workforce Investment Act, Field Report Series.* Philadelphia, PA: Public/ Private Ventures.

D'Amico, Ronald D., Deborah Kogan, Suzanne Kreutzer, Andrew Wiegand, and Alberta Baker. 2001. *A Report on Early State and Local Progress Towards WIA Implementation, Final Interim Report.* Washington, DC: U.S. Department of Labor, Employment and Training Administration.

D'Amico, Ronald, Jeffrey Salzman, and Paul Decker. 2002. *An Evaluation of the Individual Training Account/Eligible Training Provider Demonstration: Draft Final Report.* Oakland, CA: Social Policy Research Associates and Mathematica Policy Research.

Frank, Abbey, Hedieh Rahmanou, and Steve Savner. 2003. *The Workforce Investment Act: A First Look at Participation, Demographics and Services.* Update No. 1. Washington, DC: Center for Law and Social Policy.

Hollenbeck, Kevin, and Wei-Jang Huang. 2006. "Net Impact and Benefit-Cost Estimates of the Workforce Development System in Washington State." Technical Report No. TR06-020. Kalamazoo, MI: W.E. Upjohn Institute for Employment Research,

Hollenbeck, Kevin, Christopher T. King, and Daniel Schroeder. 2003. "Preliminary WIA Net Impact Estimates: Administrative Records Opportunities and Limitations." Prepared for "New Tools for a New Era!" symposium, held in Washington, DC, July 23–24.

Hollenbeck, Kevin, Daniel Schroeder, Christopher T. King, and Wei-Jang Huang. 2005. *Net Impact Estimates for Services Provided through the Workforce Investment Act.* Washington, DC: U.S. Department of Labor, Employment and Training Administration.

Isbell, Kellie, John Trutko, and Burt S. Barnow. 2000. "Customized Training for Employers: Training People for Jobs That Exist and Employers Who Want to Hire Them." In *Improving the Odds: Increasing Effectiveness of Publicly Funded Training*, Burt S. Barnow and Christopher T. King, eds. Washington, DC: Urban Institute Press, pp. 209–226.

King, Christopher T. 2004. "The Effectiveness of Publicly Financed Training in the United States." In *Job Training Policy in the United States,* Christopher J. O'Leary, Robert A. Straits, and Stephen A. Wandner, eds. Kalamazoo, MI: W.E. Upjohn Institute for Employment Research, pp. 57–100.

———. 2006. "Performance Measures Adjustment and Incentives: Key Strategies for Providing Improved Services to Harder to Serve Populations in the Age of Accountability." Background paper. Washington, DC: National Collaborative on Workforce and Disability for Youth.

———. 2008. *Does Workforce Development Work?* Working paper prepared for the Annie E. Casey Foundation's Workforce Narrative Project, January. Baltimore, MD: Annie E. Casey Foundation.

King, Christopher T., Ying Tang, Tara Carter Smith, and Daniel G. Schroeder, with Burt S. Barnow. 2008. *Returns from Investments in Workforce Services: Texas Statewide Estimates for Participants, Taxpayers and Society.* Report to the Texas Association of Workforce Boards, Ray Marshall Center for the Study of Human Resources, Lyndon B. Johnson School of Public Affairs. Austin, TX: University of Texas at Austin.

Lurie, Irene. 2003. "Field Network Studies." In *Policy into Action: Implementation Research and Welfare Reform*, Mary Clare Lennon and Thomas Corbett, eds. Washington, DC: Urban Institute Press, pp. 81–105.

McConnell, Sheena, Elizabeth Stuart, Kenneth Fortson, Paul Decker, Irma Perez-Johnson, Barbara Harris, and Jeffrey Salzman. 2006. *Managing Customers' Training Choices: Findings from the Individual Training Account Experiment.* Report to the U.S. Department of Labor. Washington, DC: Mathematica Policy Research.

Mueser, Peter R., and Deanna L. Sharpe. 2006. *Anatomy of Two One-Stops.* ADARE Project Report. Baltimore, MD: Jacob France Institute.

Mueser, Peter, Kenneth R. Troske, and Alexey Gorislavsky. 2003. *Using State Administrative Data to Measure Program Performance.* Photocopy. Columbia, MO: University of Missouri, Department of Economics.

Osborne, David, and Ted Gaebler. 1992. *Reinventing Government: How the Entrepreneurial Spirit Is Transforming the Public Sector.* Reading, MA: Addison-Wesley.

O'Shea, Daniel, and Christopher T. King. 2001. *The Workforce Investment Act of 1998: Restructuring Workforce Development Initiatives in States and Localities.* Report No. 12. Albany, NY: Nelson A. Rockefeller Institute of Government.

O'Shea, Dan, Sarah E. Looney, and Christopher T. King. 2003a. *Non-federal Workforce System Performance Measures in the States: Overview.* Report to the Center for the Study of Human Resources, Lyndon B. Johnson School of Public Affairs. Austin, TX: University of Texas at Austin.

———. 2003b. *Non-federal Workforce System Performance Measures in the States: Ten State Profiles.* Report to the Center for the Study of Human Resources, Lyndon B. Johnson School of Public Affairs. Austin, TX: University of Texas at Austin.

Peters, Thomas J., and Robert Waterman Jr. 1982. *In Search of Excellence.* New York: Harper and Row Publishers.

Rockefeller Institute of Government. 2004a. *The Workforce Investment Act in Eight States: State Case Studies from a Field Network Evaluation—Volume One: Maryland, Michigan, Missouri, Oregon.* ETA Occasional Paper 2004-02. Washington, DC: U.S. Department of Labor, Employment and Training Administration.

————. 2004b. *The Workforce Investment Act in Eight States: State Case Studies from a Field Network Evaluation—Volume Two: Florida, Indiana, Texas, Utah.* Occasional Paper 2004-03. Washington, DC: U.S. Department of Labor, Employment and Training Administration.

Saunders, Ellen O'Brien, and Bryan Wilson. 2003. *Integrated Performance Information (IPI) for Workforce Development System Planning, Oversight and Management.* Olympia, WA: Workforce Education and Training Coordinating Board.

Smith, Tara Carter, Christopher T. King, and Daniel G. Schroeder. 2008. *Local Investments in Workforce Development: Evaluation Update.* Report to the Center for the Study of Human Resources, Lyndon B. Johnson School of Public Affairs. Austin, TX: University of Texas at Austin.

Spaulding, Shayne. 2001. "Performance-Based Contracting under the Job Training Partnership Act." Master's thesis. Baltimore, MD: Johns Hopkins University.

Stevens, David W. 2003. *Mapping One-Stop Client Flows, PY 2000 (July 2000–June 2001), Title I-B Adults and Dislocated Workers, by Core (Registered), Intensive and Training Services.* Research Project No. 1, prepared for USDOL/ETA, Administrative Data Research and Evaluation Project, Washington, DC: U.S. Department of Labor, Employment and Training Administration.

Stevens, David W., and Treva Stack. 2006. *Anatomy of a One-Stop.* ADARE Project Report. Baltimore, MD: Jacob France Institute.

Trutko, John W., and Burt S. Barnow. 1999. *Experiences with Training Vouchers under the Job Training Partnership Act and Implications for Individual Training Accounts under the Workforce Investment Act: Final Report.* Washington, DC: U.S. Department of Labor, Employment and Training Administration.

Wilson, Bryan. 2005. *Integrated Performance Information for Workforce Development: A Blueprint for States.* Olympia, WA: Washington State Workforce Training and Education Coordinating Board.

4
Customized Training

David A. Long

Abt Associates

In the United States, national workforce development policy has steadily placed a greater emphasis on the involvement of the private sector in the planning and oversight of federally funded programs. WIA has required local workforce development planning and operations be led by boards chaired and largely composed of private sector leaders. However, this and other WIA provisions have not ensured the use of "demand-driven" skills training—that is, the provision of particular employee skills needed by specific firms in their current and new workers. Federal policy once shied away from such training, because it was considered the responsibility of employers to prepare their own workers in skills that are this job-specific. Now, however, local boards have the discretion to support the training they want, and there is increasing recognition that training tailored to the needs of specific employers is a vehicle both for providing good jobs to low-income and disadvantaged groups and for promoting economic growth in particular communities and industrial sectors. Recognizing this, the USDOL and private foundations in the United States have funded what can be termed "customized" training initiatives (this type of training goes by several names). These initiatives typically involve local partnerships between firms from the private sector and training providers and intermediaries from the public sector.

This chapter answers several questions about customized training, beginning with the most fundamental: What is it? And, what is the rationale for this training? Then the discussion will turn to the role of customized training in WIA. What is that role now and what might it be in the future? Finally, I will address questions regarding how much we know about delivering customized training and, if implemented well, about how effective this training can be. In answering these last two questions, I will rely primarily on research findings from four large-scale demonstrations mounted by the USDOL during the last 10 years and from a fifth major initiative funded by the Charles Stewart Mott Foundation.

WHAT IS CUSTOMIZED TRAINING?

One of economist Gary Becker's many contributions to the way we think about education and training is the distinction he drew between general and specific training. Firm-specific training is useful only to the individual sector firms providing it, while general education or training is useful to a range of firms. At the general education and training end of the continuum is the wide-ranging preparation—for example, in communication skills and word processing functions—that is not designed for a particular industry, let alone a specific firm in the industry. At the other end is the specific, in-house skills training provided by individual firms to their own employees, including on-the-job learning about the firm's procedures, structure, and culture.

Becker notes that employers have little incentive to invest in general training, because it raises the productivity of workers in other firms and not just their own, which then encourages competing employers to hire away these workers at higher wages. On the other hand, he argues that completely specific training—which can only be provided by the individual firm as on-the-job training in its own unique processes, special methods and routines, and unique uses of technologies and equipment—has no value to other employers and consequently does not bid up wages (Becker 1997). Becker's distinction is very useful, although it should be noted that there are few completely firm-specific skills and, even where they exist, such skills may actually be quite valuable to competing firms.

Along the continuum between general and specific training, customized training occupies a place closer to the latter. By definition, customized training is instruction for workers and job seekers provided by education and training institutions working closely with employers. The training curriculum is developed or adapted to meet the education and training needs of the specific firms, which often belong to a particular sector. As a result, this training often has gone by the name of "sectoral training"—particularly in the philanthropic community. This term is incomprehensible to most people. In addition, the training to which the term refers sometimes involves well-defined jobs (such as a computer technician) in firms from more than a single sector, but located in a single geographic area. Government agencies have more often attached the term "demand-driven" to this type of training, wanting to differentiate it from supply-driven training—that is, education and training provided by schools and training institutions with insufficient regard for the specific needs of employers. But the demand-driven label tells us little about what the training is. This chapter uses "customized training" instead to emphasize its responsiveness to the needs of specific local employers in filling particular skilled work positions, differentiating it from "off-the-shelf" training in various vocational fields.

Thus, customized training is designed to meet the particular requirements of an employer or group of employers. Generally speaking, it is conducted with a commitment by the employer to employ some or all successful completers of the training (or continue employing incumbent workers) and share the costs of the training, which usually include support of the training's hands-on aspects. The training is often provided through partnerships between education and training institutions and groups of firms from the same region.[1] In the United States, the institutions are often, but not always, community colleges. Typically, each partnership involves another important collaborator: a labor market intermediary such as a local Workforce Investment Board (WIB) or a community-based organization.[2] This intermediary often convenes the initial relationship between employers and training providers, and it almost always plays the role of recruiting and screening applicants for customized training when partner employers are looking to hire new skilled workers. This recruitment effort is customized in the sense that the partner employer's hiring criteria are explicitly taken into account by the intermediaries. This role played by the intermediaries turns out to be crucial to the targeting of customized training programs, because it permits programs to give priority to low-income and disadvantaged groups.[3]

The Biotech Workforce Network in the San Francisco Bay area, which trains biotech technicians, is an example of such a partnership. The original corporate partner was Genentech (the world's second largest biotech firm) and more than 25 other companies have joined the network. Two WIBs (the local boards established by WIA) created this regional partnership, secured the necessary funding, developed the program management systems and program operations procedures, and involved their respective One-Stop Career Centers in the recruitment, screening, and enrollment of participants. Two community colleges have developed training curricula and provided the training classes, and the colleges partnered with community-based organizations to recruit and provide supports for disadvantaged individuals entering the training programs. A consulting firm helped in recruiting corporate partners, developed on-the-job training models, and assisted with employer communications and technical assistance (Biotech Workforce Network 2007).

WHAT IS THE RATIONALE FOR PUBLIC INVOLVEMENT IN CUSTOMIZED TRAINING?

The rationale for public support of customized training includes four arguments. First, changes in U.S. labor demand over the last 40 years have favored more educated and skilled workers. This has partly resulted from market globalization, indicated by the rapid expansion of international trade.[4] The growth in imports during this period is associated with a loss in employment across many low-skill occupational categories, reflecting the steady shift of production overseas. At the same time, U.S. employment in medium- and high-skill occupations has been supported by the nation's increased exports.[5] Changes in demand also have resulted from technological advances, including the astonishing growth of computers and the internet. This has boosted employers' needs for workers in higher-skill occupations. There has been a corresponding reduction in the demand for less-skilled labor (that is, for workers conducting routine tasks).

The second argument is that, despite their growing need for skilled labor, employers are reluctant to invest in skills training. The growth in the supply of skilled labor has not kept pace with employers' demand, particularly in some sectors, which has created skill shortages and applied upward pressure on wages. However, it appears that increasing employee turnover has discouraged many businesses from investing in employee skills training, because employee departures reduce employers' return on such investments.[6] This is especially true of training for low-wage, entry-level workers (see, for example, Ahlstrand, Bassi, and McMurrer [2003]). As noted earlier, training that does not involve truly firm-specific skills constitutes an investment in the employee over which the employer has no control. Once trained, employees can leave a job to sell their enhanced services to another employer. While individual firms may be reluctant to invest in skills training, it is clearly in the interest of businesses collectively—that is, the U.S. economy—to make such investments. This satisfies economists' conditions for a market failure and for treating such training as a public good.

The third argument is that individuals also do not invest enough in skills training. The increased demand for skilled labor in the United States has boosted the wages paid to skilled workers relative to unskilled workers. For example, between 1979 and 2000, real wages of workers with a college degree increased 21 percent, while those with only a high school diploma fell 3 percent (Mishel, Bernstein, and Boushey 2003). The acquisition of skills has consequently become ever more critical to both the productivity and employability of workers. Even though most people are aware of the premium now paid to skilled workers, a high proportion of the U.S. workforce lacks necessary basic and occupational skills. Some of this skills gap is attributable to workers entering the labor force without first obtaining the needed skills through the education and training system. Other sources of this problem are high dropout rates and poor achievement in U.S. schools, and the limited reach of the "second-chance education" and vocational training systems. In addition, workers who lack the skills they need for labor market success typically also lack both the financial resources and the know-how to obtain the skills on their own.

Finally, while customized training arrangements provide a way for valuable workforce skill development to take place, these arrangements appear to develop slowly in the marketplace unless there is funding from government and/or private foundations to spur them on. Customized training combines occupational instruction and firm-specific training into an attractive package. However, many observers have noted the lack of collaboration, and sometimes even communication, between businesses and the education and workforce development systems. Community leaders have said it often is difficult to engage decision makers from local industries, especially small businesses lacking a dedicated human resources staff. At the same time, education and training institutions often have lacked mechanisms to facilitate such engagement by small businesses, which collectively account for more employment in the United States than do their larger brethren. A survey by the U.S. Bureau of Labor Statistics showed that while large business establishments heavily used community colleges as a source of skilled labor, particularly in some industries, a much lower proportion of small businesses took advantage of community college training resources.[7]

These arguments have led policymakers to subsidize the development of partnerships that deliver customized training. Both the USDOL and private foundations have made grants to education and training institutions and to labor market intermediaries to create these partnerships. The vision is that the funding is short-term, and partnerships will eventually become self-supporting. The training provided by the partnerships may also reduce the social costs associated with unemployment and provide greater employment opportunities to low-income and disadvantaged populations.

WHAT ROLE DOES CUSTOMIZED TRAINING PLAY IN WIA?

WIA has increased the role played by employers in the governance of the nation's training system. It has both resulted from and helped produce a corresponding move toward more demand-led rather than supply-led systems. As indicated earlier, the former are systems that respond to the immediate needs of businesses, while the latter tend to be driven by the priorities of established training providers. Customized training is a logical product of a more demand-led system.

The USDOL administers WIA, including the allocation of national program grants between local WIBs. The boards then are responsible for assessing the needs of the local economy and allocating WIA funds among potential service providers, which deliver different types of training and other services. They also oversee the One-Stop centers, where job seekers can obtain employment information, find out about available services, and be referred to the various service providers.

Unlike JTPA, WIA permits funds to support the training of incumbent workers as well as of unemployed members of the workforce. Local boards make different assessments of the skill sets workers and job seekers need and of which skills should be given highest priority in the areas they serve. At the general education end of the spectrum are the basic skills—that is, the literacy and numeracy skills—that are ideally acquired from a primary and early secondary education. Next to these are either occupational skills, which are acquired mainly in vocational and technical schools (including specialized secondary school programs and community college vocational instruction), or the professional skills obtained through additional academic study in colleges and universities. Beyond these occupation skills are the firm-specific skills acquired through work experience or training gained in the context of employment.

About 40 percent of the federal money given to local boards is spent on all types of training for adults (and many boards spend much less than this on training) (GAO 2005). While most WIA-funded training services involve occupational skills training, local boards also fund on-the-job training, an activity designed to provide firm-specific skills. Customized training can be viewed as packaging of an employer-tailored version of occupational skills training with on-the-job training (OJT) or another form of workplace activity providing hands-on experience. Local boards are free to develop customized training programs, and many of them have chosen to do so, often as an adjunct to their OJT programs. At least one WIA area in each of 32 U.S. states currently has a customized training program. On the other hand, this means that all local boards in 18 states, and many boards in the 32 states with programs, have chosen not to invest in customized training—which is their prerogative under WIA.

However, the Department of Labor has encouraged local investments in customized training, particularly through four major initiatives. The Sectoral Employment Demonstration (SED), which operated between 2000 and 2003, funded 38 local boards to operate special projects, some of which involved customized training. The High Growth Training Initiative (HGTI) has provided funding to WIBs, community colleges, and other organizations in support of customized training in 14 rapidly growing industries. The Community Based Training Initiative (CBTI) has supported similar initiatives, primarily involving community colleges.[8] HGTI and CBTI were funded under WIA's demonstration authority. The Workforce Innovation in Regional Economic Development (WIRED) Initiative entails more sweeping workforce development plans, with each WIRED grant calling for the creation of regional leadership groups, systematic assessments of regional economies (to identify target sectors), and the development of regional funding sources in advance of actually implementing skills training strategies. These activities have led most of the original 13 WIRED grantees to boost customized training (Almandsmith et al. 2008).

Congress is currently considering WIA reauthorization. Legislation has been proposed that would amend WIA, establishing a new partnership funding program similar to HGTI. The "Strengthening Employment Clusters to Organize Regional Success Act of 2009" would provide grants both to expand existing partnerships and establish new partnerships to provide customized training.[9] In addition, several organizations, including the National Governors Association, have urged Congress to make the regional workforce development promoted by WIRED a permanent part of WIA (see Ganzglass 2006).

WHAT HAVE WE LEARNED ABOUT IMPLEMENTING CUSTOMIZED TRAINING?

Successful implementation of customized training programs appears to depend, not surprisingly, on many things. This section of the chapter focuses on five themes from the implementation findings of the evaluation research on customized training: 1) informed sector choice, 2) productive partnerships, 3) recruitment and engagement of trainees, 4) curriculum development and use, and 5) effective placement and support services.

Informed Sector Choice

The available research on sector-focused customized training indicates that pertinent initiatives have consistently used three criteria to select sectors. One is observed sector growth or skill shortages created by sector growth. Sector growth has been the key criterion for sector selection in the HGTI initiative, while skill shortages were the primary factors for both the SED and the Skill Shortage Demonstration, a smaller project funded by the USDOL and completed four years ago (for discussion of this project, see Public Policy Associates [2005]). The rationale behind these related criteria is that, as discussed earlier, rapid growth in a given sector produces skill gaps when the supply of skilled labor does not keep up with growing demand. Filling such gaps serves the needs of employers, potential and existing employees, and the overall economy.

Nothing from the research evidence calls this criterion into question, but some of it underscores the need for up-to-date information on sector growth, and project responsiveness to changes in economic conditions. The need for current information results from the rapid changes in labor markets, and the studies reviewed in this chapter provide no revelations regarding the assessment of this information. The findings of the SED evaluation, as well as of the evaluation of the Sectoral Employment Initiative (SEI) funded by the Mott Foundation, emphasized the second point, noting that site programs needed to make appropriate responses when economic downturns occurred.[10] Given current economic conditions, this lesson is apropos.

Another consistent selection criterion has been the extent and concentration of local demand for specific skills. This was an important consideration for successful grantees in all the projects reviewed, largely for practical and strategic reasons. It is hard to think about capacity building—such as a new occupational training program at a community college—without reaching some threshold of skill demand.

Third, virtually all initiatives have put a priority on sectors with satisfactory wage levels and fringe benefits. Some of the grantees in the SED and Skill Shortage Demonstration had difficulty achieving their wage goals. However, it is noteworthy that the SEI sites judged most successful based on early results, and subsequently found to produce positive impacts on employment and earnings (described below), placed a high priority on participants obtaining high wages. This finding is consistent with the results of some other evaluations of workforce development programs, such as the findings for the Portland (Oregon) site in the National Evaluation of Welfare-to-Work Strategies.[11]

Productive Partnerships

The heart of each successful customized training project has been a partnership between an education and training institution, or institutions, and an engaged group of employers in the targeted sector. The partnerships have taken different forms, and have often involved additional organizations, but the ones judged to be successful have always had high employer involvement in multiple program activities. There has been variation in the level of employer involvement in particular activities, notably recruitment and screening; and, particularly in the SED, there was variation in the level of interaction among participating partners. There has been consistent employer involvement in curriculum development in programs providing specific training, although it has been more limited in some programs (for example, several of the HGTI and CBTI sites that have implemented traditional nursing programs with relatively little customization to meet the needs of particular health care providers).

The individual projects in the various customized training initiatives mentioned in this chapter have involved many types of partnerships. They typically have involved the workforce development system, local community colleges and other training institutions, employers, and other agencies or organizations within the region. There does not appear to be a single template for a successful partnership. Indeed, one of the conclusions of the SED evaluation, a demonstration in which all partnerships were led by local WIBs, was that there was no "best" project structure even in cases where the boards were always in the leadership position.

However, the research evidence suggests that communities are wise to build on the institutional relationships that are already in place. One of the important conclusions from the WIRED evaluation is that many of the strongest partnerships were already well under way before the grants were awarded. In these cases planning and goal setting had been completed, and the needed institutional relationships had been established, so the grants were used to expand preexisting projects. This also was clearly true of successful projects such as the Portland site mentioned above.

While it is sensible to build on existing collaborations, many grantees in all of the USDOL initiatives developed new partnerships. Indeed, two-thirds of the SED grantees formed new stakeholder groups that included employers, community colleges, and community organizations and/or unions and industry associations. The SED evaluators from the Urban Institute reported that, based on the metrics used in the study, most of these partnerships successfully engaged employers and other organizations in developing training (Pindus et al. 2004). Also, many of the grantees leveraged additional resources beyond the SED funding to support their implementation plans.

In developing new partnerships, labor market intermediaries appear to have played a crucial role in convening and facilitating collaboration. In some cases, this role has been played by local WIBs and their staff. This was the case, for example, in the Biotech Workforce Network described earlier. In other cases, this role has gone to a variety of private organizations, such as the ones that led projects in the SEI.

Recruitment, Screening, and Engagement

Success in recruiting and enrolling participants must be achieved in order to reach customized training initiatives' goals, namely

- meeting employers' needs—that is, increasing their supply of qualified workers and improving the skill levels of new and incumbent workers;

- meeting worker needs—identifying those needs and improving their employability and ability to advance in the labor market; and

- building the capacity of training partnerships to sustain themselves—that is, to continue to reliably identify and enroll qualified, motivated students for customized training after government or foundation funding is gone.

The findings of both the SED and the foundation-funded SEI initiative show that success in recruitment and enrollment has been a major challenge. The evaluations of both these multisite projects indicate that recruitment success has required collaboration between employers and training programs to ensure that employers' specific enrollment qualifications are met. The recruitment of disadvantaged and low-income workers has been especially challenging, leading evaluators in the Work Advancement and Support Center Demonstration (WASC) to conclude that it requires substantial staff and funding resources.[12]

Keeping participants engaged, especially disadvantaged and low-income workers, also has been challenging for training programs. Many successful programs, such as the Center for Employment Training (CET), have required a commitment from trainees to remain engaged throughout training. Retaining participants who needed income to support themselves and their families during training presents obvious difficulties. Indeed, WASC evaluators have suggested that tangible incentives are a potentially effective way to maintain engagement.

Curriculum Development and Use

Similarly, success in developing and using an appropriate sector-driven training curriculum is necessary for meeting employer needs (increased skilled worker supply and improved skill levels) as well as the needs of workers (to improve their employability and chances for advancement). Past research suggests the potential for considerable success on this important task, although this potential success is qualified by the fact that most SED, SEI, and other initiatives built on past training efforts in the same sectors, making only modest curricular modifications based on employers' input. In such cases, the curriculum also can draw on national standards and established academic materials. Success is less assured when new sectors are targeted or when new skills within a given sector are taught, and substantial collaboration between employers and training programs may be needed in these cases.

Another issue regarding curriculum is the extent to which basic skills instruction should be integrated into the training. This is a common element to the three SEI sites shown to have produced significant impacts on employment and earnings. It also is one of the notable components of the CET model, which achieved noteworthy success in preparing low-income participants for jobs with partnering employers.[13]

Placement and Support Services

Another key task if programs are to be successful is supporting participants during and after training. During training, this may involve tutoring and/or supplemental instruction (provided in most interventions described in earlier sections of this paper), providing counseling, mentoring, and/or coaching (as in the WASC project), and providing assistance with transportation, child care, books and supplies, and other participant needs (as in most projects described earlier). Often, too, counselors or advisors in strong programs have worked with participants to develop plans specifying participation expectations along with the supports that programs will provide.

After training, it is crucial to program success to get participants into appropriate jobs that utilize the training they have received. Particular sites in the various programs discussed in this paper used a range of specific approaches to achieving this objective. For example, one SEI site (in Milwaukee) often did not start particular training classes until employers made firm hiring commitments, so the movement of trainees into specific jobs was predetermined. In the welfare-to-work site in Portland, a highly effective job placement effort was used to reach this goal.

Ideally, the efforts to complete each of these three tasks should involve sufficient stakeholder collaboration to ensure that employers' needs are met and the improvements in training capabilities can be sustained.

WHAT HAVE WE LEARNED ABOUT THE EFFECTIVENESS OF CUSTOMIZED TRAINING?

Customized training is intended to have three types of effects: impacts on current and new employees, employers, and the broader economy (beyond those on immediately affected employees and employers). The available evidence on these types of effectiveness is discussed in turn.

Current and New Employees

Finding that individuals who have participated in customized training programs have improved their skills, or have experienced increased employment or earnings, does not necessarily indicate that the programs were effective. Changes in these outcomes are determined by more factors than training programs or even job skills, including the labor market conditions in the places where training programs are implemented. Over time, the earnings of individuals tend to increase without special training programs as a result of inflation, job experience, and other developments. Thus, as indicated in Figure 4.1, outcomes for training program participants—especially employment and earnings—must be compared to what these outcomes would have been without the training. The impacts are estimated as the differences between participants' earnings (and other outcomes) and those of a control group or a comparison group, which provide the counterfactual (or baseline) for impact measurement.

Until recently, none of the evaluations of customized training programs had assessed the impacts on individual outcomes. Indeed, many

Figure 4.1 Factors Determining Effects of Customized Training on Employees

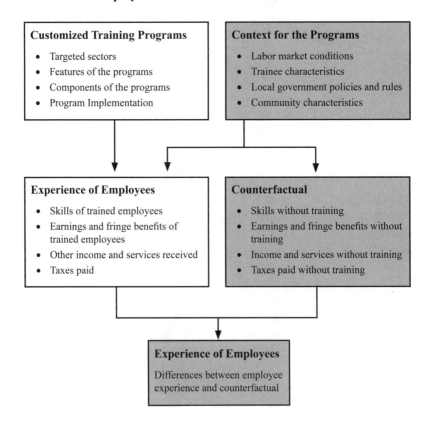

of the evaluations focused on implementation issues and did not measure individual outcomes over an extended period of time. Earlier this year, however, Public/Private Ventures released interim impact findings for individuals who participated in customized training offered by three project sites in the Sectoral Employment Initiative (SEI). In examining these results, it is important to remember that there are two forces that determine the impacts of any training programs on individuals. As shown in Figure 4.1, these are the external context for the training programs and the targeting, features, and implementation of the programs themselves. The characteristics and operational success of the programs ultimately determine whether they have impacts given their context—that is, the extent to which skills, employment, and earnings rise above what they would have been without the programs (indicated by the "counterfactual" box in the figure). However, the contextual factors are important in interpreting those impacts.

SEI was started in 1998, when nine organizations were formed to lead collaborative efforts in workforce development. Six of them concentrated on skills training for participants (in the health care, manufacturing, paralegal, and information technology industrial sectors) and three engaged in other enterprises. The final report on the SEI initiative, which was published last year, contributed to the customized training program implementation lessons summarized above (Roder, Clymer, and Wyckoff 2008). In 2003, three of the original nine SEI sites were selected to be part of the Sectoral Employment Impact Study, also funded by the Mott Foundation. The sites are operated by the Jewish Vocational Service, a community-based nonprofit in Boston; Per Scholas, a social venture in New York City; and the Wisconsin Regional Training Partnership, an association of employers and unions based in Milwaukee. Each organization has continued to operate its own customized training program. While the three sites have not followed a common program model, their programs are said to have shared several key elements.

- **Employer focus.** The programs all have focused on a sector or a small set of sectors, have maintained one-to-one contact regarding individual firms' training needs, and have used additional strategies to engage the employers. One site used an employer/union membership association to organize a group of employers from targeted sectors to define common skills needs.

- **Participant/job matching.** Throughout their recruitment, screening, and intake processes, the programs have encouraged appropriate career matches by participants. They have identified individuals with interest in and aptitude for particular sectors, and then ensured that these people had the basic skills needed for training and met the occupation-specific requirements for particular positions (e.g., had a driver's license for a construction job).

- **Skills training.** Programs have provided training on the full range of skills needed for particular jobs, including technical job-specific training, job-readiness workshops geared to particular industry settings, and basic training in English and math skills. The three programs have made all training accessible (whether they provided the components themselves or contracted part of the training to other agencies).

- **Encouraging training completion and job success.** In addition to providing training to participants, the programs offered supports such as child care, transportation, housing and financial assistance, and tutoring. Again, the programs either provided these services directly or in partnership with outside public or private agencies.

- **Adjusting to changing conditions.** All three programs have shown flexibility by making changes in occupational or industry focus, their curriculum, the mix of services they provide, and/or their collaborations (due to changes in partner agencies or funding).

The evaluation has used an experimental research design to measure program impacts on the employment, earnings, and other outcomes for participants. (The description and results of the impact study discussed in this section come from Maguire et al. [2009]).

The three programs recruited 1,285 people who met their eligibility criteria, and the recruits were randomly assigned to the treatment group, which could participate in the programs, or to a control group that could not receive services from the sites for two years but were free to seek services from other programs. Thirty-two percent of control group members indeed received other training services.

The population served by these programs appears to be at least as disadvantaged as that of WIA training programs. Sixty percent of the treatment and control group members were African American and 21 percent were Hispanic. On average, the sample members had worked seven months in the year before random assignment and about a third were employed at the time of assignment. Nearly 40 percent of the sample had received public assistance, including a quarter on welfare at the time of enrollment, and 5 percent had experienced homelessness in the last year. More than a quarter of the sample was under the age of 24 (the median participant age was 30). Three-quarters of sample members had a high school diploma or a GED, 8 percent had an associate's degree, and 9 percent had a bachelor's degree. Although there were differences across sites, the overall sample included approximately equal numbers of women and men.

Participants in sector-focused training earned 18 percent (about $4,500) more than controls during the two-year period covered by the study. The positive effect on earnings started in the eighth month following random assignment and continued through the end of the two years. Most of the increase in earnings occurred during the second year, which is not surprising given that the training was received in the first year, limiting participants' availability for work. The participants earned 29 percent more than the controls during the second year (about $4,000).

Part of the observed earnings gain is due to the training intervention's impact on employment—that is, program participants were more likely to find work and worked more consistently. During the two years over which they were followed, participants were significantly more likely to be employed, and worked on average 1.3 more months than controls. In the first several months of the follow-up period, while most treatment group members were in training, control group members were more likely to be employed. However, by month eight, after most participants had finished training, treatment group members were more likely to be employed than controls through the remainder of the two-year period. Employment rates hovered around 70 percent for treatment group members in the second year—about 10 percentage points higher than the rates for control group members. In addition, participants were significantly more likely to work all 12 months in the second year, indicating that the training helped them find steadier employment.

As valuable as these new findings are, it is worth noting two of their limitations. First, while the features of the three programs seem consistent with those of other well-implemented programs in other demonstrations, the impact results still cover only three urban programs serving only new employees and operating during a period when the economy was expanding (2004–2008). Thus, it is not clear whether comparable programs would have comparable impacts under different external conditions. Second, the impact study has only measured the effects of the training treatment as a whole. Thus, the value added by particular program components, such as the career-matching focus, cannot be established by the impact results. Other information must be taken into account in trying to draw inferences about the factors determining program impacts.

Employers

Customized training's effects on employers include increased output, improved flexibility and team performance, and a better pipeline of skilled employees. The boost in output can be generated by improved work quality, reduced time per task, improved ability to use new technology, reduced error rates and waste in production, improved coping skills, reduced absenteeism, and other results of the training. The training may also increase the task flexibility and team performance of employees, leading to potential productivity gains beyond those produced by the trained worker per se. Training programs that recruit and screen potential employees, as well as train them, provide a source of skilled employees that reduces a firm's need to either carry out these tasks on its own or to pay a human resources contractor to carry them out.

For incumbent workers who go through training, improved employee outcomes—in terms of skills, wages, performance ratings, absentee rates, and promotions—provide a reasonable, if imperfect, basis for judging the boost in output and profitability of the firms who provide the training. The available evidence indicates that this boost is substantial, far exceeding the increase in the wages they paid trained workers (Lowenstein and Spletzer 1999). Taking account of both this productivity gain and the effect of the training on employment (new hires and reduced layoffs), Hollenbeck (2008) has estimated that the total return to firms on their investments in incumbent worker training is at least 17 percent.

For new workers, however, the task is harder. In principle, the performance of new workers from customized training programs should be compared to the workers who *would have been recruited and hired* in the absence of the programs, as shown in Figure 4.2. This is virtually impossible to estimate with confidence, however, creating the need to use statistical modeling to isolate the value added by training interventions. Also, beyond the productivity and employment gains generated for incumbent workers, customized training leads to reduced recruit-

Figure 4.2 Factors Determining Effects of Customized Training on Employers

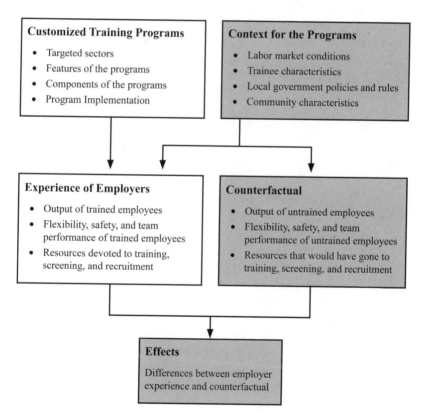

ment, screening, and hiring costs for new workers, as well as improved performance of the teams to which trained workers are assigned.

Probably the best available research evidence of the potential value of customized training to employers comes from studies of the value of in-house training provided by the employers themselves to new employees—in effect, perfectly customized training. For example, economist Lisa Lynch conducted a study almost 20 years ago on the impact of private sector training (Lynch 1992). She used data from the National Longitudinal Survey youth cohort to determine how individual characteristics, including employment histories, determine the probability of receiving training in the private sector; and, in turn, the effect of this training on wages and wage growth in young workers. Thus, the trainee experience came from survey sample members who had received training, and the counterfactual was estimated based on outcomes of sample members who had not received training and the characteristics of both trainees and sample members who had not received training.

The training studied by Lynch was employer-provided job-specific training. Lynch found that this training had a significant impact both on wage determination and on the career patterns of individuals. Indeed, she found that a year of formal private-sector training had as much effect on non-college youths (in the form of increased earnings) as did a year of college. The return to employers was even greater than the return to their employees, because employers and employees shared the gains from improved productivity due to training.

Economist Ann Bartel carried out a study of the relationship among training provided by a business to employees, the employees' subsequent wages and job performance, and the full return on investment to the company (Bartel 1995). The data came from the personnel records of a large manufacturing firm, and covered training provided in 1986–1990. The company spent about $1,950 on formal training per employee during 1990, which was more than five times the average for U.S. firms at that time. The study's sample included 19,000 observations of the firm's professional employees (about 3,800 per year). The occupations were distributed across finance, engineering, manufacturing, marketing and sales, information systems, research and development, staff services, and support services. The training itself fell into a range of core, employee development, and technical categories. The average sample member was older, more educated, and had more work experience than most of the individuals who have received the customized training described in this chapter.[14]

The study's main findings were that training led to improvements in job performance (as measured by performance rating scores), had a positive and significant effect on wage growth, and produced a positive rate of return for the firm. The training significantly increased the probability of improved job performance scores in the year following training and significantly reduced the probability of score declines. The measured effects of training on wage growth were particularly large for the employee development and technical training categories, the types of training provided to employees who were more comparable to those who participated in the demand-led training initiatives discussed in the last section of this chapter. Finally, Bartel estimated the short-term rates of return to the firm under alternative assumptions about the depreciation of job skills over time. The estimated return on dollars invested in employee development training ranged from 20 to 50 percent, and the return for technical training was between 21 and 52 percent.

Economy

Finally, customized training is thought to have additional effects on the broader economy. The effects of skills training programs on marketplace functioning are important, but hard to measure. The importance of skills acquired from schools, colleges and universities, training programs, and other sources is well documented. The pertinent economics literature shows, among other things, that differences in labor force skills explain most of the variance in economic growth among countries (Hanushek and Woessmann 2008). However, isolating the specific contribution of training programs—in particular, customized programs—is more difficult.[15] Economist David Ellwood assessed the potential effects as part of a project for the Aspen Institute (Ellwood 2003). He argues that the U.S. economy faces a future skilled labor shortage of dramatic proportions, and that the United States should address the issue head-on rather than being overtaken by it. Ellwood notes that skills training encourages economic growth and that customized training encourages particularly rapid growth because it speeds the match between the appropriately trained worker and the firm that needs the worker. Moreover, he makes the case that neither businesses nor individuals, by themselves, could undertake the job-specific training that is needed. Ellwood's prescription was demand-driven training involving government-supported partnerships within specific industries.

WHAT ARE THE CRITICAL UNANSWERED QUESTIONS?

This review of what is known about customized training indicates that a good deal has been learned from recent research on pertinent initiatives, but also that key questions remain both about such training's value and about how the training should best be structured. This concluding section lists three of the most critical open questions about customized training.

What is the return on investment in customized training?

As indicated earlier, the direct costs of customized training are shared by institutions in the public sector and firms in the private sector. Indirect costs are also borne by participants in training, who often must forgo employment or other activities while they are enrolled, as well as by private firms. A key question, therefore, is: What is the return on the investments made by these groups? Ultimately, this is the calculation that each group must make in deciding whether customized training is a good idea.

Rigorously measuring the impacts of customized training on earnings, as the SEI study has recently done, provides a good start. Much of the value of the training to participants, as well as its opportunity costs to them, is captured by these impacts. Also, part of the return on investments by public institutions is driven by the program impacts on earnings. However, these impacts tell us little about the return on investment to employers. As indicated in this chapter, the best current evidence on the *potential* return to employers comes from research on the return on training by employers themselves. Evidence regarding the actual return to employers would be much better.

What is the relationship between program effectiveness and economic conditions?

It is important to gain a better understanding of the extent to which the effectiveness of customized training depends on local and national economic conditions. One way to do this would be to assess customized training program impacts in sites facing a range of unemployment levels and local labor market circumstances, and to assess the impacts during all phases of the business cycle. Another way would be to conduct a more systematic assessment of program flexibility and responsiveness to changing economic conditions—that is, the ability of programs to make appropriate changes in occupational and sector focus, curriculum, and services as needed.

Can effective customized programs be replicated?

If we find an approach to customized training that is determined to be cost-effective, and is effective in a variety of conditions, then it will be important to determine whether the training model can be successfully replicated. This will be a challenge, as illustrated by the USDOL's experience in trying to replicate the success of CET. Despite receiving technical assistance, most sites in the CET replication project were unable to establish programs that met several operational criteria; and the sites that could not duplicate the CET model were found to produce no impacts on employment or earnings. However, if customized training does prove to be effective, this is undoubtedly a challenge that the Labor Department, as well as policymakers in other countries, would be happy to take on.

Notes

1. Because of the increased use of distance learning, there are more and more examples of partnerships where the training providers and partner firms are not in the same geographic area.
2. Labor market intermediaries serve dual customers: businesses (seeking qualified workers) and potential and current workers (seeking jobs or career advancement). In addition to local board and community organizations, intermediaries include business associations, chambers of commerce, staffing and temporary agencies,

community colleges and other educational institutions, and labor unions. For discussion, see Soukamneuth and Harvey (2008).

3. A recent survey of more than 200 workforce development organizations in the United States provides an overview of the kinds of partnerships and programs that currently deliver customized training. The programs targeted approximately 20 industries (Conway et al. 2007).

4. By the last quarter of 2008, total trade (exports plus imports) reached 31 percent of estimated GDP, according to the U.S. Bureau of Economic Analysis (BEA). This fraction is about three times what it was in 1970. News releases by the BEA can be accessed at www.bea.gov/newsreleases.htm.

5. For example, the BEA has reported that exports of education, financial services, telecommunications, professional, and business and technical services grew to $224 billion in 2007, more than 50 percent larger than the imports of $144 billion in these same service categories during the same year (Koncz and Flatness 2008).

6. While the average tenure in workers' longest job rose from 22 years in the late 1960s to 24 years in the late seventies, it has declined ever since (Stevens 2005).

7. The survey covered 1,062 establishments with more than 50 employees. Among establishments with 500 or more employees, 57 percent had used community colleges for training during the last 12 months. For establishments with 100–499 employees, the figure was 35 percent, while 27 percent of businesses with 50–99 employees used the colleges (Dougherty 2003).

8. The Urban Institute and Johns Hopkins University are evaluating this initiative. For discussion of the project and its implementation, see Nightingale et al. (2008).

9. Further details are available at www.workforcealliance.org.

10. This finding comes from the evaluation of the original initiative, which involved nine sites and focused on program implementation and participant outcomes (see Roder, Clymer, and Wyckoff [2008]). Based on interim results, three of the original sites were chosen to be part of a controlled experiment, which has produced the impact results described later in the chapter.

11. The Portland site in this evaluation, which used an experimental research design, achieved substantially larger impacts than the other sites. The program's education, training, and placement services were explicitly designed to generate jobs with satisfactory wages, fringe benefits, and good career prospects (see Scrivener et al. [1998]).

12. This was one of the early lessons from the demonstration (see Anderson, Kato, and Riccio [2006]).

13. CET, which stresses hands-on training and maintains close relationships with employers in the San Jose area, had substantially greater impacts on employment and earnings than other sites of two major evaluations (Burghardt et al. 1992; Cave et al. 1993). Later, in a 12-site demonstration that sought to replicate CET in other locations, moderate success was achieved in sites that faithfully implemented CET's model, and no impacts were found in sites that were unable to carry out the model (Miller et al. 2005).

14. For example, the average age of sample members in the SEI impact study was 30, compared to 36 in Bartel's study. Only 18 percent of the SEI sample had education

beyond high school, whereas the average sample member in Bartel's study had 4.5 years of schooling beyond high school. The SEI sample was made up of new employees, while the average sample member in Bartel's study had worked seven years with the firm (Bartel 1995; Maguire et al. 2009).

15. It is clear that additional vocational education or training—measured in months or credentials received—increases the productivity of workers (measured by earnings) (Bailey, Kienzl, and Marcotte 2004). Distinguishing the value added by particular types of vocational training is empirically difficult.

References

Ahlstrand, Amanda, Laurie Bassi, and Daniel McMurrer. 2003. *Workplace Education for Low-Wage Workers.* Kalamazoo, MI: W.E. Upjohn Institute for Employment Research.

Almandsmith, Sherry, Mary Walshok, Kay Magill, Linda Toms Barker, Pamela Surko, Mary Vencill, Tommy Smith, Hannah Betesh, and June Chocheles. 2008. *Early Implementation of Generation I of the Workforce Innovation in Regional Economic Development (WIRED) Initiative: 2007 Interim Evaluation Report.* Report submitted to U.S. Department of Labor, ETA/OGCM, Washington, DC: U.S. Department of Labor.

Anderson, Jacquelyn, Linda Yuriko Kato, and James A. Riccio. 2006. *A New Approach to Low-Wage Workers and Employers: Launching the Work Advancement and Support Center Demonstration.* New York: MDRC.

Bailey, Martin, Gregory Kienzl, and Dave E. Marcotte. 2004. *The Return to Sub-Baccalaureate Education: The Effects of Schooling, Credentials and Program of Study on Economic Outcomes.* Report prepared for the National Assessment of Vocational Education, U.S. Department of Education, Washington, DC: U.S. Department of Education.

Bartel, Ann P. 1995. "Training, Wage Growth and Job Performance: Evidence from a Company Database." *Journal of Labor Economics* 13(3): 401–425.

Becker, Gary. 1997. "The Economic Way of Looking at Life." In *Nobel Lectures, Economics, 1991–1995*, Torsten Perrson, ed. Singapore: World Scientific Publishing. http://nobelprize.org/nobel_prizes/economics/laureates/1992/becker-lecture.pdf (accessed Feb 23, 2011).

Biotech Workforce Network. 2007. "Ahead of the Curve: Responding to the Dynamic Biotech Sector." Brochure. Belmont, CA: Alameda and San Mateo Workforce Investment Boards. http://www.biotechworkforcenetwork.com/docs/BWN_Brochure.pdf (accessed August 11, 2010).

Burghardt, John, Anu Rangarajan, Anne Gordon, and Ellen Kisker. 1992. *Evaluation of the Minority Female Single Parent Demonstration: Summary Report.* Princeton, NJ: Mathematica Policy Research.

Cave, George, Hans Bos, Fred Doolittle, and Cyril Toussaint. 1993. *JOBSTART: Final Report on a Program for School Dropouts.* New York: MDRC.

Conway, Maureen, Amy Blair, Steven L. Dawson, and Linda Dworak-Muñoz. 2007. *Sectoral Strategies for Low Income Workers: Lessons from the Field.* Washington, DC: The Aspen Institute.

Dougherty, Kevin. 2003. "The Uneven Distribution of Employee Training by Community Colleges: Description and Explanation." In *The Annals of the American Academy of Political and Social Science, Vol. 586.* Philadelphia, PA: A.L. Hummel for the American Academy of Political and Social Science, pp. 62–91.

Ellwood, David. 2003. "How We Got Here." In *Grow Faster Together or Grow Slowly Apart: How Will America Work in the 21st Century?* Report to the GAO Domestic Strategy Group. Washington, DC: Aspen Institute.

Ganzglass, Evelyn. 2006. "NGA Center for Best Practices, State Sector Strategies: Regional Solutions to Worker and Employer Needs." Washington, DC: National Governors Association.

Government Accountability Office (GAO). 2005. *WIA—Substantial Funds Are Used for Training, but Little is Known Nationally about Training Outcomes.* Washington, DC: GAO.

Hanushek, Eric A., and Ludger Woessmann. 2008. "The Role of Cognitive Skills in Economic Development." *Journal of Economic Literature* 46(3): 607–668.

Hollenbeck, Kevin. 2008. "Is There a Role for Public Support of Incumbent Work On-the-Job Training?" Working Paper No. 08-138. Kalamazoo, MI: W.E. Upjohn Institute for Employment Research.

Koncz, Jennifer, and Anne Flatness. 2008. "U.S. International Services: Cross-Border Trade in 2007 and Services Supplied through Affiliates in 2006." *Survey of Current Business* (October): 16–37.

Lowenstein, Mark, and James Spletzer. 1999. "General and Specific Training: Evidence and Implications." *Journal of Human Resources* 34(4): 710–733.

Lynch, Lisa M. 1992. "Private Sector Training and Its Impact on the Earnings of Young Workers." *American Economic Review* 82(1): 299–332.

Maguire, Sheila, Joshua Freely, Carol Clymer, and Maureen Conway. 2009. *Job Training That Works: Findings from the Sectoral Impact Study.* Philadelphia, PA: Public/Private Ventures.

Miller, Cynthia, Johannes Bos, Kristin Porter, Fannie Tseng, and Yasuyo Abe. 2005. *The Challenge of Repeating Success in a Changing World: Final Report on the Center for Employment Training Replication Sites.* New York: MDRC.

Mishel, Lawrence R., Jared Bernstein, and Heather Boushey. 2003. *The State of Working America.* Ithaca, NY: Cornell University Press.

Nightingale, Demetra Smith, Lauren Eyster, John Trutko, Carolyn O'Brien, and Kate Chambers. 2008. *Implementation Analysis of the High Growth Job Training Initiative (HGJTI) Programs.* Washington, DC: Urban Institute.

Pindus, Nancy M., Carolyn O/Brien, Maureen Conway, Conaway Haskins, and Ida Rademacher. 2004. *Evaluation of the Sectoral Employment Demonstration Program: Final Report.* Report to the U.S. Department of Labor. Washington, DC: Urban Institute and Aspen Institute.

Public Policy Associates. 2005. *Incumbent/Dislocated Worker Skill Shortage II Demonstration: Evaluation Final Report.* Lansing, MI: Public Policy Associates.

Roder, Anne, Carol Clymer, and Laura Wyckoff. 2008. *Targeting Industries, Training Workers and Improving Opportunities: The Final Report from the Sectoral Employment Initiative.* Philadelphia, PA: Public/Private Ventures.

Scrivener, Susan, Gayle Hamilton, Mary Farrell, Stephen Freedman, Daniel Friedlander, Marissa Mitchell, Jodi Nudelman, and Christine Schwartz. 1998. *Implementation, Participation Patterns, Costs and Two-Year Impacts of the Portland (Oregon) Welfare-to-Work Program.* New York: MDRC.

Stevens, Ann Huff. 2005. "The More Things Change, the More They Stay the Same: Trends in Long-Term Employment in the United States, 1969–2002." NBER Working Paper No. 11878. Cambridge, MA: National Bureau of Economic Research.

Soukamneuth, Sengsouvanh, and Sandra Harvey. 2008. *Literature Review: Intermediaries and FBOCs Working Together.* Oakland, CA: Social Policy Research Associates.

5
One-Stop Management and
the Private Sector

David Heaney
MAXIMUS, Inc.

The implementation of WIA fostered the development of a wide range of solutions to address the problems of unemployment and/or underemployment among selected demographic groups including youth, adults, dislocated (redundant) workers, the disabled, older adults, veterans, and, in some cases, those families receiving public assistance under the Temporary Assistance for Needy Families (TANF) program. Many of the employment programs operating through One-Stop Career Centers have enjoyed considerable success. Their success, at least in part, appears owing to operational designs based on certain foundational principles set out in WIA. The principles place a high premium on employer-driven strategies and integrated service delivery through co-locating key providers under one roof. The act envisioned a nationwide network of One-Stop Career Centers where job seekers and employers could access all required resources in a single location. A key feature of successful programs has been their capacity to effectively leverage the strengths of this diverse set of partner organizations operating side by side. Still, while many achieved impressive outcomes under this design, many others found the new model unwieldy, difficult to manage, and driven by a disproportionate focus on business.

The foundational principles embodied in the legislation are intended to be institutionalized in the overall design of all program operations. A key differentiator between WIA and its predecessors is the role that business is intended to play in both the creation and ongoing management of the One-Stop delivery system. The One-Stop system was intended to be and is often described as "employer driven." Employers, it is reasoned, understand a community's existing and emerging labor market conditions, occupational needs, and skill sets required for in-demand jobs. The employer is, after all, the consumer who hires well-equipped job seekers. Employer need should, therefore, define and determine the content of education and training programs to prepare and equip the workforce. By designing a system around employer needs, WIA intended to create a business-friendly system.

Under the current operating model, the management of One-Stop centers may be competitively procured, which has spawned the growth of a new, albeit small, industry of One-Stop operators. These management entities are responsible for organizing and managing 12 mandated and colocated partners, together with various voluntary partners into a seamless employment service system, which will meet specific performance levels established by the Workforce Investment Board (WIB). Managing entities come from the private for-profit, nonprofit, and public sectors. After some 10 years, the number of private, for-profit companies competing for One-Stop management opportunities has noticeably dwindled to a relatively small group. Managing entities, for the most part, appear to remain the same from procurement to procurement. The reasons for this vary and will be discussed in this chapter. However, the impact of this withdrawal has limited competition, and perhaps innovative and more effective approaches to achieving better employment outcomes in more efficient and cost-effective ways.

The impact of minimal competition on service delivery arguably encourages maintenance of the status quo and stimulates little in the way of novel approaches. I personally have spoken with executives from some of the nation's largest WIBs, who express concern about the diminishing number of qualified bidders competing in their procurements. Some critics of the workforce investment system have called for the elimination of competitive procurements altogether as a means to acquire workforce services.

The discussion presented in this chapter assumes that open and fair competition between a diverse set of qualified bidders supports continuous improvement, high performance, and increased transparency. Whether limited participation by the private sector has, in fact, inhibited the creation of more effective programs cannot be established without careful evaluation of empirical data. Overall, this paper aims to encourage the development of policies which facilitate procurement processes and operational models designed to attract a greater number and more diverse set of qualified bidders from all sectors. With this in mind, I have attempted to identify some of the factors contributing to the private sector's ambivalence toward the WIA market in the United States. The aim here is to identify several significant practices that discourage private sector participation in procurements to manage One-Stop centers and to briefly comment on what this has meant to the industry. Finally, I will discuss alternative approaches which WIA reauthorization will need to address to support the engagement and retention of a diverse network of providers.

The perspective offered here is one derived principally from observation of many existing WIA-funded One-Stop operations, as well as discussions with a wide range of leaders from the field over the past decade. The perspective I bring is that of an executive from a large for-profit organization that views the current WIA market as one fraught with risk, and in this regard, not viable from a business perspective. Therefore, I have identified selected changes to the current WIA system that could increase market desirability, support increased achievement of performance outcomes, and promote greater efforts to economize through efficiency.

PRIVATE SECTOR, THIRD SECTOR, PUBLIC SECTOR: THE CHALLENGE OF STEREOTYPES

Right or wrong, there exists in every community a tension between business and government. Generally, business wants as little government interference in its affairs as possible. "Why would I go to a government agency for help with my business when their interference always makes my life more difficult?" one business owner asked in a discussion regarding WIA employer services. Again, right or wrong, third-sector (nonprofit) organizations are commonly perceived as indifferent to the "bottom line" and more focused on job seeker services than employer hiring needs. And finally, the private, for-profit sector is often viewed as indifferent to everything but the bottom line.

The overall aim of keeping the private sector engaged is to support competition that improves quality of service while creating greater economies and efficiencies for the government and taxpayer. The same, of course, might be argued in favor of retaining third-sector, organized labor, and public sector approaches—all of which bring unique solutions that offer varying degrees of value. Setting aside stereotypes and promoting policies that encourage a diverse pool of bidders supports the government's goal of obtaining "best value."

WHO DRIVES THE SYSTEM?

Under WIA, emphasis has been directed toward creating and operating an employer-driven system. The thinking is based on the notion that business leaders best understand the unique emerging labor market needs of the communities in which they operate. Many WIBs appear to have been unclear, or had only a vague sense of what "employer driven" meant and the changes it was intended to facilitate that differentiated WIA from its predecessor, the Job Training Partnership Act (JTPA). Following the passage of WIA, some WIBs actively engaged employers to help reshape their service delivery models, while others argued that greater emphasis should be placed on job seeker needs.

A broad look at the changes in the workforce delivery system suggests that relatively few WIBs have truly created an employer-driven service delivery system, instead doing what long-time providers have frequently done—build a service-rich environment to meet job seeker desires even when these are at odds with the realities of the existing market. A recent conversation with the labor commissioner from a Midwest state illustrated the challenge of supporting an employer-driven system. She explained that WIA's promotion of customer choice as a guiding principle has unintentionally created an opportunity for unnecessarily expensive training providers to exploit job seeker interests while turning a blind eye to employer hiring needs. Job seekers are encouraged to assert their right to choose, too often selecting trainers with the best television commercial but poor employment placement rates.

Visits to scores of major One-Stops further illustrate this point; while job seeker resource centers appear consistently active, many newly created Employer Services Business Centers, designed to serve employers, remain underutilized. It is true that some employers have taken advantage of One-Stop hiring assistance, but it is also true that many WIA industry observers worry that such employers often offer unsustainable employment.

Striking a balance between employer- and job-seeker-focused service delivery models seems obvious but has proven difficult to achieve. Such a balance requires the right mix of stakeholder partners engaged in service delivery. To be useful to a broader range of employers, the One-Stop Employer Services function may require a level of sophistication on par with services provided by human resources, outplacement, staffing, and consulting firms. This perhaps means better resourcing and significantly greater efforts to reach the large number of employers who do not use and indeed remain unaware of the services and benefits offered by the nation's One-Stop Career Center network. Policies to support business participation, such as requiring the board to be weighted in favor of business leadership, have done relatively little to promote greater interest in the One-Stops' capacity to help build and effectively serve their labor force.

As it stands, to portray the current workforce system as employer driven appears inaccurate. WIA policy needs to underscore the interdependent relationship between employer and job seeker. While WIA policy should clearly reflect a commitment to both job seeker and employer interests, to meet the needs of both groups, it too should facilitate the creation of service models to capture the interests of a wider range of providers who possess the appropriate expertise to meet the needs of the community's business leadership.

FISCAL CONSIDERATIONS: ADMINISTRATIVE AND PROFIT CAPS

The inclusion of private for-profits in the management of any public program inevitably raises concerns about whether profit is appropriate when using public monies and, if it is, what constitutes a fair and reasonable profit. The ambivalence felt by many WIBs is expressed in policies that include profit caps, holdbacks, administrative caps, and disproportionate risk and reward ratios.

Administrative costs are typically capped at what are often perceived to be unrealistic levels, forcing many organizations to broaden the interpretation of what can be classified as a program cost. In some ways related to stereotyping, local policy restrictions placed on a One-Stop operator's ability to earn profit and the imposition of administrative caps reflect a fundamental and pervasive ambivalence regarding the private sector's role in the workforce delivery system. On the one hand, WIA legislation was intended to engage the private sector in a leadership role, mandating that the majority of WIB members be from the private sector. On the other hand, policies that cap both profit and administrative costs can, and do, discourage private sector interest in WIA opportunities.

Caps on profit and administrative costs are intended to protect the public's interest by requiring contractors to allocate a specified percentage of the total contract value to direct service. However, when profit rules are viewed within the context of the growing demand for outcome-based, pay-for-performance contracting, risk and reward are generally disproportionate. In other words, if profit is capped at 6–8 percent (which it commonly is) and is contingent upon meeting all performance targets, then failure to meet targets should, too, be capped at 6–8 percent, instead of not compensating a provider at all.

Alternatively, if the contracting agency is concerned with not simply achieving but exceeding specific outcomes, creating a much broader upside-downside spread is likely to drive greater innovation and better outcomes. There is no reason to believe that highly prescriptive rules regarding administrative and profit limits have led to better outcomes. Instead, such restrictions may have limited competition and squelched innovative approaches by shrinking the pool of potential providers.

Unrealistically low administrative caps force bidders to "back into" their solutions. Instead of allocating time and necessary resources based on the best solution to meet contract targets, solutions must be tailored to conform to the required allocation formula. Artificial allocation formulas result in decreased transparency and accountability.

It also seems appropriate to ask what end is actually served by imposing caps. When an organization purchases, say, computer hardware through a competitive procurement, "best value" is generally tied to some combination of best product and best price. A government agency does not make a decision to buy 100 personal computers on the basis of administrative costs and profit margins associated with the production of those 100 PCs. Rather, the decision is based on the quality of the product, available funding, and the price.

If performance measures are carefully constructed, risk and profit limits can both be more expansive. Allowing bidding organizations to design and price their proposals based on their risk/reward tolerance levels should be explored. Such freedom creates a more diverse collection of bidders. At one end of the spectrum are entrepreneurs and risk takers whose solutions are designed to exceed targets, and at the other are those whose tolerance for risk is low but whose performance is deemed adequate to meet performance targets.

WIA rules might better reflect a commitment to both business and job seeker by seeking providers who will raise the bar for performance, quality, economy, and efficiency. The good news is these improvements can be accomplished without additional funds, but simply with fewer prescriptive accounting rules. Transparency and accountability are not compromised when actual administrative costs are reported, and profit earned is a consequence of performance against targets.

GOVERNANCE AND MANAGEMENT

The diverse array of WIA partners creates significant challenges. The composition of the local WIBs requires participation by representatives from a wide range of stakeholder groups, including business, labor, education, economic development, each of the One-Stops, and community-based organizations. At least 51 percent of the board must be comprised of representatives from the business community. Additionally, the board chair must be from the business community. There are, of course, trade-offs inherent in such broad representation. Predictably, the ability to make decisions on urgent matters is frequently achieved through consensus and compromises that ultimately please no one. Critics complain WIA representation requirements create an unnecessarily large, unwieldy, and ineffective board. The ideal of broad representation, collaborative program design, and consensus-driven leadership has created still more unintended consequences that impact participation, especially among those who derive no clear return on their investment of time and energy. This is particularly important at the local level where local board decisions directly impact service delivery.

The managing entity responsible for day-to-day oversight of the local One-Stop Career Center struggles with the same challenges posed by the broad participation requirements at the WIB level. The requirement for colocation of different agencies and organizations serving the same customer is intended to promote better service through easy access to services. However, both strategic and day-to-day operational management is a complicated affair where building consensus among mandated partners can make even relatively simple organizational decisions difficult. Without clear lines of authority, especially as they relate to uniform standards for quality, customer service, and performance management, the managing partner absorbs all risk without a defined path for mitigation. This is a particular challenge to for-profits where some portion of total revenue may be tied to the achievement of targets.

The degree to which One-Stop partners organize around common goals with a clear management structure directly impacts the capacity to generate revenue. Still, disparity in compensation schemes, work hours, and organizational cultures cannot all be resolved by institutionalizing the managing partner's authority. Generally, because risks and rewards tied to revenue cannot be flowed down to all partner organizations, the managing partner, whose earnings and profits are tied to performance, bears the brunt of responsibility. Failure or success regarding target achievement simply does not drive performance with the same degree of urgency as when targets are tied to revenues. The policy challenge here is daunting. How, or should, policy align the interests of all participating partner organizations so that risks and rewards are genuinely shared? How, for example, can incentive and bonus programs, generally an integral component of successful for-profit approaches, be equitably implemented across multiple organizations providing integrated services under one roof? How does a One-Stop offer extended hours (often a contractual requirement) when labor contracts and organizational policies make it difficult, if not impossible, to meet this obligation?

While current policy has created challenges for both WIBs and comprehensive One-Stops, failure to preserve broad representation at the state, local, and One-Stop levels would be regressive and counterproductive. Clarification of the One-Stop managing entity's role as managing partner with authority to make decisions regarding performance, quality, and corrective actions would facilitate the development of a more seamless service delivery model as was envisioned by the WIA legislation. Additionally, identification of best practices regarding effective governance and management models, including targeted technical assistance for new managing partners, will help generalize more successful approaches.

PROGRAM SEQUENCE

Rules that leave the provider with little discretionary authority undermine creative engagement of both job seekers and employers. The WIA requirement of sequencing movement through the "core, intensive, individual training account" tiers frustrates all parties who may clearly discern a path that leads to a desired outcome. Policies that offer providers greater discretionary authority regarding the level of service appropriate to an individual customer will improve the pace of reemployment by allowing direct service providers to route customers in a timely fashion to the best resource(s) available. Limitations on discretion and the corresponding development of prescriptive procedure is designed to ensure that services are fairly, equitably, and consistently provided. If the provider and the customer's interests are aligned, allowing greater levels of discretion supports seeking the most direct route to most favorable outcome. Limitations on discretion in favor of highly prescribed program sequences are generally most critical when a provider is able to achieve some benefit by acting in a manner not in accord with the customer's best interest. As long as both parties' interests are aligned, allowing greater discretionary authority encourages providers to redesign cumbersome business processes to offer improved customer service and capture greater efficiencies and cost savings.

PERFORMANCE MEASURES

Performance measures are designed to reflect whether a job seeker has succeeded in upgrading skills, securing employment, retaining a job, and progressing satisfactorily along a determined career track. Many critics have described these performance measures as burdensome, arguing they should be streamlined. From the perspective of managing operations, timely availability of performance data is most critical. Major gaps between a key event and the provider's ability to track that event have dramatic performance implications. The stakes are still greater where provider payments are tied to measures that are reported months after the fact. When a provider is unable to obtain information required to manage the achievement of successful outcomes tied to payment, the program is fatally flawed. Reexamining the model to determine where the fix must be applied needs to be embodied in policy change, the performance measure, how the data element is captured, who captures the data element, or the means for reporting critical data.

An equally formidable challenge pertains to vaguely defined rules that apply to program enrollment. Provider performance is measured against those whom the provider enters into the performance denominator. It is well-known that the "gatekeeper" role played by the One-Stop managing entity is essential to meeting targets. Program designs that keep those with more complex needs out of the denominator undermine the overall purpose of the One-Stop. On the other hand, an employer driven approach is clearly at odds with enrolling ill-equipped job seekers. Performance measures need to reflect enrollment in distinct service-level tracks. Additionally, policies should establish standardized assessment tools designed to help determine the most appropriate service-level track for job seeker customers. The Australian Department of Education, Employment, and Workplace Relations, which administers similar employment programs, has devised such a tool and deployed it nationwide. The level of service is determined by an independently administered assessment. Providers are paid according to a payment schedule designed to reflect the level of effort. An appeals process allows the provider to present evidence to demonstrate that the initial level of service determination may have been inadequate. The adoption of a similar approach would both support better service and offer more useful data. It also may help better define the role of certain upfront services as distinct and independent from postenrollment activities.

CONCLUSION

The foundational principles upon which the workforce delivery system in the United States is built are sound, but large-scale efforts to operationalize them are flawed. There is a significant disconnect between the aim of creating a business-driven One-Stop system and a procurement process and service delivery model that creates an environment in which it is difficult to be even marginally successful. Subtle prejudices are played out in ways that inhibit a more successful integration of mandated and voluntary partners. Fiscal rules and practices frustrate participation by for-profits and perpetuate the problems created by a limited pool of qualified bidders. Governance, management, and operations in general are heavily prescriptive and at odds with the common practice adopted by most government agencies over the past decade of paying for performance and tying profit to target achievements. Having said that, pay for performance schemes should be linked to outcomes only where operators have the flexibility to refine existing approaches as they go and change out those that simply do not work in favor of more effective practices. Performance measures need to take account of the entire population requiring service and provide meaningful information for continuous improvement.

While there exist many challenges to keeping the private sector engaged in ongoing One-Stop center management procurements, a major redesign would be significantly less productive than relatively minor changes to existing program rules. WIA included language requiring a comprehensive evaluation by 2005. Regrettably, this did not happen. The result is that relatively little information exists on what employment and training services really work and for whom. Reauthorization of WIA, therefore, should proceed with some degree of caution. Proposals that call for dismantling or radically redesigning the workforce delivery system without such an evaluation appear reckless and conflict with the current administration's promotion of evidence-based practices. Rather, continuous improvement practices (a concept that lies at the heart of WIA approaches) suggest the opportunity still exists to review the evidence we have, to highlight best (and worst) practices, to create additional forums such as this conference for the exchange of ideas, and to make an intentional effort to reengage the business community at all levels through easily improved policies derived from the right principles that support the evolution of a stronger workforce delivery system.

6
Eligible Training Provider Lists and Consumer Report Cards

Carl E. Van Horn
*John J. Heldrich Center for Workforce Development,
Rutgers University*

Aaron Fichtner
New Jersey Department of Labor and Workforce Development

Billions of public and private funds support short-term education and training for millions of Americans seeking jobs or advancement in positions they already hold. These training programs, delivered by thousands of nonprofit and for-profit education and training institutions throughout the United States, are critical components of the nation's workforce development system and especially for services funded by WIA.

WIA customers who receive individual training account (ITA) credit to pay for short-term occupational training are given wide latitude in choosing training providers. WIA requires that states develop a process for identifying qualified providers who are eligible to provide training to these job seekers, based on the employment experiences of past students. Despite the obvious appeal of such policies, most states and communities have struggled to implement performance reporting systems.

While a nationwide system of disseminating training outcomes is yet to be achieved, several states have successfully implemented robust reporting systems. This chapter examines the experiences of these states as well as the barriers to wider adoption of a more transparent and reliable reporting system. It also offers observations and recommendations for improving outcome reporting on education and training programs that are applicable to the management and assessment of training programs.

THE VALUE OF OUTCOME REPORTING ON
JOB TRAINING PROGRAMS

In the United States, short-term occupational training for un-employed and underemployed job seekers is delivered through a decentralized and wide array of education and training institutions, including two- and four-year colleges, vocational schools, community-based nonprofits, and for-profit/proprietary schools. It is estimated that more than 667,000 credentials are awarded each year by thousands of trainers who offer thousands of courses in occupations ranging from commercial truck driver training to home heath care aides (National Center for Education Statistics n.d.).

The costs of occupational training are paid by students with their own money, by federal student loan programs, by employers, and by government programs, such as WIA, that furnish grants or vouchers individuals may use to obtain training. Many of these same institutions also deliver longer-term education and training programs for students and adult workers who desire or need new skills and credentials in order to obtain jobs or be promoted to a new position.

Oversight of publicly funded education and training institutions is handled by dozens of federal and state government agencies. One of their principal responsibilities is to protect students from fraud, such as when providers offer poor training. To meet their responsibilities, state governments, which shoulder the greatest burden for oversight, have relied on licensing training suppliers. These processes typically involve an assessment or self-assessment of the provider's capabilities, includ-ing their financial statements, and a review of their facilities and the intructors' credentials. After receiving approval to accept public funds, education and training institutions usually have limited reporting ob-ligations to public agencies. Students or employers may subsequently lodge complaints with the regulators, but enforcement actions, such as revocation of a license or denial of public funds, are rare.

Licensing and accreditation procedures seldom consider the ef-fectiveness of the training delivered by those organizations. A school might, for example, continue training truck drivers, cooks, or nurses' aides for years, even if few graduates obtain jobs in those or other oc-cupations. Moreover, when information on program outcomes, such as job placements or wages earned, is made available, it is supplied by the training organization rather than by an independent organization or government agency.

WIA contained several provisions that, if implemented, would have begun to address these obvious deficiencies. While it is beyond the scope of this chapter to provide a full explanation for the failure by federal and state officials to implement these provisions, it is clear that the goals of a more transparent and accountable workforce development system were never achieved. Education and training establishments and their trade organizations marshaled opposition to performance reporting and undermined or quashed implementation throughout the country.

Nevertheless, several state governments, profiled in this chapter, forged ahead and developed comprehensive outcome reporting systems. While the specific outcome reporting schemes varied, these states typically were able to disseminate detailed information at the program and institutional level on the following three measures:

1) Program completion, including the percentage of students who complete the program, the costs per completion, and the average amount of time to completion;

2) Educational outcomes, including the percentage of individuals who obtain an industry-certified credential, certificate, license, or other indicator of job readiness; and

3) Employment outcomes, including the percentage of completers who obtain employment, who obtain employment in a related field of work, and the average wages earned by completers.

These states envisioned benefits for four key audiences: 1) resource allocators, 2) regulators, 3) individuals in need of training, and 4) employers who hire graduates and often purchase training services for their employees. Regulators could use outcome reports when making licensing decisions, ensuring that only those suppliers with proven track records would be permitted to continue to provide training. Policymakers could use outcome data when deciding which training providers should receive government funding and for which training programs. Individuals seeking training to obtain a job or get a better one could benefit by knowing how well institutions delivered training and the extent to which graduates succeeded in the labor market. Informed about program outcomes, individuals would also be better able to determine whether their investment of time and money would be worthwhile. Finally, performance information on trainers could be used by employers to inform hiring decisions or decide where to invest funds for upgrading the skills of their workforces.

ELIGIBLE TRAINING PROVIDER PROVISIONS OF WIA

WIA provided $2 billion in funding in program year 2008 to states to help unemployed and underemployed adults find jobs. The law also encourages state and local governments managing WIA to fund training programs for qualified individuals who need additional skills to obtain jobs. In program year 2007, 147,000 adults obtained such services under WIA.

Another of WIA's principal goals was to increase customer choice for individuals seeking training. Under the law's predecessor, JTPA, training services were typically obtained directly by local government agencies that selected both occupational concentrations and service providers. Each year, local workforce program managers would estimate demand for categories of training and select a provider to offer those services. Local government administrators purchased a set number of training slots and throughout the year referred individuals to those programs. Often these arrangements led to overconsumption of some training and lack of flexibility for funders, students, and employers. Consumer protection—and common sense—demanded that job seekers and program managers be afforded more flexibility and better information when choosing training options.

WIA placed greater emphasis on informed customer choice. Individuals who qualified for financial assistance for training (usually long-term unemployed and/or low-income applicants) may receive an ITA to purchase short-term occupational training. Moreover, ITA recipients are given wide latitude in selecting training providers. WIA, therefore, required that states, in partnership with local workforce areas, develop a process for identifying organizations that are qualified to offer training, based on the past performance. WIA also required that performance information be collected and calculated in a standardized manner so as to produce accurate and verifiable information.

The creation of a state eligible training provider list (ETPL) introduced the potential for greater accountability by ensuring that ITA recipients could choose a provider that met or exceeded minimum standards. The law required that performance outcomes would be calculated for individual training programs, recognizing that some providers may offer some high-quality programs as well as some of lesser quality.

WIA mandated that states use past performance information to determine if providers and their individual programs should be included on and remain on the ETPL. WIA further required that states and local workforce areas include six outcome measures when determining which programs and providers would remain on the list (see Table 6.1). Three outcome measures must be calculated for those students who receive training accounts. The other measures were to be calculated for all students enrolled in training in any program on the list, regardless of the funding source.

States were also directed to establish a consumer report card (CRC) system to disseminate the ETPL to ITA recipients and other interested stakeholders, such as Workforce Investment Boards (WIBs) that oversee the state and local programs. States were supposed to report on training outcomes (by provider and program) in the CRC system so that

Table 6.1 Required Measures for the ETPL

Measures	Outcome measures to be calculated for all students regardless of funding	Outcome measures to also be calculated for ITA recipients only
Program completion rate	Required	Required
Employment at placement	Required	Required
Wages at placement	Required	Required
Retention in employment at six months	Optional	Required
Wages at six months	Optional	Required
Rates of licensure or certification, attainment of academic degrees or equivalents, attainment of other measures industry-recognized of skills	Optional	Required

individuals who receive an ITA could make an informed choice about training providers.

Initial eligibility. States were expected to collaborate with administrators of local workforce boards to establish the process for creating the initial ETPL. Typically, training providers would submit applications to local administrators who would then decide if a provider (and their programs) met minimum eligibility requirements. WIA mandated that providers submit an "appropriate portion" of the required performance measures and that they meet "appropriate levels of performance." If the provider and the program met these requirements, they were included on the state's ETPL.

Subsequent eligibility. WIA mandated that states create a process for determining if providers and their programs should remain on the ETPL. However, local WIBs were also permitted to set their own standards, which were not to be lower than the state's standards. States and local WIBs were given significant latitude in developing and implementing these standards.

Obtaining Performance Data

WIA did not specify how training providers, states, or local workforce areas would obtain the needed performance information on training providers and programs. USDOL regulations governing WIA merely said that performance data must be verifiable and reliable. However, the regulations noted that that states could either require providers to calculate outcomes themselves (through surveys and follow-up telephone calls to past students) or utilize administrative data, such as Unemployment Insurance (UI) wage records.

Self-reported data from providers. One option for collecting information was to require training providers to assemble it. Some information, such as completion rates, may be available to providers. Often education and training institutions help place students into jobs and gather information on entering wages or salaries. However, most trainers have little or no contact with students after they are placed in their first jobs. As a result, providers would have to contact students by telephone, e-mail, or mail to inquire about postprogram employment and wages.

Use of administrative data. States could also use administrative data to calculate outcomes for providers and programs. States routinely collect quarterly earnings information for employed individuals when their employers pay their UI payroll taxes. Data collected by a state's UI Wage Record Interchange System (WRIS) provide employment and earnings data of all individuals employed in the 90 percent of jobs covered by UI. By matching the Social Security numbers in the WRIS with the Social Security numbers of program participants, this method can be used to calculate performance outcomes for government-funded workforce services. States and local WIBs are also required by WIA to use UI wage records in the calculation of employment outcomes for performance measures for overall WIA services delivered within a state or workforce development jurisdiction such as a large city or county.

UI wage records, however, were not required for use in the ETPLs because they cannot be used unless individual student or participant records with Social Security numbers are available. Participant records and corresponding Social Security numbers are collected for individuals receiving WIA services. However, individual student records are not readily available for all training providers. For example, as detailed below, some schools either do not collect Social Security numbers from program enrollees or are prohibited from sharing them outside their agencies.

IMPLEMENTATION CHALLENGES

State and local WIBs struggled to implement ETPL and consumer report provisions of WIA. In fact, more than 35 states requested and received waivers from the Employment and Training Administration. These waivers either permitted them to implement only a portion of the ETPL requirements or allotted additional time to implement the provisions. In the early years of WIA, the USDOL offered technical assistance to states to encourage the deployment of effective ETPL systems, but support from Washington, DC, evaporated during the Bush administration.

The challenges encountered by state agencies responsible for WIA fell into six broad categories.

1) Lack of cooperation of training providers. Training providers complained about what they regarded as the onerous and expensive costs associated with collecting program outcome data. Schools claimed that the benefits of being on the ETPL (in potentially increased students and revenue) might not outweigh the costs of providing the necessary information to states and local WIBs. It is impossible to know if these fears were justified or if they were just arguments used to stall and frustrate implementation. However, some policymakers were persuaded that the ETPL provisions would limit choice by restricting the number of training options available to individuals.

2) Problems of using self-reported data. Several states required training providers to collect performance information on employment outcomes through follow-up surveys. This method placed heavy financial and administrative burdens on providers, particularly for those measures that applied to all students, regardless of funding source. State and local workforce program managers also found it difficult to verify the accuracy of reported outcomes from training providers and to ensure that every provider collected reliable information from their graduates.

3) Challenges in using administrative data. Other states, including those profiled in this chapter, opted to match program participant data with UI wage records to calculate outcomes. States already collect data on students who attend and graduate from public colleges and universities and from public vocational programs. States also obtain data on individuals funded by WIA. Because these datasets usually contain Social Security numbers, they can be matched with UI wage records to obtain employment outcomes. However, states do not routinely collect student records from for-profit proprietary schools, nonprofit organizations, and for noncredit programs at public colleges. As a result, states that use administrative data to calculate outcomes must require training providers to submit student records, including Social Security numbers, to the state, so that a match with the UI wage records can be performed. Some providers, however, are reluctant to report student re-

cords due to concerns about collecting Social Security numbers from students who are worried about data security and privacy. In several states, trainers mobilized political supporters to help them block the reporting requirements.

4) Barriers to cooperation of multiple state agencies. Using administrative data to calculate outcomes involves sharing administrative data across state departments of labor and workforce development, state departments of education, and state departments or agencies that oversee higher education. Such data sharing can be difficult to accomplish given the differing policies and priorities of these agencies. In addition, the Federal Education Rights and Privacy Act (FERPA) limits sharing student data from educational institutions by state education departments. FERPA has also been interpreted in some states as prohibiting educational institutions from collecting Social Security numbers from students. A number of states have overcome these FERPA restrictions.

5) Barriers to cooperation between local WIBs and states. The WIA legislation and regulations issued by the USDOL identify conflicting roles for states and for local boards. For example, providers must apply to a local WIB that decides if the program meets its minimum standards. If the provider meets these standards, it is placed on the statewide ETPL. Training providers could apply to multiple local boards in the state to be on a statewide list that applies to all local boards, thus negating any substantive role played by the local WIB.

6) Comparing programs and providers that serve different labor markets and different students. A chief complaint from training providers is that programs throughout a state often serve very different students and labor markets. They argue that these differences may profoundly affect employment outcomes. Programs serving a local area with high unemployment rates may have lower employment outcomes than programs serving areas with low unemployment. In addition, programs serving students with low levels of formal education and limited work histories may be less successful than those enrolling people with higher levels of formal education and significant work histories. WIA

required that local WIBs take such factors into account when creating the ETPL. However, WIA did not specify the methodologies to be used and the USDOL did not provide further guidance or technical assistance to states and local WIBs.

PROMISING STATE STRATEGIES FOR IMPLEMENTING ETPLS AND CRCS

Despite these challenges, several states, including New Jersey, Texas, Washington, and Florida, successfully implemented effective ETPL and CRC systems. There is considerable evidence that these states and in some cases their local WIBs are using the information to guide individuals seeking training as well as state and local officials making resource allocation decisions. None of these states have fully implemented all of the ETPL provisions of WIA. In fact, Texas has received a waiver from the ETA, and New Jersey has recently applied for such a waiver to give the state more time to fully implement the ETPL provisions.

Nevertheless, states that successfully applied performance reporting principles, coupled with the evidence from states that either did not try or were less successful, provide valuable lessons for revisions of WIA. (See Table 6.2 for an overview of ETPL procedures in the four profiled states.)

Profile of Four State Strategies

Washington

The state of Washington has had a commitment to setting performance standards for workforce development and training programs since 1991, when the state's Workforce Training and Education Coordinating Board launched a comprehensive planning process that included state and local policymakers, education and training providers, and other stakeholders. In 1996, the state reached agreement with all stakeholders that training providers would be held accountable for key performance measures, including student completion and employment outcomes, before the passage of WIA in 1998.

As of 2010, Washington State has a fully developed ETPL system and set performance standards (see Washington State Workforce Training and Education Coordinating Board 2007, 2010). More than 400 training providers and more than 5,000 training programs were on the state's list.

Washington has made a strong commitment to assisting training providers with the ETPL process. The state has created an online system that allows training providers to apply to be on the ETPL electronically. The state has a designated staff member who assists training providers with the Web site and approval process.

Washington State has also created the Career Bridge Web site (www.careerbridge.wa.gov) as the primary online career guidance resource in the state. The site, which is heavily marketed by state staff, also functions as the state's CRC system, allowing job training consumers to search for training providers that meet their needs. The Web site attracts nearly 9,000 users each month. State officials report that training providers value the ability to reach potential students through Career Bridge.

As with New Jersey, Washington State relies exclusively on UI wage records for the calculation of outcomes. Community and technical colleges submit student records to the State Board for Community and Technical Colleges. All other providers, regardless of funding source, must submit student records to the state WIB. The state WIB then combines these student record data sets and calculates employment and earnings outcomes for providers.

The state calculates performance outcomes for providers once per year. The state has set minimum performance levels for completion rate, employment rate, and earnings and uses these levels to determine subsequent eligibility. These standards include

- Completion rate: 20 percent
- Employment rate: 50 percent
- Earnings: $3,643 in a quarter, or $9.67 per hour.

To avoid the administration of an additional complex system, local WIBs have agreed to allow the state to manage the implementation of the ETPL in Washington. Training providers apply to the state WIB for inclusion on the ETPL, bypassing the local WIBs. The state sets the minimum standards for providers and is responsible for the calculation

Table 6.2 ETPL Procedures in the Four Profiled States

	Source of data for performance measures	Source of student records	Application process	Setting of performance standards
Florida	UI wage records	Student records reported by providers for use in the ETPL.	Local WIBs accept and review all applications from training providers.	State delegates responsibility for setting minimum standards to local WIBs.
New Jersey	UI wage records	Existing student record systems for public colleges and universities and adult vocational schools and Student records reported by other providers for sole use in the ETPL.	State accepts and reviews all applications from training providers. (Local WIBs' role is limited to providing input on state ETPL procedures.)	State has not set standards.
Texas	Self-reported data from training providers or UI wage records	Student records voluntarily reported by providers that choose to use the UI wage record match.	Local WIBs accept and review all applications from training providers.	State has set minimum standards. Local WIBs can establish higher standards.
Washington	UI wage records	Existing student record systems for community and technical colleges and Student records reported by other providers for sole use in the ETPL.	State WIB accepts and reviews all applications from training providers.	State has set minimum standards. Local WIBs can establish higher standards.

of all outcome measures. Local WIBs can set higher standards for providers but have chosen not to do so.

New Jersey

Since 1998, New Jersey has implemented a robust ETPL and CRC system that includes more than 600 education and training providers who offer more than 3,000 training programs (see New Jersey Department of Labor and Workforce Development n.d.; New Jersey State Employment and Training Commission 2009). New Jersey utilizes an online application system that enables providers to submit required data to the state and facilitates state-level reviews. If approved, the submitted information is immediately uploaded to the state's CRC system (www.njtrainingsystems.org).

Approved providers are required to cooperate in the calculation of employment outcomes for their approved programs. The state uses UI wage records as the only means for calculating performance outcomes. The John J. Heldrich Center for Workforce Development at Rutgers University calculates measures on a quarterly basis. UI wage records from New Jersey are supplemented with UI wage records from other states using the WRIS maintained by the USDOL. Only those individuals who are self-employed or work for religious organizations are excluded from these data sets. The Heldrich Center estimates that well over 95 percent of training participants are captured using this method.

New Jersey relies on administrative data from the state's Commission on Higher Education and Department of Education to gather student records from public colleges and universities and from adult vocational schools. The state also uses WIA administrative data to supplement these two data sources. Providers that do not already submit student records to the state are required to do so through a secure, online reporting system established for the purpose of the ETPL. These providers include private, proprietary schools, noncredit programs at public colleges, and nonprofit organizations.

The use of Rutgers University for the matching of student records enabled the state to comply with FERPA. Rutgers functions as an agent of the state Department of Education and student record data are not shared with the Department of Labor and Workforce Development, or with any other entity.

In 2005, New Jersey enacted a law that strengthens the ETPL system in the state and expressly requires that all training providers that receive state or federal workforce funds must participate in the list process and submit required student records to the state. The state Department of Labor and Workforce Development will issue regulations in the next few months and plans to fully enforce the provisions of the law in the coming year.

Currently, the state disseminates performance information on approximately one-third of all training programs on the ETPL, primarily due to the lack of the reporting of student records by some providers and by the inclusion on the list of some relatively new programs. The state plans to aggressively enforce the list regulations in the coming year and plans to remove those providers from the list that do not report their student records. The state also plans to set performance standards for providers and programs.

In New Jersey, the ETPL process is managed centrally by the State Employment and Training Commission (the state WIB) and by the Department of Labor and Workforce Development. Local WIBs provide input into the development and implementation of the ETPL but have no formal role in its implementation.

New Jersey has made a significant investment in the creation of the ETPL and CRC systems, spending more than $1.5 million over an 11-year period on the design, implementation, and hosting of the CRC and on the calculation of performance measures. The CRC Web site (www .njtrainingsystems.org) is a prominent part of the online career guidance and workforce services made available by the state Department of Labor and Workforce Development. Current accurate counts and analysis of usage are not available. However, the Web site is widely used in the state's One-Stop Career Centers by individuals who receive an ITA and by their career counselors.

Texas

Texas has also implemented an ETPL system, but unlike New Jersey and Washington, local WIBs play a greater role in the process (Texas Workforce Commission n.d., 2009). Trainers apply to local WIBs for inclusion on the statewide ETPL using an online application system that enables providers to submit required information and facilitates local and state level reviews.

Local WIBs are allowed to set their own performance standards for training providers, as long as they exceed the minimum standards set by the state. The state set minimum performance standards for all the measures required by WIA. These standards include

- Completion rate: 60 percent

- Entered employment rate: 60 percent

- Average hourly wage at placement: Average entry level wage for occupation(s) for which training is provided

- Average quarterly wage for WIA participants: Average entry level wage for occupation(s) for which training is provided.

Unlike New Jersey and Washington, Texas requires that performance data be used to determine if a provider should be included initially on the ETPL. As specified by WIA, all higher education institutions are exempt from the performance requirements during this determination of initial eligibility. In Texas, performance measures are not used to determine if a provider should remain on the list and the state received a waiver from the USDOL to permit this approach. Once a provider has been placed on the ETPL, it is not required to submit performance information.

Texas's trainers may follow two routes for inclusion in the performance requirements of the ETPL. Providers can submit their own performance statistics and a description of the methodology used to collect the data on the employment and wage information of graduates. School records, attendance sheets, exit interviews, and follow-up letters/calls to graduates and/or employers may be used. Providers that are not interested or unable to collect such data can send their student records to the state and the state will perform a match with UI wage records for a modest fee. The fee structure uses a sliding scale based on the quantity of students. This scale begins at a cost of $100 for 150–300 student records. Local WIBs are responsible to ensure that applications submitted are complete and accurate and this includes reported performance data.

When setting performance standards, local WIBs are required to take into account local labor market conditions and the characteristics of the students served by the program when making final eligibility decisions. Workforce boards are expected to ensure center staff provide

information to WIA customers on local labor market conditions and occupations in demand, along with the statewide ETPL, which contains
relevant information they should use in making their choice of a training provider.

Florida

Florida's ETPL procedures are built on the infrastructure of the
Florida Education and Training Placement Information Program
(FETPIP) system (see Agency for Workforce Innovation n.d., 2009).
The state established the FETPIP system in the early 1990s to produce
employment outcome information for a wide variety of secondary and
postsecondary educational institutions in the state. When WIA was
passed in 1998, the state already had significant experience in using UI
wage records and student-record data.

Regional Workforce Boards (Florida's name for local WIBs) set the
procedures for initial and subsequent eligibility. However, all Regional
Workforce Boards must require that training providers participate in
the FETPIP system. Public education institutions submit their student
records to the State Department of Education. Private training providers
must submit their student records to the Commission for Independent
Education, which regulates these education and training providers. The
state does not set performance standards and delegates to the Regional
Workforce Boards the responsibility for setting such standards and for
removing poor performing providers from the ETPL.

Factors That Contributed to Implementation of the ETPL

Washington, New Jersey, Texas, and Florida share several common
features and provide important lessons for other states, for potential
revisions to WIA and its regulations.

1) Administrative data should be used to improve the quality
   and lower the cost of reporting. These four states have a long-
   standing commitment to measuring employment outcomes using UI wage records. Washington and Florida also received
   funding from the USDOL in the late 1990s that assisted them to
   build longitudinal data systems. New Jersey, prior to the passage
   of WIA, had begun the initial steps to create information on the

employment outcomes of individuals in training programs. The application of UI wage records is an efficient strategy for calculating employment outcomes. Such a strategy minimizes the burden on providers, helps ensure that employment outcomes are collected and calculated in a standard manner, and limits the ability of training providers to manipulate outcomes.

2) Cooperation/involvement of multiple state agencies with strong state leadership. The four profiled states also involved multiple agencies in building their ETPL systems. New Jersey, for example, uses data from the Department of Education and the Commission on Higher Education to calculate employment outcomes. In Washington, the State Board for Community and Technical Colleges provides student record data to the Department of Labor for use in performance outcome calculation. In each of these states, a state department or agency plays a central role in implementing the ETPL system. Local WIBs are given a clearly defined role but the systems are state run and largely implemented by the state.

3) Serving public needs. All four states created user-friendly CRC Web sites that enable individuals to explore training options and easily identify training programs that meet their needs. Washington's state ETPL is a prominent part of the Career Bridge Web site (www.careerbridge.wa.gov), which is the state's primary portal for assisting unemployed individuals and state residents to make education and training decisions. The New Jersey CRC (www.njtrainingsystems.org) is a prominent part of the state's Department of Labor and Workforce Development's suite of online tools for state residents.

New Jersey state law also requires that all training providers receiving state or federal workforce funds be included on the ETPL. By expanding the system beyond WIA, the state increased the incentive for training providers to participate.

IMPLICATIONS AND FUTURE DIRECTIONS

The experiences of the four profiled states (Washington, New Jersey, Texas, and Florida) demonstrate that the ETPL and CRC provisions of WIA can be implemented in a cost-effective manner and yield benefits to various audiences, including regulators, resource allocators, students, and employers. As federal officials consider amendments to WIA and other programs funding education and training programs, several recommendations should be carefully considered.

1) Broaden ETPL and CRC requirements beyond WIA and apply them to One-Stop partner programs, or at least to other programs administered by the ETA. WIA represents a significant investment in training resources, but other One-Stop partner programs, such as Trade Adjustment Assistance, also spend significant funds to support training. To broaden the incentive to providers to participate in the ETPL process, the ETPL system should at least apply to all training funding overseen by the ETA.

2) Assign a stronger role to states in developing the ETPLs and CRCs. Given the complexity in implementing such systems, states must play a central coordinating role in developing and implementing performance reporting. In addition, training providers rarely serve only one local workforce area. Multiple processes for each local area only increase the burden on training providers.

3) Connect ETPLs to state efforts to build longitudinal data systems for education. The U.S. Department of Education is providing significant funding to states through the American Reinvestment and Recovery Act to expand longitudinal data systems for education. A competitive solicitation, with applications due in November 2009, placed a new emphasis on connecting secondary education data with postsecondary education data and employment outcomes. The Department of Labor should work with the Department of Education to assist states that secure funding to connect these efforts to ETPL systems.

4) Provide clear federal guidance to states on the application of FERPA through a collaboration of the Departments of Labor and Education. FERPA has hindered the ability of several states to implement ETPL systems. In some cases, it has been interpreted as prohibiting state education departments and individual providers from sharing student record data for the calculations of outcomes for the ETPL. Some states have developed procedures to share data that they believe meet their interpretation of the requirements of FERPA.

5) Offer competitive funding for states to develop the infrastructure to build robust ETPL systems and CRC systems. The USDOL should consider providing funding to states on a competitive basis to assist them to develop ETPL systems. In the early years of WIA implementation, the Labor Department funded the ITA/ETPL demonstration, which provided funds of up to $500,000 on a competitive basis to six local WIBs and to seven states to assist in the development of these systems. These grants were the subject of an evaluation report completed in 2004 (Social Policy Research Associates 2004).

6) Provide technical assistance to states. The USDOL provided technical assistance to states on ETPL issues in the first few years following the enactment of WIA. Technical assistance is needed to fully develop ETPL systems.

7) Governance issues in structure of accountability. As currently structured, state and local WIBs include significant representation from training agencies that may thwart the collection and dissemination of performance outcome data. In the revisions to WIA, Congress should consider eliminating them from membership on boards that influence resource allocation and ETPL and CRC policies. Alternatively, Congress might require that the ETPLs and CRCs be developed and implemented by independent agencies, in the same manner that many state and federal programs require independent financial audits.

References

Agency for Workforce Innovation. n.d. "Florida's Eligible Training Providers." Tallahassee, FL: Agency for Workforce Innovation. http://www.floridajobs .org/etpl/TrainingProvider.asp (accessed April 22, 2010).

———. 2009. "Florida's One-Year Strategic State Plan Modification for 2009–2010." Tallahassee, FL: Agency for Workforce Innovation. http:// www.workforceflorida.com/news/reports/WIA2009/WIAPlan2009_Final .pdf (accessed April 22, 2010).

National Center for Education Statistics. n.d. "Number of Undergraduate Career Education Credentials Awarded by Title IV Postsecondary Institutions, by Control and Level of Institution and Credential Level: United States, 1997 to 2006. Table P74." Washington, DC: National Center for Education Statistics. http://nces.ed.gov/surveys/ctes/tables/P74.asp (accessed April 22, 2010).

New Jersey Department of Labor and Workforce Development. n.d. "NJ Training Opportunities: New Jersey's Guide to Education and Training Opportunities." Trenton, NJ: New Jersey Department of Labor and Workforce Development. http://www.njtrainingsystems.org (accessed April 22, 2010).

New Jersey State Employment and Training Commission. 2009. *New Jersey Workforce Investment System Unified State Plan Modification PY 2009 July 1, 2009, to June 30, 2010.* Trenton, NJ: New Jersey State Employment and Training Commission. http://www.njsetc.net/publications/NJStatePlanPY2009.pdf (accessed August 17, 2010).

Social Policy Research Associates. 2004. *An Evaluation of the Individual Training Account/Eligible Training Provider Demonstration Final Report.* Oakland, CA: Social Policy Research Associates.

Texas Workforce Commission. n.d. "Eligible Training Provider Certification, Rules and Programs." Houston, TX: Texas Workforce Commission. http:// www.twc.state.tx.us/customers/serpro/serprosub3.html (accessed August 17, 2010).

———. 2009. "Strategic State Workforce Investment Plan (modification submitted June 30, 2009) for Title I of the Workforce Investment Act of 1998 and the Wagner-Peyser Act." Houston, TX: Texas Workforce Commission. http://www.twc.state.tx.us/boards/wia/state_plan/state_plan.html (accessed April 22, 2010).

Washington State Workforce Training and Education Coordinating Board. 2007. *State Plan Modification for Title I-B of the Workforce Investment Act and the Wagner-Peyser Act, July 1, 2007 to June 30, 2010.* Olympia, WA:

WSWTECB. http://www.wtb.wa.gov/Documents/StatePlan2009-2010.pdf
(accessed April 22, 2010).
————. 2010. "Governor's Procedure for Determining Training Program Eligibility." Olympia, WA: WSWTECB. http://www.wtb.wa.gov/etp.pdf (accessed April 22, 2010).

Part 3

Performance Management

7
The Challenges of Measuring Performance

William S. Borden
Mathematica Policy Research

Both the WIA reauthorization process and the planning efforts of the European Social Fund (ESF) would benefit from a review of the recent experiences of performance management of employment training programs in the United States. This chapter presents an operational perspective on how performance systems are designed and implemented. It also discusses the challenges to effective performance management—challenges that are little known except to the state and federal staff managing the performance systems, and that are often not clearly understood. There is very little that is easy and straightforward about measuring program performance. Seemingly simple concepts such as enrollment, exit, employment, earnings, and whom and when to count must be defined very precisely for performance results to have meaning. This chapter assumes that the reader is familiar with WIA and its performance measures.

The design and implementation of effective performance management involve many conceptual and operational issues. This analysis briefly touches on many of them to illustrate how involved the process is and to alert program managers to the areas that they need to address. Each of these issues requires more extensive discussion than the scope of this chapter allows. Performance management raises interesting and significant questions about organizational and human motivation, the dynamics of state-federal political power sharing, and the management of government programs. Policymakers tend to underestimate the challenges they face and sometimes lack the commitment necessary to make performance management processes as effective as they should be. The Employment and Training Administration (ETA) has corrected some of the problems that occurred early on, but there are still some operational aspects that need improvement. The pursuit of effective and fair performance management inevitably encounters challenges for which there are no easy solutions.

Research on employment and training programs focuses primarily on evaluations of the impact of public investment in job training services, but there are other factors to consider when analyzing the WIA performance management system; there is a clear dichotomy between its program management objectives and its evaluative objectives. This analysis argues that some form of performance tracking and data validation is necessary for managing a complex national system of job training programs, even if the outcome data were not used to determine funding. Despite the great value of effective performance management, there are limits to using performance management data to drive funding decisions.

It is also important to look beyond WIA and take a comprehensive approach to assessing performance management of job training services by examining the programs that serve special populations. Policymakers need to consider how to provide efficient and effective service to everyone, but especially people with disabilities, veterans, youth, and older workers, since the costs to serve them greatly exceed those of serving job seekers in general. This broader perspective also helps inform the debate about consolidating services under a universal program like WIA and provides the most useful information for the European Commission as it looks at performance management and service delivery alternatives. Choices must be made about whether to manage services under a more unified governance structure or as independent governance structures. In the United States, there is a somewhat confusing mix of approaches, with WIA and the Employment Service (ES) at the core and considerable fragmentation and overlap beyond that.

This analysis will draw broadly on lessons learned from implementing performance measurement systems for WIA, the ES, the Senior Community Service Employment Program (SCSEP), and the Vocational Rehabilitation (VR) program at the Department of Education, among others.[1]

We begin the chapter with a conceptual framework for analyzing performance management issues. This includes discussion of the goals of performance systems, the limitations on measuring government program performance, and how measures are designed and defined. These concepts form the building blocks for designing a performance system. The next section of the chapter then discusses the distinction between using informal processes to manage performance and effective performance management. It covers the importance of implementing rigorous standardization, validation, and monitoring processes for effective performance management, and looks at the ETA's great progress in this area despite continuing problems.

The following section examines the challenges and benefits of involving stakeholders in the design and implementation of the performance measures. It analyzes the problems that occur when stakeholders are more concerned about meeting their goals than improving their results, as well as their somewhat exaggerated reaction to the burdens imposed by performance systems.

The final section discusses key aspects of the WIA performance management experience to date, including how the measures have evolved and the use of wage records to measure outcomes.

A CONCEPTUAL FRAMEWORK FOR ANALYZING PERFORMANCE MANAGEMENT ISSUES

Performance Management versus Program Evaluation

As Barnow and Smith (2004) point out, program evaluation and performance management derive from different sources and motives and have deeply committed adherents. This analysis takes the position that managing very large-scale and far-flung programs involving thousands of staff, millions of customers, and billions of dollars requires comprehensive management information systems. In other words, tracking and measuring customer flow, services, and outcomes is inherently desirable and even necessary to managing any modern organization. Therefore, the question is not whether we should track customer flow and services and measure performance, but whether and how we should use the data to determine funding, incentives, and sanctions.

Some in the evaluation community argue that there are risks in drawing conclusions from administrative performance data; this concern is supported by a detailed understanding of data quality and measurement validity issues (Barnow and Smith 2004). The ETA's experience in implementing performance management systems over the 10 years since the passage of WIA has shown that it is difficult to measure performance well, and that using inaccurate performance data to drive policy and incentives leads to misallocated resources. Putting more emphasis on using results to reward and sanction states than on ensuring that the results are valid and meaningful also leads to understandable yet often undesirable behavior by program operators.

Performance management systems and research evaluation methods both have their strengths and weaknesses. Performance data are much more efficient, systematic, comprehensive (they are produced for all customers), and timely, but they are somewhat crude and imprecise tools for measuring program impacts. Effective performance management systems, however, are essential to good evaluation, particularly since performance management is the main reason that reliable data are available on programs. Some research efforts are abandoned because of incomplete and flawed data sets, while other research projects draw erroneous conclusions because of bad administrative data. There is an increasing tendency to leverage the efficiency of analyzing administrative data versus more expensive experimental designs. In fact, both are needed. Even selecting stratified samples of participants for randomization requires clean and complete participant data sets with accurate enrollment and exit dates and customer characteristics.

Underlying Premises of Performance Management

First, we need to define precisely what the goals of a government program performance management system are and what constitutes a performance measure. We must also examine the motives and roles of the various actors in such politically and technically complex systems.

Two premises underlie the increasing emphasis on accountability in government performance. The first is that public funds must be spent wisely and produce a return on taxpayer investment. The second is that measuring the effectiveness of a business process is critical to managing a modern organization.

Behind the first premise is the implicit assumption that government agencies must be under pressure to perform just as in private enterprise—where profit and loss determine success, rewards, and even survival. This underlying "Darwinian" notion that competition is good and that programs should demonstrate results to justify their existence is accepted by both major political parties. The Bush administration greatly advanced this approach to federal management and reflected the program management approaches used in Texas and Florida, the most advanced states in using performance outcomes to drive funding decisions.

But the notion that measuring the performance of a government program can substitute for the competitive pressures of the marketplace has many limitations. In the extreme, this idea takes the form of performance-based budgeting, where funding is directly correlated to performance, and programs can be totally defunded based on measured outcomes. In theory this makes sense, if there are valid measures and accurate performance data. The reality, however, is that measures frequently do not accurately reflect underlying program performance, and even more often the data are inaccurate and inconsistent across operational entities. Accounting for all the factors affecting WIA performance is impossible to do with great precision. We must control for variations both in the type of barriers to employment in the population served and in the employment opportunities available in an area, and then we must implement rigorous data validation methods. Without such steps, cutting budgets or defunding programs or operational entities based on program performance would be irrational and unfair. Such extreme approaches to using performance outcomes would also encourage program operators to engage in creaming: developing too-easily-reached goals and underserving the target population by focusing on those most likely to be deemed a success, instead of serving those most in need of services yet less likely to succeed.

Monopolies, Competition, and Privatization

There is another flaw in the application of the competitive approach: some programs enjoy natural monopolies. For example, one might conclude that if Ohio's program was ineffective and Michigan's was effective, people in Ohio should seek services from Michigan or Michigan staff should replace Ohio staff. Obviously, the Darwinian "perform or die" theory breaks down in this application. So, if we cannot put the Ohio program out of business, how do we act on our performance data? Do we provide increased funding to Michigan as a reward (presumably not needed), or do we cut Ohio's funding as a penalty (and probably damage their performance further)? We are left with the industrial quality control concept that we have used performance management to identify superior and unacceptable performance. Using the performance information, we can now intervene to provide technical assistance to Ohio and transplant best practices and methods from Michigan to Ohio. Finally, we must continue to track Ohio's improvement until its performance becomes acceptable. This is an appropriate application of performance management in a government setting.

There are two situations in which the monopoly problem does not interfere with applying market forces to government performance management. First, programs that provide similar services to the same population can compete against each other. Since there are many overlapping job training programs, this is possible and indeed has been discussed by the Office of Management and Budget (OMB), as we shall soon see. Every Bush administration budget since 2000 contained no funding for the National Farmworker Jobs Program (NFJP) and maintained that WIA should be the vehicle to provide these services.[2] All the programs for special populations are mandatory One-Stop partners, but there is a wide diversity in the integration of these programs into the one-stop setting. Most operators of programs for hard-to-serve populations believe that their clients would not be well served by WIA. This sentiment derives partly from the instinct for self-preservation and partly from the common belief among social workers that the population they serve is unique and cannot be well served by a more general program. It is true that a One-Stop operator might choose to prioritize services to customers that are more likely to gain employment unless counterbalancing incentives are built into the system. The VR program, managed by the Department of Education, operates very differently from the labor programs and has not adopted common employment measures or data validation activities.

Second, services can be privatized and the public entity defunded. Some states have done this with large programs, and it is a common feature at the local level.[3] So the ultimate application of market principles is to privatize services and make all provider payments contingent on performance. This was used to some degree with performance-based contracting of training providers and is a feature of the Pathways to Work program in the United Kingdom. However, this approach puts tremendous pressure on the providers to manipulate their performance rates and puts unrealistic expectations on the ability of the oversight agency to act on high-quality data that fairly measure performance. If effective performance management methods are used, performance-based budgeting would be an effective incentive in some settings.

The second premise underlying performance management systems is that measuring the effectiveness of a business process (job training and placement services) is critical to managing a modern organization. Performance management techniques derive from industrial quality control techniques that measure the rate of defects in an industrial process (as popularized by W.E. Deming). The quality movement is based on the notion that processes that are measured work better than processes that are not measured (Blalock and Barnow 2001). Performance data are a vital tool for program managers at all levels to identify successful processes and methods, determine what works, share best practices, identify areas in need of improvement through technical assistance, and forecast future customer flows and costs. It is common sense that program managers at all levels should have data on customer flow, services, and outcomes. The complexity and cost associated with collecting and analyzing high-quality program data, however, leads too many state and federal officials to avoid these challenges and instead put minimal effort into performance data.

Both objectives of prudent public investment and improved service provisions have implications for understanding the potential limitations of measuring the performance of government programs. We can place performance management objectives on a continuum ranging from tracking and performance data solely for better management to the other extreme of basing all funding decisions solely on performance outcomes. Finding the middle ground is appropriate. Although there are limits to how much a performance management system can tell decision makers about program costs and benefits, there are compelling reasons to track enrollments, services, and outcomes carefully. Doing so provides valuable information to managers at all levels of the system, from Congress and the OMB through the federal agency, and to the state and the local area or grantee. In large, diverse systems like WIA and the other programs under discussion, the forces of fragmentation and inconsistent data are so great that only a very strong and standardized performance management system can overcome or at least neutralize them. We can thus see that it is more useful to think of performance data primarily as a management tool and secondarily as an evaluation tool.

Defining a Performance Measure

To serve the second premise—identifying relatively good or bad performance and measuring improved or decreased performance—a measure must produce a rate of success and not simply a count of activities. Thus, a measure can be used to distinguish better and worse performance in meeting program objectives of a single operating entity (One-Stop, Workforce Investment Board [WIB], state, program) over time, and also compare performance between operating entities at all levels. Standards that identify minimally acceptable performance must be associated with measures. Failure to meet these standards would trigger remedial steps, such as technical assistance, and even punitive actions, such as sanctions. Standards for superior performance could trigger rewards such as incentives and documentation of best practices. A performance measure that does not produce a rate of success cannot accomplish these essential functions.[4]

Programs should set standards for minimum acceptable performance by analyzing the range of outcomes across reporting entities (states, in the case of WIA). One simple axiom is that the minimum acceptable level is what 85 percent of states achieve; the theory being that if the bulk of states can achieve this performance, then it is a practical goal, and the trailing 15 percent should strive to improve. For example, the UI program sets performance goals based on the actual distribution of state performance rates. Another approach is to set different goals for different sets of customers based on their barriers to employment. Separate performance calculations should be produced anyway for significant customer groups such as low literacy, people with disabilities, and those with poor work histories. As we will discuss later, however, absolute performance outcomes should be adjusted to account for differences in customers and labor markets. This approach makes data validation even more essential as program operators have incentives to exaggerate their customers' barriers. The ETA has adopted a negotiation approach to setting standards and has moved away from using national performance means and standardized adjustment mechanisms.

Measuring Processes, Outputs, and Outcomes

Another aspect of performance management is whether to measure processes or outcomes. Process measures are very indirect and are therefore usually unreliable for assessing actual performance. Process measurement operates on the assumption that adhering to good processes will produce a better result, but execution of the process can be highly variable. Many of the process measurement approaches popular two decades ago have resulted in a checklist approach: items are checked off when manuals are written or staff are given various responsibilities. These continuous-improvement approaches are good means to an end, but they cannot substitute for measuring actual program results.

Measuring intermediate outcomes, sometimes referred to as program outputs, can be useful and can resemble process measures. For example, measuring program attendance, grade advancement, test scores, customer satisfaction, and the timeliness and quality of customer services provides prompt feedback to program managers and helps predict actual outcomes. These intermediate outcomes or program outputs should be secondary to actual program outcomes (such as long-term employment and earnings).

Another school of thought focuses on societal rather than individual outcomes. This approach would use poverty levels and measures of community well-being to evaluate program effectiveness. This is a laudable objective and should be a component of an overall evaluation strategy, but it does not fit well within the performance management paradigm. Performance management relies on reasonably direct feedback to program operators at all levels about the effectiveness of service delivery strategies on customer outcomes in order to improve management decisions. Societal outcomes result in too broad a range of sources to provide direct feedback to management, but they should be taken into account when determining long-term policy direction.

The Impact of Performance Management on Customer Selection

The general intent of the programs is to channel scarce funds to those who need services most because they have the most or the highest barriers to employment. Performance outcomes, however, are based on success, which is least likely for those with the highest barriers. How does the program operator respond to this dilemma? Clearly it would be rational to choose to serve the people most likely to succeed. This could be considered a socially useful impact of performance management on program behavior if the operator is selecting between two people to serve: one with barriers but whose success is feasible and one with more barriers whose success is unlikely. Society may benefit more if the operator chooses to serve the person with the highest chance of success. In VR, for example, states are instructed not to serve people considered "too significantly disabled" to become employed. If the choice is between someone with barriers where success is feasible and someone with relatively few barriers where the service would not be a significant factor in employment, then society would not benefit from the incentive to serve the least-needy customers.

The correct means to rectify this potentially bad incentive is to adjust performance outcomes to provide more credit for achieving success with a customer with higher barriers. This leads us back to the conundrum that measuring barriers can be subjective and unreliable. It also raises the question of how we perform the adjustment. Computing performance separately for different classes of customers based on barriers provides the clearest information to program operators. Or we can adjust performance after the fact, based on regression models. Either approach, if done well, would produce the same results, though there are other adjustment factors to consider.

Adjusting Performance Outcomes

An effective performance management system must produce objective and systematic results. The system must account for the high degree of variability in both customers served and in labor markets. So the system must adjust performance results to provide credit for serving those with the most barriers and for variations in labor market conditions across geographic areas. Here some type of objective regression model is necessary. In 1998, the ETA decided to abandon the JTPA regression model, whose complexity had made it unpopular at both the state and the federal levels, in favor of a negotiation process. Negotiation provides flexibility, but it does not allow for systematic and consistent performance goals across states. Instead, the outcome of the process is a function more of the toughness of the negotiator than of a method for developing consistent, reasonable performance goals. In addition, states could also try to manipulate the negotiation process by using various approaches to developing JTPA baseline data that would produce the lowest performance, thus ensuring that they could easily meet WIA improvement targets. The weakness of the negotiation approach was illustrated when the ETA chose to train regional staff on negotiation skills rather than on how to interpret state baseline performance estimates so that initial WIA goals were set more accurately.

EFFECTIVE PERFORMANCE MANAGEMENT AND ITS COSTS

Effective Performance Management Methods

There is a significant difference between collecting and calculating performance data using informal methods and using formal performance management methods to ensure that performance results are meaningful and usable. Federal performance management processes should emulate management information systems approaches used to manage large business enterprises. The software development industry has developed formal methods to ensure that systems function properly from the original source of the data to the distribution of results to end users. Rarely are federal performance systems designed with understanding of the risks to data quality and the methods needed to overcome them. Each time a system is set up, the same long process of finding out what does not work takes place over several years before usable performance data are obtained. Sixteen years after the passage of the Government Performance Results Act (GPRA), the technical state of federal performance management is still dismal.

The contrast between ineffective and effective performance management can best be illustrated by SCSEP. Attempts to draw samples for customer satisfaction surveys for SCSEP failed because there were few usable case management data on who the customers were. This and other deficiencies in the performance reporting system led the SCSEP program to develop a sophisticated national case management system. The SCSEP system contains real-time data on all customers, services, and outcomes, and has robust analytical and reporting functions. The availability of these detailed, individual-level performance management data enabled the SCSEP program to smoothly transfer 12,000 participants (as a result of the national grantee competition of 2006), to develop timely and comprehensive management reports for all levels of the system, and to report on participants funded by the American Recovery and Reinvestment Act in real time with virtually no additional effort. Prior to this investment, most SCSEP performance data reports were aggregated essentially by hand at local offices and then reaggregated at the state level before being submitted to the ETA. There was no audit trail and thus no way to determine or support the reliability of the data. Through the use of thorough and effective performance management methods, SCSEP has gone from having few reliable performance data at all to having among the best data of all federal programs.

However, this drastic progress in SCSEP (and to a lesser extent in other ETA programs using less extensive methods) has come with significant expense at the federal level. Federal managers at all levels find it difficult to justify the costs of high-quality data systems for several reasons. First, they view performance management narrowly as a reporting function and not a performance enhancement process. Second, they tend to focus only on the costs to the federal agency budget rather than the overall cost of the program to the taxpayers. This is a funding allocation issue that Congress should address. Finally, it is hard to convey the complex technical risks and complexities of collecting data from such a large and highly fragmented system, where there are incentives to interpret data rules in such a way as to optimize program performance outcomes. Investments in standardized data processing technology are the only means to develop high-quality data sets and result in considerable cost savings overall.

Performance management is a much simpler and more efficient process for federally run programs than for state-run programs because there are fewer operational entities. Therefore, there are considerable costs involved in allowing states to administer their own programs—even make their own rules in some cases (such as UI, Medicaid, and SNAP)—and in trying to achieve usable national data. It is possible to map or translate state variations to a federal data template to make the data more consistent, but this requires significant effort and expense. Given the high turnover in state staff, getting all states to understand and operate using consistent data rules is a never-ending task. This task would seem to be even more challenging for Europe.

The large number of Congressional committees that have control of sources of employment program funding cause the overall system to be highly fragmented, with considerable overlapping services and more costly reporting processes. The One-Stop system is intended to be seamless to the customer but certainly not to the program managers, accountants, or performance and reporting staff. The fragmented funding streams result in higher implementation costs because One-Stops have to collect data to report to many programs and agencies with varying and even conflicting definitions of customer characteristics (such as multiple definitions of *veteran*). Thus it is necessary to step back and look at the whole range of programs serving the population needing employment supports while acknowledging that specialized programs may be more effective in serving difficult populations.

Having consistent and reliable data across all states and local workforce areas is essential to using the data to manage programs. Without reliable and consistent data, the entire performance process is at best a waste of effort and at worst a source of bad policy (rewarding inferior and punishing superior performance). Most program operators at the state and local levels are diligent and honest, but there are some who see performance as a game, not a management tool, and find clever ways to manipulate their performance outcomes. The most fundamental challenges to obtaining reliable and consistent performance data are lack of precision and clarity in data requirements and lack of standardized and sophisticated data processing and calculation tools.

Defining Data Elements

The risks to reliable and consistent data are twofold: 1) caseworkers will interpret and thus enter information into the case management systems very differently, and 2) the data will be processed very differently by software developed separately by every state or grantee. Some of the WIA measures were ill defined early on, but in 2001 ETA did launch an ambitious data validation effort that has resulted in data that are considerably more reliable.

The first step in obtaining reliable data is to write clear, objective definitions and to define precise source documentation to verify the validity of a data element. This is much more difficult than one would think. When asked to validate data, we have responded by asking policymakers for the criteria to use to distinguish valid from invalid data and what source documentation we can use to make the determination. Policymakers are often stumped by these very difficult questions. Measures and their component data elements should not be used if they cannot be defined and validated.

There were some definitional problems in the original WIA youth measures for credential and skill attainment. The skill attainment measure was intended to give credit for youth that advanced in a skill area over a one-year period. The first operational step was to limit the number of possible skills attained to a maximum of three per youth per year. This put a cap on local areas setting large numbers of easily attained goals for a single customer. The next step was to define a skill attainment. Some felt that this was too difficult because of the wide variation in capabilities of the youth being served. An easy skill for one youth might be a huge challenge for another. This is obviously true, so ETA decided to provide flexible parameters for what constituted a skill attainment. Case managers used this flexibility to decide subjectively, on a case-by-case basis, what constituted a skill attainment and, in so doing, created inconsistent definitions of skill attainments across states and WIBs. Thus, from the first day it was difficult to compare the skill attainment results across reporting entities. Considerable effort was made to program the calculations, to train the states and local areas, and to collect all the required data and discuss what it all meant. In fact, such vaguely specified measures end up costing more than clearly defined ones, because there is never any closure to the discussions on how to calculate the measures and what to make of the results. This is an example of how effort and resources can be wasted if performance measures are vaguely defined or performance data are inconsistent and unreliable.

The credential attainment measure met a similar fate. The first problem was that some decision makers believed they needed to show strong results early in the implementation of WIA in order to demonstrate the effectiveness of the program. This view led to a loose definition of credentials, which encouraged states to define them so as to ensure that most customers would attain them. One state manager said it was "like a license to print our own money." Needless to say, the measure produced unreliable data.

Fortunately, the advent of common-measures discussions by the OMB in 2003 allowed ETA to correct these definitional problems. Partly based upon the lessons of the skill attainment and credential rates, the OMB and the ETA decided to develop new measures that would overcome some of the deficiencies of the original ones. They defined *credential* more strictly by eliminating work readiness credentials and focusing more on credentials and certificates that reward improvement in occupational skills. They also merged the credential rate with the diploma rate, which led to the new attainment of a degree or certificate rate. In addition, they replaced the skill attainment rate with a literacy and numeracy gains measure that required that states use U.S. Department of Education–approved standardized tests to determine whether or not an individual youth had improved his/her skills. This change created a well-defined measure but presented a complex challenge to write detailed specifications for calculating the measure accurately, given the almost infinite number of possible sequences of test scores and exceptions. Once the programming was done, testing the accuracy of the calculations consumed hundreds of hours of staff time.

Manipulating Performance

Performance outcomes can be manipulated during the enrollment and exit processes. A casual observer would not see how difficult it is to define enrollment date and exit date, which drive all performance calculations. Some states' first reaction to the launch of WIA was to impose more restrictive criteria on enrollment. They did not want to be held accountable for outcomes for customers who received very inexpensive services. The lower enrollment did not reflect the number of people being served, just the number for which the state was accountable in the performance system. This was done by redefining "staff-assisted services." Because WIA and ES are universal-access programs with a broad range of services, from self-service only (e.g., using the job-seeking aids on Web sites or at One-Stops without assistance) to staff-assisted training, there was significant discussion early on about at what point in the continuum of services a customer should be formally included in the performance system. The ETA instructed states to include customers when they received significant staff-assisted services. Some states, however, defined staff-assisted services very broadly, while others defined them very narrowly. Enrollment numbers fell sharply in some areas. It is not clear whether particular types of customers (such as incumbent workers, where earnings gains would be most difficult to achieve) were more likely to be left out of the reporting system or not. Measuring performance outcomes for customers who received little or no staff-assisted service and may have never visited a One-Stop is problematic. On the other hand, there has been very significant public investment in self-service facilities, so it is appropriate to determine whether the investment has led to better outcomes. Self-service utilization measures might be good complements to outcome measures for this customer group.

Another, more direct way of distorting outcomes was to manipulate exit dates. One dilemma states faced when they converted from JTPA to WIA was what to do with hundreds of thousands of JTPA customers who had never exited from JTPA but were no longer receiving services. The records of these customers had gone to the "data graveyard," never to be included in performance outcomes. States were instructed to purge these unmeasured customers from the system to allow WIA to start with a clean slate, and the concept of "soft exit" was developed to prevent a reoccurrence of the problem. States were instructed to generate an exit date for any customer who had not received a service for 90 days. There was much discussion about whether the exit date would be the last date of service or 90 days later, and also about how to avoid exiting customers in long-term training programs. The obvious means of manipulating performance is to avoid exiting customers until they have been placed in jobs. It is impossible to enforce rigorous standards or consistency across states for these issues because there is no way to tell from the case management files whether there were real continuing services provided or if the customer was being "held" in the system until job placement.

Defining Employment and Earnings

Defining employment and retention and earnings is not straightforward. Traditionally programs using manual follow-up methods have used fairly rigorous definitions. For example, SCSEP required exited customers to be employed for 60 of the first 90 days after exit to be counted as placed. Other programs set minimum levels of hours per week to exclude very partial employment or looked at average hourly wage and even whether the employment was related to the training provided. The universal use of wage record data under WIA raised a new set of issues. Wage records were quite thorough (all wages reported from multiple employers could be easily captured and aggregated) but did not provide details on employment and only reported quarterly totals. The number of hours worked, the hourly wage, and the occupation were generally not available, and it was not known if someone worked one day in the quarter or 90 days. Therefore, it was decided that the total earnings in the quarter after exit would define "entered employment." The threshold for total dollars required was discussed, and finally the ETA determined that any amount would qualify, making a very low barrier for placement.

The wage record system does not operate to serve employment program research or performance assessment, but to determine employer UI tax rates. It would be useful but difficult to obtain more detail on employment from employers, but given the high degree of automation of payroll systems, especially for larger employers, it may be feasible at some point in the future.

The earnings gain measure raised a host of additional definitional and technical problems. States had considerable concern about how enrolling laid-off, high-wage manufacturing sector workers would produce sharp earnings decreases after services when they were placed in lower-paying service industries. Some initial analyses of dislocated worker earnings replacement rates, however, showed earnings gains of over 300 percent. These spectacular results derived from customers who had already received services for a year or more prior to enrollment in WIA and thus had zero preprogram earnings. Defining the dates to use to calculate preprogram earnings, determining the actual dislocation date, and then collecting the correct quarters of wage record data proved to be very problematic. States approached these issues in various ways and with various levels of success, leading to inconsistent results.

A related issue involved measuring earnings gains from the first quarter after exit to the third quarter after exit. This did not seem to be a meaningful measure because it only measured earnings increases over a very short period when raises would not likely be provided. This measure was supported by the Temporary Assistance to Needy Families (TANF) program, where there were by definition no preprogram earnings. Ultimately the ETA abandoned pre- and postprogram earnings measures and now reports only average postprogram earnings.

The lessons from the early implementation of WIA are clear: do not attempt to measure something you cannot define or validate, and make sure the calculations are reliable and well tested.

Reporting and Validating Performance Data

The ETA has been in the forefront of federal performance management and data validation efforts since the 1970s for two reasons. First, the U.S. Supreme Court ruled in 1969 that the USDOL had to ensure that UI claimants received payments on time, and this required measuring the timeliness of UI activities. Second, it was discovered that the allocation of administrative funds to state UI agencies was inequitable because of inconsistencies in how states counted their activities. UI conducted a significant upgrade to its performance management and data validation systems in the 1990s and set the model for the rest of the federal government to follow, which generated a healthy culture of data quality and standardization in the state workforce agencies.

With the passage of WIA, the ETA sought to bring standardized reporting and data validation to the workforce programs, and such systems were gradually put in place starting in 2002. The data validation process asks whether the data used to calculate performance are correct and whether the performance measures were calculated correctly. This process led to much more rigorous definitions of data elements, as well as the development of standardized reporting software that states could use to edit files, perform reporting and performance calculations, and receive immediate feedback on data problems and performance. It also served to enhance the quality of program data and greatly speed the availability of performance data to the ETA, the OMB, Congress, and the research community. In addition, the reporting and data validation software provided basic analytical functionality so that states could explain in detail the changes in performance over time. Some states made extensive use of the analytical capabilities of the software to educate their local areas about how the measures worked.

Performance calculations are highly complex, and extensive testing is required to ensure their accuracy.[5] Before the use of standardized data calculations at a federal level, each state calculated its own performance at considerable expense and with inconsistent methods and results. Initially, the ETA was committed to the standardized reporting and data validation methods and processes, especially in light of USDOL Office of Inspector General (OIG) reports on deficiencies in ETA data (see OIG 2001a,b; 2002a,b; 2003; 2005). The standardized software required continued investment to maintain because of the large number of changes in the performance measures and because the software had to be enhanced to meet growing state analytical and diagnostic needs. States embraced the concept of accurate and consistent performance calculations and data edits and liked the immediate feedback they received on their data quality and performance.[6] Further, the total cost of using standardized software was far less overall than the cost of having each state program its own calculations, not to mention that the separately calculated performance data would be unreliable.[7]

In addition to editing files, calculating performance, and providing basic analytical functionality for states, the data validation software samples customer records for validation of data elements. In the validation process, state monitoring staff review a small sample of records against supporting documentation maintained at the local area. The software contains sampling algorithms that make the state monitoring process as efficient as possible for creating estimates of errors for each data element by state. State staff generally found the data validation process to be very helpful and efficient for monitoring data quality at the local level. Unfortunately, the software does not yet compute the standard error rate for each data element, so the ETA cannot set or enforce data accuracy standards.[8]

Federal Performance Monitoring

The ETA's regional offices have always monitored state programs. There are two basic forms of monitoring: 1) *process monitoring* consists of reviews of required state functions to ensure that they meet federal standards, and 2) *data monitoring* involves reviewing samples of records against source documentation and is thus identical to the data validation effort conducted by states. In 2006, the ETA designed a process by which federal regional monitoring staff would review a subsample of the records reviewed by the state staff to ensure that states were applying the data validation rules consistently. The federal staff would enter their results for the subsample into the data validation software, which would then generate a report to ETA on the state's accuracy. This monitoring process has not yet been implemented. The recent OIG report (2009) concluded that "without an effective monitoring process, ETA has no assurance that data validation is operating as designed so that the data can be relied upon for accurately reporting performance results" (p. 11).

Some ETA regional office staff developed their own data-monitoring processes, but they are implemented inconsistently, and not all regions monitor data systematically. Therefore, there is no systematic check on whether the states are performing the data element validation consistently and correctly. With no data accuracy standards, no precise calculations of state error rates, and no check that states are performing the validation correctly, the reliability of WIA data is still not clear. This is unfortunate because states still incur the full burden to perform annual data validation. This annual validation exercise does allow state staff to conduct effective data monitoring of local areas and thus facilitates the detection of data problems and discussion of remedies.

THE CHALLENGES AND BENEFITS OF STAKEHOLDER INVOLVEMENT

The process of designing performance measures starts with the funding legislation. Congress requires that recipients of funding submit certain performance outcomes to justify continued funding. Statutes also normally contain some language about remedial or punitive steps that will be taken if programs fall short of performance goals. Of course, Congress does not operate in a vacuum, and the legislation reflects input from the executive branch (the OMB and agencies) as well as from lobbyists for the state agencies and population-specific interest groups.[9] Statutory language about measures is usually very general, so agencies must add further levels of detail to "operationalize" the measures, including the specific data elements that must be reported and how the measures are to be calculated. Effective performance measurement requires strong leadership from the federal government both in defining the measures and objectives and in providing the definitional structure and necessary performance management tools. In some programs with immature performance management processes, program operators are given the latitude to define or choose their own measures. This approach may be politically popular, but it rarely produces any usable results and does not lead to program improvement. States and grantees look to the federal partner for leadership and structure but still want input on the operational details.

Soliciting Feedback and Consulting Program Operators

Both aspects of the dual rationale for measuring performance—accountability and program improvement—make it desirable that program operators "buy in" to the system. Obviously, the program management and program improvement rationale for measuring performance is advanced when program operators find the results meaningful and helpful. Even the program accountability rationale works best when operators find the measures to be legitimate. Therefore, the programs discussed in this chapter have sought extensive consultation from program operators (states, local areas, and grantees) during the design process and during the phase of the process when the measures are being operationalized.

At the end of 1998, the ETA produced an initial draft of the approach to measuring WIA, but it did not contain clear and well-defined measures, and thus was not well received by the states. Therefore, during the spring of 1999 there ensued a series of consultative meetings attended by federal and state staff. Six early adaptor states launched WIA on July 1, 1999, and representatives of these states met with federal staff over a series of months to hammer out the details. The first complete set of technical performance specifications was published in March 2000, before the other states implemented WIA on July 1, 2000. Input from state staff was very helpful in operationalizing the measures because of their rich knowledge of program operations and workforce data. Feedback on the technical aspects of the measures continued to be received during conferences and meetings for the next two years. Other programs had similar if less extensive consultations. All the ETA programs relating to WIA established performance workgroups to seek input from state and grantee staff.[10]

Fear of Performance Management

The performance measures were seen by some states, local areas, and grantees primarily as a threat rather than as a management tool. This perception greatly influenced their input on how the measures should be designed. It is logical that those at risk of sanctions from measured poor performance would become defensive and try to reduce the effectiveness of the measurement system itself. This defensive impulse leads to actions to evade the implications of the measures and to resist measurement in a number of ways. As mentioned in the data validation discussion above, state WIA staff play a dual role in the performance system and are sometimes defensive because they are being measured as states and sometimes supportive of effective performance methods because they oversee local areas.

The essence of the resistance to effective federal performance methods was documented in a Government Accountability Office (GAO) report (2005) on WIA, which said that "collecting uniform performance data at the national level [and] giving states and localities the flexibility they need to implement programs" are "competing objectives" (p. 1). This is based on a misunderstanding actively pushed by people who resist performance processes to muddy the true role of performance management techniques in improving government services.

We must distinguish clearly between service delivery and program management. Performance management systems track common events such as enrollment date, customer characteristics, limited service dates, exit date, and outcomes. Performance management systems do not specify how services are delivered. Therefore, there is no inherent conflict between allowing program operators creativity and flexibility in customer outreach and providing services and tracking customer characteristics and flow through the system and measuring outcomes. Local program operators and grantees are fond of saying that they can either serve people or enter case management data, but they cannot do both. This is all too often a defensive reaction to fear of being measured and a reflection of inadequate management capacity. That is why it is so important to focus initially on building strong data capacity through effective performance management tools and methods rather than on the punitive aspects of performance management.

The Relative Burden of Federal Performance Requirements

Despite the complaints about the burden of federal data requirements, many states collect far more detailed performance data and invest in more sophisticated performance management systems than anything imposed by the ETA. There is wide variation among states, grantees, and local program operators in their level of sophistication and the level of case management data they collect. The goal of the federal performance management system, including the key data validation component, should be to raise every state and grantee to a minimum acceptable level of data management and data reliability. There will always be states with more sophisticated performance systems than are practical for the federal partner to develop.

Tracking participants, services, and outcomes is essential to any effective program management at all levels of the system and would be done for the most part in the absence of any federal performance and data validation initiatives. From having overseen the development of the Paperwork Reduction Act requests for performance and data validation for many years, it has become clear that little information is collected solely for performance purposes, and that none of it constrains program operators from employing innovative and diverse service delivery methods.

Once we accept that program operators must know whom they are serving and what services they are providing, the only aspect of performance management that is a true burden is collecting outcome data. It is less important to the basic management of the program to track extended outcomes as required by WIA retention rates than to track customers and services. But if those long-term outcome data can be collected efficiently through wage records or some other form of already existing high-quality administrative data, then measuring even long-term outcomes becomes very cost-effective. There is also a strong argument to be made that long-term follow-up services are an expensive but essential part of an effective service delivery strategy, especially for the hardest-to-serve populations. The WIA Youth program and SCSEP both require long-term follow-up to support customers after exit, but this is resisted in the VR program even though the need for long-term support is evident in that population.

Another source of resistance to performance management is the concern that the population served is too varied and complex to permit effective measurement of the actual performance of a program operator. This becomes a problem when the emphasis is on incentives and sanctions and not program management, because program operators do not trust that the measures are fair. This notion is reinforced by the "social worker" mindset that is especially pervasive in programs serving special hard-to-serve populations. Many staff in these programs assert that all programs must be run well and must be effective because program staff are sympathetic to the population being served. There are thus three complementary threads to the resistance to effective performance management: 1) collecting data is a burden, 2) performance measures cannot accurately reflect the quality of services rendered, and 3) staff are well intentioned and therefore must be left alone to perform their work.

To be fair, local program operators and grantees often operate under stressful conditions. They serve very difficult populations with inadequate and declining funding levels and operate under the weight of threatening and somewhat crude performance measures. It is therefore critical that the performance system be sold primarily as a means to achieving better management and analysis capacity.

There is one critical area of performance management in which program operators are forced to bear a true burden for which no relief is likely to be found. That burden comes with requirements to collect data validation documentation from the most difficult-to-serve populations, such as homeless youth, people with disabilities, very low-income older workers, and non-English-speaking customers. Collecting such documentation is important to program integrity, not only because these are important program eligibility criteria, but also because programs are given extra credit for serving these people. SCSEP measures, for example, give credit to the grantees for specific categories of customers (disabled, homeless, low literacy skills, and frail), and in the VR program the category of "severely disabled" is critical to program intake and performance outcomes. In addition, programs allow performance outcome exemptions for medical conditions and even for medical conditions of family members; this is a major issue for the integrity of performance outcome data for SCSEP, which serves many people over age 70. It is very convenient to avoid a negative performance outcome by classifying the customer as excluded from performance.

Collecting documentation to show that customers meet criteria for extensive barriers to employment or exclusion from performance represents a true burden for case managers. Medical conditions, disability, homelessness, homeless youth, and family income are all very difficult areas to document. For example, how do you prove you are homeless? The only approach that we have found is to allow—in lieu of actual evidence—"self-attestation" in the form of documents the customers sign testifying as to their conditions. This will continue to be a challenge to effective performance management for the foreseeable future.

Measuring Accountability

Once we get past the "data are a burden" argument, we find a more subtle and valid tension between simplicity and clarity in measures and determining the program's actual accountability for outcomes. With a defensive mentality, program operators view performance measures as directly measuring their accountability or their effort in serving each individual customer. In fact, it is impossible to design measures that can account for all the factors bearing on success with a single customer. Performance management is a statistical process that assumes that measures of a sufficient number of outcomes can distinguish between more successful and less successful processes and methods.

Not understanding how performance management works, program operators seek direct measures of their accountability and thus want the measures to be designed to account for every exception. One state staff person argued that their state should not be held accountable when a customer failed to show up for services and had a negative outcome. I responded with two questions: 1) Why would more people fail to show up for services in your state than in other states? 2) If customers did tend to show up less in your state than in other states, was that not a valid finding about the quality of your services? Performance goals are always set well below 100 percent so that the system accounts for such "failures" that cannot be directly attributable to a program operator's deficiencies.

The impulse to design measures that account for individual customer circumstances leads to exponential increases in complexity. Each additional factor that a measure must consider to define success, such as excluding outcomes where customers became ill, doubles the number of possible outcomes. Some accountability factors are significant enough to incorporate into the measure design, and more sophisticated measures are practical if standard automated tools are used to perform data analysis and calculate measures. But ironically, once program operators have succeeded in adding factors to better measure what they are directly accountable for, they often complain that the measures have become too complex to understand or to explain to their local stakeholders. So, there is a tricky balance between designing detailed measures of actual accountability and designing measures that are easy to understand and explain.

THE WIA PERFORMANCE SYSTEM

The Evolution of WIA Measures

Stakeholder concerns had a direct and significant impact on the early WIA measures, where there was significant input from states and local areas. The initial WIA measures were very simple, but within a year they had become much more complex. One example of a change that added complexity but greatly strengthened the measure was in the treatment of youth who were placed in postsecondary education but not in employment. Originally, since it was considered that the Department of Labor could not reward an educational placement, the postsecondary education placement without employment was classified as a negative outcome. In other words, placing a youth in Harvard was bad, but placing him at McDonald's was good. After further discussion it was decided that postsecondary placement without employment would become a "neutral outcome," where the record was excluded from the placement calculation completely.

In 2003, the OMB launched a common-measures initiative for federal employment programs to try to standardize performance calculations across the many federal job training programs. This effort was prompted by the breakdown of the competitive approach to program funding. The Bush administration sought to use program outcome data to determine which programs were effective and which were ineffective and should be defunded or folded into more effective programs. This attempt was confounded by the lack of comparability of performance data across the data sets. For example, SCSEP defined a successful placement as 30 days of continuous employment within the first 90 days after exit, while WIA defined it as any earnings at all in the quarter after exit. The disparate definitions of success and performance goals across programs made it an even greater challenge to control for differences in the populations served.

The ETA embraced the OMB initiative and launched a second round of state-federal discussions over how to implement the new common measures. Other programs within ETA, including VR and even SCSEP, resisted the common measures, arguing that their populations were special and that they could not be expected to achieve results comparable to those of the mainstream programs. SCSEP has since adopted the common measures, but VR has still not implemented them. The common measures are a good step toward effective performance management at the national level across training programs and do not constrain programs from using other performance management tools.

The Use of Wage Records

In the absence of a good source of data on postprogram earnings like the UI wage record system, it would be very difficult to develop an efficient and effective performance management system, especially for such large-scale programs as WIA and ES. UI wage records are reasonably reliable because they are official tax records and are subject to some audit controls. They are not perfect, however, for a number of reasons, including uncovered employment, failure to report by employers, and errors in reporting that prevent matches of wages to participant records, but they do supply the vast majority of the data needed to measure outcomes. The ETA must continue to allow states to collect "supplemental" earnings data collected directly from program customers to compensate for the gaps in wage record data. This is particularly important, because the need for supplemental data varies widely by region. Wage record data are significantly less complete in agricultural areas; areas with a larger "underground economy" (such as Hawaii and Puerto Rico, where employment in tourist-related industries is more informal); and in areas with a high concentration of contract labor, such as the movie and software industries. Another critical issue is providing states with access to wage data collected by other states. Until recently, the ETA had experienced mixed success in establishing such a system, but privacy and legal concerns have rendered interstate wage data useless for performance management purposes. States can send files of Social Security numbers and receive aggregate rates of matches with a national wage file (including federal and military employment) to obtain more accurate entered employment, retention, and earnings data; however, this data is not provided at the customer level and is useless for analyzing and improving performance. Many states have had bilateral wage-record-sharing agreements since WIA began and can continue to use these more detailed data to analyze their performance at the customer level.

Not all employment and training programs can access the state wage record file; this is either because some are nongovernmental entities or because it is too cumbersome to negotiate access with the UI agency. SCSEP, for example, still conducts manual follow-up with each exiter up to three times to obtain postexit earnings data, which must be carefully documented for data validation. This additional burden can be seen as adding value because it allows grantees to provide follow-up employment support services. The Pathways to Work project in the United Kingdom planned to conduct extensive provider follow-up because there were no available earnings data equivalent to the UI data in the United States.

One of the major problems with reliance on wage data for performance management is that the files are not complete and available until about six to nine months after entry into the employment activity being measured. This prevents timely feedback to program operators, but it is still a far more cost-effective approach than expensive and unreliable informal follow-up data as gathered under JTPA. The six- to nine-month lag in the availability of complete employment outcome data is an unfortunate reality and does limit the benefits of the analytical feedback loop to program operators, which is a key aspect of an effective performance management system.

Although outcome data are the primary source for performance management, additional data are helpful for some programs where customers receive services over a long period of time. This is especially an issue in the WIA younger youth program where customers may be enrolled for five years or more and to some degree in SCSEP and VR as well. These programs would benefit from intermediary progress measures to provide more timely feedback to program operators on their performance. The literacy and numeracy gain measure in the WIA Youth program is an ideal measure not only because it is well-defined but also because it provides continuous feedback on youth progress to program operators.

CONCLUSION

This chapter introduced some of the challenges of effective performance management. We can conclude that top priority should be placed on establishing a solid foundation of collecting and processing data consistently and accurately to help Congress, program managers, and local One-Stop administrators to understand who is being served and what their outcomes are. There are many technical aspects to developing this foundation, and this chapter has only touched on them. An effective performance management system requires enlightened federal leadership with a sound understanding of the potential and limitations of performance system and a commitment to effective performance management. Federal staff must take the lead in promoting the value of performance management to the other levels of the system and firmly enforce performance objectives.

Only when the foundation for effective performance management is securely in place should policymakers take punitive action on the findings. They should concentrate initially on identifying superior and inferior performers, analyzing which processes and methods produce

the best results, and providing technical assistance to the poor performers. The least emphasis should be on rewards and sanctions. These
motivational devices can be useful but are often rushed into play before
the data are reliable or well understood and thus engender resistance
to performance management and inappropriate behavior by program
operators.

Notes

1. The Performance Management Group at Mathematica Policy Research has been
   involved in designing and implementing performance management and data
   validation systems for WIA, the Trade Adjustment Assistance Act, the Labor
   Exchange (or the ES), the National Farmworker Jobs Program, the Senior Community Service Employment Program, the Unemployment Insurance Program,
   and the Vocational Rehabilitation Program. The group also works on TANF and
   Supplemental Nutrition Assistance Program (SNAP) performance reporting and
   on assessing performance for Medicaid and Education Department grants.
2. Congress always restored NFJP funding.
3. WIA requires the local boards to contract the operation of the One-Stop centers,
   although public entities often hold the contracts.
4. Counts are sometimes used as performance measures, for example, if there is no
   real process to measure, such as program outcomes after a spell of services, or
   if the designer of the measures just wants to demonstrate results by adding up
   events that are considered to have social value. In these situations, the counts are
   not really performance measures in a technical sense and should not be confused
   with actual performance data. Such counts can be converted to rates if they reflect
   underlying performance and not increases in funding.
5. The data reporting and validation software calculates over 1,600 individual cells
   on various WIA and ES reports, as well as tens of thousands of additional calculations needed for other reporting, validation, and analytical functions. These
   calculations, reports, and functionality are documented in more than 500 pages
   of specifications and high-level requirements. The software also applies roughly
   300 edit checks to the data. Extensive testing is done to ensure that the calculated
   results are correct for every state regardless of numerous variations in data files
   submitted by the states.
6. The feedback was immediate when states loaded their customer files (e.g., the
   WIASRD) into the software, but was still constrained by data lags associated with
   wage records.
7. Many states have invested in performance software and use the federal validation
   software for testing and to validate their performance reports. Even if the state calculations are determined to be incorrect by the data validation software, the ETA
   uses data from the state calculations and not the validated calculations in its report

to Congress. Approximately 20–25 states use the federal software to generate their performance reports. Given budget cuts and the focus on other priorities, the ETA reduced the funding for the maintenance of the reporting and data validation software for WIA and ES. The functionality for states has diminished since 2005, and many of the suggestions states made for enhancing the software have not been implemented. The Office of Inspector General (2009) concluded that "with the lack of software upgrades, the effectiveness and efficiency of using the data validation software as a tool to improve the accuracy and reliability of WIA performance data has been compromised" (pp. 3, 11).

8. The UI data validation program does have data accuracy standards and computes reliable estimates of error, taking sampling error into account.

9. The National Association of State Workforce Agencies represents the state agencies that administer WIA and most related programs. The VR program is represented by the Council of State Administrators of Vocational Rehabilitation.

10. SCSEP, ES, NFJP, and the Division of Indian and Native American Programs all convened performance workgroups in 2000 and 2001.

References

Barnow, Burt S., and Jeffrey Smith. 2004. "Performance Management of U.S. Job Training Programs: Lessons from the Job Training Partnership Act." *Public Finance and Management* 4(3): 247–287.

Blalock, Ann B., and Burt S. Barnow. 2001. "Is the New Obsession with Performance Management Masking the Truth about Social Programs?" In *Quicker, Better, Cheaper? Managing Performance in American Government,* Dall Forsythe, ed. Albany, NY: Rockefeller Institute Press, pp. 487–519.

Government Accountability Office. 2005. *Workforce Investment Act: Labor and States Have Taken Action to Improve Data Quality, but Additional Steps Are Needed.* GAO-06-82. Washington, DC: GAO.

Office of Inspector General. 2001a. *Job Training Partnership Act Title II-C Out-of-School Youth Performance Audit.* Report No. 06-01-001-03-340. Washington, DC: U.S. Department of Labor.

———. 2001b. *Improving Trade Act Programs.* Report No. 0401-009-330. Washington, DC: U.S. Department of Labor.

———. 2002a. *Workforce Investment Act Performance Outcomes Reporting Oversight.* Report No. 06-02-006-03-309. Washington, DC: U.S. Department of Labor.

———. 2002b. *Audit of the Unemployment Insurance Data Validation Pilot Program.* Report No. 22-02-005-03-315. Washington, DC: U.S. Department of Labor.

————. 2003. *Workforce Investment Act Evaluation of Youth Program Enrollments, Services, and Recorded Outcomes*. Report No. 06-03-006-03-390. Washington, DC: U.S. Department of Labor.

————. 2005. *GPRA Data Validation Review Trade Adjustment Assistance Program*. Report No. 22-05-007-03-330. Washington, DC: U.S. Department of Labor.

————. 2009. *Audit of Workforce Investment Act Data Validation for the Adult and Dislocated Worker Programs*. Report No. 03-090003-03-390. Washington, DC: U.S. Department of Labor.

8
Lessons from the WIA Performance Measures

Burt S. Barnow
George Washington University

Since the late 1970s, major federal workforce development programs in the United States have included performance management systems that assess how well the programs are performing at the national, state, and local levels. The use of performance management in workforce programs predates the more general congressionally mandated performance requirements of the Government Performance and Results Act (GPRA). This chapter draws on the previous work of the author and others in assessing the lessons of the past 30 years of experience with performance management in workforce programs. Although the chapter focuses on the U.S. system, the lessons should apply to programs in other countries as well.

The chapter first discusses what performance management is in the context of workforce programs. Next, performance management is contrasted and compared with program evaluations. Policy officials would like to implement performance measures that are based on program impact; the next section describes why that is generally not possible to do and presents empirical findings on the success of such efforts. The following section describes how the performance management system used for U.S. workforce programs can lead to unintended results and summarizes some of the research on this topic. This is followed by a discussion of whether standards should be absolute or adjusted for factors such as participant characteristics and economic conditions. The final section presents lessons for countries that are considering establishing a performance management system.

Although related, the concepts of performance measurement and evaluation are distinct and serve different purposes (see Blalock and Barnow [2001]). Performance measurement is a management tool that is used to monitor implementation on a real-time basis. Performance measures may track data that indicate fidelity in program implementation, inputs (such as participant characteristics) that are considered important to the program's purpose, process measures (e.g., use of "best practices"), outputs expected from the program, and sometimes short-term gross outcome measures. Program evaluation, on the other hand, is intended to answer specific questions about programs. Process studies document what happened while the program was implemented, impact evaluations assess what difference in outcome measures was due to the intervention, and cost-benefit analyses assess whether the benefits of a program exceed the costs.

If the program has limited capacity, participant characteristics may be a useful performance measure, and one or more measures could be established to track the characteristics of customers served.[1] Process measures rather than output or outcome measures are sometimes used. For example, if particular practices are known to be more effective or less expensive than the alternatives, a case can be made for including process measures of performance. In the current health care reform debate in the United States, some advocates argue that costs can be driven down by requiring providers to use best practices or by providing financial incentives to do so; similar arguments can be raised in setting standards for education. In the past, however, some in the workforce field have argued that so long as the grant recipients are held accountable for the desired results, they should be free to adopt the approach they believe is best rather than relying on processes prescribed by the federal government.[2] A reasonable approach might be to monitor use of best practices and provide technical assistance, rewards, and sanctions only when an organization fails to achieve satisfactory outcomes.

In a system characterized by delegation of authority from the central government to lower levels of government (state and local government for many U.S. programs, but the concepts apply to a system of grantees or for-profit contractors as well), the goals of the level of government providing the funds may not be aligned with the goals of the level of government providing the services. By instituting a performance management system that provides rewards and sanctions based on how well the lower level of government meets the goals of the funding agency, the so-called principal-agent problem can be (in theory) resolved.

The differences between performance measurement and evaluation often are matters of depth of analysis and causality. Because of the need for rapid feedback, performance measurement activities generally track easy-to-collect data on inputs, activities, and outputs. Data for performance measurement generally come from management information systems maintained by the programs and from administrative data collected for other purposes.[3] Evaluations are usually conducted less often and with greater resources; a process study, for example, can make use of extensive interviews to document program implementation. Performance management activities cannot usually afford the time and resources required for tracking long-term outcomes and establishing and tracking a control group or comparison group, so performance measures are usually based on gross postprogram measures (such as earnings during a postprogram period), while evaluations can estimate program impact (by, for example, comparing earnings of participants after participation with earnings of a control group of applicants that was excluded from the program through random assignment). For example, performance measures for a vocational training program can include placement rates, wages at placement, and perhaps short-term follow-up measures of employment and earnings for participants, but an impact evaluation will focus on the change in employment and earnings due to the program, usually for a significantly longer period. Both types of activities are important for management and policy development, but, as discussed below, one should avoid reading more into performance results than is actually there.

PERFORMANCE MANAGEMENT FOR U.S. WORKFORCE DEVELOPMENT PROGRAMS

In the United States, implementation of GPRA has led various programs to embrace alternative concepts of why performance management is useful. According to the statute, GPRA was designed to hold "federal agencies accountable for achieving program results." In particular, GPRA requires that agencies develop performance measures and standards for the programs they administer, as well as strategic plans to achieve their goals.

A performance management system must include three components: 1) measures of performance, 2) standards for acceptable performance, and 3) feedback on performance. As discussed below, measures for U.S. workforce programs have attempted to focus on program impacts, but that need not be the case.

The USDOL established performance measures long before such measures were mandated under GPRA. Performance measures were first established in the late 1970s for CETA. JTPA, which was the major national workforce program in the 1980s and 1990s, had statutory provisions calling for measuring performance as the impact of the program on employment and earnings relative to program cost.[4] Specifically, Section 106 of JTPA, which provided the requirements for performance standards, stated

> The Congress recognizes that job training is an investment in human capital and not an expense. In order to determine whether that investment has been productive, Congress finds that it is essential that criteria for measuring the return on this investment be developed; and that the basic return on investment is to be measured by long-term economic self-sufficiency, increased employment and earnings, reductions in welfare dependency, and increased educational attainment and occupational skills.

The JTPA statute suggested but did not require that measures for adults include the employment rate in unsubsidized employment, employment retention for six months, an increase in earnings and/or the wage rate, a reduction in welfare dependency, and acquisition of skills. In practice, the performance measures used for JTPA were primarily program outcomes that, at best, served as proxies for program impact. Initially, the measures focused on the status of participants at the time of exit from the program or shortly thereafter, but by the time the program was replaced by WIA, a follow-up period of 13 weeks was used for most measures. The statute originally also called for cost measures, but as described below, this requirement was repealed in 1992.[5]

Under WIA, the Office of Management and Budget (OMB) has advocated that all programs with a workforce goal have "common measures," but agencies other than the USDOL have resisted adopting the common measures. Currently, the common measures for adults and dislocated workers are:

- Entered employment rate: Of those not employed at the date of participation, the number of participants who are employed in the first quarter after the exit quarter divided by the number of participants who exited during the quarter.

- Employment retention rate: Of those who are employed in the first quarter after the exit quarter, the number of participants who are employed in both the second and third quarters after the exit quarter divided by the number of participants who exited during the quarter.

- Average earnings: Of those participants who are employed in the first, second, and third quarters after the exit quarter, total earnings in the second quarter plus total earnings in the third quarter divided by the number of participants who exited during the quarter.[6]

For Youth programs, the common measures use a broader concept of a successful outcome by including training and education, and the measures include attainment of a certificate or degree and literacy and numeracy gains.

ADJUSTMENTS TO PERFORMANCE STANDARDS

U.S. workforce investment programs have varied in their approach to adjusting performance standards, both among programs and over time. This section first describes how performance standards have been adjusted for major U.S. workforce investment programs and then summarizes the pros and cons of adjusting standards.[7]

For the primary workforce investment programs administered by the USDOL, JTPA in the 1980s and 1990s, and WIA beginning in 2000, state and local area standards were subject to adjustment, but the approach has varied greatly. Initially under JTPA, governors had three options for adjusting standards for the service delivery areas (SDAs) within their jurisdiction: using the national standards established by the Secretary of Labor, using regression models developed by the USDOL to adjust standards for variation in participant characteristics and economic conditions, or developing their own adjustment system.

The legislation was later amended to make it relatively difficult for governors to use any adjustment mechanism other than the national model. Under WIA, standards were established at the state level through negotiations, although some have commented that USDOL officials imposed standards on the states with no opportunity to truly negotiate; states can determine local workforce area standards in any manner they choose.[8]

Although many public programs, including all that are administered by federal agencies, are required to establish performance standards, there are few cases where adjustments to performance standards have been considered, and even fewer where they have actually been applied. The concepts of fairness and equity have been set forth to argue both for and against the use of performance adjustments. The most oft-cited reason for adjusting standards is to "level the playing field," or to make performance management systems as fair as possible by establishing expectations that take account of different demographic, economic, and other conditions or circumstances outside of public managers' control that influence performance. It has also been argued, however, that it is not acceptable to set lower expectations for some programs than others, even if they serve more disadvantaged populations or operate in more difficult circumstances. For example, do we perpetuate inequities in education if less rigorous standards for reading and math performance are established for schools serving poorer children? Or if a single standard is set for all, could governments instead direct more resources to those programs that face more difficult conditions or disadvantaged populations to help put them on a more level playing field?

Another argument of those advocating adjustments to performance standards is that they better approximate the value added of programs (rather than gross outcome levels or change). For policymakers or program managers, having a better understanding of the contributions of program activities to performance (net of factors that are not influenced by the production or service processes) may contribute to more effective use of the performance information to improve program operations and management. The use of adjusted performance measures is also more likely to discourage (if not eliminate) "gaming" responses, in which program managers attempt to influence measured performance in ways that do not increase impacts (e.g., by altering who is served and how). A system that adjusts for population characteristics and other such factors will reduce the efficacy of these gaming strategies and the misspent effort and resources associated with them. As described below, there is ample evidence that workforce investment programs have responded to performance management systems by cream skimming from the pool of eligible individuals.

Of course, these benefits may be contingent on program managers understanding and having confidence in the adjustment mechanisms. Regression-based performance adjustment models have been criticized for having low explanatory power (as measured by R^2) and flawed specifications, suggesting that sometimes adjustments may be biased or unreliable. The argument that a low R^2 implies that the statistical model is not useful is in most cases false. A low R^2 means that there is a lot of noise in predicting the overall level of the dependent variable, not necessarily that the estimates of the effects of specific explanatory variables are unreliable. Indeed, one may obtain statistically significant coefficients for the adjustment factors even with a low R^2, implying that there are important factors that have a strong effect on predicted performance and should be accounted for in measuring performance.

While there are merits in the arguments both for and against the use of performance adjustments, few public programs appear to even consider or attempt to develop adjustments for performance standards. Until more experimentation with performance adjustments takes place in public programs, we will continue to be limited in our ability to understand not only whether they have the potential to improve the accuracy of our performance assessments, but also if they contribute to improved performance over time as public managers receive more useful feedback about their programs' achievements (or failures) and what contributes to them.

In their assessment of adjusting performance standards, Barnow and Heinrich (2010) conclude with the following recommendations. First, policymakers and program managers should, at a minimum, give more consideration to the concept of adjusting performance standards. Specifically, programs should ask if they can make a strong case for having the same standard for all jurisdictions or entities regardless of the context or circumstances in which they operate. Second, statistical modeling should be viewed as one tool in the adjustment process (and not the only technique to be applied). There is no single approach to statistical modeling or to combining statistical analysis with other methods such as negotiation or subgroup performance analysis that will work best for all programs. In fact, Barnow and Heinrich (2010) suggest that statistical modeling should be viewed as a complement rather than a substitute for negotiating performance standards. In Washington State, for example, statistical models are a starting point for negotiations of local WIA performance standards, and at the national level, the USDOL is now providing guidance on how changes in circumstances (such as the unemployment rate) can affect outcomes. Likewise, if regression models produce counterintuitive findings or findings that are contrary to other policies of interest, the models, data, and time frame should be investigated and refined accordingly or discarded. Finally, the use of statistical modeling for performance adjustments does not negate the use of other incentives for guiding program managers or the incorporation of other performance management system features or requirements such as "continuous performance improvement."

EVIDENCE ON THE EFFECTS OF PERFORMANCE MANAGEMENT IN WORKFORCE INVESTMENT PROGRAMS

The ETA has had substantial experience with performance standards, and a number of studies have been conducted on the impacts of performance management on participants served, activities, costs, and program impacts. While most analysts note the strong rationale for developing performance measures for government programs, there has been considerable controversy in the literature regarding the benefits of performance management systems, particularly as they have been applied since enactment of the GPRA in 1993. This section of the report reviews the literature on performance standards for workforce programs; most of the research was conducted on the performance standards system used under JTPA, WIA's predecessor.[9] Although much of the literature on performance management points to its salutary effects, there is little doubt from the literature that instituting performance standards can have a strong impact on program behavior, and not always in the desired direction. This section summarizes the literature on performance standards in employment and training programs in five key areas: 1) the impact of performance standards on who is served, 2) the impact of performance standards on the services provided, 3) the relationship between performance measures and program impacts, 4) strategic responses by state and local programs to performance standards, and 5) lessons learned by the ETA and states/localities on the use and effects of efficiency measures/standards.

The Impact of Performance Standards on Who Is Served

The majority of the employment and training literature on performance incentives addresses the question of their effect on who gets served. Under JTPA, local SDAs had strong incentives to serve persons likely to have good labor market outcomes, regardless of whether those outcomes were due to JTPA because the performance measures used focused on postprogram levels of employment and earnings. Similar incentives guide the WIA program. In fact, the absence of a regression model to adjust standards for serving individuals with labor market barriers should make these incentives stronger under WIA than they were under JTPA.

The literature divides this issue into two parts. First, do SDAs (called WIBs under WIA) respond to these incentives by differentially serving persons likely to have good outcomes, whether or not those good outcomes result from the effects of the program? This is the literature on "cream skimming." Second, if there is cream skimming, what are its impact effects? Taking the best among the eligible could be economically efficient if the types of services offered by these programs have their largest net impacts for this group. In what follows, the literature on each of these two questions is reviewed.

Do employment and training programs cream skim?

Several papers examine whether or not JTPA program staff cream skimmed in response to the incentives provided by the JTPA performance system. The key issue in this literature is the counterfactual: to what group of nonparticipants should the participants be compared in order to determine whether or not cream skimming has occurred? In all cases, the studies proceed by comparing observable characteristics correlated with outcomes, such as education levels or participation in transfer programs such as Aid to Families with Dependent Children (AFDC) or Temporary Assistance for Needy Families. A finding that participants have "better" characteristics relative to nonparticipants in the form of higher mean years of schooling or lower average prepro-gram transfer receipt, is interpreted as evidence of cream skimming.

Anderson et al. (1992) and Anderson, Burkhauser, and Raymond (1993) compare the characteristics of JTPA enrollees in Tennessee in 1987 with the characteristics of a sample of individuals eligible for JTPA in the same state with data constructed from the Current Population Survey. The literature suggests that less than 5 percent of the eligible population participated in JTPA in each year (see the discussion in Heckman and Smith 1999), which allows wide scope for cream skimming. Both papers find modest evidence of cream skimming. In particular, the Anderson, Burkhauser, and Raymond (1993) analysis of program participation and postprogram job placement suggests that if eligible persons participated at random, the placement rate would have been 61.6 percent rather than 70.7 percent, a fall of 9.1 percentage points.

Heckman and Smith (2004) address the issue of self-selection versus selection by program staff using data from the Survey of Income and Program Participation on JTPA eligibles combined with data from the National JTPA Study. They break the participation process for JTPA into a series of stages—eligibility, awareness, application and acceptance, and participation—and look at the observed determinants of going from each stage to the next. They find that some differences between program eligibles and participants result primarily from self-selection at stages of the participation process, such as awareness, over which program staff have little or no control. The evidence in Heckman and Smith (2004) suggests that while cream skimming may be empirically relevant, comparing the eligible population as a whole to participants likely overstates its extent, and misses a lot of substantive and policy-relevant detail.

The paper by Heckman, Smith, and Taber (1996) presents a contrasting view. They use data from the Corpus Christi, Texas, SDA, the only SDA in the National JTPA Study for which reliable data on all program applicants are available for the period during the experiment. In their empirical work, they examine whether those applicants who reach random assignment (i.e., were selected to participate in the program) differ from those who do not in terms of both predicted outcome levels (earnings in the 18 months after random assignment) and predicted program impacts (projected into the future and discounted). The authors find strong evidence of negative selection on levels combined with weak evidence for positive selection on impacts. They attribute the former to a strong "social worker mentality" toward helping the hard-to-serve among the eligible that was evident in interactions with program staff at the Corpus Christi site. WIA offers an interesting contrast to JTPA because the WIA performance standards are not adjusted by a regression model, and they therefore do not hold programs harmless for the characteristics of their participants. Because programs now have stronger incentives to enroll individuals with few barriers to employment, we would expect to observe enrollment shift toward this group. An internal (USDOL 2002) study finds that this is precisely what appears to be occurring, at least in the area scrutinized:

> A brief survey of States by our Chicago Regional Office indicated that WIA registrations were occurring at only half the level of enrollment achieved by JTPA. While some of this may be due to start up issues, there are indications that the reduced registration levels are due to a reluctance in local areas to officially register people in WIA because of concerns about their ability to meet performance goals, especially the "earnings gain" measure. It appears that local areas in these States are selective in whom they will be accountable for. Some local areas are basing their decisions to register a person on the likelihood of success, rather than on an individual's need for services.

A study by the U.S. Government Accountability Office (GAO 2002) confirms these problems. The GAO report, based on a survey of 50 states, indicated "many states reported that the need to meet performance levels may be the driving factor in deciding who receives WIA-funded services at the local level."

Overall, the literature provides modest evidence that program staff responded to the incentives provided by the JTPA performance standards system to choose participants likely to improve their measured performance whether or not they benefited from program services, and studies of the implementation of WIA indicate that, if anything, the situation has been exacerbated by the performance management system used for WIA. At the same time, the evidence from the Corpus Christi SDA indicates that staff concerns about serving the hard-to-serve could trump the performance incentives in some contexts.

What are the impact implications of cream skimming?

A number of studies have examined the efficiency implications of cream skimming by estimating the correlation between performance measures and program impacts. Barnow and Smith (2004) summarize the evidence from the seven studies that comprise this literature. The seven papers examine a variety of different programs, ranging from the MDTA program of the 1960s to the Job Corps program of today. Most rely on experimental data for their impact estimates. With one exception (Zornitsky et al. 1988), the findings are negative or mixed regarding the relationship between outcome-based performance measures of the type typically used in employment and training programs and program impacts. The Zornitsky et al. findings refer to a program, the AFDC Homemaker–Home Health Aide Demonstration, which differs from programs such as JTPA and WIA in that it provided a homogeneous treatment to a relatively homogeneous population. Taken together, the literature clearly indicates that, in the context of employment and training programs, commonly used performance measures do *not* improve program impact by inducing service to those who will benefit most. At the same time, the literature indicates that cream skimming likely has a very small effect, if any, on program earnings impact.

Effects of Performance Incentives on Services Provided

At least two papers examine the effect of performance incentives on the types and duration of services offered in an employment and training program, holding constant the characteristics of persons served.[10] Marschke's (2002) analysis uses the variation in performance incentives facing the training centers in the National JTPA Study to identify the effects of performance incentives on the types of services received by JTPA participants. Marschke (2002) finds evidence that changes in the performance measures employed in JTPA led SDAs to alter the mix of services provided in ways that would improve their performance relative to the altered incentives they faced. In some cases, these changes led to increases in efficiency, but in others they did not. Marschke (2002) interprets his evidence as indicating that SDAs' service choices are responsive at the margin, but that existing performance measures do a poor job of capturing program goals such as maximizing the (net) impacts of the services provided.

More recently, Courty and Marschke (2004) demonstrate that the JTPA performance management system affects the duration of training for some participants because program managers manipulate the duration of services for some participants in order to be able to count them on their performance measures for a specific program year. Courty and Marschke (2004) find that these manipulations reduced the overall mean impact of the employment and training services provided by JTPA.

Relationship between Performance Measures and Program Impact

Performance measures for a program may be of intrinsic interest, or they may be a proxy for some underlying factor of interest that is not easy to measure in a relatively quick and inexpensive manner. For example, Blalock and Barnow (2001) note that programs may wish to use program impact as a performance measure, but accurately measuring impact requires many years and the presence of a randomly assigned control group or a carefully selected comparison group. Because this is not generally compatible with obtaining quick, inexpensive measures, programs often rely on proxy measures such as postprogram earnings or the pre-post change in earnings. If the goal is to have performance measures serve as a proxy for impact, then it is necessary to assess how well the types of measures that are practical and have been used for the JTPA and WIA programs correspond with program impact.

Two studies have explored this issue for JTPA in recent years, and another study looked at the Job Corps. Barnow (2000) and Heckman, Heinrich, and Smith (2002) both made use of the fact that the National JTPA Study provided experimental impact findings in 16 local areas and included the data needed to construct performance measures similar to those used by ETA. However, the approach used to measure performance does not include a control group or even a comparison group, so it is not surprising that the performance measures used are at best weakly correlated with program impact.[11]

The recent evaluation of the Job Corps that was based on a classical experimental design provided Schochet and Burghardt (2008) with an opportunity to analyze how closely the Job Corps's performance standards track the program's impacts. Job Corps is a primarily residential program for highly disadvantaged out-of-school youth. Schochet and

Burghardt indicate that during the evaluation period, program years 1994 through 1996, the performance measures included eight measures in three broad areas: 1) program achievement (reading and math gains, GED attainment rate, and vocational completion rate); 2) placement measures (placement rate, average wage at placement, and the percentage of placements related to training); and 3) quality/compliance measures (ratings of federal monitors). Because of the random assignment used to assign treatment status, impact can be estimated as the difference between treatment and control group values on the outcome measures. Schochet and Burghardt (2008) compare program impacts for Job Corps centers ranked in each third of the performance distribution. They conclude, "Our results indicate that at the time of the National Job Corps Study, measured center performance was not associated with impacts on key education, crime, and earnings outcomes."

Strategic Responses to Performance Incentives

In addition to the substantive responses to performance incentives considered above, in which local programs changed what they actually did, local programs can also attempt to change their measured performance without changing their actual performance. This behavior is referred to as a strategic response, or as "gaming" the performance system. Regardless of their differing goals, all types of organizations have an incentive to respond strategically to performance incentives, provided the cost is low, as doing so yields additional resources to further their own goals. The literature provides clear evidence of such gaming behavior under JTPA.

One important form of strategic behavior under JTPA was the manipulation of whether or not participants were formally enrolled. Under the JTPA incentive system (and WIA as well), only persons formally enrolled counted toward site performance. In addition, for the first decade of JTPA's existence, local programs had substantial flexibility in regard to when someone became formally enrolled. Clever SDAs improved their performance by basing enrollments on job placements rather than the initiation of services. For example, some SDAs boosted performance by providing job search assistance without formally enrolling those receiving it in the program. Then, if an individual found a job, the person would be enrolled, counted as a placement, and terminated, all in quick succession. Similarly, SDAs would send potential trainees to employers to see if the employer would approve them for an on-the-job training slot; enrollment would not take place until a willing employer was found.

There are several pieces of evidence regarding the empirical importance of this phenomenon. The first is indirect, and consists of the fact that USDOL found it enough of a problem to change the regulations. Specifically, in 1992, the USDOL required that individuals become enrolled once they received objective assessment and that they count as a participant for performance standards purposes once they received any substantive service, including job search assistance.

Other evidence comes from the National JTPA Study. As part of their process analysis of the treatments provided at the 16 SDAs in the study, Kemple, Doolittle, and Wallace (1993) conducted interviews of nonenrolled members of the experimental treatment group at 12 of the 16 sites. These results (available in Table 3.2 of their report) show that 53 percent of nonenrolled treatment group members received services, most often referrals to employers for possible on-the-job training (36 percent of all nonenrollees) and job search assistance (20 percent of all nonenrollees). They report that ". . . most of the study sites enrolled individuals in classroom training when they attended their first class or in OJT when they worked their first day." There is also evidence that this type of behavior has continued under WIA. The U.S. Government Accountability Office (2002, p. 14) notes that "all the states we visited told us that local areas are not registering many WIA participants, largely attributing the low number of WIA participants to concerns by local staff about meeting performance levels."

The flexibility of JTPA also allowed strategic manipulation of the termination decision. Because performance standards in JTPA were based on exiters, SDAs had no incentive to terminate individuals from the program who were not successfully placed in a job. By keeping them on the rolls, the person's lack of success would never be recognized and used against the SDA in measuring its performance. As the USDOL explains in one of its guidance letters, "Without some policy on termination, performance standards create strong incentives for local programs to avoid terminating failures even when individuals no longer have any contact with the program."[12]

Problems with local programs retaining participants on the rolls long after they stopped receiving services go back to the days of JTPA's predecessor, CETA. In one of their guidance letters, the USDOL observed that "monitors and auditors found that some participants continued to be carried in an 'active' or 'inactive' status for two or three years after last contact with these programs." For Title II-A of JTPA, the USDOL limited the period of inactivity to 90 days, although some commentators suggested periods of 180 days or more.[13]

The ETA's Experience with Efficiency Measures

The ETA also has previous experience with efficiency standards under JTPA. Under the original JTPA statute, Section 106(b)(4) required that efficiency measures be prescribed for the JTPA Adult Program and that the efficiency measures be related to the outcome measures used. The National Commission for Employment Policy (NCEP) commissioned an evaluation of the effects of JTPA performance standards on participants, services, and costs (see Dickinson et al. [1988]). The study included quantitative statistical analysis of JTPA Annual Status Report data linked to data on the characteristics of local program areas, as well as qualitative analysis based on interviews with 30 local programs and 87 service providers in eight states.

For the most part, the study found that the JTPA performance standards had the desired effects of holding programs harmless for differences in participant characteristics and local economic conditions. However, the study found that the cost standards had intrinsic problems and created some undesirable effects on participants served:

> This evaluation found that the federal standards for the entered employment rate and wage rate for adults generally did not have unintended effects on clients or services . . . The federal cost standards, however, had the most unintended effects and were the least comparably measured of all the federal performance measures. The evaluation found that SDAs in states that placed more weight on the federal cost standard tended to serve fewer hard-to-serve clients and that [local areas] concerned about exceeding the cost standards tended to design less intensive services. At the same time, this evaluation found serious measurement problems with the cost standards. We found large differences in the extent to which [local programs] were leveraging JTPA funds, either by

using funds from other programs to help fund JTPA Title II-A programs or by using service providers that had alternative funding sources. As a result, it is difficult to compare the cost of services received by JTPA participants across *local programs*. (p. 5)

Based on their findings from both the quantitative and qualitative components of the study, the authors recommended that alternatives to the cost measures be explored. The authors note that as a result of concern about the unintended impacts of the cost standards, the ETA set more lenient cost standards in PY 1988, but they conclude that this policy change would not eliminate the disincentive problems in states that emphasize exceeding rather than meeting standards. In response to the research findings, the NCEP made a number of recommendations for changing the statutory provisions of JTPA dealing with performance standards. Taking note of the study's findings regarding the undesirable incentives and comparability of cost issues, the commission's first recommendation was that ". . . Section 106(b)(4), which requires the Secretary [of Labor] to prescribe performance standards relating gross program expenditures to various performance measures, be amended to direct that cost-efficiency be monitored by states."

In August 1992, the JTPA statute was amended, and the amendments repealed the federal requirement for efficiency standards and prohibited governors from using efficiency standards in making awards to local areas. WIA has no prohibitions against the use of cost standards, and in response to requests by the OMB, the USDOL currently has a contractor exploring the use of cost measures for 11 workforce programs administered by the ETA.

CONCLUSIONS AND LESSONS FOR THE EUROPEAN COMMISSION

This final section presents conclusions based on the research and lessons I suggest for countries about to introduce a performance measurement system for its workforce investment programs.

Do not confuse performance measurement with program evaluation. Performance measurement is used as a management tool, and it cannot and should not be expected to serve as a substitute for program evaluation. Performance must be monitored on a continuous basis to assess whether key elements of the program are being implemented as planned and if immediate program outcomes are consistent with the long-term results expected. As a management tool, performance measurement should provide quick feedback on the operation of a program, but in most cases, performance measures cannot and do not measure program impacts.

There are often good reasons to adjust performance standards to take account of program goals, participant characteristics, and environmental conditions. Performance is generally a function of many factors, so it is likely that programs in different locations will vary in important ways that can affect their performance. U.S. programs that use adjustment mechanisms refer to the adjustments as "leveling the playing field"—an effort to judge programs in different circumstances appropriately. When WIA abandoned the statistically based adjustment procedures used for the predecessor JTPA program, the states and local governments indicated strong dissatisfaction with the new approach.

Programs need not have the same performance measures or standards. In the United States, the OMB has attempted to impose common measures on all programs with a workforce orientation. The programs often differ, however, in significant ways, and there is no reason why programs with different participants, activities, and/or economic conditions should necessarily have identical measures. For example, the Senior Community Service Employment Program, sometimes referred to as the Older Worker program, provides community service opportunities to poor older individuals who would like to work. It can be debated whether placement in an unsubsidized job is a good measure of performance for the program, but it is very unlikely that if the entered employment rate is used as a measure that the standard should be the same for programs serving customers with fewer barriers to employment.

Be cautious in establishing performance measures with large rewards and/or sanctions. This is an extremely important lesson from the literature on U.S. workforce investment program performance management research. The literature on performance management for U.S. workforce programs clearly indicates that the measures are sometimes only weakly related to outcomes of interest such as program impact and that state and local programs can manipulate their data to raise their measured performance without actually increasing the value of what they do—in short, they spend resources trying to look good instead of doing good. Worse, there is strong evidence that programs sometimes engage in cream skimming and reduce their services to those most in need. Thus, for workforce programs it is wise to avoid "high stakes" performance measures if the programs can behave strategically to affect their measured performance.

The U.S. experience indicates that too much emphasis on efficiency can lead to programs avoiding customers who require expensive service strategies and to too much emphasis on less expensive service strategies. Research on the use of cost measures for U.S. workforce investment programs indicates that in the past there was widespread agreement that cost measures led to deleterious consequences. Efficiency is, however, a very important goal, particularly when past studies have indicated that only a small fraction of those eligible for workforce programs can be served at current budget levels. Thus, the current concern about taking cost into consideration when measuring the performance of workforce programs is appropriate. The question is how best to balance the need to use resources efficiently with the knowledge that placing too much emphasis on cost issues can lead to providing the wrong mix of services. I would recommend monitoring and discussing efficiency with those who perform poorly on such measures, but given the negative experiences with the use of cost measures for workforce programs in the United States, I would recommend against establishing formal efficiency measures.

Performance management is still in a formative stage; legislation should not be overly prescriptive on the measures, standards, and incentives. Deliberations on the structure of the performance management system should include input by all the relevant stakeholders. When performance management was first introduced in the U.S. workforce investment system, meetings involving representatives of states, localities, training providers, academics, and others were held over the course of several years before a formal system with rewards and sanctions was implemented. This process paved the way for statistical models to be used to adjust for variations across states and local areas. Over time, these work groups explored changes, such as using longer-term measures and using administrative data rather than survey data. The inclusionary process helped lead those involved to have a voice in the system and led them to support the resulting system. In contrast, when the performance management system was changed significantly for the implementation of the WIA program with little if any discussion with stakeholders, there was a strong rejection of the new system. Performance measures are much less likely to drive performance in the manner intended if those being graded consider the system grossly unfair.

Notes

1. The performance management system for JTPA required local programs to classify at least 65 percent of participants served as "hard to serve" to qualify for performance bonuses.
2. The JTPA Advisory Committee explicitly rejected the idea of dictating process to state and local governments: "In the business world, it is now widely accepted that the excellent companies define their expected results explicitly, and tightly measure performance against them, while allowing their producers to have discretion in how they attain those results. We suggest that JTPA emulate this model" (JTPA Advisory Committee 1989, p. 27).
3. In the United States, data on employment and earnings for workforce programs come from administrative data maintained by states to determine eligibility and benefit levels for unemployment insurance. Such data are not perfect, though, as self-employment earnings and off-the-books employment (and sometimes employment in other states or for government) are not covered. It is inexpensive to use relative to conducting a survey, and it avoids recall issues.
4. During this period the Work Incentive Program (WIN), which provided employment and training services to welfare recipients, also had a performance management system that distributed some of the funding to states based on their success on measures such as welfare grant reductions, the entered employment rate, wage rates of WIN participants who obtained jobs, and job retention. See U.S. GAO (1982).
5. For a discussion of the JTPA performance management system in its later years, see Social Policy Research Associates (1999).
6. See Training and Employment Guidance Letter 17-05, Attachment A. Available at http://wdr.doleta.gov/directives/attach/TEGL17-05_AttachA.pdf (accessed on October 24, 2009).
7. This section is based on Barnow and Heinrich (2010).
8. See Social Policy Research Associates (2004) and Barnow and King (2005) for a discussion of state and local perceptions of performance management under WIA.

9. For a more in-depth review of the literature on performance standards in workforce programs, see Barnow and Smith (2004); most of this section is based on Barnow and Smith (2004). For a critical review of the performance management movement, see Radin (2006).

10. The effects of cost standards on services are covered in a later section.

11. A related problem is that performance measures must use short-term postprogram earnings to measure performance, but the impact of a program is best measured over a longer period. Barnow and Smith (2004) review the literature on the relationship between short-term earnings impacts and long-term impacts, and they find that most studies find a very weak relationship between the two.

12. See TEIN, 5-93, available at: http://wdr.doleta.gov/directives/corr_doc.cfm?DOCN=770.

13. Pascal Courty and Gerald Marschke conducted several studies that verify gaming behavior by local programs participating in the National JTPA Study. See Barnow and Smith (2004) for a review of these studies.

References

Anderson, Kathryn, Richard Burkhauser, and Jennie Raymond. 1993. "The Effect of Creaming on Placement Rates under the Job Training Partnership Act." *Industrial and Labor Relations Review* 46(4): 613–624.

Anderson, Kathryn, Richard Burkhauser, Jennie Raymond, and Clifford Russell. 1992. "Mixed Signals in the Job Training Partnership Act." *Growth and Change* 22(3): 32–48.

Barnow, Burt S. 2000. "Exploring the Relationship between Performance Management and Program Impact: A Case Study of the Job Training Partnership Act." *Journal of Policy Analysis and Management* 19(1): 118–141.

Barnow, Burt S., and Carolyn Heinrich. 2010. "One Standard Fits All? The Pros and Cons of Performance Standard Adjustments." *Public Administration Review* 70(1): 60–71.

Barnow, Burt S., and Christopher T. King. 2005. *The Workforce Investment Act in Eight States.* Report prepared for the U.S. Department of Labor. Albany, NY: The Nelson A. Rockefeller Institute of Government. http://www.rockinst.org/pdf/workforce_welfare_and_social_services/2005-02-the_workforce_investment_act_in_eight_states.pdf (accessed July 13, 2010).

Barnow, Burt S., and Jeffrey Smith. 2004. "Performance Management of U.S. Job Training Programs: Lessons from the Job Training Partnership Act." *Public Finance and Management* 4(3): 247–287.

Blalock, Ann B., and Burt S. Barnow. 2001. "Is the New Obsession with 'Performance Management' Masking the Truth about Social Programs?" In *Quicker, Better Cheaper? Managing Performance in American Gov-*

ernment, Dall Forsythe, ed. Albany, NY: Rockefeller Institute Press, pp. 487–519.

Courty, Pascal, and Gerald Marschke. 2004. "An Empirical Investigation of Gaming Responses to Explicit Performance Incentives." *Journal of Labor Economics* 22(1): 22–56.

Dickinson, Katherine, Richard W. West, Deborah J. Kogan, David A. Drury, Marlene S. Franks, Laura Schlictmann, and Mary Vencill. 1988. *Evaluation of the Effects of JTPA Performance Standards on Clients, Services, and Costs*. Research Report No. 88-15. Washington, DC: National Commission for Employment Policy.

Government Accountability Office (GAO). 1982. "An Overview of the WIN Program: Its Objectives, Accomplishments, and Problems." GAO/HRD-82-55. Washington, DC: GAO.

———. 2002. "Workforce Investment Act: Improvements Needed in Performance Measures to Provide a More Accurate Picture of WIA's Effectiveness." GAO-02-275. Washington, DC: GAO.

Heckman, James J., Carolyn Heinrich, and Jeffrey Smith. 2002. "The Performance of Performance Standards." *Journal of Human Resources* 37(4): 778–811.

Heckman, James J., and Jeffrey Smith. 1999. "The Pre-Programme Dip and the Determinants of Participation in a Social Programme: Implications for Simple Programme Evelation Strategies." *Economic Journal* 109(457): 313–348.

———. 2004. "The Determinants of Participation in a Social Program: Evidence from JTPA." *Journal of Labor Economics* 22(2): 243–298.

Heckman, James J., Jeffrey Smith, and Christopher Taber. 1996. "What Do Bureaucrats Do? The Effects of Performance Standards and Bureaucratic Preferences on Acceptance into the JTPA Program." In *Advances in the Study of Entrepreneurship, Innovation and Economic Growth*, Vol. 7, Gary Libecap, ed. Greenwich, CT: JAI Press, pp. 191–218.

Job Training Partnership Act Advisory Committee. 1989. *Human Capital: JTPA Investments for the 90's*. Washington, DC: U.S. Department of Labor.

Kemple, James, Fred Doolittle, and John Wallace. 1993. *The National JTPA Study: Site Characteristics and Participation Patterns*. New York: Manpower Demonstration Research Corporation.

Marschke, Gerald. 2002. "Performance Incentives and Bureaucratic Behavior: Evidence from a Federal Bureaucracy." Department of Economics Discussion Paper 02-07. Albany, NY: University at Albany, SUNY.

Radin, Beryl. 2006. *Challenging the Performance Movement*. Washington, DC: Georgetown University Press.

Schochet, Peter Z., and John A. Burghardt. 2008. "Do Job Corps Performance

Measures Track Program Impacts?" *Journal of Policy Analysis and Management* 27(3): 556–576.

Social Policy Research Associates. 1999. *Guide to JTPA Performance Standards for Program Years 1998 and 1999.* Menlo Park, CA: Social Policy Research Associates.

———. 2004. *The Workforce Investment Act after Five Years: Results from the National Evaluation of the Implementation of WIA.* Oakland, CA: Social Policy Research Associates.

U.S. Department of Labor (USDOL). 2002. *Summary Report on WIA Implementation.* Washington, DC: Employment and Training Administration.

Zornitsky, Jeffrey, Mary Rubin, Stephen Bell, and William Martin. 1988. *Establishing a Performance Management System for Targeted Welfare Programs.* National Commission for Employment Policy Research Report 88-14. Washington, DC: National Commission for Employment Policy.

9
Recent Advances in Performance Measurement of Federal Workforce Development Programs

Randall W. Eberts
Timothy J. Bartik
Wei-Jang Huang
W.E. Upjohn Institute for Employment Research

The purpose of performance measurement is to enable federal, state, and local workforce agencies to track the progress of program participants in achieving the core goals of programs under WIA: finding a job, retaining a job, and receiving adequate earnings. Performance measures are also used to hold management accountable for the effectiveness of the services delivered to help participants achieve those goals. The ETA has established three measures to capture these three goals for adult and youth programs: 1) entered employment, 2) job retention, and 3) earnings levels. Each state negotiates with the USDOL to set state targets, and the states in turn negotiate with each of the roughly 600 local Workforce Investment Boards (WIBs) to determine local performance targets.

As this practice of setting standards evolved over the past decade, states and WIBs increasingly found that negotiations were not taking into account factors that affected their performance but were beyond their control and not related to the services they provided. These factors include the conditions of the local labor market and the personal characteristics and work history of participants in their programs. Without accounting for differences in these factors across states and across WIBs, those entities with more favorable labor market conditions or more capable participants are likely to have higher outcomes, and those for which these factors are unfavorable can expect lower outcomes. Differences in these outcomes are not the result of how well service providers have met the needs of their customers, but of factors outside their control and extraneous to the effectiveness of their service delivery. Therefore, the measures are not fulfilling their intent of measuring the value added of the workforce system, and may even distort decisions by administrators of whom to enroll in workforce programs.

In response to these concerns about the measurement and setting of performance goals, the ETA has contracted with the W.E. Upjohn Institute for Employment Research to adjust national performance targets for differences (actual and forecasted) in unemployment rates. To make adjustments, the Institute estimated the relationship between individual participants' performance outcomes and local unemployment rates. These adjustments are incorporated in President Obama's annual budget request and the national performance targets.[1]

In addition, the ETA, through the help of the Upjohn Institute, is exploring procedures to adjust state and local WIA performance targets for factors that affect performance outcomes but are outside the control of state and local administrators. This procedure provides a systematic, transparent, and objective method to set WIA performance targets; it helps to level the playing field by making the targets neutral with respect to the observed characteristics of WIA participants and of the local labor market conditions in which they seek employment. It also provides a more accurate measure of the value added of WIA programs at both state and local levels by controlling for observed factors that affect outcomes but are unrelated to the services provided by the workforce development system.

The purpose of this chapter is to describe the two procedures of adjusting performance targets for economic conditions and personal characteristics. The first procedure adjusts the national performance targets for changes in unemployment rate, and the second adjusts state and local performance targets for differences in local market conditions and personal characteristics. The contribution of both sets of factors is estimated using one general model that relates performance outcomes (the common measures) to unemployment rates and personal attributes. The chapter is divided into two major parts. The first part describes the general methodology and then provides estimates of these effects for each of the common measures for each of the three WIA programs. The second part demonstrates how these estimates can be used to adjust performance outcomes at the national and state levels for differences in these factors.

ACCOUNTING FOR DIFFERENCES IN LABOR MARKET CONDITIONS AND PERSONAL ATTRIBUTES

Adjusting for differences in labor market conditions and personal characteristics is not new for the workforce system programs. WIA's immediate predecessor, JTPA, used statistical analysis to adjust performance targets for a list of factors which were deemed outside the control of administrators. The adjustment procedure that the ETA has adopted to adjust national performance measures and that the ETA is considering to adjust state and local performance targets is similar in many respects to what was followed under JTPA.[2] For each program and performance measure, a state's targets are set according to the extent to which the values of participant characteristics and of local labor market measures at the state level differ from those at the national level. The difference for each factor is weighted by each factor's contribution to the respective performance outcome. The summation of the weighted differences constitutes the adjustment factor. Adding the adjustment factor to the national target yields the adjusted performance target for each state. Consequently, under this procedure, a state serving a hard-to-serve population would be given a lower performance standard than a state serving a less hard-to-serve population, all else the same. Although the targets for these two states are set at different levels, it presumably takes the same level of effort on the part of each state to meet their respective standards. Thus, local administrators are not penalized for serving a harder-to-employ group of participants. The major differences between this procedure and that used under JTPA are the way in which the weights are estimated and the consistent framework that allows the local workforce investment areas (LWIAs) and state targets to add up to the national target. JTPA adjustments were based on data aggregated at the local workforce board level; the current procedure is based initially on the outcomes of individual participants of the workforce programs, as they search for employment within their local labor markets.

METHODOLOGY AND RESULTS

The study derives direct estimates of the effects of unemployment rates on performance measures for various programs using detailed data of WIA participants.[3] As a result, the estimates capture actual relationships between changes in unemployment rates and performance. Estimates are based on the experience of individual participants in the local labor markets in which they are searching for employment. Using data at the local level provides a much stronger correspondence between the labor market outcomes of program participants and the economic conditions they are facing. As data become more aggregated, such as at the state or national level, the alignment weakens, since the economic conditions of local labor markets vary widely from the state and national averages. The conditions faced by individuals looking for work in Detroit, Michigan, are much different from those seeking employment in Grand Rapids, Michigan, just as the conditions are much different, on average, for individuals in Illinois versus those in Texas. Using individual participant data also provides the ability to control for differences in the demographic characteristics of individuals. To isolate the effects of unemployment rates on performance, it would be ideal to place an identical person in each of the labor markets to observe his or her outcomes. Controlling for differences in educational attainment, prior employment history, and perceived barriers to employment through statistical means moves the analysis closer to that ideal situation. The data used to estimate these relationships are obtained from the WIA Standardized Record Data (WIASRD). Data are obtained quarterly from the years 2000–2008. The exact length of time depends upon the program and performance measure.

Estimation methodology

Separate estimates are obtained for the following programs within WIA: Adult, Dislocated Worker, and Youth. Estimates of the effect of unemployment rates on performance measures are robust across the various programs and appear reasonable in the magnitude of their impact. Results reveal a negative relationship between unemployment rates and both entered employment rate and retention rate, which are statistically significant. For these two performance measures, estimates range from a reduction of 1.0 percentage point to a reduction of 1.8 percentage points for an increase of a 1.0-percentage-point change in unemployment rates. This can be interpreted in the following way: an estimate of −1.8 means that a 1.0-percentage-point change in the unemployment rate, say, from 6 percent to 7 percent, is expected to reduce the entered employment rate by 1.8 percentage points. If the entered employment rate was 70 percent at an unemployment rate of 6 percent, then an increase in the unemployment rate from 6 to 7 percent would lower the expected entered employment rate from 70.0 percent to 68.2 percent.[4]

Estimates of the relationship between program outcomes and business cycles were conducted at the local labor market level, as defined by the Workforce Investment Board (WIB) service area. A separate model is estimated for each performance measure in each program. The estimation equation is written generally as

(9.1) $Y_{isq} = B_0 + B_1 * X_{isq} + B_2 * D_{sq} + \text{error term,}$

where Y is the outcome variable for individual i in WIBs (counties) in year-quarter q, X denotes the person's individual attributes, and D is the local unemployment rate in WIBs (counties) during year-quarter q. B represents the estimated coefficients.

Of specific interest is the estimated coefficient B_2, which shows the statistical relationship between unemployment rates (D) and the performance-related outcomes (Y). In order to account for the possibility that the effects are not contemporaneous, we tested several lag structures. We settled on a lag structure that enters the unemployment rates in the quarter in which the performance target is recorded. For example, retention rate is measured the second and third quarter after exit. Therefore, for the estimation of the effect of unemployment rates on retention rates, we entered the unemployment rates that corresponded with the second and third quarters after exit for each individual. In addition, since retention represents a change in status from holding a job to not holding one, we used the change in unemployment rates from quarter to quarter to reflect the changing labor market conditions on keeping a job. For the average earnings measure, which is defined as the earnings in the second and third quarters after exit, the unemployment rates are entered for those two quarters plus the first quarter after exit, since the participant had to be employed the first quarter to be counted in this measure.[5] For the "credentials and employment" performance measure, the effects over four quarters (from the quarter of exit through the third quarter after exit) are used to estimate the effect of unemployment rates. Therefore, for performance measures that span more than one quarter, the full effect of unemployment rates on the measure is computed by adding the coefficients on the unemployment rates for each relevant quarter. The statistical significance is estimated using a t-test for the combined effects of the relevant coefficients.[6]

The dependent variable is a dichotomous variable that takes on the value of 1 if the outcome is achieved and 0 if not. For example, entered employment is defined as having positive earnings in the first quarter after exit. The dependent variable takes a value of 1 for individuals for whom positive earnings are observed in their wage record for that quarter, and 0 otherwise. Thus, the samples include two types of outcomes—1 or 0—and not a continuous range of percentages. Therefore, the effect of unemployment rates on entered employment is estimated as the effect of unemployment rates on the probability of finding employment (e.g., achieving a 1). Aggregating the effects across the sample of individuals included in the analysis translates the results from the effect on the probability of getting a job to the effect on the percentage of people entering employment, which is the performance measure for the WIA system.

In addition to the unemployment rate as an explanatory variable in the estimation equation, individual characteristics of participants, as denoted by the Xs, are also included in the equation. These variables include measures of education, age, race/ethnicity, disability, gender, and employment history prior to registration. Most of these variables are entered as categorical variables. Since characteristics affect the performance measures and these characteristics may change over a business cycle, it is important to control for these variables in order to isolate the net effect of business cycles on performance.

For simplicity and ease of computation, the models are estimated using linear probability models, even when the dependent variable is a 0-1 variable.[7] Logit and probit estimation techniques are generally recommended for estimating equations with 0-1 dependent variables. However, using logit or probit makes it more difficult to interpret results and creates some complexities in calculating adjustments. For example, because logit and probit are nonlinear models, the adjustment factor cannot be calculated using sample means of local areas but rather requires calculating probabilities for all observations using the full set of data. Econometricians have shown that the drawbacks of linear probability models, compared with logit and probit techniques, may be minimal.[8] A fixed-effects model is estimated by including 0-1 variables for each of the WIBs. The fixed-effects model controls for idiosyncratic differences between each of the units (e.g., WIBs or states). By including these 0-1 variables, the estimation captures the response of program participants to changes in unemployment rates over time and not the long-run differences across local labor markets (as represented by WIB service areas or states). This response to short-run changes in unemployment rates over time is the response we are trying to predict during the next few years, as the economy moves through this business cycle.

Zero-one variables indicating the year and quarter are also included to control for national time trends. Zero-one variables indicating the quarter (regardless of year) are entered to capture seasonal variation in the performance measures that may be due to regular occurrences throughout the year, such as shopping patterns and plant closings to retool for new products.[9]

Although the database includes tens of thousands of participants (generating variation in the dependent variable), the unemployment rate varies only at the WIB level. Therefore, in all cases, more than one individual participant experiences the same unemployment rate at the same time in the same local labor market. In addition, because these individuals are within one labor market (one grouping of individuals), there may be intragroup correlation. With the possible presence of intragroup correlation and fewer relevant observations (than the total), the typical computation of standard errors of the coefficients may be biased. To correct for this we use cluster sandwich estimators, a standard procedure in the statistical analysis package that we employ.[10] However, we do not take into consideration the possibility of spatial correlation between the geographical units, which could arise from interregional linkages of industries (supply chains) and household commuting patterns.

Data sources and variable definitions

For the WIA programs, participant outcomes and attributes are derived from the WIASRD. This allows us to consider the program outcomes from the third quarter of 2000 (which is the beginning of PY2001) to the most recent data available, third quarter 2007.

The variable definitions, taken directly from WIASRD, are displayed in Appendix 9A (see Social Policy Research Associates [2008]). WIASRD includes for each WIA participant a host of personal characteristics, employment outcomes, and educational outcomes (e.g., credentials and attainment of degree or certification). It also includes a selected set of services received through the workforce programs and participation in other non-WIA programs, such as cash assistance and unemployment insurance.

Unemployment rates were collected monthly at either the WIB level or the county level from the first quarter of 2000 to the first quarter of 2008. During that time, the national unemployment rates varied from 4.0 (2000) to 6.0 (2003) on an annual basis and from 3.6 (October 2000) to 6.5 (January and June 2003) on a seasonally unadjusted monthly basis. It was not until December 2008 that the monthly seasonally unadjusted unemployment rate exceeded the rates posted during 2003. However, this variation at the national level does not reflect the breadth of experience in local labor conditions across the thousands of counties and the hundreds of WIBs. During that time, unemployment rates among counties with total employment of more than 100,000 ranged from 1.1 to 14.9 percent, as shown in Figure 9.1.[11] Therefore, despite the relatively tight band of unemployment rates at the national level, the estimates of the effect of unemployment rates on labor market outcomes of program participants are based on a broad range of unemployment rates and occur at levels that are more than double what we experienced in the recent deep recession.

ESTIMATION

Each performance measure for each WIA program was estimated by separate regressions. The equations are similar with respect to the explanatory variables included, except for the way in which the unemployment variables are entered. The full results are reported by major program. For the sake of brevity, the results for the WIA Adult program

Figure 9.1 Range of Unemployment Rates for All U.S. Counties, 2000–2008 Quarterly

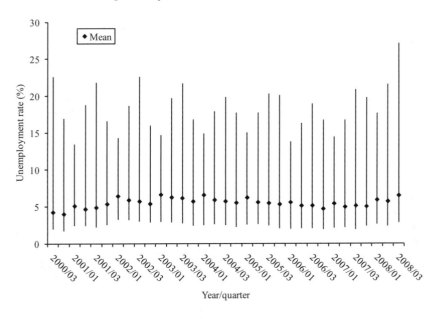

NOTE: The bold dot is the median unemployment rate for all counties for each quarter.
SOURCE: Bureau of Labor Statistics, various years.

are explained in detail and the results from the other two programs are displayed in Appendix 9B.[12]

Four performance measures are included in the analysis for the WIA Adult worker program. The means and standard deviations of the variables are displayed in Table 9.1 for each of the performance measures. The reason for the slight difference in sample statistics is that the performance measure definitions do not include the same participants. This is due to the number of quarters of earnings required to construct the performance measure, and to the definitions themselves. For example, entered employment and retention are computed from different groups of individuals, for several reasons. Entered employment requires that the participant not have worked at the time of registration; retention includes both those who worked and those who did not work. Retention requires wage record information for two quarters after exit; entered

Table 9.1 Means and Standard Deviations of Variables Used in WIA Adult Estimation

| | WIA Adult | | | |
	Entered employment	Retention	Average earnings	Credential and employment
Dependent	0.762	0.838	11,643	0.534
variable	(0.426)	(0.369)	(8,306)	(0.499)
female	0.554	0.573	0.586	0.571
	(0.497)	(0.495)	(0.493)	(0.495)
black_female	0.191	0.188	0.190	0.193
	(0.393)	(0.391)	(0.392)	(0.394)
age20				
age21				
age26_35	0.288	0.300	0.303	0.300
	(0.453)	(0.458)	(0.459)	(0.458)
age36_45	0.249	0.245	0.245	0.244
	(0.432)	(0.430)	(0.430)	(0.430)
age46_55	0.158	0.147	0.148	0.143
	(0.365)	(0.354)	(0.355)	(0.350)
age56_65	0.049	0.043	0.041	0.043
	(0.217)	(0.202)	(0.199)	(0.202)
agegt65	0.007	0.005	0.004	0.005
	(0.083)	(0.068)	(0.063)	(0.073)
hispanic	0.229	0.224	0.226	0.215
	(0.420)	(0.417)	(0.418)	(0.411)
asian	0.036	0.035	0.037	0.037
	(0.186)	(0.184)	(0.188)	(0.188)
black	0.342	0.317	0.308	0.326
	(0.475)	(0.465)	(0.462)	(0.469)
hi_pacific	0.003	0.003	0.003	0.003
	(0.052)	(0.054)	(0.055)	(0.056)
indian	0.006	0.007	0.006	0.008
	(0.080)	(0.081)	(0.079)	(0.088)
multi	0.015	0.013	0.013	0.008
	(0.123)	(0.114)	(0.113)	(0.088)
lths	0.178	0.150	0.137	0.159
	(0.382)	(0.357)	(0.343)	(0.366)
ba	0.067	0.070	0.073	0.063
	(0.250)	(0.254)	(0.260)	(0.243)
beyondba	0.016	0.016	0.016	0.015
	(0.126)	(0.125)	(0.126)	(0.120)

Table 9.1 (continued)

| | WIA Adult | | | |
	Entered employment	Retention	Average earnings	Credential and employment
somecoll	0.176	0.193	0.200	0.180
	(0.381)	(0.395)	(0.400)	(0.384)
ged	0.064	0.061	0.057	0.065
	(0.245)	(0.240)	(0.232)	(0.247)
cert	0.000	0.000	0.000	0.000
	(0.019)	(0.016)	(0.015)	(0.014)
otherpostdegcert	0.008	0.007	0.007	0.003
	(0.088)	(0.081)	(0.083)	(0.053)
assoc	0.013	0.011	0.012	0.006
	(0.115)	(0.103)	(0.107)	(0.075)
disabled	0.118	0.118	0.115	0.095
	(0.323)	(0.323)	(0.319)	(0.294)
veteran	0.071	0.064	0.062	0.062
	(0.256)	(0.245)	(0.241)	(0.242)
empreg11	0.452	0.550	0.586	0.513
	(0.498)	(0.498)	(0.493)	(0.500)
empreg10	0.076	0.074	0.070	0.073
	(0.264)	(0.261)	(0.256)	(0.260)
empreg01	0.091	0.081	0.078	0.082
	(0.288)	(0.273)	(0.268)	(0.274)
wp	0.363	0.343	0.349	0.261
	(0.481)	(0.475)	(0.477)	(0.439)
exit_wib_ur				6.294
				(2.096)
f1_wib_ur	6.182		6.052	6.360
	1.989		(1.951)	(2.085)
f2_wib_ur			6.045	
			(1.974)	
f3_wib_ur			6.009	
			(1.985)	
diff12		0.000		
		(0.819)		
diff23		−0.034		
		(0.794)		
N	429,329	400,523	310,066	395,240

SOURCE: WIASRD and Bureau of Labor Statistics.

employment requires such information for only one quarter after exit. Thus, retention cannot be computed at the same time as entered employment for the same set of individuals, since the second-quarter earnings have not yet been determined.

Estimates of the factors that are expected to affect the four performance measures are displayed in Table 9.2. Most of the coefficients are statistically significant and have the expected sign, including the unemployment rates. For example, the estimated relationship between entered employment and unemployment rates is −0.018. An estimate of −0.018 means that a 1.0-percentage-point change in the unemployment rate—say, from 6 percent to 7 percent—is expected to reduce the entered employment rate by 0.018 percentage points. If the entered employment rate was 0.70 (the dependent variable is measured as a rate [0.70], not as a percentage [70.0 percent]) at an unemployment rate of 6 percent, then an increase of the unemployment rate from 6 to 7 percent would lower the expected entered employment rate from 0.70 to 0.682. If the unemployment rate doubled, then the entered employment rate would fall by −0.036 points (2 × −0.018).

A similar relationship is found for retention. In this case the unemployment rate is entered as a change from one quarter to the next, as indicated by the variables diff12, the change in unemployment rates from the first quarter after exit to the second quarter after exit, and diff23, the change in unemployment rates from the second quarter after exit to the third quarter after exit. Since the performance measure for retention spans two quarters, the full effect of unemployment rates is estimated by adding together the two coefficients. The sum of the two coefficients is shown at the bottom of the table along with the t-test result that the combined estimate is different from zero. For retention, unemployment rates have a negative and statistically significant effect, reducing the retention rate by nearly one point.

For average earnings, the effect of unemployment rates is derived by adding the coefficients associated with the three quarters of unemployment rates, f1_wib_ur, f2_wib_ur, and f3_wib_ur. The total effect is a reduction of $266 on an average base of $11,643. The estimate is statistically significant.

The credentials and employment performance measure follows a similar pattern but exhibits a larger effect from an increase in unemployment rates than was found for the other performance measures. In this

Table 9.2 Estimates of the Effect of Unemployment Rates and Other Factors on the WIA Adult Program Performance Measures

	(1) Entered employment	(2) Retention	(3) Average earnings	(4) Credential and employment
female	0.000542	0.0167***	−2653.4***	−0.0218***
	(0.25)	(9.22)	(−23.27)	(−6.95)
black_female	0.0157***	0.0252***	1484.3***	0.0184***
	(4.65)	(7.29)	(19.04)	(3.95)
age26_35	−0.00345	0.00948***	1456.8***	0.0116***
	(−1.53)	(5.53)	(34.75)	(4.29)
age36_45	0.0137***	0.00743***	1744.9***	0.00128
	(−5.13)	(3.60)	(26.52)	(0.33)
age46_55	−0.0330***	0.00619*	1605.6***	−0.0140**
	(−10.54)	(2.20)	(13.53)	(−3.00)
age56_65	−0.0854***	−0.0194***	513.9**	−0.0447***
	(−19.55)	(−4.95)	(2.86)	(−6.29)
agegt65	−0.202***	−0.0806***	−3229.4***	−0.0832***
	(−18.28)	(−7.45)	(−13.43)	(−5.59)
hispanic	0.0205***	0.0136***	−1312.7***	−0.0289***
	(8.22)	(6.05)	(−15.44)	(−4.62)
asian	0.0193**	0.0388***	−608.7***	0.0266*
	(3.24)	(10.33)	(−4.47)	(2.27)
black	−0.0283***	−0.0394***	−3344.9***	−0.0657***
	(−9.15)	(−12.81)	(−33.34)	(−10.47)
hi_pacific	0.0267*	0.0263*	−401.6	0.0120
	(2.03)	(2.39)	(−1.42)	(0.85)
indian	−0.0491***	−0.0274***	−712.7***	−0.0350***
	(−5.67)	(−3.62)	(−3.84)	(−3.71)
multi	−0.0130*	−0.0167**	−1942.5***	−0.00650
	(−2.04)	(−2.65)	(−10.42)	(−0.56)
lths	−0.0488***	−0.0505***	−1483.8***	−0.0436***
	(−12.09)	(−21.96)	(−26.86)	(−13.40)
ba	0.0218***	0.0258***	4164.5***	−0.0153
	(6.37)	(10.19)	(34.74)	(−1.63)
beyondba	0.0123*	0.0113*	6665.3***	−0.0348***
	(2.06)	(2.29)	(18.76)	(−4.31)

(continued)

Table 9.2 (continued)

	(1) Entered employment	(2) Retention	(3) Average earnings	(4) Credential and employment
somecoll	0.0130***	0.0139***	1675.5***	0.00334
	(5.55)	(8.53)	(29.57)	(1.05)
ged	−0.0195***	−0.0398***	−877.9***	−0.0153**
	(−6.41)	(−14.97)	(−11.47)	(−2.94)
cert	−0.0239	−0.0436	−1412.7	0.000824
	(−0.62)	(−0.90)	(−1.86)	(0.02)
otherpostdegcert	−0.0282*	0.0174*	3159.2***	0.0428
	(−2.10)	(2.55)	(10.03)	(0.85)
assoc	0.00414	0.0191**	1516.7***	−0.0699***
	(0.62)	(3.23)	(8.06)	(-5.29)
disabled	−0.0960***	−0.0291***	−1918.2***	−0.0351***
	(−17.39)	(−8.24)	(−20.71)	(−5.99)
veteran	−0.00735	−0.0139***	155.6	0.00302
	(−1.80)	(−4.15)	(1.06)	(0.60)
empreg11	0.140***	0.0868***	1563.6***	0.0322***
	(44.64)	(46.36)	(31.33)	(11.04)
empreg10	0.0740***	0.0226***	−160.2**	−0.00419
	(23.43)	(8.57)	(−3.02)	(−1.34)
empreg01	0.0690***	0.0260***	263.2***	0.00622*
	(23.42)	(10.26)	(4.19)	(1.96)
wp	0.00671	0.00510	−72.24	−0.0232***
	(1.57)	(1.66)	(−0.71)	(−3.52)
exit_wib_ur				−0.000246
				(−0.05)
f1_wib_ur	−0.0180***		−111.0	−0.0114
	(−5.75)		(−1.71)	(−1.90)
f2_wib_ur			−104.2	−0.00645
			(−1.63)	(−1.11)
f3_wib_ur			−50.41	−0.0170**
			(−0.83)	(−2.81)
diff12		−0.00417**		
		(−3.22)		
diff23		−0.00347**		
		(−2.81)		

Table 9.2 (continued)

	(1) Entered employment	(2) Retention	(3) Average earnings	(4) Credential and employment
_cons	0.860***	0.760***	11,108.5***	0.687***
	(31.43)	(30.88)	(19.99)	(10.83)
N	429,329	400,523	310,066	395,240
adj. R^2	0.073	0.035	0.198	0.275
Combined unemployment rate	−0.0180***	−0.008**	−265.7**	−0.352***
Effect	(−5.75)	(−3.98)	(3.16)	(−4.51)

NOTE: t-statistics are in parentheses. Asterisks indicate statistical significance in which $p < 0.05$ (*), $p < 0.01$ (**), and $p < 0.001$ (***). Year-quarter time dummy variables, quarter time dummy variables, and WIB dummy variables are also included in the estimation, but, to conserve space, the coefficient estimates are not shown.
SOURCE: Authors' analysis of WIASRD data and Bureau of Labor Statistics unemployment rates.

case, a 1.0-percentage-point increase in unemployment rates reduces the rate of attaining credentials and employment by 0.036 points. The estimate is obtained by summing the coefficients over four quarters: exit_wib_ur (the quarter of exit) through f3_wib_ur (the third quarter after exit). The estimate of the combined effect is statistically significant. With the mean rate of credentialing and employment at 0.53, this effect results in a 6.6 percent reduction in that performance measure.

The estimated relationships between participant characteristics and performance measures offer a broad perspective on the ability of participants with different backgrounds and employment barriers to achieve the outcomes defined by the performance measures. For example, the results suggest that participants who are black, older, disabled, have less than a high school education, and have an inconsistent work history are less likely to find and retain employment. For those who do find work, they earn less and find it more difficult to attain credentials and employment. The single largest positive effect on all four performance measures is a person's past employment history. Individuals who have positive earnings for both quarters before registration are much more successful in finding and retaining a job and in obtaining higher earnings than those with no prior employment during that period. For example, a person with prior employment in those two quarters experienced an entered employment rate that was 0.14 points higher than someone without employment during that same period, holding all other characteristics constant. If the entered employment rate is 0.70 for those without prior employment, the rate for those with prior employment is 0.84—a sizable difference. Furthermore, we find that 45 percent of the participants in the entered employment group have two quarters of prior employment.

The largest negative effect relates to older workers. Participants older than 65 are far less likely to find a job than those in the 18–25 age range. However, very few participants fall into the over-65 age range.

PERFORMANCE ADJUSTMENT PROCEDURES

Adjusting National Performance Targets

Using the estimates reported in the previous section, performance targets for each of these programs are adjusted by the estimated effects of the change in unemployment rate from year to year. The unemployment rate assumptions of the President's FY 2010 Budget Request are used in the calculations. The calculations start in PY 2007 (FY 2007 for Trade Adjustment Assistance [TAA]) and extend through PY 2014. The actual performance rate was used as the base in PY 2007. The adjusted target for the following year was calculated by multiplying the previous year's performance target by the change in unemployment rates times the appropriate estimate of the effect of the unemployment rate change on the performance measure. This adjustment factor is then added to the previous target.

Using the WIA Adult entered employment rate as an example, the calculation for PY 2008 is

$$EER_{(PY\,2008)} = EER_{(PY\,2007)} + EER_{(PY\,2007)} \times (-1.8/76.2) \times (UR_{PY\,2008} - UR_{PY\,2007}).$$

The estimated effects are converted into percentage changes ($-1.8/76.2$ in this case) so that their effect is proportional to the magnitude of the target, which varies by program. Repeating this procedure each year thereafter yields the entered employment performance targets for the WIA Adult program, as shown in Table 9.3. This procedure is also used to adjust performance targets for retention and earnings levels.

Displaying the adjusted performance targets along with the unemployment rate assumptions, Figure 9.2 shows how the targets adjust with changes in the unemployment rates. As the unemployment rate assumptions increase from PY 2007 to PY 2008, the adjusted target declines, reflecting the experience (as estimated in the analysis) that it is more difficult to find a job in tougher economic times. As the unemployment rate assumptions begin to fall after PY 2009, the performance targets gradually increase but do not return to their PY 2007 levels because the unemployment rate assumption remains slightly higher in PY 2014 than in the base period of PY 2007. Notice that the GPRA targets are considerably higher than the adjusted targets throughout this period.

Figures 9.3 and 9.4 show similar patterns for the other two adjusted performance measures because they are all driven by the unemployment rate assumptions. The only difference among the three measures in the change from year to year is related to the weights derived from the estimates, which are different for each performance measure.

Adjusting State Performance Targets

The second step uses the national adjusted target as the departure point for setting state performance targets. A state's ability to meet the national target depends upon the effectiveness of its services as well as the characteristics of its participants and the labor market conditions, both relative to the national average. Therefore, a state's target should be adjusted by the weighted difference in participant characteristics and labor market conditions. The weights are the contribution of each factor to participant outcomes. States with participants who have characteristics more favorable to finding and retaining jobs will be expected to achieve higher rates of entered employment and retention, and the adjustment procedure raises the targets for these measures accordingly. Such characteristics that lead to higher performance levels are higher educational attainment, more work experience, and younger in age, to name a few. States whose participants are less likely to have these attributes will be less likely to achieve such high performance levels and the procedure lowers targets accordingly.

Table 9.3 Example of Adjustment Procedure for WIA Adult Program

WIA Adult program	Program year							
	2007	2008	2009	2010	2011	2012	2013	2014
UR assumptions (%)	4.9	7.2	8.1	7.6	6.6	5.5	5.0	5.0
Entered employment (%)								
GPRA target	70.0	70	70	70	71	72	73	
Unemployment rate adjusted target		66.2	64.8	65.6	67.1	68.8	69.7	69.7
Retention rate (%)								
GPRA target	84.0	84.0	84.0	84.0	85.0	86.0	87.0	
Unemployment rate adjusted target		81.7	80.8	81.3	82.3	83.3	83.8	83.8
Earnings ($)								
GPRA target	13,575	13,575	13,575	13,575	13,914	14,262	14,619	
Unemployment rate adjusted target		12,862	12,597	12,741	13,032	13,360	13,512	13,512

NOTE: GPRA = Government Performance and Results Act.

SOURCE: Unemployment rate assumptions are from the President's FY 2010 Budget Request, GPRA targets are based on published guidance from the Office of Management and Budget, and unemployment rate–adjusted targets are derived from the analysis.

Figure 9.2 WIA Adult Entered Employment Performance Adjustment

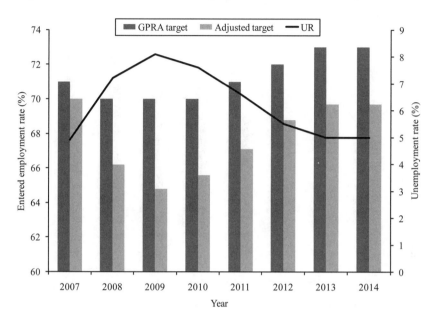

SOURCE: Unemployment rate assumptions are from the President's FY 2010 Budget Request, GRPA targets are based on published guidance from the Office of Management and Budget, and unemployment rate–adjusted targets are derived from the analysis.

Thus, using the adjusted target rather than an unadjusted target offers a better measure of the value added of a state's WIA program. Without the adjustment, a state may be credited with higher value added when in fact the difference between actual performance and the unadjusted target was due to factors that were outside the control of the state and local administrators and so happened to be favorable to the outcomes. Conversely, state performance outcomes may fall short of their targets not because of their value added but because of the unfavorable attributes or local labor market conditions that they have experienced. To emphasize the point, it is conceivable that two states with identical value added, in terms of the effectiveness of their programs to the participants they serve, may have entirely different outcomes relative to an unadjusted target for the reasons just described. Adjusting

Figure 9.3 WIA Adult Retention Rate Performance Adjustment

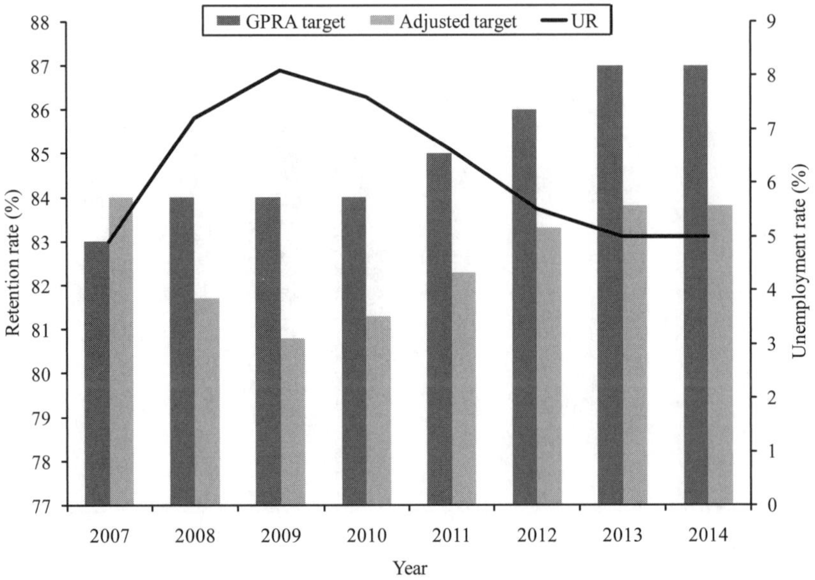

SOURCE: Unemployment rate assumptions are from the President's FY 2010 Budget Request, GPRA targets are based on published guidance from the Office of Management and Budget, and unemployment rate–adjusted targets are derived from the analysis.

the targets reduces this misrepresentation of a state's performance and provides a more systematic, objective way to scrutinize the reasons for the differences.

The key elements for computing state performance targets are displayed in the worksheet in Table 9.4. To illustrate the steps required to calculate the adjusted performance targets, only a few of the factors actually used to calculate performance targets are displayed in the table. The full set of variables is listed in Appendix 9B. Adjusting state performance targets requires three elements: 1) the state value for each factor (column A); 2) the national value for each factor (column B); and 3) the estimated weights for each factor (column D). The difference in the national and state values (column C) is multiplied by the weight (column E). The weighted differences are summed and added to the national adjusted target.

Figure 9.4 WIA Adult Earnings Level Performance Adjustment

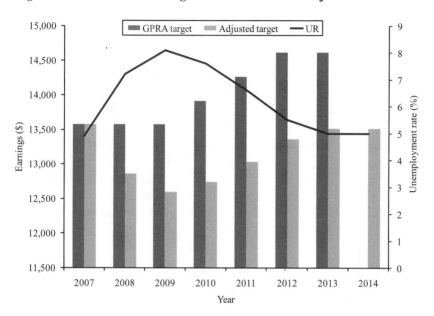

SOURCE: Unemployment rate assumptions are from the President's FY 2010 Budget Request, GPRA targets are based on published guidance from the Office of Management and Budget, and unemployment rate–adjusted targets are derived from the analysis.

To fill out the worksheet, the state will need information about each characteristic for the program year at both the state level and the national level. Obviously, the characteristics of the exiters are not available prior to the beginning of the program year. The most recent data can be used when they become available. At the beginning of the program year, the most recent data are from the previous program year. The actual date of availability depends upon the performance measure. Table 9.5 summarizes the data availability from the WIASRD as of May 2009. Using WIASRD has the advantage of a consistent data set for all three levels: nation, state, and LWIA. To avoid surprises, the adjustments should be updated whenever new data are available. This was the method used under JTPA. Under that program, the actual end-of-year performance standards were not computed until the end-of-year data were finally available.

Table 9.4 Hypothetical Example of Computing Adjusted Performance Target for State A

WIA Adult entered employment (%)	State A	National	Difference (A−B)	Effect on EE	Adjustment: weighted difference (C × D)
Unemployment rates	12.6	8.3	+4.3	−1.8	−7.74
High school dropout	10.3	4.6	+5.7	−0.049	−0.279
BA degree	7.6	1.8	+5.8	+0.022	+0.128
Disabled	6.4	4.9	+1.5	−0.096	−0.144
Work experience	39.0	64.0	−25.0	+0.14	−3.50
			Total adjustment (add column E)		−11.5%
			Adjusted national EE rate		64.8%
			Adjusted performance target for State A		53.3%

NOTE: For purposes of illustration, only a few of the many factors included in the estimation are displayed in the table. The actual state adjustments shown in Table 9.6 include all variables used in the regressions.

Table 9.5 Data Requirements and Availability as of May 2009

		PY07 (7/1/07–6/30/08)	PY08 (7/1/08–6/30/09)	PY09 (7/1/09–6/30/10)
Unemployment rates	National	Actual	Actual (3 qtrs.)	Assumed
	State	Actual	Actual (3 qtrs.)	N/A: S/N Diff
	WIB	Actual	Actual (3 qtrs.)	N/A: W/S Diff
Personal characteristics	National	W07 (1st qtr.)	N/A: W07	N/A: W07
	State	W07 (1st qtr.)	N/A: W07	N/A: S/N Diff
	WIB	W07 (1st qtr.)	N/A: W07	N/A: S/N Diff

NOTE: W07 denotes PY 2007 data from WIASRD; N/A indicates that current data are not available for that program year; the data source after the N/A indicates the suggested source; S/N Diff indicates that historical differences between a state and the nation will be used; W/S Diff indicates that historical differences between a WIB and its state nation will be used.

Table 9.6 displays the actual, negotiated, and adjusted performance measures for entered employment for the Adult WIA program for PY 2006. PY 2006 is the latest year for which complete data are available from WIASRD. The adjusted performance targets are calculated using the characteristics displayed in Table 9A.1. We find that the difference between the actual level and the adjusted performance target has a wider spread between the maximum difference and the minimum than the difference between the negotiated target and the actual performance level. However, the number of states in which the target is greater or less than the actual level is the same for the negotiated level and the adjusted level.

Adjusting Performance Targets at the Local WIB Level

The third step follows the same procedure as the second, except that it is for each local WIB instead of each state. The reference point is the state and the differences in characteristics are between the state and each local WIB. The same weights are used for local WIB performance target calculations as for the state performance target calculations. By using the same weights for each approach and the same weights as for the state and national performance adjustments, all targets from the WIB to the state to the nation easily add up. If the data come from different data sources, for whatever reason, then targets will not add up. Also, if different weights are estimated for each state (or even for each ETA administrative region), the targets will not add up.

SUMMARY

The procedure for adjusting performance targets at the national, state, and local levels provides a systematic, transparent, and objective way to set national, state, and WIB performance targets for WIA programs. Using the same information that is collected and compiled for WIA performance monitoring along with measures of local labor market conditions, targets can be adjusted for factors that are outside the control of state and local administrators. The adjustment factors, since they relate to factors that are familiar and understandable to administra-

Table 9.6 Comparison of Actual, Negotiated, and Adjusted Performance Measures for Entered Employment in the Adult WIA Program, PY 2006

State	ETA report Negotiated level	ETA report Actual level	Negotiated minus actual	Adjusted target	Adjusted target minus actual
Nation	79.2	70.2	9.0	79.2	9.0
Alabama	73.0	71.3	1.7	79.6	8.3
Alaska	74.0	72.2	1.8	74.7	2.5
Arkansas	89.0	92.0	−3.0	80.2	−11.8
Arizona	76.0	81.6	−5.6	79.2	−2.4
California	74.0	79.3	−5.3	76.6	−2.7
Colorado	82.0	82.6	−0.6	78.6	−4.0
Connecticut	79.0	80.5	−1.5	79.5	−1.0
DC	68.5	77.5	−9.0	66.4	−11.1
Delaware	82.0	82.4	−0.4	81.3	−1.1
Florida	71.0	82.9	−11.9	83.3	0.4
Georgia	84.0	76.1	7.9	78.6	2.5
Hawaii	76.0	71.9	4.1	84.2	12.3
Idaho	87.0	96.5	−9.5	81.5	−15.0
Iowa	83.0	79.0	4.0	78.7	−0.3
Illinois	75.0	77.3	−2.3	77.0	−0.3
Indiana	82.0	86.8	−4.8	79.5	−7.3
Kansas	76.0	82.1	−6.1	81.4	−0.7
Kentucky	78.0	88.7	−10.7	77.4	−11.3
Louisiana	82.0	67.4	14.6	77.1	9.7
Maine	88.0	72.2	15.8	80.2	8.0
Maryland	91.0	78.3	12.7	81.5	3.2
Massachusetts	79.0	79.7	−0.7	77.5	−2.2
Michigan	85.0	86.2	−1.2	74.8	−11.4
Minnesota	86.0	87.5	−1.5	80.6	−6.9
Missouri	80.0	88.6	−8.6	78.7	−9.9
Mississippi	77.0	62.4	14.6	74.9	12.5
Montana	82.0	85.6	−3.6	82.4	−3.2
Nebraska	86.0	78.2	7.8	81.2	3.0
Nevada	76.0	77.5	−1.5	79.1	1.6

Table 9.6 (continued)

State	ETA report Negotiated level	ETA report Actual level	Negotiated minus actual	Adjusted target	Adjusted target minus actual
New Hampshire	80.0	69.2	10.8	80.8	11.6
New Jersey	82.0	83.7	−1.7	80.6	−3.1
New Mexico	78.0	84.5	−6.5	80.4	−4.1
New York	65.0	62.1	2.9	80.2	18.1
North Carolina	80.0	75.9	4.1	78.5	2.6
North Dakota	74.5	75.8	−1.3	80.2	4.4
Ohio	75.0	79.4	−4.4	77.5	−1.9
Oklahoma	85.0	71.1	13.9	82.3	11.2
Oregon	83.0	85.6	−2.6	79.5	−6.1
Pennsylvania	82.5	76.3	6.2	80.1	3.8
Puerto Rico	78.0	91.0	−13.0	66.2	−24.8
Rhode Island	82.0	81.7	0.3	78.1	−3.6
South Carolina	83.0	80.4	2.6	76.6	−3.8
South Dakota	78.0	80.6	−2.6	79.8	−0.8
Tennessee	83.0	84.2	−1.2	80.9	−3.3
Texas	82.0	75.1	6.9	80.2	5.1
Utah	66.0	66.6	−0.6	80.2	13.6
Vermont	83.0	77.3	5.7	75.2	−2.1
Virginia	77.5	78.0	−0.5	80.6	2.6
Washington	81.8	81.5	0.3	78.9	−2.6
West Virginia	80.0	72.2	7.8	80.2	8.0
Wisconsin	74.0	76.8	−2.8	78.8	2.0
Wyoming	89.0	81.7	7.3	77.8	−3.9
			min	−13.0	−24.8
			max	15.8	18.1
			mean	0.7	−0.1
			#Target>Actual	23	23
			#Target<Actual	30	30

SOURCE: Authors' calculations and ETA annual performance reports.

tors, can be easily scrutinized by all parties in order to better understand how they affect their programs' outcomes and what might happen if they change. For example, the effects on performance of a mass layoff event triggering a spike in a WIB's unemployment rate or an influx of disadvantaged workers with lower educational attainment can be assessed by using this procedure. The adjusted performance targets also provide a more accurate measure of the value added of the WIA programs.

Notes

The first part of this chapter was extracted from Bartik, Eberts, and Huang (2009). The assistance of Wei-Jang Huang and Phyllis Molhoek is greatly appreciated.

1. The USDOL's Employment and Training Administration issued Training and Employment Guidance Letter 09-08 Change 1 on June 5, 2009. This guidance letter revises the Government Performance and Results Act performance measures for federal workforce development programs to take into account the effect of the recession on participants' labor market and educational outcomes. As described in the guidance letter, the performance targets of the various workforce development programs have been developed for use for the years PY 2008 through PY 2010. They are intended to be used for PY 2009 performance target negotiations and are included in the President's Budget Request for FY 2010.
2. For a detailed description of the JTPA adjustment procedures, see Social Policy Research Associates (1999).
3. Adjustments in performance targets were estimated and computed for all 13 federal workforce development programs, including WIA, Wagner-Peyser Employment Service, and Trade Adjustment Assistance programs.
4. For the analysis, the performance measures are expressed as rates, not percentages. That means that instead of entered employment being expressed as 70 percent, for example, we express it as 0.70. The explanatory variables are also expressed as rates. However, for the performance adjustment calculations, we follow the standard approach of the USDOL and describe the performance targets in percentage terms.
5. Retention rate is also contingent on being employed the first quarter after exit, but since it is capturing the ability to retain a job, we looked at the change from quarter to quarter, encompassing the first three quarters after exit.
6. We also explored whether or not the unemployment rate exerts different effects on performance measures depending upon the magnitude of the unemployment rate. That is, we addressed the possibility that unemployment rates might have a nonlinear effect on performance measures. We introduced this possibility by specifying unemployment rates in two different ways. First, we entered unemployment rates as a quadratic, and second, we entered unemployment rates as

a set of categorical variables, each capturing different ranges of unemployment rates. In both cases, we could not reject the fact that unemployment rates have a linear effect on performance measures. Therefore, a 1.0-percentage-point change in unemployment rates produces the same point change in performance measures (or dollar change in earnings) no matter the level of unemployment rates.

7. Two problems associated with the linear probability model are heteroscedasticity and the predicted values extending beyond the limits of 0 and 1.

8. Wooldridge (2002) states in his textbook that the linear probability model "often seems to give good estimates of the partial effects on the response probability near the center of the distribution of x" (p. 455). He adds that "if the main purpose is to estimate the partial effect of x on the response probability, averaged across the distribution of x, then the fact that some predicted values are outside the unit interval may not be very important" (p. 455). In order to test the sensitivity in the estimates when using a linear probability model instead of the preferred logit estimation technique, we ran both techniques for entered employment and retention performance measures for the WIA Adult program. Our particular focus was on the coefficient estimates related to unemployment rates. We found that the two techniques yielded virtually identical estimates. Using the linear probability model, the estimated coefficient on the unemployment rate for entered employment was -0.018 with a t-statistic of -5.75; using the logit technique, the estimated coefficient was -0.0178 with a z-statistic of -5.66. For the retention rate, the combined estimated coefficient on the unemployment rates was -0.0076 using the linear probability technique and -0.0075 using the logit technique. Therefore, these results help to assuage concerns about the linear probability approach yielding biased estimates, and they are consistent with the position expressed by Wooldridge and others.

9. A reviewer of the draft suggested that we consider the possibility of spatial dependence in the estimation. This could arise for several reasons and as a consequence may bias the estimate or affect the statistical significance of the coefficient estimates. Spatial dependence basically recognizes that some local labor markets may be interdependent because of linkages among regions. These linkages could be due to commuting patterns, commodity flows, or similarity in industrial or occupational mix in that they compete regionally or nationally for workers with similar qualifications. Spatial dependence is a complex issue with no straightforward approach, since different regions across the country may be related in different ways. Therefore, we do not attempt to address this issue in the analysis and have no clear intuition whether it may bias the estimates or by how much.

10. We use STATA to estimate the model. The procedure to calculate standard errors is found in Rogers (1993).

11. In our sample, 102 counties had total employment that surpassed 100,000 at any time during the period considered in the analysis.

12. The estimates described in this section and in Appendix 9B are derived from a sample of 11 of the largest U.S. states. These estimates were used to adjust national targets, which were included in the President's 2010 Budget Request. A sample of states was used because of the need to derive estimates quickly in order to meet the deadline of submitting the president's budget. Since then, we have reestimated

the models including all states and Puerto Rico. The results are qualitatively the same, and these estimates are used for the state target adjustments, shown in the next section.

Appendix 9A

Variable Definitions

Table 9A.1 Dependent Variable Description

Dependent variable	Description of coding
Entered employment	= 1 if participant is employed (positive earnings) in the first quarter after exit and was not employed at registration
Retention	= 1 if participant is employed (positive earnings) in the first quarter after exit and in both the second and third quarters after exit
Average earnings	Summation of earnings in the second and third quarter after exit for those employed in those quarters plus the first quarter
Credential and employment (adult)	= 1 if attained a credential after exit and employment in the first quarter after exit
Credential or employment (youth)	= 1 if participant entered postsecondary education, advanced training, military service, or a qualified apprenticeship or entered employment the first quarter after exit
Attainment of degree or certificate	= 1 if participant entered postsecondary education, advanced training, or military service on or before the third quarter after exit
Literacy and numeracy gain (youth)	= 1 if there is at least one posttest with a functioning level greater than the corresponding pretest function level and the pretest function level was between 0 and 6

SOURCE: Definition of variables as described in WIASRD public use document, selected years.

Table 9A.2 Explanatory Variable Definitions

Explanatory variables	Description of coding
female	= 1 if participant is female, 0 otherwise.
black_female	= 1 if participant is female and black.
age26_35	= 1 if participant is between the ages of 26 and 35.
age36_45	= 1 if participant is between the ages of 36 and 45.
age46_55	= 1 if participant is between the ages of 46 and 55.
age56_65	= 1 if participant is between the ages of 56 and 65.
agegt65	= 1 if participant is over the age of 65.
hispanic	= 1 if participant indicates that he/she is a person of Cuban, Mexican, Puerto Rican, South or Central American, or other Spanish culture in origin, regardless of race.
asian	= 1 if participant's origin is any of the original peoples of the Far East, Southeast Asia, India, etc.
black	= 1 if participant indicates that he/she is a person having origins in any of the black racial groups of Africa.
hi_pacific	= 1 if participant indicates that he/she is a person having origins in any of the original peoples of Hawaii or other Pacific Islands.
indian	= 1 if participant indicates that he/she is a person having origins in any of the original peoples of North and South America and who maintains cultural identification through tribal affiliation or community recognition.
multi-racial	= 1 if participant indicates more than one ethnic/race category, except Hispanic.
white	= 1 if participant indicates that he/she is a person having origins in any of the original peoples of Europe, the Middle East, or North Africa.
lths	= 1 if participant completed no or some elementary/ secondary school grades and did not receive a high school diploma or GED.
highschool	= 1 if participant indicates that he/she attained a high school diploma.
ba	= 1 if participant indicates that he/she received a bachelor's degree or equivalent.
beyondba	= 1 if participant indicates that he/she received a degree beyond a bachelor's degree, such as a master's, PhD, or professional degree.

Table 9A.2 (continued)

Explanatory variables	Description of coding
somecoll	= 1 if participant indicates the he/she completed some college but did not receive a degree.
ged	= 1 if participant indicates that he/she attained a GED or equivalent.
cert	= 1 if participant indicates that he/she attained a certificate of completion or attendance.
otherpostdegcert	= 1 if participant indicates that he/she attained other postsecondary degree or certification.
assoc	= 1 if participant indicates that he/she attained an associate's diploma or degree.
disabled	= 1 if participant indicates that he/she has any disability, such as a physical or mental impairment that substantially limits one or more of the person's life activities, as defined in the Americans with Disabilities Act of 1990.
veteran	= 1 if participant served in the active U.S. military and was released with other than a dishonorable discharge, or if participant was a spouse of any U.S. military personnel who died or is missing in action, was forcibly detained, or has a total permanent disability.
empreg11	= 1 if participant is employed (positive wage record quarterly earnings) in both the second and third quarters before registration.
wp	= 1 if participant is coenrolled in ES (for those in WIA programs).
empreg10	= 1 if participant is employed (positive wage record quarterly earnings) in second quarter but not third quarter before registration.
empreg01	= 1 if participant is employed (positive wage record quarterly earnings) in the third but not the second quarter before registration.
unemp	The unemployment rate by WIB or county by quarter entered as a percentage (e.g., 6.5).

SOURCE: Definition of variables as described in WIASRD public use document, selected years, and as defined and derived by the authors using the WIASRD variables.

Appendix 9B

Estimation Results for WIA Dislocated Workers and Youth Programs

DISLOCATED WORKER PROGRAM

The results for the WIA Dislocated Worker program, shown in Table 9B.2, yield patterns of effects similar to those found for the Adult WIA program, shown in Table 9.2. Unemployment rates have a negative and statistically significant effect on all four performance measures. The magnitude of the effects is slightly smaller than that found for the WIA Adult program participants but is in the same general range. For example, a 1.0-percentage-point increase in unemployment rates lowers the entered employment rate by 0.008 points, compared with 0.018 points for the Adult WIA program participants. As seen in Table 9.6, which displays the mean characteristics of the Dislocated Worker participants, dislocated workers are better educated and more strongly attached to the workforce. These traits may explain their ability to weather economic downturns a little better. As with the WIA Adult program, prior employment and age exhibited the largest effects on the performance measures.

Older Youth

Results for the WIA Older Youth program are in the range of estimates established by the two previously described programs. The means and standard deviations of the variables used in the estimation are displayed in Table 9B.3. Unemployment rates negatively affect the four performance measures, but they are found to be statistically significant only for entered employment, as shown in Table 9B.4. As with the two adult programs, prior employment history has the largest effect on the four performance measures, increasing significantly the likelihood of finding and retaining a job and of holding a job with higher earnings. Unlike the two adult programs, age is not a large factor, but education is important. Those without a high school degree—nearly half the participants—are at a significant disadvantage in their employment prospects.

Table 9B.1 Means and Standard Deviations of Variables Used in the Estimation of WIA Dislocated Worker Program

	WIA Dislocated Worker			
	Entered employment	Retention	Average earnings	Employment and credential
Dependent variable	0.822	0.887	14,328	0.563
	(0.383)	(0.317)	(9434)	(0.496)
female	0.514	0.513	0.518	0.505
	(0.500)	(0.500)	(0.500)	(0.500)
black_female	0.119	0.117	0.119	0.115
	(0.323)	(0.322)	(0.323)	(0.320)
age20				
age21				
age26_35	0.232	0.240	0.242	0.243
	(0.422)	(0.427)	(0.428)	(0.429)
age36_45	0.319	0.326	0.329	0.327
	(0.466)	(0.469)	(0.470)	(0.469)
age46_55	0.277	0.275	0.274	0.267
	(0.447)	(0.446)	(0.446)	(0.443)
age56_65	0.090	0.077	0.073	0.080
	(0.286)	(0.267)	(0.261)	(0.271)
agegt65	0.007	0.004	0.004	0.006
	(0.085)	(0.066)	(0.060)	(0.076)
hispanic	0.207	0.206	0.206	0.196
	(0.405)	(0.404)	(0.405)	(0.397)
asian	0.048	0.045	0.045	0.050
	(0.213)	(0.207)	(0.207)	(0.219)
black	0.205	0.200	0.200	0.201
	(0.403)	(0.400)	(0.400)	(0.401)
hi_pacific	0.002	0.002	0.002	0.003
	(0.049)	(0.049)	(0.048)	(0.050)
indian	0.005	0.005	0.005	0.005
	(0.070)	(0.069)	(0.069)	(0.072)
multi	0.009	0.009	0.009	0.006
	(0.096)	(0.095)	(0.094)	(0.076)
lths	0.109	0.105	0.101	0.102
	(0.312)	(0.306)	(0.302)	(0.303)
ba	0.120	0.117	0.116	0.118
	(0.325)	(0.321)	(0.321)	(0.323)
beyondba	0.033	0.031	0.030	0.033
	(0.180)	(0.172)	(0.170)	(0.178)

Table 9B.1 (continued)

| | WIA Dislocated Worker | | | |
	Entered employment	Retention	Average earnings	Employment and credential
somecoll	0.229	0.231	0.232	0.235
	(0.420)	(0.422)	(0.422)	(0.424)
ged	0.043	0.044	0.043	0.044
	(0.203)	(0.204)	(0.204)	(0.205)
cert	0.000	0.000	0.000	0.000
	(0.012)	(0.012)	(0.012)	(0.009)
otherpostdegcert	0.005	0.005	0.005	0.002
	(0.071)	(0.071)	(0.072)	(0.050)
assoc	0.015	0.014	0.014	0.007
	(0.123)	(0.116)	(0.116)	(0.086)
disabled	0.101	0.110	0.109	0.083
	(0.302)	(0.313)	(0.312)	(0.276)
veteran	0.086	0.086	0.084	0.088
	(0.281)	(0.281)	(0.278)	(0.283)
empreg11	0.742	0.755	0.767	0.736
	(0.437)	(0.430)	(0.423)	(0.441)
empreg10	0.039	0.039	0.037	0.037
	(0.193)	(0.193)	(0.188)	(0.190)
empreg01	0.067	0.064	0.062	0.068
	(0.251)	(0.244)	(0.241)	(0.253)
wp	0.348	0.340	0.342	0.259
	(0.476)	(0.474)	(0.474)	(0.438)
exit_wib_ur				6.119
				(1.924)
f1_wib_ur	5.970		5.953	6.160
	(1.863)		(1.816)	(1.919)
f2_wib_ur			5.969	
			(1.824)	
f3_wib_ur			5.942	
			(1.835)	
diff12		0.021		
		(0.804)		
diff23		−0.026		
		(0.802)		
N	408,234	322,098	266,915	311,452

SOURCE: WIASRD and Bureau of Labor Statistics.

Table 9B.2 Estimates of the Effect of Unemployment Rates and Other Factors on the WIA Dislocated Worker Program Performance Measures

	(1) Entered employment	(2) Retention	(3) Average earnings	(4) Credentials/ employment
female	−0.00392*	0.00634***	−3861.5***	−0.0352***
	(−2.25)	(4.76)	(−65.96)	(−15.05)
black_female	0.0189***	0.0118***	1649.4***	−0.00344
	(5.31)	(4.04)	(19.73)	(−0.78)
age26_35	0.000243	0.0119***	1707.8***	0.0187***
	(0.10)	(4.97)	(30.08)	(4.61)
age36_45	−0.00823**	0.0137***	2154.0***	0.0106*
	(−3.13)	(5.86)	(35.81)	(2.51)
age46_55	−0.0224***	0.00710**	1622.9***	−0.00374
	(−8.12)	(2.91)	(24.73)	(−0.82)
age56_65	−0.108***	−0.0227***	13.06	−0.0311***
	(−28.92)	(−6.86)	(0.14)	(−5.86)
agegt65	−0.277***	−0.110***	−4181.1***	−0.0712***
	(−26.83)	(−9.41)	(−15.90)	(−6.30)
hispanic	0.0213***	0.00549**	−1572.8***	−0.0160***
	(9.60)	(2.66)	(−22.69)	(−4.19)
asian	−0.0258***	0.00709*	−540.2***	0.0164*
	(−7.29)	(2.16)	(−4.30)	(2.15)
black	−0.00603*	−0.0179***	−3526.8***	−0.0253***
	(−1.98)	(−7.09)	(−38.06)	(−5.26)
hi_pacific	−0.00205	0.0146	−671.8	−0.0281
	(−0.18)	(1.20)	(−1.85)	(−1.78)
indian	−0.0341***	−0.0112	−1004.8***	−0.0271*
	(−3.72)	(−1.31)	(−4.38)	(−2.11)
multi	0.00438	−0.0139	−1770.1***	−0.00960
	(0.48)	(−1.87)	(−9.24)	(−0.83)
lths	−0.0323***	−0.0252***	−1618.0***	−0.0381***
	(−13.08)	(−10.52)	(−31.68)	(−9.11)
ba	−0.00127	0.0000558	5115.2***	−0.0222***
	(−0.58)	(0.03)	(58.41)	(−4.83)
beyondba	−0.0261***	−0.0120**	9812.3***	−0.0308***
	(−6.70)	(−3.26)	(41.70)	(−3.93)

Table 9B.2 (continued)

	(1) Entered employment	(2) Retention	(3) Average earnings	(4) Credentials/ employment
somecoll	−0.00249	−0.00144	1440.9***	−0.00821**
	(−1.65)	(−1.02)	(33.68)	(−3.17)
ged	−0.00297	−0.0159***	−517.3***	−0.000521
	(−0.92)	(−5.60)	(−7.39)	(−0.09)
cert	−0.0413	0.0437	−496.2	−0.0369
	(−0.86)	(1.06)	(−0.56)	(−0.34)
otherpostdegcert	−0.0119	0.00390	3429.9***	0.00300
	(−1.40)	(0.45)	(9.35)	(0.11)
assoc	−0.0265***	−0.00393	2086.3***	−0.0357**
	(−4.27)	(−0.73)	(7.96)	(−3.25)
disabled	−0.0532***	−0.0281***	−1332.8***	−0.0412***
	(−11.74)	(−6.93)	(−10.80)	(−4.85)
veteran	−0.0103***	−0.0114***	181.8*	−0.00298
	(−4.42)	(−5.20)	(2.57)	(−0.92)
empreg11	0.0743***	0.0434***	745.4***	0.0145***
	(24.08)	(20.43)	(12.92)	(3.68)
empreg10	0.0560***	0.00356	−107.2	0.00791
	(13.19)	(0.95)	(−0.99)	(1.41)
empreg01	0.0293***	0.0110***	−4.378	−0.00896
	(7.68)	(3.49)	(−0.05)	(−1.79)
wp	0.0142***	−0.000527	−74.17	0.0155**
	(3.86)	(−0.26)	(−0.89)	(2.72)
exit_wib_ur				−0.00169
				(−0.37)
f1_wib_ur	−0.00983***		28.42	−0.00484
	(−3.63)		(0.48)	(−0.89)
f2_wib_ur			−166.7*	−0.00391
			(−2.33)	(−0.76)
f3_wib_ur			14.97	−0.00643
			(0.29)	(−1.13)
diff12		−0.00582***		
		(−4.65)		
diff23		−0.00429***		
		(−3.39)		

(continued)

Table 9B.2 (continued)

	(1) Entered employment	(2) Retention	(3) Average earnings	(4) Credentials/ employment
_cons	0.876***	0.806***	14682.2***	0.668***
	(27.17)	(34.71)	(25.92)	(9.55)
N	408,234	322,098	266,915	311,452
adj. R^2	0.058	0.019	0.196	0.210
Combined UR	−0.00983***	−0.010***	−123.33**	−0.017**
Effect	(−3.63)	(−5.16)	(−2.34)	(−2.55)

NOTE: Asterisks indicate statistical significance in which $p < 0.05$ (*), $p < 0.01$ (**), and $p < 0.001$ (***). Year-quarter time dummy variables, quarter time dummy variables, and WIB dummy variables are also included in the estimation, but, to conserve space, the coefficient estimates are not shown.

SOURCE: Authors' analysis of WIASRD data and BLS unemployment rates.

Table 9B.3 Means and Standard Deviations of Variables used in the Estimation of the WIA Older Youth Program

	Older Youth			
	Entered employment	Retention	Average earnings	Employment and credential
Dependent variable	0.727	0.811	6970	0.582
	(0.445)	(0.392)	(5,300)	(0.493)
female	0.591	0.603	0.618	0.593
	(0.492)	(0.489)	(0.486)	(0.491)
black_female	0.252	0.247	0.246	0.247
	(0.434)	(0.432)	(0.431)	(0.431)
age20	0.320	0.324	0.322	0.320
	(0.467)	(0.468)	(0.467)	(0.467)
age21	0.227	0.237	0.243	0.228
	(0.419)	(0.425)	(0.429)	(0.420)
hispanic	0.306	0.311	0.330	0.298
	(0.461)	(0.463)	(0.470)	(0.457)
asian	0.026	0.024	0.023	0.028
	(0.159)	(0.152)	(0.151)	(0.164)
black	0.416	0.392	0.377	0.405
	(0.493)	(0.488)	(0.485)	(0.491)
hi_pacific	0.003	0.003	0.004	0.004
	(0.058)	(0.057)	(0.060)	(0.060)
indian	0.006	0.006	0.005	0.007
	(0.080)	(0.076)	(0.074)	(0.081)
multi	0.010	0.010	0.009	0.009
	(0.100)	(0.100)	(0.096)	(0.096)
lths	0.472	0.409	0.366	0.457
	(0.499)	(0.492)	(0.482)	(0.498)
ba	0.001	0.002	0.002	0.002
	(0.037)	(0.042)	(0.044)	(0.041)
beyondba	0.000	0.001	0.000	0.001
	(0.018)	(0.024)	(0.022)	(0.023)
somecoll	0.044	0.058	0.068	0.046
	(0.205)	(0.234)	(0.251)	(0.210)
ged	0.037	0.041	0.039	0.036
	(0.189)	(0.197)	(0.194)	(0.187)
cert	0.002	0.001	0.001	0.002
	(0.041)	(0.036)	(0.036)	(0.041)

(continued)

Table 9B.3 (continued)

| | Older Youth | | | |
	Entered employment	Retention	Average earnings	Employment and credential
otherpostdegcert	0.001	0.002	0.002	0.000
	(0.032)	(0.042)	(0.048)	(0.020)
assoc	0.000	0.001	0.001	0.000
	(0.020)	(0.027)	(0.028)	(0.013)
disabled	0.165	0.160	0.155	0.165
	(0.371)	(0.367)	(0.362)	(0.371)
veteran	0.004	0.005	0.005	0.005
	(0.064)	(0.070)	(0.073)	(0.068)
empreg11	0.323	0.407	0.454	0.350
	(0.467)	(0.491)	(0.498)	(0.477)
empreg10	0.104	0.108	0.106	0.104
	(0.305)	(0.310)	(0.308)	(0.305)
empreg01	0.108	0.104	0.102	0.103
	(0.310)	(0.305)	(0.303)	(0.304)
wp	0.292	0.288	0.297	0.260
	(0.455)	(0.453)	(0.457)	(0.438)
exit_wib_ur				6.392
				(2.195)
f1_wib_ur	6.386		6.306	6.428
	(2.171)		(2.166)	(2.200)
f2_wib_ur			6.313	
			(2.195)	
f3_wib_ur			6.293	
			(2.209)	
diff12		0.012		
		(0.858)		
diff23		−0.019		
		(0.853)		
N	73,488	57,610	38,657	80,326

SOURCE: WIASRD and Bureau of Labor Statistics.

Table 9B.4   Estimates of the Effect of Unemployment Rates and Other Factors on WIA Older Youth Program Performance Measures

	(1) Entered employment	(2) Retention	(3) Average earnings	(4) Credentials/ employment
female	−0.0269***	−0.00582	−839.3***	0.0268***
	(−6.15)	(−1.40)	(−10.98)	(5.43)
black_female	0.0470***	0.0173*	314.6**	−0.00203
	(6.86)	(2.44)	(2.73)	(−0.27)
age20	−0.000806	−0.00692	330.4***	−0.00224
	(−0.21)	(−1.84)	(5.57)	(−0.59)
age21	0.000126	−0.00230	724.6***	0.00518
	(0.03)	(−0.57)	(10.44)	(1.20)
hispanic	0.0325***	0.0268***	271.8**	−0.00751
	(5.66)	(4.75)	(3.08)	(−1.17)
asian	0.00519	0.0251	−108.6	−0.00640
	(0.35)	(1.94)	(−0.58)	(−0.47)
black	−0.0468***	−0.0327***	−1155.0***	−0.0553***
	(−6.71)	(−4.75)	(−10.52)	(−7.46)
hi_pacific	0.000369	0.0168	−134.6	−0.00589
	(0.01)	(0.56)	(−0.39)	(−0.19)
indian	−0.0239	−0.0139	−281.7	−0.0561*
	(−1.11)	(−0.60)	(−0.62)	(−2.50)
multi	−0.0252	−0.0278	−550.0*	−0.0289
	(−1.64)	(−1.57)	(−2.28)	(−1.66)
lths	−0.100***	−0.0776***	−1,138.1***	−0.0203***
	(−24.61)	(−19.38)	(−17.56)	(−4.25)
ba	−0.00655	0.000401	3629.0***	0.0147
	(−0.19)	(0.01)	(4.23)	(0.49)
beyondba	0.0566	0.0215	3530.3*	−0.0000878
	(0.93)	(0.39)	(2.42)	(−0.00)
somecoll	0.0451***	0.0305***	1,273.4***	0.0327***
	(6.05)	(4.90)	(9.87)	(3.50)
ged	−0.0393***	−0.0442***	−708.0***	−0.0330***
	(−4.59)	(−5.34)	(−5.54)	(−3.32)
cert	−0.149**	−0.0510	−2384.9***	−0.0908*
	(−3.06)	(−0.93)	(−5.87)	(−2.03)
otherpostdegcert	0.0599	0.0712**	1700.5*	0.0303
	(1.64)	(3.12)	(2.06)	(0.34)

Table 9B.4 (continued)

	(1) Entered employment	(2) Retention	(3) Average earnings	(4) Credentials/ employment
assoc	0.0420	−0.0510	6731.1*	−0.0141
	(0.75)	(−0.80)	(2.23)	(−0.13)
disabled	−0.0740***	−0.000386	−1,291.5***	0.00578
	(−9.10)	(−0.06)	(−13.86)	(0.74)
veteran	0.0315	0.0356	512.6	−0.0156
	(1.33)	(1.82)	(1.37)	(−0.63)
empreg11	0.146***	0.0791***	833.1***	0.0170***
	(35.31)	(21.78)	(13.57)	(4.39)
empreg10	0.0872***	0.0275***	33.25	−0.00903
	(15.42)	(4.63)	(0.38)	(−1.64)
empreg01	0.0754***	0.0246***	50.53	0.00129
	(13.28)	(4.30)	(0.65)	(0.23)
wp	0.0394***	−0.0103*	−272.4**	0.0346***
	(5.66)	(−1.96)	(−3.04)	(3.67)
exit_wib_ur				−0.0231**
				(−2.85)
f1_wib_ur	−0.0174***		−50.38	0.00893
	(−4.91)		(−1.07)	(1.12)
f2_wib_ur			−43.49	−0.00977
			(−0.84)	(−1.24)
f3_wib_ur			−7.105	0.00902
			(−0.15)	(1.14)
diff12		−0.00400		
		(−1.57)		
diff23		−0.00213		
		(−0.87)		
_cons	0.732***	0.774***	7453.1***	0.398***
	(19.94)	(28.53)	(12.64)	(3.79)
N	73,488	57,610	38,657	80,326
adj. R^2	0.088	0.039	0.092	0.164
Combined UR	−0.0174***	−0.006	−101	−0.0142
Effect	(−4.91)	(−1.64)	(−1.87)	(−1.86)

NOTE: Asterisks indicate statistical significance in which $p < 0.05$ (*), $p < 0.01$ (**), and $p < 0.001$ (***). Year-quarter time dummy variables, quarter time dummy variables, and WIB dummy variables are also included in the estimation, but, to conserve space, the coefficient estimates are not shown.

SOURCE: Authors' analysis of WIASRD data and BLS unemployment rates.

References

Bartik, Timothy J., Randall W. Eberts, and Wei-Jang Huang. 2009. *Methodology for Adjusting GPRA Workforce Development Program Performance Targets for the Effects of Business Cycles*. Washington, DC: U.S. Department of Labor, Employment and Training Administration.

Rogers, W.H. 1993. "Regression Standard Errors in Clustered Samples." *Stata Technical Bulletin* 13: 19–23; reprinted in *Stata Technical Bulletin Reprints* 3: 88–94.

Social Policy Research Associates. 1999. *Guide to JTPA Performance Standards for Program Years 1998 and 1999*. Report prepared for the Office of Policy and Research, Employment and Training Administration, U.S. Department of Labor. Oakland, CA: Social Policy Research Associates.

———. 2008. *WIASRD Data File Public Use, Including Data Quality Revision, Record Layout, Selected Years*. Report prepared for the Office of Performance and Technology, Employment and Training Administration, U.S. Department of Labor. Oakland, CA: Social Policy Research Associates.

Wooldridge, Jeffrey M. 2002. *Econometric Analysis of Cross Section and Panel Data*. Cambridge, MA: MIT Press.

10
Financial Performance Incentives

Stephen A. Wandner
Urban Institute

Michael Wiseman
George Washington University

High performance incentive grants were incorporated into a number of domestic federal programs in the 1990s. Section 503 of WIA authorizes the Secretary of Labor to award incentive grants to states that exceed performance levels for programs authorized by Title I of WIA, the Adult Education and Family Literacy Act (AEFLA), and the Carl D. Perkins Vocational and Technical Education Act (Perkins). The WIA incentive process was designed with the intent to reward "good" performance by state government programs implementing workforce investment, adult literacy, and vocational education programs.

Financial incentives based on program performance also appeared in a number of other federal government programs around the same time. Domestic social programs such as Temporary Assistance for Needy Families (TANF) and the Food Stamp Program (FSP, since the beginning of the 2009 fiscal year called Supplemental Nutrition Assistance Program, or SNAP) have also used financial incentives to attempt to improve program performance. However, there is growing evidence that incentives may in some instances actually harm performance by rewarding behaviors that result from programs being more focused on receiving the reward than improving program design, delivery, and outcomes. Incentive programs raise many issues, including choice of how large funding should be and possible conflict between the use of bonuses and the ethos of public service.

This chapter examines high performance bonuses (HPBs) in WIA, TANF, and FSP/SNAP. It examines the design of the HPB programs, the issues that they raise, and lessons that have been learned from the experience of implementing and operating them. The chapter concludes that the HPBs have not worked as intended and that a different approach improving program performance should be used in the future for both the WIA program and TANF. On balance, the FSP/SNAP program looks better, but the objectives of the program make it easier to conduct.

WIA HPBs

WIA is a federal–state program.[1] The federal government provides grants to states to operate the programs, and the states pass most of these funds to local workforce investment boards. Workforce services are provided by about 3,000 One-Stop Career Centers that are located throughout the country. WIA programs provide core, intensive, and training services. Services may include job matching, labor market information, assessment and counseling, and other job search services, as well as training services. While all workers can receive core services, state workforce agencies determine which workers to serve beyond the core services and the mix of services target groups are to receive.

The WIA program was enacted for five years and expired in 2003. Since that time the program has been continued by Congress through the appropriation process. Unsuccessful proposals to reauthorize the program were introduced in 2003, 2005, and 2007. The program seems unlikely to be reauthorized before 2011 or 2012.

The Program

HPBs have been offered since the inception of the WIA system. States can receive bonuses for amounts between $750,000 and $3 million per year if they meet the WIA HPB criteria, depending on fund availability. The potential bonuses are of the same amount, regardless of the size of the state. To receive an HPB, a state must achieve at least 80 percent of the annual negotiated target for each of the 17 WIA performance measures that are specified by statute. They must also achieve an average of at least 100 percent of the negotiated performance targets for the major performance measures groupings for adult, dislocated worker, youth, and customer satisfaction measures.

The WIA program makes financial incentives available as a way to reward performance that exceeds the expected level of negotiated performance for participants in Title 1B of the WIA Adult, Dislocated Worker, and Youth programs. WIA law authorizes the states to use their incentive bonuses to carry out an innovative program consistent with the requirements of any one or more of the programs within Title I of WIA, the Adult Education and Family Literacy Act, or the Perkins Act. These provisions allow states great flexibility in using these funds, and the governors and state agencies are not limited to only one type of innovative program. States find this money attractive because it not only recognizes them for exceeding negotiated performance goals but also provides funds for special projects that might not otherwise be implemented due to budget limitations.

WIA financial incentives are complicated because they are a reward for meeting conditions for three separate programs. The annual awards are determined on the basis of WIA program performance in conjunction with performance for the Adult Education and Family Literacy Act and the Carl D. Perkins Vocational and Technical Education Act programs. States must meet the criteria established by each individual program before they are deemed eligible to apply for a grant. A state may demonstrate outstanding performance under WIA requirements but be removed from consideration for an award because it falls short with respect to program performance for literacy and/or Perkins education programs.

WIA HPBs are given for exceeding performance targets, which are set by negotiations led by USDOL regional office staff in the six USDOL regional offices for the USDOL national office. Regional staff members negotiate targets with the states based on factors that are considered to be under their control. If a state has higher unemployment levels or serves a more disadvantaged population, however, its performance targets should be adjusted downward to accommodate for these factors outside of their control. The negotiation process is intended to "level the playing field" between states, so that adjustments are made for differences between states with respect to anticipated economic and demographic characteristics.

Issues

Experience with the WIA HPB has drawn attention to a number of issues.

Behavioral issues in responding to WIA performance targets. Barnow and Smith (2004) review the incentives to state workforce agencies and local WIBs to take actions that can improve their WIA performance measurement results. Barnow and Smith examine four substantive behavioral measures that the WIA system can take:

1) selection of participants who are likely to have good performance outcomes (cream skimming),

2) selection of services and service mix provided to improve performance,

3) encouragement of workforce agency employees to work harder and smarter, and

4) provision of incentives to contractors and subcontractors providing services.

In addition, state workforce agencies can make strategic decisions about how to improve performance by "gaming" the system. In particular, under both JTPA and WIA, local and state performance outcomes could be improved by making determinations about who is formally enrolled in the program, and how and when enrollees are exited out of the program. For example, formal enrollment can be delayed until workers are placed in jobs or become employed. Exiting workers out of the program can be accelerated or delayed to maximize performance outcomes (Barnow and Smith 2004).

Jacobson (2009) documents the high cost of retaining WIA program participants in some localities until a time when their exiting is most beneficial for workforce agency performance measurement purposes. The cost of this extended retention of participants is the time it takes program staff to maintain periodic telephone contact with the WIA participants rather than providing them with additional employment services and, secondarily, that this behavior continues solely to improve measured program performance outcomes.

Thus, it appears that state workforce agencies have many tools at their disposal to improve their measured WIA program performance, if they wish to make use of them. A number of state workforce agencies and local WIBs do make use of these techniques.

Incentives for states. While the WIA HPBs are a small proportion of total WIA resources available to states, the incentive for states varies greatly because each state is eligible for the same bonus amount. Small states will find the HPB to be much larger in proportion to their state WIA formula grant than is the case for larger states.

Accuracy of the HPB data. Heinrich (2007) assesses whether the current HPBs work by looking at two questions. First, she examines the accuracy of the data used for the measures. Second, she assesses whether the performance award system properly recognizes and rewards high performing states. With respect to the first issue, her answer is affirmative: she finds that the data used by the system are reasonably accurate.

Does the HPB properly reward high performing states? With respect to the issue of whether the system properly recognizes high performers, Heinrich (2007) provides a negative answer for a number of reasons. As we saw above, a core factor in establishing an objective WIA performance targeting system is that the targets need to be set to establish a level playing field between states. Not surprisingly, she finds that the negotiation process—determined by USDOL regional staff without an objective methodology—does not properly take into consideration economic and demographic characteristics and service mix as they differ between states. In particular, she finds no adjustment to performance targets for differences with respect to education and race.

Heinrich finds that the negotiation process between regional and state staff establishes the bonus threshold and therefore plays a key role in the outcomes of HPBs. States that negotiate higher performance targets relative to other states are less likely to receive the bonuses. Thus, the negotiation process is crucial to success in obtaining an HPB.

Heinrich also looks at whether there has been a relationship between performance and the size of the bonus awarded. She again reaches a negative conclusion. She finds that some states not receiving a bonus appear to have performed better than those that did. States receiving higher bonuses did not necessarily perform better than those receiving low bonuses.

Declining Funding of WIA Incentive Grants, 1999–2007

The statutory provisions for the WIA HPB have not changed over time, so the HPB program specifications have been unchanged for over a decade. The only change in the program has been its funding amount. Because the USDOL has not sought appropriations for the HPB beginning in federal FY 2004 for federal PY 2003, funding availability has declined and has derived only from the Adult Education and Family Literacy Act and the Carl D. Perkins Vocational and Technical Education Act programs.

The USDOL started awarding incentive grants in 1999. The size of the grant awards is determined by WIA Section 503(c)(1), which sets the range of incentive grant awards from $750,000 to $3 million, depending upon the amount of appropriated funds available. If the amount available for grants is insufficient to award the minimum grant to each eligible state, the minimum and maximum grant amounts are adjusted by a uniform percentage as required by WIA Section 503(c)(2). For PY 1999 through PY 2002, the Department of Labor requested and received funding for the incentive grants, and state workforce agencies received funding from the department.

In its FY 2004 budget request, the USDOL did not request funds for WIA incentives. The Bush administration proposed revisions to the incentive grant process as part of its unsuccessful WIA reauthorization proposal of 2003. Had they been enacted, the new incentive grants awarded by the secretary would have been based on performance for statewide and local workforce programs authorized by Title I-B of WIA. The secretary would base the award on performance of states with respect to the performance measures, and/or the performance of the state in serving special populations (which could include the level of service and the outcomes and other appropriate factors).

In its FY 2005 budget submission, the USDOL requested $12 million to be awarded to states that successfully addressed barriers to employment of special populations (e.g., those with disabilities, individuals with limited English proficiency, homeless individuals, veterans, older Americans, and participants transitioning from welfare to work) and placed these individuals into good jobs. The department, however, did not propose a quantifiable way to measure delivery of services to these populations. The OMB denied the request for FY 2005 funds, and the USDOL has not requested incentive funds since then.

For PY 2006 only the Adult Education program provided funds for incentives. However, states were still required to meet the criteria established by all three programs in order to qualify. Thus, the amount of money available for incentives has been drastically reduced from a high of $29.8 million in 2001 to $9.8 million in FY 2007. The amount of the incentive grant for the PY 2006 performance awards was based on the size of the state's programs, as measured by the state's relative share of the combined Title I, AEFLA, and Perkins III formula grants awarded to that state.

For PY 2007, the Adult Education program was again the sole contributor to state incentive grants amid some changes to performance management and at a slightly lower funding level. In 2007, the Labor Department revised performance measurement requirements for determining eligibility of states for receiving incentive grants. In addition to changes to WIA performance reporting, the 2007 reauthorization of the Perkins Act removed the requirement that funds be reserved for WIA performance bonuses. Therefore, the Department of Education no longer sets aside Perkins Act funds for the purpose of funding incentive grants to states. The remaining funding is provided only by the Adult Education program, and 11 states were awarded incentive grants for a total of $9.76 million in 2007.

For PY 2008, USDOL guidance was issued based on state-negotiated performance levels that would have had an impact on states' eligibility to qualify for incentive grants. The Labor Department continued to facilitate the grant review and award process, and the Office of Adult Vocational Education within the Department of Education continued to fund these grants. In PY 2008, 10 states were awarded incentive grants, for a total of $9.76 million.

Variation in State and Regional Receipt of the WIA HPBs

The receipt of WIA financial incentives varies widely by state and by region (see Table 10.1). The variation is so great that it points toward exogenous influences on program performance such as fluctuations in economic conditions or changes in the demographics of state and local participants. These wide swings in program performance relative to

Table 10.1 WIA High Performance Bonuses: Eligible States and Funding Levels, PY 1999–2008

Program year/number of states eligible	Amount of incentive money available	Bonus range	Eligible states
1999/6	**$10,084,000** $2M from the USDOL $8.1M from the Dept. of Education	$843,351–$2,645,125	Florida, Indiana, Kentucky, Texas, Utah, Vermont
2000/12	**$27,580,600** $12M from the USDOL $15.5 M from the Dept. of Education	$750,000–$3,000,000	Connecticut, Florida, Idaho, Illinois, Indiana, Kentucky, Maine, Massachusetts, Michigan, North Dakota, Texas, Wisconsin
2001/16	**$29,760,422** $13.2M from the USDOL $16.5 M from the Dept. of Education	$750,000–$3,000,000	Colorado, Florida, Illinois, Kentucky, Louisiana, Maryland, Montana, Nebraska, North Dakota, Oklahoma, South Carolina, South Dakota, Tennessee, Texas, Washington, Wyoming
2002/23	**$24,422,000** $7.9M from the Dept. of Education $16.9M from the Dept. of Education	$750,000–$3,000,000	Alabama, Colorado, Florida, Georgia, Iowa, Illinois, Kentucky, Louisiana, Maryland, Michigan, Minnesota, Missouri, Mississippi, Montana, North Carolina, North Dakota, Nebraska, New Hampshire, Oklahoma, Oregon, South Dakota, Tennessee, Texas

2003/19	**$16,247,000** Funded by Dept. of Education (AEFLA & Perkins)	$772,770–$1,076,445	Alabama, Colorado, Delaware, Georgia, Iowa, Indiana, Louisiana, Maryland, Michigan, Minnesota, Missouri, Nebraska, Nevada, North Dakota, Oregon, Pennsylvania, South Carolina
2004/23	**$16,605,048** From the Dept. of Education (AEFLA & Perkins)	$646,569–$941,250	Arizona, Colorado, Connecticut, Delaware, Georgia, Illinois, Indiana, Iowa, Kentucky, Maryland, Massachusetts, Michigan, Minnesota, Nebraska, Nevada, North Dakota, Oklahoma, Oregon, Pennsylvania, South Carolina, Tennessee, West Virginia, Wisconsin
2005/10	**$16,353,187** From the Dept. of Education	$912,966–$3,000,000	Arizona, Delaware, Illinois, Iowa, Massachusetts, Missouri, Oregon, Tennessee, Virginia, Washington
2006/8	**$9,968,489** Funded by AEFLA only	$821,995–$2,148,397	Arizona, Connecticut, Illinois, Missouri, Montana, Ohio, South Carolina, South Dakota
2007/11	**$9,760,451** Funded by AEFLA only—no longer funded through the Carl D. Perkins Act	$761,088–$1,099,410	Florida, Illinois, Indiana, Iowa, Kansas, Kentucky, Minnesota, New York, North Carolina, Ohio, South Dakota
2008/10	**$9,760,450** Funded by AEFLA only	$784,251–$1,405,909	Colorado, Connecticut, Illinois, Iowa, Kentucky, Minnesota, Missouri, Nebraska, New York, Tennessee

annual targets could be minimized through objective methods of target setting accounting for external factors.

There has been a strong concentration in the distribution of incentive grants by state and region during the PY 1999 through PY 2007 period. During those nine years, states have been eligible for incentive awards 125 times. Five states in three regions were eligible for (and received) an incentive award five or more times since PY 1999 (see Table 10.2).

Thus, these 5 states have collectively received 31 awards, or nearly 25 percent of all awards. On the other hand, 9 states received no awards (Alaska, Arkansas, California, the District of Columbia, Hawaii, New Jersey, New Mexico, Puerto Rico, and Rhode Island), and 12 states have received only one award (Idaho, Kansas, Maine, New Hampshire, Nevada, New York, Pennsylvania, Utah, Virginia, Vermont, West Virginia, and Wyoming) through 2007.

There have been large differences among USDOL regions with respect to award eligibility. The 9 states in Region 1 (Connecticut, Massachusetts, Maine, New Hampshire, New Jersey, New York, Puerto Rico, Rhode Island, and Vermont) were eligible to receive 10 awards, or about 8 percent of all of the awards. At the other extreme, in Region 5 (Iowa, Illinois, Indiana, Kansas, Michigan, Minnesota, Missouri, Nebraska, Ohio, and Wisconsin), the 10 states were eligible for 37 awards, or about 30 percent of the total awards.

These regional variances, with awards concentrated heavily in some regions and not in others, suggest that there might be greater incentives or pressure in some regions for states to obtain awards than in others. As previously stated, there is no uniform method in place to adjust for differences among state economic and labor market environments, so when regions of states consistently achieve a significantly higher number of awards, there is a likelihood of strategic behavior in pursuit of these monetary awards.

Consequences

While establishing monetary incentive strategies was popular at the outset of the WIA program, this strategy has not proved to be an effective way to encourage exemplary performance. In fact, it may have resulted in reduced services to populations most in need.

Table 10.2 States Receiving the Largest Number of WIA High Performance Bonuses, 1999–2008

Region	State	Number of awards
5	Illinois	9
3	Kentucky	8
3	Florida	6
5	Iowa	6
4	North Dakota	5

Since the core performance measures of WIA are based on the ratio of the numbers of program participants who exit the program ("exiters") who obtain and retain employment to those exiters who do not, the temptation to reduce the numbers of exiters who do not successfully gain employment is high. The risk of using a monetary bonus based on performance results is, therefore, that states will engage in manipulative reporting, or "gaming," or even elect to serve those individuals with a high likelihood of success (creaming).

The relationship between WIA monetary incentives and the mainline WIA programs is weak. State plans providing information on the intended use of received bonuses indicate that incentive grant awards go toward new programs or increases in services rather than to individuals involved in frontline service. This proposed usage does not provide a direct incentive to individual frontline employees for providing exemplary or increasingly effective services, since these individuals do not receive any monetary return on their investment in improving services.

Thus, it is very possible that individual level service might be negatively impacted by offering monetary incentives for achieving performance goals. Providing monetary services without adjusting for the characteristics of the population served reduces the incentive to serve disadvantaged populations, whether measured by education, disability, or race/ethnicity.

As can be seen in Table 10.1, the annual awards have been declining over time. The number of states eligible for the awards has declined in recent years. The overall annual award amount also has been steadily diminishing since the beginning of the WIA program, and funding for these incentives has ceased altogether from the USDOL.

The WIA HPB continues despite lack of support from the Labor Department because the Adult Education Program continues to provide HPB funding. Though there has been no department funding since FY 2004, the USDOL continued to participate in the HPB process because of statutory requirements.

TANF HPB

The TANF program provides a minimum income for families with children. TANF was established in 1996 by the Personal Responsibility and Work Opportunity Reconciliation Act (PRWORA) as a successor to the Aid to Families with Dependent Children (AFDC) program. The 1996 legislation identified one TANF goal as ending "the dependence of needy parents on government benefits by promoting job preparation, work, and marriage." To promote attainment of this end, the law authorized payment of bonuses to "high performing states based on a formula to be established by the Department of Health and Human Services" (DHHS) in consultation with the National Governors Association, the American Public Welfare Association (an organization largely representing state social service agency directors that is now called the American Public Human Services Association), and other interested parties. These HPBs were distributed by the DHHS to states for accomplishments from federal fiscal year 1998 through 2004. Funding for the program ceased in 2005.

Experience with the HPB offers a case study of a policy intended to provide positive incentives for local program operators to improve performance in pursuit of public objectives. The purpose of case studies is generally to gain insight into the myriad details that bedevil implementation of policy and to offer lessons of experience. To this end we provide an overview of the program and identify issues and lessons.

Our conclusion is that the indicators upon which the TANF HPB was based have numerous shortcomings and, possibly as a result, there is no evidence that the TANF HPB affected state policy or program effectiveness. However, the program leaves an institutional legacy that, while difficult to replicate elsewhere, may prove valuable as the current administration attempts to renew interest in social policy innovation.

The Program and Its Evolution

To understand the HPB, it is important to understand the federal context. TANF is a joint federal–state venture in which states design and operate their assistance programs under broad federal guidelines. Benefit levels are determined by states, as are many other eligibility conditions and compliance requirements. Funding is from a combination of a state's own revenues and a fixed federal contribution determined largely by the amount the state received for AFDC during that program's last years. In FY 2004 combined expenditure of federal and state funds for TANF amounted to $25.8 billion, of which $14.4 billion came from the federal government. Forty-seven percent of the total went for income support; the remainder was spent on services, including work supports for cash recipients and others meeting TANF-related need standards.

The HPB fiscal stakes were small. The bonuses averaged about $200 million per year, less than 1 percent of total outlays. The program was voluntary, and no state was allowed to receive in any year an amount greater than 5 percent of its TANF block grant. Nevertheless, the program was evidently viewed by states as worth the effort required to compete. In the first year of competition, 46 states competed; 49 and 50 participated for FY 1999 and FY 2000, respectively, and thereafter generally 50 of the 51 states engaged.

As required by PRWORA, the HPB criteria were developed in consultation with the National Governors Association, the American Public Human Services Association, and a variety of other interested parties (DHHS 1999). The bonus awards for FYs 1998, 1999, and 2000 were based on four work measures: Job Entry, Success in the Labor Force (a measure based on employment retention and earnings gains), and improvement from the prior fiscal year in each of these measures. For each, the 10 states with the highest performance received awards. It was unusual for states to gain awards in all four categories, and therefore it was possible for more than 10 states to receive recognition on at least one dimension. The awards for FY 1998 went to 27 states (more than half of states entering the competition). Twenty-eight states won bonuses for performance in FY 1999, and 27 states did so in for FY 2000. States were not obligated to compete on all performance measures, but eventually most states chose to do so.

Over time, the program evolved. In 1999, the DHHS began efforts to expand the criteria used for awarding the HPB to include measures of state success in raising participation in support programs for working families and in promoting family formation and stability (DHHS 1999, p. 68202), which caused an increase in the numbers of indicators used. Beginning with the awards made for performance in FY 2001 and continuing through FY 2004, the bonus criteria included, in addition to the four employment-related measures, indicators for 1) participation of low-income working families in the FSP, 2) participation of former TANF recipients in the Medicaid program or in the State Children's Health Insurance Program (SCHIP), 3) a child care subsidy measure, and 4) a family formation and stability measure. Additionally, a quality component was added to the child care subsidy measure beginning in FY 2003.

Initially, states competing on work measures were required to collect, compile, and submit quarterly performance reports derived from earnings data reported by employers to state workforce agencies (SWAs) as part of the Unemployment Insurance system. SWA data cover only quarterly earnings and do not include hours of work, wage rates, or information on the monthly pattern of work within a quarter. Measures of Job Entry and the two components of Success in the Labor Force (job retention and earnings gain) were constructed from these data. Methods clearly varied, and the performance results submitted by states to the DHHS were not audited. The consequence was uncertainty about the reliability of state-reported achievements, which was further undermined by some exceptional accomplishments. One state won $6 million in the initial round for achieving a job entry rate in FY 1998 of 88.4 percent, 3.4 standard deviations above the participating state mean of 42.6 percent. Significantly, the greatest variance in state performance was associated with the Job Entry rate, the measure that offered under DHHS instructions the greatest opportunity for variation in state interpretation, data sources, and computation procedures.

Beginning with FY 2001, federal policy changed. Instead of carrying out computations themselves, competing states were required to submit monthly lists of adult TANF recipients, identified only by their Social Security number. These data were then matched against the National Directory of New Hires (NDNH) maintained by the DHHS. The NDNH is also based on employer wage reports. NDNH data is broader than what is available from state systems in that it includes federal employment and provides information on jobs held in one state by residents of another (in general state SWA data do not). Use of the NDNH leveled the information and computational playing field for the HPB employment measures.

Addition of the new performance categories required changes in the allocation of the $200 million annual bonus among measures. However, the employment measures continued to account for about 70 percent of all bonus funds distributed. The additional categories increased the number of opportunities for winning a bonus from 4 to 10. When awards for FY 2001 and FY 2002 were announced in late September 2003, 46 states won some amount of bonus money. In the last report (for FY 2004), 42 states gained recognition in some category; 24 were recognized in 2 or more. The awards for FY 2004, the last performance year for awards, are summarized in Table 10.3.

The TANF program itself was reauthorized by the Deficit Reduction Act of 2005, but this legislation eliminated funding for the TANF HPB program. During the reauthorization debate, virtually no effort was made by either the states or the Bush administration to see the HPB program extended. Somewhat oddly, the DHHS is still required to calculate the basic HPB employment, Food Stamp, and employment measures for states that submit the necessary data. The child care and Medicaid measures have been dropped (although indicators for these programs have been developed in other contexts).

Issues

Implementation and operation of the HPB raised a number of issues common to all performance measure programs, including those coupled with fiscal incentives.

What to measure. At least at first blush, the HPB performance measures sound appropriate—surely job entry, success in the labor force, and family formation and stability sound like good things. However, as often happens, the details pose problems. Consider the Job Entry rate. Nominally this would seem to refer to the rate at which adults receiving TANF moved in some time period from unemployment to some standard of employment. Since the NDNH data record only

Table 10.3 TANF High Performance Bonus Categories and Awards, FY 2004

Component	Indicator definition	Source	U.S. average (%)	Best performing state	Best state score	Award ($, millions)	Total awards ($, millions)
Success in the labor force							
2004 levels							
Job entry	Ratio of measure of recipients entering employment to total unemployed recipients (%)	NDNH[a]	34.9	Virginia	46.7%	7.3	48.1
Job retention	Proportion of currently employed recipients with earnings in first and second subsequent quarters (%)	NDNH	59.0	Hawaii	72.2%	n/a[b]	n/a
Earnings gain	Increase in aggregate earnings between current, second following quarter, currently employed recipients (%)	NDNH	36.9	South Dakota	81.4%	n/a	n/a
Success in labor force	Average rank on job retention and earnings gain measures	Calculated	n/a	Wyoming	1(rank)	0.4	36.9
2003–2004 change							
Job entry	Change in Job entry rate (Δ%)	Calculated	1.2	Virginia	8.2%	0.7	29.5
Job retention	Change in Job Retention Rate (Δ%)	Calculated	−0.5	Louisiana	12.4%	n/a	n/a
Earnings gain	Change in Earnings Gain Rate (Δ%)	Calculated	4.3	Georgia	31.4%	n/a	n/a
Success in labor force	Change in average rank on Job Retention and Earnings Gain measures		n/a	Georgia	1(rank)	4.0	22.2

Supporting services

2004 levels

Medicaid/SCHIP enrollment	Proportion of TANF leavers who retain enrollment in Medicaid/SCHIP for at least four months (%)	State reports	77.5	Pennsylvania	96.0%	4.7	6.3
Food Stamps	Proportion of low-income working households with children under 18 participating in Food Stamp Program (%)	Census Bureau	37.4	Maine	61.7%	3.0	6.3
Child care subsidies	Measure (with quality adjustment) of proportion of eligible children served under state's federally funded child care program (%)	State reports	n/a	Rhode Island	1(rank)	0.2	10.6

2003–2004 change

Medicaid/SCHIP enrollment	Change in Medicaid/SCHIP Enrollment Rate (Δ%)	Calculated	n/a	New Hampshire	7.3%	1.1	14.8
Food Stamps	Change in FSP Participation Rate (Δ%)	Census Bureau	2.3	Delaware	12.6%	0.3	14.8

Family formation and stability

Children living with both (married) parents	Change in proportion of children under 18 residing in married family couple groups (Δ%)	Census Bureau	−0.1	Arizona	5.1%	0.3	10.6

(continued)

Table 10.3 (continued)

Component	Indicator definition	Source	U.S. average (%)	Best performing state	Best state score	Award ($, millions)	Total awards ($, millions)
Family formation and stability							
Total high performance bonus ($, millions)							200.0

NOTES: [a]National Directory of New Hires. [b]n/a = Measure not applicable.
SOURCE: Administration for Children and Families (2009), Appendix 5. Indicator descriptions are paraphrased and corrected for errors in the source.

quarterly earnings, identification of a job entry using the NDNH must be completed on the basis of variation in quarterly earnings. The Job Entry rate is a measure of the percentage of the number of unduplicated unemployed adult recipients who entered employment for the first time during the performance year (i.e., job entries). An adult is considered to have entered employment for the first time in a calendar quarter if he/she had no earnings in any of the prior quarters of the performance year (Administration for Children and Families 2009, Table 5.1). The formula is[2]

$$\frac{\text{Sum of job entries in quarters 1–4}}{\begin{array}{c}\text{Unduplicated number of unemployed}\\ \text{adult recipients in performance year}\end{array}} \times 100.$$

It is easy to come up with scenarios in which people lose jobs, take up TANF, and are helped to find new employment, but never count in the data as a job entry using this formula. On the other end of the list of awarded outcomes (see Table 10.3), the measure actually used for "family formation and stability" was simply an estimate of the number of children under 18 residing in "married family couple groups" as a percentage of all children resident in a state. It is unclear why states should receive a *TANF* "high performance" bonus on this measure when TANF typically involves less than 5 percent of children at any point during the year.[3]

Control for context. No adjustment is made in any of the performance measures for variation in state economic and social environment. In particular, it seems likely that the ability of states to move unemployed recipients into jobs will be affected by local unemployment rates as well as the skills, education, and experience of the caseload. The DHHS initially argued that its own analysis suggested that "these specific factors do not determine entry rate to any significant degree" (DHHS 2000, p. 52843). Subsequent analysis, using NDNH data, suggests otherwise (Wiseman 2006).

At times, the DHHS argued that inclusion of measures of change compensated states in part that were disadvantaged by economic or social factors. Even when states could not outcompete others on levels of achievement, they presumably had a better chance in accomplishing improvement. The problem with change measures is that any year's set of changes is likely in part the consequence of random factors and, over time, some regression to the mean can be expected. The larger the state, the more likely it is that such factors cancel out and that year-over-year change includes less "noise." Something of this phenomenon may be observed in the data: Winning states in the change-in-job-entry category tend to be smaller than those winning on the basis of current rates.

What is welfare about? Historically, social assistance systems have generally been intended first and foremost to alleviate need. Federal law does not set benefit levels, and as a result, there is exceptional interstate variation in the amount of TANF benefits. In 2004, a TANF recipient family of three received a monthly grant of $786 in California and $288 in Indiana. (About 30 percent of this disparity was offset by variation in Food Stamp benefits.) Yet both states received roughly the same HPB amount, and California received no credit for lifting dependent recipients much closer to the national poverty standard. Over the life of the HPB, the median state TANF benefit declined by 10 percent in real terms. It seems reasonable to argue that performance in employment promotion and across other dimensions should be evaluated in light of income support accomplishments.

Source of data. A virtue of the NDNH data is that they cover all adults and the universe of jobs outside of the shadow economy. There are no problems of statistical inference. The data for Medicaid/SCHIP come from the states' own management information systems and also present no problems of statistical inference. However, the data on FSP participation, participation in subsidized child care, and children's family environment are derived from sample surveys, notably the Current Population Survey (CPS). For all but the largest states the CPS sample is too small for reliable estimates of these measures, and the problems were compounded in estimation of year-to-year changes. Perhaps not surprisingly, the DHHS summary tables for measure achievement by state on these dimensions never include estimated standard errors or cautionary notation.

Both the NDNH and census-based data take a long time to accumulate. Typically, awards were announced almost a year after the last quarter included in the performance data. (The awards for FY 2004 were announced in October 2005.) The result is a substantial temporal disconnect between the performance that was being rewarded and its actual identification.

How to respond. The nature of the TANF HPB indicators made it difficult for states to deliberately target the outcomes measured. However, some policies taken for other purposes appear to have influenced the HPB outcomes. The original TANF legislation included a federal requirement that states achieve certain target rates of participation of recipient adults in work-related activities. The impact of these targets was diminished because they were reduced in response to caseload decline and, for a variety of reasons, the total number of TANF cases fell by over 50 percent between FY 1996 and 2004. Nevertheless, some states took precautionary steps to reduce the challenge posed by the participation requirement. One strategy, sanctioned by regulations, was to create a Separate State Program (SSP) outside of TANF and wholly funded from state revenues. Persons difficult to engage in work because of disability or other problems were then served through these programs, and such expenditures were included in assessing state compliance with federal "maintenance of effort" regulations intended to sustain state contributions to the public assistance effort. Despite this selection, the TANF participation rate was calculated only for participants in federally subsidized TANF. Given that employability was generally a criterion for moving people to SSPs, introduction of such programs probably raised performance as measured by the employment-related indicators. In 2004, 32 states had SSPs, accounting for about 12.6 percent of all adult recipients. Wiseman (2006) presents evidence that, other things equal, states with SSPs had higher rates of job entry, suggesting some prizes were won by artful selection. However, the selection appears to have been motivated by the participation requirement, not the HPB competition.

Missing feedback. Performance assessment programs are generally intended not only to identify exceptional achievement but to provide feedback from assessment to improvement. The feedback occurs in at least three ways. The first is that the systems are generally intended to enhance the information available to operators. The TANF HPB program, based as it was on information not available to state and local-level program managers, did not do this for the key employment indicators. The second is that such systems provide points of reference for judging accomplishment by comparison to peers. Given lack of adjustment in the HPB measures for factors likely to influence outcomes regardless of management strategy, caution would be essential in making cross-state comparisons using HPB data.

A third feedback dimension occurs at the national management level and is notably absent from later years of HPB operation. This is use of the data and experience to make improvements in the indicators and to seek better practice in TANF employment policy. After the shift to use of the NDNH and census data for performance assessment after 2000, no significant changes occurred in the choice of indicators or methods of measurement. Moreover, no systematic attempt was launched to determine the basis for success as flagged by the bonuses awarded. If policymakers believed that the HPB bonus system uncovered genuine managerial accomplishment, then it would have been reasonable to investigate what it was that the states flagged as "top 10" were doing that led to this accomplishment and whether and how the technique(s) might be transferred. No such efforts were mounted.

Consequences

Analysts have made no attempt to assess the effect of the presence of the HPB on the trajectory of TANF policy at the state level. There simply is no reasonable control against which performance and response to the HPB stimulus might be assessed. Managers appreciated the public acknowledgment that award announcement occasioned, and coming outside of state budget cycles, the prizes themselves in many cases provided flexible resources for special projects. But the reality was that bonuses were spread across 10 indicators, even the DHHS seemed confused about how they were defined (see Note 2), and payments turned not only on what any state accomplished, but also on unknown developments elsewhere. Under these circumstances, altering policy for the coming year in pursuit of a small award to be obtained more than two years in the future made little sense. The absence of evidence of effectiveness contributed to lack of enthusiasm for continuation beyond FY 2004.

What seems clear in both the case of the WIA and TANF performance incentive bonus is that they are sought after, and in some cases they appear to be the cause of selective behavior either by states (in the case of TANF SSPs) or the programs within a state (creaming and gaming in the case of WIA). For both WIA and TANF, employing a method of setting performance targets that could essentially level the playing field with respect to economic conditions and program participant characteristics would go a long way in making the HPB a more successful incentive to improve instead of alter program performance.[4]

Additionally, the effectiveness of both the TANF and WIA HPB programs has suffered due to a weak causal relationship; the performance indicator used to measure TANF program success has been a moving target, and there is no correlation between statewide program performance and the size of the HPB in WIA. Lacking a distinctive connection between cause (high program performance) and effect (bonus award), the HPB tactic, while it in many cases does reward well-functioning programs, does not appear for either TANF or WIA to be eliciting the purely motivated and zealous program behavior it was designed to. On a positive note, these are not insurmountable problems to fix. Clearing up the muddiness of TANF performance metrics and the arbitrariness of WIA HPB award amounts could increase the effectiveness of the HPB approach.

FOOD STAMP/SUPPLEMENTAL NUTRITION ASSISTANCE PROGRAM HPB

SNAP is the most important means-tested income support program in the United States. It is administered nationally by the Food and Nutrition Service of the U.S. Department of Agriculture (USDA) and operated locally by state governments or by county governments with state supervision. Before October 2008, SNAP was called the Food Stamp Program (FSP). The Farm Security and Rural Investment Act of 2002 ("The Farm Bill") included provision for an HPB for states exhibiting exemplary administrative performance. This section summarizes the architecture and operation of the FSP/SNAP HPB and compares it to its inspiration, the HPB introduced for the TANF program in 1996. The conclusion is that, in part because of certain programmatic advantages, the FSP/SNAP HPB is the better designed and operated, but the program's small size and universal availability make its impact difficult to assess.

Background

The SNAP benefit is delivered by electronic benefits transfer and collected when recipients use a special debit card to purchase food. In FY 2008, state and federal outlays on (then) FSP benefits and administration totaled $37.7 billion; in contrast state and federal expenditures on TANF benefits amounted to just $25 billion, and only about half of this was for income support. At any time, slightly less than 10 percent of the U.S. population resides in a SNAP-recipient household; because of turnover (eligibility is determined on a monthly basis), a larger proportion of the population receives benefits at some time during the year. SNAP's importance lies in its universality: The program lacks most of the categorical restrictions imposed for eligibility on other forms of income support.

SNAP is an entitlement, meaning that all persons who meet federal eligibility standards have a legal right to benefits. Accordingly, funding responds to meet demand. The federal government pays all benefit costs, but the costs of administration are shared roughly equally between the federal and state governments. This arrangement invites lax administration. Since state governments pay a substantial fraction of administrative costs but no share of benefits costs, without other incentives they have little motivation for excellence, save an institutional adherence to eligibility rules. This incentive problem is addressed by a well-developed, sample-based quality control system that provides both data on characteristics of SNAP recipients and information on accuracy of eligibility and payments determination. States are liable for the costs of errors made, including both costs that accrue to the federal government and the cost to participants of being paid less than the benefits to which they are entitled. Sanctions are assessed against states with error rates that are persistently high relative to the national average.

States and advocates have long argued that the Food Stamp quality control system reduced the incentive for states to promote access to food stamps by households whose circumstances raised the likelihood of eligibility and computation errors. In particular, households with earnings are more likely to experience income fluctuation and to create difficulties for benefit calculation. While households with earnings might be administratively problematic, the "working poor" were considered an important target for FSP (and, more recently, SNAP) outreach, since USDA take-up estimates suggested that the rate of program participation was particularly low among eligible working households (Leftin and Wolkwitz 2009). In 2002 Congress attempted to address some of these issues, both by modifying benefit computational requirements to reduce the likelihood of error and by shifting the focus of administrative assessment from errors to outreach and achievement. The FSP/SNAP HPB is part of that effort.

THE HPBs

The 2002 Farm Bill authorized the Food and Nutrition Service (FNS) to "establish performance measures relating to actions taken to correct errors, reduce rates of error, improve eligibility determinations, and other indicators of effective administration; measure states' performance against these performance measures; and award performance bonus payments totaling $48 million for each fiscal year to state agencies that show high or most improved performance relating to the performance measures" (FNS 2005, p. 6314).

The FNS responded with four bonus categories. Three categories—best payment accuracy, best negative error rate, and application processing timeliness—cover administrative matters. The fourth, program access, involves outreach. Levels and changes are both measured for everything but processing timeliness. Features of the awards for FY 2008 are summarized in Table 10.4 below. Total state FSP administrative expenses for FY 2008 were about $3 billion, so, at $48 million, the bonuses amount to less than a 2 percent increment in aggregate. For the individual state winners, however, the gain can be quite significant.

The payment accuracy indices are simply the sum of sample-based estimates of the dollar value of overpayments and underpayments during the year. The FNS Web site reports the components of this measure for each state. On average, the overpayments component is four times the size of the underpayments amount. The official reports give no information on precision of estimates, but the sampling strategy is simple

Table 10.4 Food Stamp Program High Performance Bonuses, FY 2008

Category	Definition	State average (%, unweighted)	Awards made	Best state	Best state score (%)	State award ($, millions)	Total awards ($, millions)
Payment accuracy	Sum of erroneous under- and overpayments as proportion of total benefits (%)	5.0	8	Florida	0.8	7.2	24.0
Payment accuracy improvement	Change in payment accuracy measure, FY 2007–FY 2008 (Δ %)		3	Georgia	−5.6	4.1[a]	
Negative error rate	Proportion of applications or cases denied, suspended, or terminated in error	11.0	4	Nebraska	0.0	0.7	6.0
Negative error rate improvement	Change in negative error measure, FY 2007–FY 2008 (Δ %; negative identifies error decline)	0.02	2	Oklahoma	−6.5	2.3	
Application processing timeliness	Proportion of approved applicants given benefit access within target time (30 days for normal cases, 7 days for cases qualified for expedited processing)	87.8	6	Montana	98.0	0.3	6.0
Program access	Ratio of average monthly number of SNAP participants over calendar year to number of persons in families with incomes less than 125 percent of the federal poverty standard (%)	58.6	4	Missouri	90.0	2.6	12.0
Program access improvement	Change in program access measure, 2007–2008 (Δ %)	3.8	4	Maryland	10.0	1.4	
Total							48.0

[a]Georgia won awards in both level and improvement categories.
SOURCE: FNS; definitions paraphrased.

and samples for all states are large enough to produce equivalent precision.[5] No agency can win money for both "best" and "most improved," so Georgia, which scored in both categories, got only one award. The FNS gives each winning state agency a base award of $100,000, and the remainder is distributed in proportion to average monthly caseload. The result is that Florida ended up receiving $7.2 billion and the Virgin Islands got $148,000. The "federalist" character of this exercise is evident in the "national average." This is not, as might be presumed, an estimate of the accuracy of all payments in aggregate. It is the arithmetic average of state estimates, so the Virgin Islands receive the same weight as California. The national payment accuracy rate would be a measure of FNS performance, and that's not in accord with the HPB concept.

The "negative error rate" calculations refer not to costs but prevalence of mistakes in actions involving denial, suspension, or termination of benefits. This, too, is sample based. Perhaps the most striking thing in Table 10.4 is the "national average." Again, this is not the national average for transactions of this sort, but rather the average achievement across states. These data pose political problems, since each negative error involves denial of benefit to a family in need, and some states have rates that are very high—in one case 17 percent. The negative error rates are the only components of the bonus system for which the full "league table" of outcomes for all states is not published on the Web.

Application timeliness is relatively straightforward. One issue concerns definition of when the benefit is received. FSP/SNAP participants may not use their benefit immediately, just as cash recipients may not begin spending immediately. The timeliness definition works with the point at which the new recipient's electronic benefits transfer card can be used.

It is common to claim that take-up rates for the FSP/SNAP are low, and the FNS has long been criticized for not effectively promoting outreach. The program access index is part of the agency's response. The index is the ratio of persons living in households receiving FSP/SNAP benefits to an estimate of persons living in families with incomes less than 125 percent of the national poverty standard (FNS 2009). This denominator is intended to approximate roughly the number of persons actually eligible for benefits; various adjustments are made to both the numerator and the denominator to reflect special state circumstances (for example, distribution of food assistance by means other than SNAP in Native American reservations). Calling this measure the program access *index* rather than program access *rate* reflects the agency's concern that it not be misinterpreted. Over time the program access index has been improved, most notably by shifting the base of state poverty estimates from the CPS to the much larger American Community Survey. The American Community Survey sample size is about 3 million households per year, compared to roughly 100,000 in the CPS Annual Social and Economic Supplement.

While the American Community Survey may be much larger than the CPS, it contains much less data on household characteristics and sources of income—factors important in determining FSP/SNAP eligibility. The FNS contracts with a consulting firm, Mathematica Policy Research, to develop more sophisticated estimates of state FSP/SNAP participation rates using the CPS. In one of the few applications of Bayesian techniques to empirical study of U.S. welfare policies, the Mathematica Policy Research team uses shrinkage estimators to combine observations from state CPS subsamples with regression-based predictions of participation based on other states' experience (Cunningham, Castner, and Schirm 2009). The results are mixed. In FY 2006 (the latest year for which the CPS-based participation estimates are available), the correlation between state ranking on the program access index and ranking on estimated participation rates was 0.86; three of the top four prizewinners would have still won had the (presumably) superior participation rate measure of access been employed. For change, the results are much different: The correlation is ~0.4 and only one state appears in both the top four "most improved" lists. What appears to be happening is that the Bayesian shrinkage estimator for state participation rates takes out a lot of "noise" in the data, noise that without adjustment may be interpreted as change.

To the agency's credit, the FNS is aware of these problems and has published analyses of them (cf. FNS 2006). The argument for the program access index as currently calculated is that the number is available by the statutory deadline of September of the year following the performance year. This is a work in progress; the challenge is to find an indicator with a more credible connection to genuine improvement in achieved participation rates.

Net Effects

Has the bonus system actually improved performance? It is difficult to judge, both because of the absence of a counterfactual and because changes over time in eligibility standards have reduced the rigor of eligibility definition. Nevertheless, the story is mixed. Average state achievement on the Payment Error Rate has fallen from 6.63 in FY 2003 to the 5.01 recorded for FY 2008 in Table 10.4. On the other hand, the average negative error rate has increased from 7.6 to 11.0. Access, as measured both by the program access index and estimated participation rates (through 2006), is also up, both for all families and the subset with earnings. This of course could simply be the product of publication of the "league tables" of state achievement on the various dimensions used for HPB assessment. But the bonuses do serve to draw attention to data and add to whatever motivation exists for state operators to seek improvement opportunities.

The Missing Element

If there is a shortcoming here, it is in the absence of an openly debated agenda for evaluation and refinement. However, the FNS does engage in a number of forums in which federal and state officials confer—most notably the meetings of what is now called the American Association of SNAP Directors. The problems with the program access and other measures are openly addressed in its sponsored research. Nevertheless, there is little institutional apparatus either for developing a vision of where the management system should be headed or refinement of the performance indicators for assessing progress toward that goal.

SNAP program administration is an interesting contrast to WIA and TANF in that there is a tremendous amount of control on the part of the program or state administrators to improve performance over the four metrics in use. The metrics, however, are designed to have this effect. In essence, the proper or improved functioning of SNAP *is* the goal, whereas the expected levels of performance for WIA and TANF apply to the participants of the program (e.g., employment, or reemployment rates), who are strongly influenced by behavioral and economic factors and labor market conditions. Awarding a program a monetary bonus for performance metrics specific to the functioning of that program (i.e., SNAP) may create an environment more conducive to improved program performance using HPBs. Regardless, rewarding program rather than participant behavior has allowed SNAP to make a much stronger connection between the annual performance levels and the amount of the incentive award.

LESSONS LEARNED FROM HPB PROGRAMS

While there are similarities and differences between the three HPB programs we have examined, there are a number of lessons that can be learned from their use.

Inadequate Emphasis on Best Practice

Arguably the greatest failing of the TANF HPB was that after one major round of reform, it went nowhere. An important indicator of the quality of management systems is the presence of procedures for feedback, assessment, and improvement. It is virtually impossible to predict in advance all problems and opportunities that will arise in context of development of performance assessment and incentive systems. Any plan for implementation of a performance assessment and bonus system should include provisions for review and adjustment.

WIA programs similarly missed an opportunity to exemplify bonus award winners as leaders in best practices. As shown in Table 10.1, HPBs have been awarded to a narrow set of states from year to year, and therefore do not appear to be encouraging the spreading of performance-enhancing practices which would lead to a wider set of states achieving bonuses.

By contrast, in the SNAP program, the clear connection between nationally rewarded outcomes and local management is emphasized by the FNS on its Web site, where the data on achievement are followed by links to information on "promising practices" for improving access, outreach, improving payment accuracy, and managing recent increase in demand for SNAP benefits.[6] Improvement of local management is promoted by FNS regional offices.

Insufficient Focus on Objectives

The WIA monetary incentives are small and are likely to have weak impacts on state workforce agencies serving moderate to large numbers of participants. Typically, incentives to improve performance are higher with high bonus amounts, but in the case of WIA, even if all states were to apply for and receive the maximum incentive grant award, this total amount would be a very small percentage of annual WIA funding. With a weak link between award amounts and program performance, the objective of improved program efficacy is lost, particularly in large states.

The TANF HPB indicators are distinctly ad hoc and seem to miss essentials. This creates a sense of arbitrariness in the factors determining which states receive awards. It also creates an unstable link between program performance and HPB achievements. Indicators need to be motivated by a philosophy of what the system is attempting to accomplish in order to improve program performance.

Only the SNAP program shows promise in connecting the HPB with the program objectives. The SNAP bonus program has a direct connection with what is done and what should be monitored at the "ground level," i.e., where SNAP eligibility is assessed and benefits are calculated and delivered.

Negative Impact on Program Operation

WIA differs from previous workforce development programs like JTPA in discontinuing use of state or local regression analysis, which factored in prevailing regional labor market and economic conditions that affect workforce program outcomes in setting targets. Instead, states make adjustments for these exogenous factors through a negotiation process in setting performance targets. Offering incentive grants may apply pressure at the state level to encourage manipulative behavior to negotiate lower performance targets to increase the likelihood of achieving the performance levels required to qualify for incentive grants.

What this pressure does at the programmatic level is to discourage frontline service to those participants hardest to serve, which are often those most in need, in order to secure higher levels of performance. This effect of programmatic disinclination to offer services or to process claims for challenging populations occurs in both the WIA and the TANF programs.

Greater Care Needed Regarding Data Use and Validity

In the case of TANF, greater caution should be exercised with regard to statistical inference. It is doubtful that any honest governmental purpose is served by ignoring the shortcomings of sample-based achievement estimators. Where possible, data on the target "universe" are better, but such data often come with their own problems. In any event, statistical inference based on data to which operators have access is better than numbers that cannot be audited.

The FSP/SNAP bonus systems rest on a good deal of statistical inference. A substantial effort is made to report precision of estimation and to acknowledge the role of random factors in affecting interstate comparisons. The data on participation rates, for example, are reported in a league chart that includes confidence intervals around point estimates (see Cunningham, Castner, and Schirm 2009, p. 2).

All of the three SNAP operations-related performance indicators used to award HPBs are subject to, and indeed derived from, a uniform, sample-based audit. This methodology diminishes the potential for bias and for results skewed by exogenous factors, which reduces the risk of creating an award program with unreasonable benchmarks. One drawback, however, is that HPBs have been awarded to high performing states relative to a national average which, given the wide variation in state performance levels, decreases the sensitivity of this approach in determining HPB awards.

The WIA HPB, by contrast, does not make use of statistical inference. State submissions of performance data for the HPB program are accepted by the USDOL, subject to a data validation process administered for each state.

Institutional Development Can Be an Important Product

The primary original purpose of the NDNH was the creation of a database to support pursuit across state borders of noncustodial parents obligated to provide child support. Performance assessment for TANF is something quite different, and manipulation of NDNH data for this purpose has required substantial administrative investment. Though the TANF HPB is not currently in use, the apparatus developed for analysis of the NDNH has been used for other DHHS policy research.

In 2008, a new administration was elected with a new social policy agenda. Since the January 2009 inauguration, a new leadership team was installed at the DHHS. As of the end of 2010, the social policy objectives beyond universal health care had yet to be announced in detail, but planning was under way for the next reauthorization of TANF, scheduled for 2010 but deferred until 2011. TANF is the responsibility of the DHHS Administration for Children and Families (ACF). In anticipation of reauthorization, ACF working groups were established both to review performance measures and to develop a new set of incentives for innovation in social policy, in part following the lead of the Department of Education's "Invest in Education" fund. It appears likely that data from the NDNH, restructured in light of HPB performance, will play a role in these developments.

Similarly, the WIA program will await reauthorization until at least 2011 or 2012. There has been no indication of whether the HPB is to be recommended for continuation in the new legislation or not.

CONCLUSIONS

Offering monetary bonus awards as an incentive to improve performance—once a favored approach in the business world—has had inconclusive impacts on governmental program performance, and might actually be encouraging programs to alter their behavior to improve their chances of gaining a bonus at the expense of not serving their customers.

Though PYs 2000–2002 were the highest for receipt of WIA HPBs, there isn't a clear legacy of improved program performance resulting from use of this incentive system. The states that received WIA bonuses have done so sporadically and have received differing amounts from year to year, and state-by-state comparisons of HPBs between states within the same year reveal little logic in how the amounts are assigned. At best, this type of incentive appears to have minimal impact on improving program performance, and at worst, might decrease program effectiveness. When an HPB is offered through the WIA program, the temptation intensifies to either selectively report on only favorable performance data or to strategically negotiate performance levels to increase the probability of qualifying for a bonus. In addition, the incidences of gaming the system in WIA to obtain monetary performance incentives has resulted in reduction of services to difficult-to-serve populations for which job entry (a primary performance indicator) is particularly challenging.

TANF programs show some reporting patterns that also indicate that select reporting has been occurring in order to increase the reported performance rates. Since TANF does not offer the same opportunity that WIA does to negotiate expected performance levels for each state, those states characterized by a depressed economy have been at a disadvantage in qualifying for a bonus. States have been further alienated from any benefits of a monetary bonus because of insufficient or invalid data, and inconsistent data requirements in TANF have lent an air of arbitrariness to the award of these financial incentives. The temporal gap between program performance and bonus award is wide due to reporting delays and, since no effort has been made to exemplify the top performers in encouraging overall performance increases, it isn't even clear from the federal administration of TANF that these bonuses are a useful tool for increasing program performance levels.

The SNAP program offers a more promising bonus model and, compared to WIA and TANF, it has large strategic advantages. The objective of the program is near-immediate: delivering a well-defined benefit to a target population each month. This means that outcomes can be observed very soon after the management actions that do or do not produce them. Moreover, the foundation of assessment is a well-designed audit program for procedures that are intended to be identical nationwide. That said, the transparency developed for assessment procedures and the ongoing assessment of measure validity seems admirable and worthy of study by social assistance agencies in other departments and, for that matter, other countries. It is possible that the unusual name and character of the SNAP/FSP has caused the program to be overlooked by those from abroad looking for promising practice in social assistance governance.

Federal funding of HPBs in WIA and TANF has in fact significantly diminished or ceased by this point, and funding for the SNAP bonus has never been large. Overall, the challenges in estimating the merit of these awards based on inconsistent data sources, the fact that the bonuses do not provide any monetary gain to local service providers, and the pressure they place on programs to alter their reporting or service behavior in a nonaltruistic direction makes HPBs in government programs an inefficient use of federal resources.

Notes

1. As used in this chapter, the term *state* includes the District of Columbia.
2. Actually, this definition, taken from the Labor Department's Annual TANF report, is incorrect. The numerator in the actual calculation is the sum across four quarters of unduplicated TANF recipient adults with earnings in the current quarter but no earnings in the quarter preceding divided by the unduplicated sum across four quarters of TANF recipient adults who meet the unemployment criterion, i.e., have no reported earnings in the previous quarter (see Wiseman [2006] for more detail).
3. A higher proportion of children receive TANF assistance at some point during the year.
4. A pilot program is under way at the USDOL to test the effect of economic and demographic characteristics on local and state workforce program performance. It is possible this pilot program will affect the WIA HPB should it remain available for state employment and training programs.
5. The 1/100th of a percent difference between Mississippi and North Carolina is undoubtedly not significant, and the 3.22 percent payment error rate for the marginal winning "state," the Virgin Islands, was hardly different from the runner-up, Colorado, at 3.32, so chance clearly plays a role.
6. See http://www.fns.usda.gov/snap/government/program-improvement.htm.

References

Administration for Children and Families (ACF). 2009. *Temporary Assistance for Needy Families (TANF): Eighth Annual Report to Congress.* Washington, DC: Administration for Children and Families, U.S. Department of Health and Human Services.

Barnow, Burt S., and Jeffrey A. Smith. 2004. "Performance Management in U.S. Job Training Programs." In *Job Training Policy in the United States,* Christopher J. O'Leary, Robert A. Straits, and Stephen A. Wandner, eds. Kalamazoo, MI: W.E. Upjohn Institute for Employment Research, pp. 21–55.

Cunningham, Karen E., Laura A. Castner, and Allen L. Schirm. 2009. *Empirical Bayes Shrinkage Estimates of State Food Stamp Program Participation*

Rates in 2004–2007 for All Eligible People and the Working Poor. Final report to the U.S. Department of Agriculture, Food and Nutrition Service. Alexandria, VA: U.S. Department of Agriculture.

Department of Health and Human Services (DHHS). 1999. "Notice of Proposed Rulemaking, High Performance Bonus." *Federal Register* 64(233): 68201–68226.

————. 2000. "Bonus to Reward State for High Performance under the TANF Program: Final Rule." *Federal Register* 65(169): 52814–52855.

DiMartini, Traci. 2007. "Workforce Investment Act High Performance Bonuses." Unpublished manuscript.

Food and Nutrition Service (FNS). 2005. "Food Stamp Program: High Performance Bonuses, Final Rule." *Federal Register* 70: 6313–6323.

————. 2006. "Estimating the Number of People in Poverty for the Program Access Index: The American Community Survey vs. the Current Population Survey." Alexandria, VA: U.S. Department of Agriculture, Food and Nutrition Service. http://www.fns.usda.gov/snap/rules/Memo/2006/080206a.pdf (accessed October 29, 2010).

————. 2009. "Calculating the Snap Program Access Index: A Step-by-Step Guide." Alexandria, VA: U.S. Department of Agriculture, Food and Nutrition Service. http://www.fns.usda.gov/ora/menu/Published/snap/FILES/Other/pai2008.pdf (accessed January 5, 2010).

Heinrich, Carolyn J. 2007. "False or Fitting Recognition? The Use of High Performance Bonuses in Motivating Organizational Achievements." *Journal of Policy Analysis and Management* 26(2): 281–304.

Jacobson, Louis. 2009. "Strengthening One-Stop Career Centers: Helping More Unemployed Workers Find Jobs and Build Skills." Discussion Paper No. 2009-01. Washington, DC: Brookings Institution, The Hamilton Project.

Leftin, Joshua, and Kari Wolkwitz. 2009. *Trends in Supplemental Nutrition Assistance Program Participation Rates: 2000–2007.* Alexandria, VA: U.S. Department of Agriculture, Food and Nutrition Service, Office of Research and Analysis.

Wiseman, Michael. 2006. "TANF Job Entry: State Performance and State Policy." Paper presented at the Twenty-Eighth Annual Research Conference, Association for Public Policy and Management, held in Madison, Wisconsin, November 2–4.

Part 4

Impact Evaluations

11
Ten Years of WIA Research

Paul T. Decker
Mathematica Policy Research

To remain competitive in today's global economy, U.S. workers increasingly need a strong foundation in core work competencies and advanced technical skills. In the past two decades, however, concerns have mounted about the widening gap between U.S. employers' need for skilled labor and the availability of workers with the requisite skills. In one national survey, more than 80 percent of U.S. manufacturers reported a shortage of skilled workers, and nearly half viewed the skill levels of their employees as poor (National Association of Manufacturers and Deloitte Consulting 2005). This skills shortage contributes to the growing earnings gap between those who are educated and skilled and those who are not (Heckman and Krueger 2003; Katz and Autor 1999; Lemieux 2006a,b). The continuing poor performance of U.S. youth—compared to their counterparts in other countries—in mathematics, science, and literacy suggests that the skills shortage is unlikely to attenuate in the near future (U.S. Department of Education 2004).

In response to rising concerns about our nation's ability to meet these growing demands on the U.S. workforce, Congress made historic reforms to the public workforce investment system in 1998, and enacted WIA. Congress viewed WIA as a way to end "business as usual" in the workforce investment system. WIA consolidated JTPA's fragmented system of employment and training programs and provided universal access to basic services. It also promoted customer choice, gave state and local agencies more flexibility in service design, strengthened local accountability for customer outcomes, engaged businesses, and fundamentally changed the services provided to youth. WIA is currently the largest source of federally funded employment and training, serving over 2 million people annually through its Adult, Dislocated Worker, and Youth programs, at a cost of $3 billion (U.S. Department of Labor 2007).

This chapter describes the existing research on WIA and related programs. During the implementation of WIA, the USDOL initiated three large studies of the new program: 1) the National Evaluation of WIA Implementation (D'Amico et al. 2005); 2) the Evaluation of the ITA/Eligible Training Provider Demonstration (D'Amico and Salzman 2004); and 3) the ITA Experiment (McConnell et al. 2006). Other studies have focused on implementation and early operations of the program as well as impacts on participants. Studies of earlier programs, including JTPA, may also have relevance for assessing the potential benefits of WIA.

In the remainder of this chapter, I discuss findings from studies of WIA implementation and early operations. The next two sections review estimated effects of WIA and related programs on the earnings and employment of participants, including both the adult and dislocated worker target populations. Then I describe findings from the ITA Experiment, which assessed the effects of different models for structuring and administering ITAs, the training vouchers used under WIA to fund training. The final section provides a summary and interpretation of the findings.

RESEARCH ON WIA IMPLEMENTATION

Several studies have examined implementation of WIA during the six years after it became fully operational.[1] My summary of the major findings from these studies is organized around seven key principles of the WIA program.

1) Service coordination. WIA has generally succeeded in increasing service coordination through local One-Stop service centers, but there have been challenges. Perhaps the greatest has been determining the appropriate contribution of various program partners to support the One-Stop infrastructure; to date, WIA's mandatory partners have made only limited financial contributions. Other challenges to coordination include conflicting goals among partners and practical obstacles that impede partnerships, such as lack of common data systems.

2) Customer empowerment. Local workforce investment agencies have enthusiastically embraced customer choice by offering a wide range of core and intensive services and establishing ITAs to facilitate customer choice of training. However, use of the eligible training provider list (ETPL) has had its weaknesses. For example, some providers have been unwilling to supply the information required to be on the list, and others have furnished data of questionable reliability (D'Amico and Salzman 2004).

3) Universal access. State and local agencies have made great progress toward the goal of universal access. It has been challenging, however, for states to provide adequate core services with available resources. Tensions have arisen between emphasizing core and intensive services for a wide range of customers and providing more extensive training for a smaller group. Reaching the most disadvantaged customers—including those with limited English proficiency, ex-offenders, those with limited computer literacy, and residents of sparsely populated rural areas—has also been difficult (Dunham 2003).

4) Accountability. Officials at state and local agencies expressed the following concerns about WIA's performance measures as first implemented: the 17 performance goals were too numerous and complex, the data used to measure performance were of uncertain reliability and received too late by agencies to use in managing the program, and local agencies tended to focus on "managing" the performance system to "make the numbers." Responding to these issues and the need for common performance measures in a wide range of programs, the USDOL replaced WIA performance measures in 2005 with the Common Measures. These measures apply to the performance of all Labor Department programs administered by the Employment and Training Administration, as well as employment and training programs administered by other federal departments.[2]

5) Engaging the private sector. Workforce agencies' level of success in connecting with the private sector has varied. Some have been successful, but others are struggling with engaging businesses in planning and providing them with high-quality services.

6) Local flexibility. States and local agencies have embraced the flexibility WIA provides; as a result, service design and delivery structures vary markedly. Particularly large differences across sites occur in how adults and dislocated workers move through the system's tiered service levels, how priority for target groups is established, and how much emphasis is placed on training.

7) Youth program improvement. WIA's changes to youth programs have generally been implemented. Nonetheless, agencies have faced challenges in identifying eligible providers of youth services, finding and retaining at-risk, out-of-school youth, verifying and documenting WIA eligibility, locating qualified mentors, enlisting youth and parents to serve on youth councils, and using interim performance measures.

RESEARCH ON THE IMPACTS OF WIA AND RELATED PROGRAMS ON DISADVANTAGED ADULTS

Although no large-scale experimental evaluation of WIA's impacts on participants has been conducted to date, some recent nonexperimental studies, described below, shed light on the impacts on participant employment and earnings. Furthermore, a long history of research on related employment and training programs can help assess WIA's likely effects. Much of this earlier research has been summarized elsewhere (see LaLonde [1995] and King [2004], for example), so here I focus most of my attention on the recent work.

Pre-1995 Evidence

Studies of WIA and its predecessors—MDTA, CETA, and JTPA—and other employment and training programs targeted to disadvantaged workers date back to the 1970s. LaLonde (1995) summarizes research generated prior to 1995. Evidence from these studies suggests that earlier government training programs generated modest increases in participant earnings. For example, LaLonde argues that the studies of MDTA and CETA show that these programs increased postprogram earnings for disadvantaged adult women but had mixed or even negative effects on disadvantaged men. Based on this evidence, LaLonde concludes that conventional employment and training services provided by WIA's predecessors benefited women, but other and perhaps more intensive services were needed for men.

For disadvantaged women, experimental evidence summarized by LaLonde demonstrates that earnings gains are generated by a variety of employment and training strategies—including some that are quite inexpensive—and that gains, although modest, can persist for several years. Programs associated with successful outcomes for women include the National Supported Work Demonstration, which tested a supported work experience strategy to increase long-term AFDC recipients' earnings (Hollister, Kemper, and Maynard 1984). Furthermore, Supported Work's positive effects on earnings persisted for at least seven years (Couch 1992) after the program ended. Some low-cost job search assistance interventions have also been found to significantly increase the postprogram earning of disadvantaged women, and in some cases the effects have been surprisingly persistent (Friedlander 1988).

Post-1995 Evidence

A critical turning point in the creation of evidence on the efficacy of employment and training programs was USDOL's National JTPA Study (Bloom et al. 1993). The study used a research design based on random assignment of applicants to a treatment group offered JTPA services or to a control group denied access to JTPA. Furthermore, the study sample was intended to be nationally representative, so that findings could be generalized to the program nationwide. This was one of the first large-scale efforts to assess the effects of an ongoing national workforce development program using random assignment. Although the study was unsuccessful in recruiting a nationally representative sample, the researchers succeeded in implementing the random assignment design and obtaining internally valid and reliable estimates of the JTPA programs overall as well as impacts of different service strategies.

Findings from the National JTPA Study showed that the program generated a modest increase in the earnings and employment of both disadvantaged women and men who enrolled in the program. Bloom et al. (1997) reported that JTPA increased total earnings among women enrollees by an average of $2,738 (converted to 2005 dollars) over the

10 quarters following random assignment (see top of Table 11.1). For disadvantaged men, JTPA generated a somewhat smaller increase in earnings—$2,383, on average. As a percentage of control group means, the earnings increase for women—which was 15 percent—was substantially larger than the increase for men—8 percent. After accounting for program costs, the net benefits per enrollee, reported in the final column of Table 11.1, were nearly identical for women ($763 per enrollee) and men ($781 per enrollee). Estimated impacts on postassignment employment rates, reported in Bloom et al. (1993), were also modest. For women, JTPA increased the rate of employment over the six quarters after random assignment by 3.5 percentage points, while the impact for men was a bit larger at 4.8 percent.

In the national study, JTPA counselors referred eligible applicants to one of three service strategies—1) classroom training in occupational skills, 2) a mix of on-the-job training (OJT) and job search assistance (JSA), and 3) other services, which could include job search assistance, basic education, work experience, or other miscellaneous offerings, but not classroom training in occupational skills or OJT. Bloom et al. (1997) found that the estimated impacts of JTPA on adult enrollees varied a bit by service strategy subgroup, at least for women, as shown in Table 11.1. For women, the OJT/JSA strategy and the other services strategy produced significantly positive impacts, increasing earnings per enrollee by $3,416 and $5,886, respectively. In contrast, the point estimate for the group recommended to classroom training in occupational skills was substantially smaller, at $939, and not statistically significant. For men, the estimates were moderate and consistently positive across the three service strategies; however, none of these estimates was statistically significant, even though the overall impact estimate for men was positive and statistically significant.

Subsequent analyses of the National JTPA Study sample by the GAO (1996) highlight the persistence of JTPA impacts on earnings. The GAO extended the follow-up period for measuring program impacts by compiling Social Security earnings records on the sample members, which allowed calculation of JTPA impacts five to six years after random assignment. The analyses demonstrate that earnings impacts persisted beyond the first 10 postassignment quarters in the original study. Over the first five to six years postassignment, JTPA increased earnings by an average of $4,021 per woman assigned to the treatment group and $3,996 per man. Because only about two-thirds of assignees actually enrolled in JTPA, the long-run effects per enrollee were larger—over $5,000, on average, for both women and men.

After WIA replaced JTPA in 1998, a number of studies attempted to examine impacts related to the new program. An early example is the ITA Experiment, sponsored by the USDOL to examine the relative effects of different methods of administering ITAs, the primary vehicle for funding training under WIA. The experiment, discussed in more detail below, was based on a research design in which WIA training applicants were randomly assigned to three ITA models being tested. In contrast to the National JTPA Study, the ITA Experiment made no attempt to deny services to any applicants. In the past year, however, the USDOL initiated a new experimental study of WIA impacts, based on random assignment of applicants to a group that has access to all WIA services or to one or more groups with limited or no access (similar to what was done in the National JTPA Study). The study (Bellotti et al. 2009) is designed to measure the impacts and cost-effectiveness of WIA services on the adult, dislocated worker, and youth populations. It is based on a nationally representative sample of WIA applicants, similar to what was intended in the National JTPA Study, to generate impact estimates that are representative of the program as it operates across the country.

Study designs that include random assignment provide unbiased estimates of WIA impacts with a known degree of precision, based on differences in outcomes between treatment and control groups. However, the need to randomly assign new WIA applicants requires time to build the needed sample and measure the outcomes of interest over an appropriate observation period. It will be at least a few years before the new experimental study will generate useful impact estimates.

In contrast, studies that do not rely on random assignment can work with retrospective data to measure outcomes for prior WIA applicants and matched comparison groups, assuming such data are available. The program administrative data in the Workforce Investment Act Standardized Record Data (WIASRD) can be combined with state UI claims records, state UI wage records, and state ES records to support this kind of retrospective research. Two groups of researchers—one led by Carolyn Heinrich (Heinrich et al. 2009) and one led by Kevin Hollenbeck (Hollenbeck et al. 2005; Hollenbeck 2009)—have used administrative data to conduct nonexperimental studies of WIA impacts on participant

Table 11.1 Estimated Effects of WIA and Related Programs on Earnings and Employment of Disadvantaged Adults

Program	Source	Population or service strategy	Estimated mean effects or range of effects (per enrollee unless noted)	Estimated social net benefits per enrollee
JTPA	Bloom et al. (1997)	Women	$2,738*** total earnings in 10 quarters after assignment (15 percent of control group mean)	$763
		Men	$2,383* total earnings in 10 quarters after assignment (8 percent)	$781
		By service strategy		
		Classroom training		
		Women	$939 total earnings	
		Men	$1,918 total earnings	
		OJT/job search assistance		
		Women	$3,416** total earnings	
		Men	$2,109 total earnings	
		Other services		
		Women	$5,886*** total earnings	
		Men	$1,403 total earnings	
	Bloom et al. (1993)[a]	Women	0.0 to 5.3 percent employed per quarter over 6 quarters after assignment (3.5 percent employed anytime in 6 quarters)	
		Men	1.9 to 8.9 percent employed per quarter over 6 quarters after assignment (4.8 percent employed anytime in 6 quarters)	
	GAO (1996)[a]	Women	$4,021 total earnings per assignee over 5 to 6 years after assignment; 1.3 to 3.1 percent employed per year over 5 years after year of assignment	

		Men	$3,996 total earnings per assignee over 5 to 6 years after assignment; 0.3 to 3.7 percent employed per year over 5 years after year of assignment
WIA	Heinrich et al. (2009)	**WIA overall**	
		Women	$482*** to $638*** per quarter for 16 quarters post-entry; 5.0** to 13.1** percent employed per quarter
		Men	$320*** to $692*** per quarter for 16 quarters post-entry; 4.9** to 11.8** percent employed per quarter
		WIA core/intensive	
		Women	$216*** to $575*** per quarter; 3.5** to 14.6** percent employed per quarter
		Men	$148* to $673*** per quarter; 4.6** to 12.3** percent employed per quarter
		WIA training vs. WIA core/intensive	
		Women	−$223*** to $928*** per quarter; −5.6** to 9.5** percent employed per quarter
		Men	$194** to $1,301** per quarter; −2.0** to 13.5** percent employed per quarter
	Hollenbeck et al. (2005)	**WIA overall**	
		Women	$887*** per quarter for 8 quarters postexit; 10.6*** percent of time employed
		Men	$773*** per quarter for 8 quarters postexit; 6.2*** percent of time employed

(continued)

Table 11.1 (continued)

Program	Source	Population or service strategy	Estimated mean effects or range of effects (per enrollee unless noted)	Estimated social net benefits per enrollee
WIA	Hollenbeck et al. (2005)			
		WIA trainees vs. WIA and ES nontrainees		
		Women	$874*** per quarter postexit; 6.5*** percent of time employed	
		Men	$623*** per quarter postexit; 2.1*** percent of time employed	
	Hollenbeck (2009)[b]	Adults	$459*** per quarter postexit	$1,446

NOTE: Bloom et al. (1993, 1996) and GAO (1996) are experimental studies; Heinrich et al. (2009), Hollenbeck et al. (2005), and Hollenbeck (2009) are nonexperimental. Earnings impacts are adjusted to 2005 dollars. *significant at the 0.10 level (two-tailed test); **significant at the 0.05 level (two-tailed test); ***significant at the 0.01 level (two-tailed test).

[a] The authors do not report significance tests for the estimates presented here.

[b] Numbers presented here are based on average estimates for Hollenbeck's (2009) studies 2 and 4 (see his Tables 4 and 5).

earnings and employment. Both of these efforts have carefully matched various groups of WIA participants to comparison groups of individuals who did not participate in WIA, usually drawn from the population of UI recipients or ES registrants.

While the strength of this method is the ability to work with retrospective data, the weakness is that impact estimates may be biased if the comparison groups differ from WIA participants in ways that are not observed or cannot be adequately controlled for in the statistical methods. The prevalence of bias in nonexperimental estimates of the impacts of employment and training programs and related policy interventions is well documented (see, for example, Fraker and Maynard [1987]; Glazerman, Levy, and Myers [2003]; LaLonde [1986]; and Peikes, Moreno, and Orzol [2008]). Furthermore, it is usually difficult to determine the direction of the bias (Glazerman, Levy, and Myers 2003). Nonetheless, recent refinements in methodology and data may have increased the probability that nonexperimental methods can generate unbiased estimates under some conditions (Dehejia and Wahba 1999; Heckman, LaLonde, and Smith 1999). While the Heinrich et al. and Hollenbeck et al. teams use broadly similar data and the same estimation methods, their approach to handling the data diverges, largely due to characteristics of the data made available to the two teams. I will highlight how these variations may explain resulting differences in the impact estimates generated.

For disadvantaged adults, the evidence on WIA impacts in Heinrich et al. (2009), Hollenbeck et al. (2005), and Hollenbeck (2009) suggests that WIA generates increases in earnings and employment that persist for at least a few years, and these increases tend to be larger than those estimated for JTPA. Heinrich et al. estimate that WIA's overall effect is to increase earnings for men and women by $320 to $692 per quarter for 16 quarters postprogram-entry. WIA also boosts employment rates over this same period by 5–13 percentage points per quarter, on average (see Table 11.1). The earnings impacts tend to be a bit higher for women—starting at around $550 in the first quarter and generally fluctuating between $450 and $650 for the remainder of the 16 quarters. In contrast, the initial effects are large for men—about $700 and $550 in the first and second quarters—but subsequently fluctuate between $300 and $500 per quarter. Despite the difference in the point estimates, we cannot conclude from these findings that WIA impacts are larger for women, given the uncertainty associated with the nonexperimental methods and the standard errors associated with the point estimates. Regardless, the time pattern of the estimates shows that for both men and women, earnings increases occur immediately—in the first quarter after program entry.

The corresponding estimates of WIA's overall impacts on earnings presented in Hollenbeck et al. tend to lie above the top end of the range of estimates presented in Heinrich et al. The Hollenbeck et al. estimates, presented in Table 11.1, imply that WIA overall increased earnings for women by $887 per quarter over the first eight quarters after program exit. Over the same period, WIA increased the share of time women were employed by 10.6 percentage points. For men, WIA increased earnings by $773 per quarter and employment by 6.2 percent.

The Hollenbeck et al. estimates tend to be higher partly because program exit point is used to begin the observation period. Measuring outcomes from the exit point, which Hollenbeck et al. had to do because of available data, effectively ignores the opportunity costs WIA participants incur if program participation keeps them from going back to work quickly and reduces their earnings. In contrast, using the point of program entry to begin the observation period, employed by Heinrich et al. and other studies discussed in this paper, allows earnings impact estimates to fully capture opportunity costs associated with forgone earnings. Hollenbeck addresses this issue by separately calculating comprehensive net benefit estimates for WIA using another data set, treating forgone earnings as part of program costs. His estimate of WIA's social net benefits per adult participant is $1,446 for the 10 quarters following program exit. This implies that for adult participants the postexit earnings increase that Hollenbeck attributes to WIA participation is large enough to outweigh the sum of any forgone earnings participants incurred and the direct costs of the program.

Both the Heinrich et al. and Hollenbeck et al. studies attempt to separate the effects of WIA training from the effects of other WIA services. For adults, estimates from both studies suggest the impacts of training average several hundred dollars per quarter after the initial quarters, as shown in Table 11.1. The Heinrich et al. estimates of the WIA training impacts on quarterly earnings are near zero shortly after program entry but increase over the 16 quarters in the observation period. In contrast, in the Hollenbeck et al. estimates, there is no lag in earnings impacts, and estimates averaged over the observation period tend to lie near the high end of the (wide) range of the Heinrich et al. estimates shown in Table 11.1. Again, using the program exit point to begin measuring impacts is one reason Hollenbeck et al.'s estimates tend to be higher. Also, Hollenbeck et al. (2005) use a broader comparison group, including ES-only participants as well as WIA nontrainees, which may imply that the difference between the trainee and nontrainee groups in terms of services received goes beyond just WIA training. Regardless, both sets of estimates imply that the average marginal effects of WIA training on adult earnings are positive.

Table 11.1 also presents the Heinrich et al. (2009) estimates for WIA core and intensive services. The range of estimated effects of core and intensive services on quarterly earnings seems broadly similar to the range of estimated training effects shown, but the patterns differ markedly. In the case of WIA core and intensive services, the effects occur immediately and then decline quickly over time, while the WIA training effects appear gradually and then increase over time. The declining pattern for core and intensive impacts, combined with concerns about the accuracy of the nonexperimental methods in estimating core and intensive services, lead the authors to conclude that the true program impacts of the WIA core and intensive services are likely to be no more than $100 to $200 per quarter.

IMPACTS OF WIA AND RELATED PROGRAMS ON DISLOCATED WORKERS

Pre-1995 Research

LaLonde (1995) asserted that at the time his article was written, relatively little was known from either nonexperimental or experimental evaluations about the impact of training on the earnings and employment of dislocated workers. Although these workers were served under JTPA Title III (and subsequently under the Economic Dislocation and Worker Adjustment Assistance [EDWAA] Act), they were not part of the National JTPA Study. Two key demonstrations from this period targeted dislocated workers—the Texas Worker Adjustment Demonstration conducted in 1984 to 1987 (Bloom 1990), and the New Jersey UI Reemployment Demonstration conducted in 1986 to 1987 (Corson et al. 1989). Both demonstrations used an experimental design to test the effect of one treatment that entailed JSA offered to all participants, as well as an alternative treatment that combined JSA with an offer of classroom training or OJT.[3] Both demonstrations found that the JSA-only treatments speeded reemployment and increased earnings, although the impacts were usually short lived. One exception occurred for women in the Texas demonstration, whose earnings impacts persisted for a full year after random assignment. In both demonstrations, the alternative treatment that offered training on top of JSA had no greater effect on outcomes than the JSA-only treatments. Based largely on these findings, Congress mandated that state UI agencies create Worker Profiling Reemployment Services (WPRS) systems, to identify unemployment insurance recipients likely to face long unemployment spells (based on a statistical recipient "profiling" model). WPRS also directed UI recipients to mandatory reemployment services as a condition of continued benefit payments.

Post-1995 Research

In the 1990s, the USDOL continued to test JSA's effects on dislocated workers. These efforts included an extended demonstration of a mandatory JSA intervention for profiled UI recipients (Decker et al. 2000) as well as a large-scale evaluation of the WPRS program shortly after its implementation (Dickinson, Kreutzer, and Decker 1997). These studies confirmed findings from the earlier demonstrations showing that mandatory reemployment services provided to UI recipients likely to face long unemployment spells expedited their reemployment. Both studies also suggested that a customized approach to JSA, where some participants receive less intensive services and others receive more, could generate impacts similar to those resulting from a consistent, one-size-fits-all approach. A similar study in Kentucky confirmed the efficacy of WPRS-mandated JSA services, with somewhat larger estimated impacts (Black et al. 2003).

In contrast to the substantial body of evidence on JSA's effects for dislocated workers, the effects of more intensive classroom training or OJT have not been fully tested for this group using an experimental design. In the mid-1990s, the USDOL initiated an experimental evaluation of dislocated workers served under Title III of JTPA (EDWAA). However, the evaluation was abandoned after WIA replaced JTPA.

Despite the lack of experimental evidence on training for dislocated workers, a number of nonexperimental studies of this group may be relevant to WIA. For example, Decker and Corson (1995) examined the effects of training provided to Trade Adjustment Assistance (TAA) program participants. This study of the TAA program, which serves workers who lose their jobs as a result of increased import competition, was based on a national sample of TAA trainees in the late 1980s. Estimates of the impact of TAA training on earnings in the 12th quarter after participants' initial UI claims was positive, at least for a post-1988 sample of TAA trainees, but small relative to the size of the training investment and not statistically significant (see Table 11.2).[4] Based on these findings the authors concluded that TAA did not substantially increase earnings of TAA trainees, at least in the first three years after the initial UI claim. In contrast, Jacobson, LaLonde, and Sullivan (2005) found a positive effect of community college on the earnings of older dislocated workers, based on a sample from Washington State in the early 1990s. Their estimates imply that one academic year of community college retraining raised earnings of men 35 or older by 7 percent and earnings of women 35 or older by 10 percent, translating into substantial net social benefits in both cases, as shown in Table 11.2. Although these results do not relate directly to the effects of any government intervention, they may provide guidance for how dislocated workers can be served effectively. Both the Decker and Corson (1995) and Jacobson, LaLonde, and Sullivan (2005) studies attempt to address a number of challenges common to nonexperimental research on dislocated workers, including how to treat trainees who enter training only after a substantial unemployment spell. Both studies also demonstrate that earnings impact estimates can vary substantially, depending on the methods or specifications used to address these challenges.

More recently, the studies of WIA conducted by Heinrich et al. (2009), Hollenbeck et al. (2005), and Hollenbeck (2009) have directly estimated WIA's effects on dislocated workers. Their findings provide limited evidence at best that either WIA services overall or WIA training efforts are effective for this group. Impacts presented by Heinrich et al. and reported in Table 11.2 imply that WIA reduces earnings in the early

Table 11.2 Estimated Effects of WIA and Related Programs on Earnings and Employment of Dislocated Workers

Program	Source	Population or service strategy	Estimated mean effects or range of effects (per enrollee unless noted)	Estimated social net benefits per enrollee
TAA	Decker and Corson (1995)	All trainees, pre-1988	−$308 in quarter 12 after initial unemployment insurance claim	
		All trainees, post-1988	$527 in quarter 12 after initial unemployment insurance claim	
Community college	Jacobson, LaLonde, and Sullivan (2005)[a]	Men 35 or older	7 percent	$3,587
		Women 35 or older	10 percent	$9,607
WIA	Heinrich et al. (2009)	**WIA overall**		
		Dislocated women	−$226*** to $417*** per quarter for 16 quarters postentry; −2.0** to 7.8** percent employed per quarter	
		Dislocated men	−$199*** to $363*** per quarter for 10 quarters postentry; 0.2* to 6.3** percent employed per quarter	
		WIA core/intensive		
		Dislocated women	−$3 to $482*** per quarter; 1.5*** to 7.8** percent employed per quarter	
		Dislocated men	−$28 to $364*** per quarter; 2.4** to 6.1** percent employed per quarter	
		WIA training vs. WIA core/intensive		
		Dislocated women	−$1,126*** to $69 per quarter; −14.0** to 1.9** percent employed per quarter	

Dislocated men	−$828*** to −$33 per quarter; −9.8** to 0 percent employed per quarter
Hollenbeck et al. (2005) **WIA overall**	
Dislocated women	$1,137*** per quarter for 8 quarters postexit; 15.2*** percent of time employed
Dislocated men	$1,010*** per quarter for 8 quarters postexit; 11.8*** percent of time employed
WIA trainees vs. WIA and ES nontrainees	
Dislocated women	$476*** per quarter postexit; 7.1*** percent of time employed
Dislocated men	$403*** per quarter postexit; 5.0*** percent of time employed
Hollenbeck (2009)[b] Dislocated Workers	$541*** per quarter postexit −$8,148

NOTE: All studies in this table are nonexperimental. Earnings impacts are adjusted to 2005 dolllars. *significant at the 0.10 level (two-tailed test); **significant at the 0.05 level (two-tailed test); ***significant at the 0.01 level (two-tailed test).

[a] The authors do not report significance tests for the estimates presented here.

[b] Numbers shown here are based on average estimates for Hollenbeck's (2009) studies 2 and 4 (see his Tables 4 and 5).

quarters after program entry, but participants catch up to their nonparticipant counterparts, eventually achieving average quarterly earnings about $400 higher than nonparticipants three to four years after program entry. However, concerns about the estimation methodology lead the authors to discount the positive impact estimates and conclude that gains from participation are, at best, very modest, even three to four years after entry. Table 11.2 also shows that evidence of a marginal effect of training on dislocated workers is particularly disappointing, with quarterly estimated earnings impacts consistently negative or near zero through the four-year postentry observation period.

In contrast to Heinrich et al. (2009), Hollenbeck et al. (2005) find positive and strong impacts of WIA overall on dislocated workers, averaging $1,137 per quarter for women and $1,010 per quarter for men. Not only are the impacts strong and positive, but they occur immediately, with the largest effects seen in the initial quarters of observation. The stark difference between these estimates and the Heinrich et al. estimates is probably attributable to methodological differences. As explained previously, the use by Hollenbeck et al. of the exit point to begin the observation period effectively ignores any forgone earnings during the period of program participation. Forgone earnings might be particularly high for dislocated workers, since they often have a stable work background with relatively high earnings. Hollenbeck (2009) shows that once forgone earnings and other program costs are taken into account, WIA generates a large net loss for society of −$8,148 per participant when it is targeted to dislocated workers (Table 11.2).

EVIDENCE ON INDIVIDUAL TRAINING ACCOUNTS AND OTHER TRAINING VOUCHER PROGRAMS

A key component of WIA is the use of ITAs, a form of training vouchers, to fund training. For many years, the USDOL and local workforce investment agencies have experimented with using vouchers to fund training. Under JTPA, many local workforce investment areas were already testing vouchers (D'Amico and Salzman 2004; Trutko and Barnow 1999). For example, when Eastern Airlines went bankrupt in 1991 and laid off about 13,000 workers, the Atlanta Regional Commission could not accommodate all workers who needed training, so it issued vouchers that participants could use to purchase training themselves. A study of nine sites that used vouchers for training under JTPA found that eight managed the system through the use of a "constrained-choice" voucher model, in which the local workforce agency screened providers, limited occupational choices, provided assessments and counseling on training choices, and retained authority to reject a participant's training choice (Trutko and Barnow 1999). Administrators in these sites felt that with a "pure" voucher model, absent assessment or restrictions on training choices, some participants would make poor training choices and waste resources. In contrast, the ninth site—the Michigan Thumb Area Employment and Training Consortium—granted customers broader choices, effectively giving them a checking account that they could use to purchase education, training, or support services.

In anticipation of WIA, the USDOL sponsored the Career Management Account demonstration in the mid-1990s to test the feasibility of using vouchers to provide training for dislocated workers. Most of the 13 agencies in the demonstration chose to manage their vouchers in a manner resembling the "constrained-choice" model described earlier. Findings showed that vouchers were a feasible way to provide training, likely to work just as well as a contracted-training system, and led to more satisfied customers and staff (Public Policy Associates 1999).

In 1998, the WIA legislation incorporated training vouchers to empower customers to choose their own training and training providers. Under JTPA, workforce agencies typically contracted with providers for training slots and then directed customers who needed training to these providers. In contrast, WIA customers who need training receive a voucher or ITA and can choose and pay for their program, subject to limitations states and local workforce agencies establish.

WIA gives states and local workforce agencies considerable flexibility in implementing ITAs. It requires only that ITAs support training supplied by a provider on a state's ETPL and that training be for an occupation considered "in demand," as defined by states and local workforce agencies. A study of the early implementation of ITAs (D'Amico and Salzman 2004) finds that most local workforce agencies chose an ITA model in which counselors guided investigation of training options, but customers made final training decisions. The study also finds that the ETPL was a critical tool for informing customer decisions; at the same time, it gave states control over determining acceptable providers. The study points out the natural tension between these two objectives—controlling provider access to WIA requires excluding some providers from the list, but informing customers requires including enough providers for the list to be useful.

The USDOL launched the ITA Experiment in 1999 to provide states and local workforce agencies with a systematic assessment of alternative approaches for structuring and administering ITAs, and for estimating effects of different approaches. The experiment randomly assigned 8,000 training-eligible WIA customers in eight sites to one of three ITA approaches. The approaches varied according to how intense required counseling was (if any was required); whether counselors could reject a customer's choice; and whether the ITA amount was fixed or set by the counselor, as shown in Table 11.3. The following approaches were tested:

- **Approach 1: Structured customer choice.** This most directive approach required customers to receive intensive counseling, and counselors had considerable discretion to customize the amount of the ITA investment. On one hand, counselors were expected to constrain customers by steering them to training with a high expected return, and they could reject customers' choices that did not fit this criterion. On the other hand, counselors also had much greater discretion to set higher ITA amounts (up to a maximum of $8,000 in most sites) if they felt expensive training was a sound investment for certain customers.

- **Approach 2: Guided customer choice.** This approach, similar to what most workforce agencies adopted in the transition to WIA, involved mandatory counseling. However, counseling was less intensive than under the preceding approach. Counselors could not reject customers' choices if the chosen provider was on the state's approved list. The amount of the ITA award was fixed at $3,000–$5,000, depending on the site.

- **Approach 3: Maximum customer choice.** This approach, the least structured of the three, did not require customers to participate in counseling after being found eligible for WIA-funded training, but they could request and receive it. Customers received a fixed ITA award of $3,000–$5,000, depending on the site (as in the preceding approach). Counselors could not reject customers' choices if the provider was on the state's approved list.

These three approaches reflected the spectrum of voucher models emerging in the early days of WIA, with the second approach most similar to the informed-choice model most sites used in the transition to WIA. To make the experiment as informative as possible, the structured and maximum customer choice approaches encouraged sites to "push the envelope" in their offerings—to adopt models that most sites would not have adopted on their own.

These alternative ITA approaches generated different levels of participation in WIA training, with greater service requirements leading to both lower participation rates and slower entry into training. Customers assigned to the least restrictive model, maximum customer choice, were significantly more likely to attend an ITA orientation and to eventually use an ITA, as shown in Table 11.4. Attendance rates for this approach were 5–7 percentage points higher than for the other two approaches. These findings suggest that the mandatory counseling associated with the other two approaches deterred some customers from pursuing an ITA. Furthermore, analysis of the timing of training reveals that customers with maximum choice entered training about two weeks sooner, on average, than those assigned to the more directive approaches (not shown in table).

Although maximum choice customers were more likely to pursue an ITA, they were much less likely to participate in counseling after the orientation. Postorientation counseling was voluntary for these customers, and only 4 percent chose to take advantage of the counseling offered. Nonetheless, there is no evidence that these customers made poor train-

Table 11.3 The Three Approaches Tested in the ITA Experiment

	Approach 1: Structured customer choice	Approach 2: Guided customer choice	Approach 3: Maximum customer choice
Award amount	Customized	Fixed	Fixed
Counseling	Mandatory, most intensive	Mandatory, moderate intensity	Voluntary
Could counselors reject customers' program choices?	Yes	No	No

336

Table 11.4 Summary of Estimated Relative Effects in the ITA Experiment

Outcomes	Group means			Estimated impacts		
	Structured choice A1	Guided choice A2	Maximum choice A3	Between A1 and A2	Between A3 and A2	Between A1 and A3
Participation						
Attended orientation (%)	69	67	74	2	7***	−5***
Received counseling beyond orientation (%)	66	59	4	7***	−55***	62***
ITA take-up rate (%)	59	58	66	1	7***	−6***
Average ITA award ($, among recipients)	4,625	2,861	2,888	1,764***	27	1,736***
Training participation (%)	64	64	66	1	3	−2
Weeks of training	19	16	18	3**	2**	1
Earnings and benefits						
Earnings in follow-up period ($, 15 months)	17,032	16,464	15,724	568	−740	1,308*
UI benefits received ($)	3,412	3,266	3,483	146	217**	−71
Relative net social benefits ($)	—	—	—	−407	−1,169	—

NOTE: *significant at the 0.10 level (two-tailed test); **significant at the 0.05 level (two-tailed test); ***significant at the 0.01 level (two-tailed test). A1 = Approach 1; A2 = Approach 2; A3 = Approach 3.
SOURCE: McConnell et al. (2006).

ing or employment choices (McConnell et al. 2006). In fact, they chose occupations, training courses, and training providers that were quite similar to those selected by customers assigned to the other two approaches, who routinely received counseling prior to entering training.

The structured choice approach—Approach 1—was the most directive, but these customers' training choices were similar to those of customers in the other approaches, largely because counselors were reluctant to be directive of any customers. Despite the guidance given to counselors regarding Approach 1, counselors tended to defer to customer preferences, failed to steer customers to high-return training, and rarely denied training. They also found it difficult to constrain expenditures. Despite guidance to counselors that average training expenditures should be similar across approaches, counselors awarded much higher ITA amounts to structured choice customers—$4,625 per trainee—than to customers assigned to the other approaches—$2,861 and $2,888 per trainee, respectively (Table 11.4). They also reported that being directive was not in the best interest of customers and that they had insufficient information on which to judge customers' choices.

Although the ITA take-up rate was higher under maximum choice than under the other approaches, the rate of training participation was similar—approximately two-thirds of customers assigned to each approach participated in training during the 15-month postassignment follow-up period. As a result, the degree to which the customers assigned to the more directive approaches were less likely to pursue an ITA was offset by their finding other ways to support participation in training. Despite the similarity across approaches in training rates, the average duration of training was longer among trainees in Approaches 1 and 3 than in Approach 2.

The relative effects of the ITA approaches on earnings and UI benefit receipt during the 15-month follow-up period were modest. Individuals assigned to structured choice, the most directive model, had somewhat higher total earnings during the postassignment follow-up period than individuals assigned to maximum choice, the least directive model. The difference in earnings between these groups is $1,308, as is shown in Table 11.4, which represents 8 percent of the mean earnings for the maximum choice customers. Average earnings for guided choice customers fell between averages for the other two approaches. Average UI benefits received were lowest for this group, and the difference between the Approach 2 and 3 groups was $217, on average, and statistically significant.

Finally, after accounting for the relative costs as well as the relative benefits of the three approaches, McConnell et al. (2006) report that estimates of net benefits were highest for guided choice and lowest for maximum choice, but the differences are not statistically significant. The findings provide no strong evidence that society would either benefit or be harmed by a general move from Approach 2 to either Approach 1 or Approach 3. However, both switches would be costly from the government perspective. The switch from guided choice to structured choice would increase costs because customers receive much larger ITAs on average. Maximum choice would also increase costs relative to guided choice, because the government provides ITAs to a higher proportion of customers and pays out more in UI benefits under the former.[5]

To explore further the use of vouchers, the USDOL launched the personal reemployment account (PRA) demonstration in 2004 in seven states. PRAs were vouchers designed to provide an incentive to reemployment and increase customer choice by removing counseling requirements and restrictions on choice of providers. They were offered to UI recipients as an alternative to participation in WIA. PRAs differed from ITAs in six ways: 1) they were offered only to UI recipients likely to exhaust their benefits (rather than to dislocated and adult workers); 2) they were limited to $3,000; 3) they could be used to pay for intensive and supportive services as well as for training; 4) they could be used to pay providers that were not on the ETPL; 5) customers could receive 60 percent of their unused PRA balance as a reemployment bonus if they became reemployed in their first 13 weeks of UI receipt; and 6) the full amount of the account was fully obligated for the customer for one year (in contrast with ITAs, from which specific obligations are based on training commitments).[6]

Three findings from the PRA demonstration are relevant to WIA (Kirby 2006). First, echoing the findings of the ITA Experiment, few customers used their PRAs to pay for counseling or other intensive services. Second, many customers chose to use their PRAs to pay for supportive services—in five of the seven sites, customers spent more on supportive services than on any other service. Third, sites found it challenging to satisfy the requirement that the full PRA amount be obligated for one year, given that many accounts were inactive for long periods.

Building on lessons from these previous generations of training vouchers, former President Bush proposed in 2006 a new version of the training voucher—career advancement accounts (CAAs). Like the other training voucher initiatives, these accounts aimed to expand customer choice and streamline the delivery of training services, freeing up resources to meet the growing education and training needs of the workforce. Eight states received CAA demonstration grants in 2006 and piloted CAAs (see Rosenberg et al. [2007] for an assessment of the early experiences in four states). In partnership with the U.S. Department of Defense, the USDOL also offered CAAs to the spouses of military personnel in 18 military installations in eight states (Needels and Zaveri 2009).

CONCLUSION

As WIA has passed the 10-year mark and faces the need for reauthorization, now is a good time to review the research related to the program and think about the implications for the future of WIA and workforce development policy. The findings from studies of WIA implementation suggest that the program has largely been successful in meeting many of its key process objectives, such as greater service coordination and customer empowerment. But meeting these objectives was neither easy nor quick, and at least in the early days of WIA, there were challenges to accomplishing the program's objectives that had not yet been fully resolved. Presumably state and local agencies have continued to make progress toward the WIA objectives since the early implementations studies. For example, the potential trend toward greater use of sectoral workforce development programs, in which workforce development programs support training opportunities by operating on both the supply and demand sides of the labor market, may imply that local workforce agencies are more engaged with the private sector now than they were in the early days of WIA.[7] Hence, further analysis would be useful, depending on the timing of reauthorization and how much the reauthorized program would differ from the current program. It would be particularly useful to have updated studies of WIA operations prior to any major overhaul of the system.

Although the USDOL has initiated a new evaluation of WIA that will be based on an experimental design, the studies of WIA to date have been based exclusively on nonexperimental methods. The findings from these studies imply that for adult participants, WIA services generate an increase in earnings and employment for both women and men, and the effects tend to persist for at least a few years. These findings are broadly consistent with the findings from the experimental study of WIA's predecessor, JTPA. In contrast, the results for dislocated workers are less promising—researchers either find little evidence that WIA services or WIA training substantially increase earnings of dislocated workers, at least in the first four years after program entry (Heinrich et al. 2009), or they find that earnings increases due to WIA are far smaller than the combination of the opportunity costs and direct costs associated with WIA services, at least by 10 quarters after program exit (Hollenbeck 2009) .

These nonexperimental studies of WIA are carefully executed with state-of-the-art methods; however, it's not clear whether they can have fully addressed well-known concerns about selection bias in the absence of random assignment to WIA. Furthermore, the data available for these studies have various limitations that constrain the conclusions that can be drawn based on the findings. Hence, it is too early to declare WIA a success for adults or a likely failure for dislocated workers based on the existing literature. The recently initiated WIA evaluation will address most of these issues by applying experimental methods to a nationally representative sample of participants to assess the program effects.

For one aspect of WIA—the ITA—we already have a set of findings that are based on an experimental assessment of different approaches to structuring and administering ITAs. Most local agencies have gravitated toward what we call a "guided customer choice" model, with mandatory training counseling but ultimately customer-driven training choices. The experiment tested both more and less counseling-prescriptive alternatives to the "guided choice" model. The findings from the experiment show that despite the flexibility allowed to local areas in how closely they can manage training decisions through ITAs, local staff are reluctant to be prescriptive in guiding training decisions even when they are given the clear authority. Furthermore, when limits on ITA amounts are eased and counselors are given the authority to customize the amount of training support made available to each participant, counselors tend to be generous in their awards across the board, and the amount of the average ITAs increases substantially. Counselors are particularly reluctant to deny an ITA to any eligible participant based on their training choice. At the other end of the spectrum of prescriptiveness, when counseling requirements are removed and participants are free to make training decisions on their own, very few participants seek counseling to guide them. At the same time, since these participants face fewer requirements, they are also more likely to pursue and ultimately receive an ITA.

Overall, the findings from the ITA Experiment suggest that in the current WIA context, deviations from the "guided choice" model of providing ITAs would generate, at most, modest changes in earnings and other participant outcomes (at least when measured over 15 months after training eligibility determination), while at the same time the alternatives would generate higher administrative and training costs for local areas. Hence, the evidence supports the widespread use of the "guided choice" model by local agencies in the current environment. If there is a strong desire among policymakers for the workforce development system to be more or less prescriptive in guiding the use of ITAs, policymakers will need to make it an explicit goal of the system rather than simply provide the flexibility that allows for it at the local level, as is done under WIA.

Notes

This is a revised version of a paper prepared for the November 2009 conference, "What the European Social Fund Can Learn from the WIA Experience," cosponsored by European Commission Directorate-General for Employment, Social Affairs and Equal Opportunity and the University of Maryland School of Public Policy. I thank Doug Besharov and Phoebe Cottingham for their suggestions and Luis Rodriguez for research assistance. I also thank Peter Mueser for providing the data used in Heinrich et al. (2009).

1. The most extensive and comprehensive study of WIA implementation was conducted by Social Policy Research Associates and involved visits to 40 local areas in 21 states (D'Amico et al. 2005). The Rockefeller Institute of Government (Barnow and King 2005), Berkeley Policy Associates (Macro, Almandsmith, and Hague 2003), and the GAO (2002, 2004a,b) have also conducted studies.

2. See USDOL, Training and Employment Guidance Letter 17-05, available at http://www.doleta.gov/Performance/quickview/WIAPMeasures.cfm.

3. Although the treatments in the Texas and New Jersey demonstrations were similar, the target populations and conditions of participation differed somewhat. The New Jersey project targeted new UI recipients across the state who had worked for their previous employer for more than three years and mandated their participation in JSA as a condition for continued receipt of UI benefits. In contrast, the Texas demonstration targeted voluntary participants in select local JTPA Title III programs.

4. For the average TAA trainee, training lasted substantially longer than a year, and average training expenditures under TAA at the time were substantially higher than under JTPA.

5. The USDOL has initiated a long-term follow-up study, being conducted by Mathematica, of the ITA Experiment. The study looks at outcomes six to seven years after random assignment (Perez-Johnson et al. 2008).

6. Supportive services can include financial assistance needed to meet a condition of employment or generate a specific job offer; logistical support for training, intensive services, or job search (for example, child care and transportation costs); and general expenses in support of job search activities. In the demonstration, all states allowed PRA expenditures in categories 1 and 2, but only some states allowed PRA expenditures in category 3.

7. Glover and King (2010) describe the expanding role of sectoral approaches in the workforce development system in recent years.

References

Barnow, Burt, and Christopher T. King. 2005. *The Workforce Investment Act in Eight States*. Contract No. AK-12224-01-60. Report prepared for the U.S. Department of Labor, Washington, DC. http://www.rockinst.org/WorkArea/showcontent.aspx?id=10156 (accessed November 22, 2010).

Bellotti, Jeanne, Andrew Clarkwest, Ronald D'Amico, Kate Dunham, Kenneth N. Fortson, Sheena M. McConnell, Karen E. Needels, Linda C. Rosenberg, Peter Z. Schochet, and Andrew Wiegand. 2009. *The Workforce Investment Act Evaluation: Design Report*. Report submitted to the U.S. Department of Labor, Employment and Training Administration, Washington, DC. Princeton, NJ: Mathematica Policy Research.

Black, Dan A., Jeffrey A. Smith, Mark C. Berger, and Brett J. Noel. 2003. "Is the Threat of Reemployment Services More Effective Than the Services Themselves? Experimental Evidence from Random Assignment in the UI System." *American Economic Review* 93(4): 1313–1327.

Bloom, Harold S. 1990. *Back to Work: Testing Reemployment Services for Dislocated Workers*. Kalamazoo, MI: W.E. Upjohn Institute for Employment Research.

Bloom, Harold S., Larry L. Orr, Stephen H. Bell, George Cave, Fred Doolittle, Winston Lin, and Johannes Bos. 1997. "The Benefits and Costs of JTPA Title II-A Programs: Key Findings from the National Job Training Partnership Act Study." *Journal of Human Resources* 32(3): 549–576.

Bloom, Harold S., Larry L. Orr, George Cave, Stephen H. Bell, and Fred Doolittle. 1993. *The National JTPA Study: Title II-A Impacts on Earnings and Employment at 18 Months.* Bethesda, MD: Abt Associates.

Corson, Walter, Paul T. Decker, Shari M. Dunstan, and Anne R. Gordon. 1989. "The New Jersey Unemployment Insurance Reemployment Demonstration project: Final Evaluation Report." Unemployment Insurance Occasional Paper 89-3. Washington, DC: U.S. Department of Labor.

Couch, Kenneth. 1992. "New Evidence on the Long-Term Effects of Employment and Training Programs." *Journal of Labor Economics* 10(4): 380–388.

D'Amico, Ronald, Kate Dunham, Jennifer Henderson-Frakes, Deborah Kogan, Vinz Koller, Melissa Mack, Micheline Magnotta, Jeffrey Salzman, Andrew Wiegand, Dan Weissbein, and Gardner Carrick. 2005. "The Workforce Investment Act after Five Years: Results from the National Evaluation of the Implementation of WIA." Employment and Training Occasional Paper 2004-05. Washington, DC: U.S. Department of Labor.

D'Amico, Ronald, and Jeffrey Salzman. 2004. *An Evaluation of the Individual Training Account/Eligible Training Provider Demonstration: Final Report.* Oakland, CA: Social Policy Research Associates.

Decker, Paul, and Walter Corson. 1995. "International Trade and Worker Displacement: Evaluation of the Trade Adjustment Assistance Program." *Industrial and Labor Relations Review* 48(4): 758–774.

Decker, Paul, Robert B. Olsen, Lance Freeman, and Daniel H. Klepinger. 2000. "Assisting Unemployment Insurance Claimants: The Long-Term Impacts of the Job Search Assistance Demonstration." Office of Workforce Security Occasional Paper 2000-02. Washington, DC: U.S. Department of Labor, Employment and Training Administration.

Dehejia, Rajeev H., and Sadek Wahba. 1999. "Causal Effects in Non-experimental Studies: Re-evaluating the Evaluation of Training Programs." *Journal of the American Statistical Association* 94(448): 1053–1062.

Dickinson, Katherine P., Suzanne Kreutzer, and Paul T. Decker. 1997. *Evaluation of Worker Profiling and Reemployment Services Systems.* Report to Congress. Washington, DC: U.S. Department of Labor, Employment and Training Administration.

Dunham, Kate. 2003. *Rural One-Stops: Issues in WIA Implementation.* Report prepared for the U.S. Department of Labor. Oakland, CA: Social Policy Research Associates.

Fraker, Thomas, and Rebecca Maynard. 1987. "The Adequacy of Comparison Group Designs for Evaluations for Employment-Related Training Programs." *Journal of Human Resources* 22: 194–227.

Friedlander, Daniel. 1988. *Subgroup Impacts and Performance Indicators for Selected Welfare Employment Programs*. New York: MDRC.

Glazerman, Steven M., Dan M. Levy, and David Myers. 2003. "Nonexperimental versus Experimental Estimates of Earnings Impacts." *Annals of the American Academy of Political and Social Science* 589(1): 63–93.

Glover, Robert W., and Christopher T. King. 2010. "Sectoral Approaches to Workforce Development: Toward an Effective U.S. Labor Market Policy." In *Human Resource Economics and Public Policy: Essays in Honor of Vernon M. Briggs Jr.*, Charles J. Whalen, ed. Kalamazoo, Michigan: W.E. Upjohn Institute for Employment Research, pp. 215–252.

Heckman, James J., and Alan B. Krueger. 2003. *Inequity in America: What Role for Human Capital Policies?* Cambridge, MA: MIT Press.

Heckman, James J., Robert J. LaLonde, and Jeffrey A. Smith. 1999. "The Economics and Econometrics of Active Labor Market Programs." In *Handbook of Labor Economics*, Vol. 3, Orley Ashenfelter and David Card, eds. Amsterdam: Elsevier.

Heinrich, Carolyn J., Peter R. Mueser, Kenneth R. Troske, Kyung-Seong Jeon, and Daver C. Kahvecioglu. 2009. "New Estimates of Public Employment and Training Program Net Impacts: A Nonexperimental Evaluation of the Workforce Investment Act Program." Working paper. Columbia, MO: University of Missouri.

Hollenbeck, Kevin. 2009. "Workforce Investment Act (WIA) Net Impact Estimates and Rates of Return." Paper presented at the European Commission–sponsored meeting "What the European Social Fund Can Learn from the WIA Experience," held in Washington, DC, November 7.

Hollenbeck, Kevin, Daniel Schroeder, Christopher T. King, and Wei-Jang Huang. 2005. "Net Impact Estimates for Services Provided through the Workforce Investment Act." Employment and Training Administration Occasional Paper 2005-06. Washington, DC: U.S. Department of Labor.

Hollister, Robinson, Peter Kemper, and Rebecca Maynard. 1984. *The National Supported Work Demonstration*. Madison, WI: University of Wisconsin Press.

Jacobson, Louis, Robert J. LaLonde, and Daniel Sullivan. 2005. "The Impact of Community College Retraining on Older Displaced Workers: Should We Teach Old Dogs New Tricks?" *Industrial and Labor Relations Review* 58(3): 398–415.

Katz, Lawrence F., and David H. Autor. 1999. "Changes in the Wage Structure and Earnings Inequality." In *Handbook of Labor Economics*, Vol. 3, Orley Ashenfelter and David Card, eds. Amsterdam: Elsevier, pp. 1463–1555.

King, Christopher T. 2004. "The Effectiveness of Publicly Financed Training in the United States: Implications for WIA and Related Programs." In *Job Training Policy in the United States*, Christopher O'Leary, Robert A. Straits, and Stephen A. Wandner, eds. Kalamazoo, MI: W.E. Upjohn Institute for Employment Research, pp. 57–100.

Kirby, Gretchen. 2006. *Implementing Personal Reemployment Accounts (PRAs): Early Experiences of the Seven Demonstration States.* Interim evaluation report. Washington, DC: Mathematica Policy Research.

LaLonde, Robert J. 1995. "The Promise of Public Sector–Sponsored Training Programs." *Journal of Economic Perspectives* 9(2): 149–168.

———. 1986. "Evaluating the Econometric Evaluations of Training Programs with Experimental Data." *American Economic Review* 76(4): 604–620.

Lemieux, Thomas. 2006a. "Post-secondary Education and Increasing Wage Inequality." NBER Working Paper No. 12077. Cambridge, MA: National Bureau of Economic Research.

———. 2006b. "Increased Residual Wage Inequality: Composition Effects, Noisy Data, or Rising Demand for Skill." *American Economic Review* 96(3): 461–498.

Macro, Bronwen, Sherry Almandsmith, and Megan Hague. 2003. *Creating Partnerships for Workforce Investment: How Services are Provided under WIA.* Revised final report for Understanding the Role of Intermediaries under WIA. Oakland, CA: Berkeley Policy Associates.

McConnell, Sheena, Elizabeth A. Stuart, Kenneth N. Fortson, Paul T. Decker, Irma L. Perez-Johnson, Barbara D. Harris, and Jeffrey Salzman. 2006. *Managing Customers' Training Choices: Findings from the Individual Training Account Experiment.* Final report prepared for the U.S. Department of Labor. Washington, DC.

National Association of Manufacturers and Deloitte Consulting. 2005. *2005 Skills Gap Report—A Survey of the American Manufacturing Workforce.* Retrieved from http://www.nam.org/~/media/Files/s_nam/docs/235800/235731.pdf.ashx. Washington, DC: The Manufacturing Institute and Deloitte Consulting.

Needels, Karen, and Heather H. Zaveri. 2009. *Findings from the Military Spouse Career Advancement Accounts Demonstration Study.* Draft final report prepared for the U.S. Department of Labor, Employment and Training Administration. Princeton, NJ: Mathematica Policy Research.

Peikes, Deborah N., Lorenzo Moreno, and Sean Michael Orzol. 2008. "Propensity Score Matching: A Note of Caution for Evaluators of Social Programs." *American Statistician* 62(3): 222–231.

Perez-Johnson, Irma, Patricia Nemeth, Kenneth Fortson, and Quinn Moore. 2008. *The Evaluation of the Individual Training Account Experiment: OMB*

Supporting Statement. Revised draft. Princeton, NJ: Mathematica Policy Research.

Public Policy Associates. 1999. *Dislocated Worker Program Report: Findings from the Career Management Account Demonstration.* Washington, DC: U.S. Department of Labor, Employment and Training Administration.

Rosenberg, Linda, Karen Needels, Timothy Silman, and Sheena McConnell. 2007. *An Early Glimpse of the Career Advancement Account Demonstration in Four States.* Princeton, NJ: Mathematica Policy Research.

Trutko, John, and Burt Barnow. 1999. *Experiences with Training Vouchers under the Job Training Partnership Act and Implications for Individual Training Accounts under the Workforce Investment Act: Final Report.* Washington, DC: U.S. Department of Labor, Employment and Training Administration.

U.S. Department of Education. 2004. *International Outcomes of Learning in Mathematics, Literacy, and Problem Solving: PISA 2003 Results from the U.S. Perspective.* NCES 2005-003. Washington, DC: U.S. Department of Education, National Center for Education Statistics.

U.S. Department of Labor. 2007. *Workforce System Results: January 1–March 31, 2007.* Washington, DC: U.S. Department of Labor, Employment and Training Administration. http://www.doleta.gov/Performance/Results/Quarterly_report/quarterly_report_03-31-07.pdf (accessed November 22, 2010).

U.S. Government Accountability Office (GAO). 1996. *Job Training Partnership Act: Long-Term Earnings and Employment Outcomes.* GAO/HEHS-96-40. Washington, DC: GAO. http://www.gao.gov/archive/1996/he96040.pdf (accessed November 22, 2010).

———. 2002. *Workforce Investment Act: Youth Provisions Promote New Service Strategies, but Additional Guidance Would Help Program Development.* GAO 02-413. Washington, DC: GAO. http://www.gao.gov/new.items/d02413.pdf (accessed November 22, 2010).

———. 2004a. *Labor Actions Can Help States Improve Quality of Performance Outcome Data and Delivery of Youth Services.* GAO-04-308. Washington, DC: GAO. http://www.gao.gov/new.items/d04308.pdf (accessed November 22, 2010).

———. 2004b. *Workforce Investment Act: States and Local Areas Have Developed Strategies to Assess Performance, but Labor Could Do More to Help.* Washington, DC: GAO. GAO-04-657. http://www.gao.gov/new.items/d04657.pdf (accessed November 22, 2010).

12
Short-Term Net Impact
Estimates and Rates of Return

Kevin Hollenbeck
W.E. Upjohn Institute for Employment Research

This chapter contrasts and compares the net impacts of workforce development programs estimated in four independent studies done in three states. These estimates were computed using a nonexperimental methodology in which individuals who had been served by the workforce system in the state were statistically matched to individuals who had encountered the Employment Service. The impetus for these studies was a commitment on the part of these states to public accountability and data-driven performance monitoring and management.

In three of the studies from which the net impacts that are reported here emanate, rates of return have been calculated for the workforce development programs that include a full accounting of the opportunity costs of participants' training investments, tax liabilities incurred due to increased earnings, as well as changes in earnings-conditioned transfers such as unemployment compensation, TANF benefits, Food Stamps, and Medicaid.

The contributions of this chapter are fourfold: 1) to compare and contrast the net impacts on employment and earnings across four independent studies; 2) to show the decomposition of the net impacts into employment rates, hours, and wage rates; 3) to present rates of return to individuals, states, and society; and 4) to point out policy implications of the work.

The next section of the chapter provides detail about the programs that were examined in these studies, the specific outcomes for which net impact estimates were generated, and the analysis periods. All four studies used administrative data from multiple workforce development programs, but this chapter focuses on the programs offered by the public job training system (administered and funded by WIA and its

347

predecessor JTPA). The succeeding section will present the results of the studies for those programs—net impacts and rates of return. Next, we discuss briefly how the net impact and rates of return estimates compare to other studies in the literature. The final section presents some policy implications of the work.

PROGRAMS, OUTCOMES, AND TIME PERIODS

This chapter draws from four studies. Each study examined a slightly different set of workforce development programs covering different time periods. Table 12.1 displays the various programs and time periods. The first two studies, done in Washington, focused on approximately the same programs: federal job training for adults, dislocated workers, and youth; a state-supported program for dislocated workers; apprenticeships; and four types of educational programs: adult basic education, high school career and technical education, community college job prep, and private career schools. In the second study in Washington, rehabilitative services programs were added to the scope of work. The programs analyzed for the study done in Virginia overlapped these programs somewhat: they included the federal job training programs for adults, dislocated workers, and youth; community college career and technical education; adult education; and rehabilitative services. In addition, this study included trade adjustment assistance, welfare-to-work, and Food Stamp Employment and Training (FSET). In Indiana, we estimated the net impacts of the federal job training programs for adults, dislocated workers, and youth; community college career and technical education; and trade adjustment assistance.

As noted in Table 12.1, the time periods in which the participants were in the programs varied across the studies. The studies defined participation year by when the individual exited from the program. All of the studies used the entire universe of program exiters: in 1997–1998 and 1999–2000 for the first Washington study; in 2001–2002 and 2003–2004 for the second Washington study; 2004–2005 for the Virginia study; and 2005–2006 for Indiana. To be clear, someone who participated in a program for three years and who exited sometime during

349

Table 12.1 Programs Analyzed and Year of Participation, by Study

Program		Study 1 Exit year		Study 2 Exit year		Study 3 Exit year	Study 4 Exit year
		1997/1998	1999/2000	2001/2002	2003/2004	2004/2005	2005/2006
Federal Job Training (Adults)	JTPA II-A	X	X				
	WIA I-B			X	X	X[a]	X
Federal Job Training (Youth)	JTPA II-C	X	X				
	WIA I-B			X	X	X	X
Dislocated Workers	JTPA III	X	X				
	WIA I-B			X	X	X[a]	X
Comm. and Tech. College Worker Retraining		X	X	X	X		
Secondary Career and Tech Ed.		X	X	X	X		
Community College Job Prep.		X	X	X	X	X	X
Private Career Schools			X	X	X		
Adult Ed./Literacy		X[b]	X[b]	X[b]	X[b]	X	
Rehab. Services							
Vocational Rehabilitation				X	X	X	
Blind and Visually Impaired				X	X	X	
Apprenticeships		X	X	X	X		
Welfare-to-Work	TANF					X	
	FSET					X	
Trade Adjustment Assistance					X	X	X

NOTE: Year of participation is defined as year of exit from services. Study 1 is Hollenbeck and Huang (2003) (Washington State); Study 2 is Hollenbeck and Huang (2006) (Washington State); Study 3 is Hollenbeck and Huang (2008) (Virginia); and Study 4 is Hollenbeck (2009) (Indiana).

[a] Combined in this study.

[b] Adult basic education as delivered by community and technical colleges only.

1997–1998 is considered to be a 1997–1998 participant, as is someone who both entered and exited in 1997–1998.[1]

In all studies, the net impacts of participation in the workforce development programs on employment and earnings were estimated. The data came from the quarterly wage record data generated from the UI system, and thus are measured over a calendar quarter. In Washington, the wage record data include hours worked in a quarter, so for the studies undertaken for that state, we estimated the net impacts on hours worked per quarter and hourly wages. Virginia had an interest in the extent to which participants earned credentials either during program participation or within a year of exit, so that outcome was analyzed in the Virginia study.[2] The Indiana study focused on employment and earnings as well as posttraining unemployment compensation benefits.

The Washington studies also examined the net impact of program participation on the receipt of unemployment compensation benefits, public assistance benefits (TANF and Food Stamps), and Medicaid enrollment. These data were supplied by the state agencies that administer those programs. Table 12.2 summarizes the outcomes that were examined in the studies. As the table notes, all of the studies focused on two outcome time periods: a short-term outcome and a longer-term outcome. In Washington, these were 3 full quarters after exit and 8–11 full quarters after exit in the first study (9–12 full quarters in the second study); in Virginia, 2 and 4 full quarters after exit, respectively; and in Indiana, 3 and 7 full quarters after exit.

SUMMARY OF RESULTS

Net impacts. Table 12.3 provides a summary of the short-term net impacts of the programs on employment rates, quarterly hours of employment, average wage rates, and quarterly average earnings. All of the results in the table for studies 1, 2, and 4 are regression-adjusted, and all of the outcomes, except for employment, exclude zero values.[3] For the Study 3 results, the employment rates are differences in means and the quarterly earnings results are differences in nonzero medians between the program participants and matched comparison groups. The wage rate and earnings impacts are in 2005$. Note that these results

Table 12.2 Outcomes Examined and Time Periods, by Study

Outcomes	Study 1 and Study 2	Study 3	Study 4
Employment	Defined as ≥ $100 in a quarter	Defined as ≥ $50 in a quarter *or* enrolled in school if ≤18	Defined as ≥ $100 in a quarter; ≥ $50 in a quarter (youth)
Earnings	Quarterly earnings totaled across all employers	Quarterly earnings totaled across all employers	Quarterly earnings totaled across all employers
Hours worked per quarter	Hours totaled across all employers	Not available	Not available
Hourly wages	Earnings divided by hours worked	Not available	Not available
Credential completion	Not available	Credential earned while in program or within 12 months of exit	Not available
Unemployment compensation	Benefits of at least $1 in quarter	Not available	Benefits of at least $1 in quarter
TANF/Food Stamp benefits	Benefits received by assistance unit that included participant of at least $1 in quarter	Not available	Not available
Medicaid eligibility	State Medicaid administrative data indicated participant was "enrollee" during at least one day in quarter	Not available	Not available
Time periods			
Short-term	3 full quarters after exit	2 full quarters after exit	3 full quarters after exit
Long-term	8–11 full quarters after exit in Study 1; 9–12 full quarters after exit in Study 2	4 full quarters after exit	7 full quarters after exit

NOTE: Study 1 is Hollenbeck and Huang (2003) (Washington State); Study 2 is Hollenbeck and Huang (2006) (Washington State); Study 3 is Hollenbeck and Huang (2008) (Virginia); and Study 4 is Hollenbeck (2009) (Indiana).

Table 12.3 Short-Term Net Impact Estimates for WIA (or JTPA)

Program	Study	Employment rate	Quarterly hours	Wage rate ($)[b]	Quarterly earnings ($)[b]
				Outcome	
Federal Job Training (Adults)					
JTPA II-A	1	0.109***	23.0**	0.77	349***
WIA I-B	2	0.097***	52.2***	1.49***	711***
WIA I-B	3	0.034***	—[a]	—[a]	146***
WIA I-B	4	0.148***	—[a]	—[a]	549***
Federal Job Training (Youth)					
JTPA II-C	1	0.061***	−15.3	−0.47	−175**
WIA I-B Youth	2	0.042**	4.7	0.20	66
WIA I-B Youth	3	−0.039**	—[a]	—[a]	62
WIA I-B Youth	4	0.034	—[a]	—[a]	24
Dislocated Workers					
JTPA III	1	0.075***	19.6***	−0.55	278***
WIA I-B	2	0.087***	58.4***	1.04***	784***
WIA I-B	4	0.170***	—[a]	—[a]	410***

NOTE: Study 1 is Hollenbeck and Huang (2003) (Washington State); Study 2 is Hollenbeck and Huang (2006) (Washington State); Study 3 is Hollenbeck and Huang (2008) (Virginia); and Study 4 is Hollenbeck (2009) (Indiana). *statistically significant at the 0.10 level; **statistically significant at the 0.05 level; ***statistically significant at the 0.01 level.

[a] Virginia and Indiana wage record data do not include hours so no results for quarterly hours or wage rate.

[b] In 2005$/2006$.

include all participants—those individuals who completed their education or training and those who left without completing.

In examining the first column of data, one can easily discern that most of the programs have statistically significant positive net impacts on short-term (3 or 4 quarters after exit) employment rates.[4] The levels of the impacts are generally in the 5–15 percentage point range. WIA seems to be generally successful at getting participants employed. The farthest right-hand column of results shows the net impacts on quarterly earnings (for individuals with earnings). Whereas the estimates are generally positive, there is more variability in the levels and statistical significance of the earnings impacts than for employment. For example, the Youth program has earnings impacts that are essentially zero, despite reasonably robust employment rate impacts.

Table 12.4 displays the results for longer-term outcomes. These results reflect the extent to which the short-term impacts are retained. The results are not substantially different from those in Table 12.3. This suggests that for the most part, the programs' outcomes do not depreciate during the first few years after exit. The programs result in a statistically significant positive employment net impact, and all of them, save federal job training for youth, have statistically significant and positive earnings impacts.

Rates of return. In addition to the net impact analyses, we conducted benefit-cost analyses for the workforce development programs in both Washington studies and in the Indiana study. The benefits that were calculated included the following:

- increased lifetime earnings (discounted)
- fringe benefits associated with those earnings
- taxes on earnings (negative benefit to participants; benefit to society)
- reductions in UI benefits (negative benefit to participants; benefit to society)
- reductions in TANF benefits (negative benefit to participants; benefit to society)
- reductions in Food Stamp benefits (negative benefit to participants; benefit to society)
- reductions in Medicaid benefits (negative benefit to participants; benefit to society).

Table 12.4 Long-Term Net Impact Estimates of WIA (or JTPA)

			Outcome		
Program	Study	Employment rate	Quarterly hours	Wage rate ($)[a]	Quarterly earnings ($)[a]
Federal Job Training (Adults)					
JTPA II-A	1	0.074***	23.9***	0.68**	658***
WIA I-B	2	0.066***	35.7***	0.67**	455***
WIA I-B	4	0.137***	—[b]	—[b]	463***
Federal Job Training (Youth)					
JTPA II-C	1	0.053**	2.3	-0.71	117
WIA I-B Youth	2	0.103***	31.1***	0.77***	325***
WIA I-B Youth	4	0.023	—[b]	—[b]	47
Dislocated Workers					
JTPA III	1	0.073***	26.6***	-0.10	1,009***
WIA I-B	2	0.064***	48.8***	0.97***	771***
WIA I-B	4	0.165***	—[b]	—[b]	310***

NOTE: Study 1 is Hollenbeck and Huang (2003) (Washington State); Study 2 is Hollenbeck and Huang (2006) (Washington State); and Study 4 is Hollenbeck (2009). *statistically significant at the 0.10 level, **statistically significant at the 0.05 level, ***statistically significant at the 0.01 level.

[a] In 2005$/2006$.
[b] Data not available.

The costs included the following:

- forgone earnings (reduced earnings during the period of training)
- tuition payments
- program costs.

Most of these costs and benefits were derived from the net impact estimates. The details about how these costs and benefits were estimated or calculated are in Appendix 12A.

Table 12.5 displays the estimated benefits and costs for the JTPA and WIA programs analyzed in the two Washington studies and for WIA in the Indiana study for the first 10 quarters after program exit and for the average working lifetime. The table entries represent financial gains (positive benefits or negative costs) or costs (negative benefits or positive costs) for the average participant. The costs and benefits are shown from three perspectives: 1) for the individual, 2) for the public (taxpayers), and 3) for society as a whole. The latter is the sum of the first two. The dollar figures are in constant 2005$/2006$ and have been discounted at 3 percent.

The top panel shows that the discounted (net) benefits to the participants over the first 10 quarters after exit are generally in the range of $2,800–$5,000. The costs to participants are fairly negligible for the Adult and Youth programs, but they are quite large (in the form of forgone earnings) for dislocated workers. Concomitantly, the short-term returns on investment for disadvantaged adult and youth participants in this time period are quite substantial—they are either positive or incalculable because the costs were nonpositive, whereas the return for dislocated workers is negative in all of the studies.[5]

For the public, benefits are generally in the $2,400–$6,000 range and are typically less than the public costs of providing services. For almost none of the programs is the rate of return for the public positive in the first 10 quarters. This suggests that these programs do not fully pay off within the first 10 quarters after a participant exits.

Taxes and income-conditioned transfers are transfers between participants and the public, so they offset each other in the calculation of benefits and costs to society as a whole. Thus the benefits to society in the cost-benefit analysis are simply the earnings and fringe benefits of participants, and the costs are the participants' forgone earnings and the financial cost of providing the program services. In the first 10 quarters,

Table 12.5 Discounted Benefits and Costs and Rates of Return for Federal Job Training Programs over First 2.5 Years after Exit and over Working Lifetime, by Program

Program	Study	Private			Public			Social		
		Benefits ($)	Costs ($)	ROI (%)	Benefits ($)	Costs ($)	ROI (%)	Benefits ($)	Costs ($)	ROI (%)
PANEL A: Over first 2.5 years after exit										
Federal Job Training (Adults)										
JTPA II-A	1	1,106	403	8.24	3,989	3,791	1.36	5,095	4,194	3.07
WIA I-B	2	4,173	−1,111	—	3,113	5,744	−15.36	7,286	4,633	9.94
WIA I-B	4	2,804	1,350	10.54	2,916	4,132	−10.29	5,720	5,482	0.85
Federal Job Training (Youth)										
JTPA II-C	1	−3,646	384	—	1,864	2,605	−4.69	−1,782	2,989	—
WIA I-B Youth	2	3,313	0	—	−1,151	6,617	—	2,163	6,617	−15.96
WIA I-B Youth	4	671	495	6.03	113	6,550	—	784	7,045	−27.96
Dislocated Workers										
JTPA III	1	4,944	13,640	−12.49	882	2,885	−12.29	5,826	16,525	−12.45
WIA I-B	2	4,258	10,746	−10.72	5,770	7,081	−5.59	10,028	17,827	−9.38
WIA I-B	4	1,993	6,440	−15.76	2,376	6,426	−21.31	4,369	12,866	−17.83
PANEL B: Over working lifetime										
Federal Job Training (Adults)										
JTPA II-A	1	62,744	403	20.52	25,092	3,791	9.26	87,836	4,194	13.23
WIA I-B	2	38,928	−1,111	—	6,241	5,744	0.21	45,170	4,633	15.14
WIA I-B	4	15,825	1,350	16.32	4,084	4,132	−0.04	19,909	5,482	7.60

Federal Job Training (Youth)									
JTPA II-C	1	30,235	384	3.08	6,770	2,605	6.08	37,005	2,989	3.61
WIA I-B Youth	2	29,002	0	—	8,282	6,617	0.07	37,284	6,617	4.55
WIA I-B Youth	4	7,055	495	13.27	1,184	6,550	-1.73	8,239	7,045	0.22
Dislocated Workers									
JTPA III	1	81,327	13,640	5.19	25,719	2,885	6.81	107,046	16,525	5.53
WIA I-B	2	49,201	10,746	5.00	18,440	7,081	5.15	67,641	17,827	5.04
WIA I-B	4	15,398	5,440	2.64	10,310	6,426	1.50	25,708	12,866	2.13

NOTE: Study 1 is Hollenbeck and Huang (2003) (Washington State); Study 2 is Hollenbeck and Huang (2006) (Washington State); Study 4 is Hollenbeck (2009) (Indiana). Table entries are for average participant. Benefits include earnings, fringe benefits, and income-related transfer payments. Costs include tuition and fees (if any), forgone earnings, and public program costs per participant. $ figures are in real 2005$/2006$. — = return on investment (ROI) could not be calculated because of 0 or negative benefits or costs.

the societal benefits exceed the costs for the WIA Adult program, but not for the Youth or Dislocated Worker programs.

The lower panel of the table displays estimated benefits, costs, and return on investments of the average individual served by a program through their working lifetime. Here we extrapolated benefits from the average age of exiters until age 65. For individuals, the discounted (net) lifetime benefits tend to be substantial, especially in the two Washington State studies. The costs (identical to the costs given in Table 12.5) are much less than these benefits, so the participants' returns on investment range from about 2.5 percent (quarterly) to over 20 percent (quarterly).[6] The benefits accruing to the public over the average worker's lifetime are dominated by tax payments on increased earnings. Given that those earnings tend to be quite substantial, it is not surprising that the public benefits tend to exceed the public costs, and there tend to be positive returns to the public for the programs. For society, the story is quite similar. The benefits far exceed the costs, and the returns are therefore quite handsome.

Validity. The net impacts and rates of return presented here are, in general, quite substantial. Are they believable? Does participation in WIA endow clients with these sorts of returns? One question that might be raised is the extent to which the methodological approach is responsible for the positive findings. While it is generally agreed that a random assignment approach is methodologically superior to the matching estimators used in the above-mentioned studies, it should be noted that according to the U.S. Government Accountability Office (1996), the National JTPA Study (NJS) that used a random assignment process resulted in a 13 percent earnings impact for adult men and a 15 percent earnings impact for adult women. The comparable estimate in Table 12.4—an earnings impact of $658 (2005$/2006$) is about a 22 percent impact (mean quarterly earnings are $2,946 for this group). The Washington State results reported here are larger than the NJS, but both studies imply quite large returns.

Another issue that might be raised is that the author of this chapter is also an author of all of the WIA impact studies cited above. The U.S. Department of Labor funded a quasi-experimental evaluation of WIA whose results are reported in Heinrich, Mueser, and Troske (2008). For the WIA Adult program, these authors report a significant quarterly earnings impact of about $600 for women and $450 for men (2005:1 $).

The comparable result reported in Table 12.4 is about $450 for the total population. For the WIA dislocated worker program, these authors report a significant quarterly earnings impact of about $380 for women and $220 for men.[7] The comparable results reported in Table 12.4 are $771 in Washington State and $310 in Indiana for the total population. Note that Mueser, Troske, and Gorislavsky (2007) use several quasi-experimental approaches to estimate the impact of JTPA in the state of Missouri, and their preferred specification results in an earnings impact of about 14 percent for men and 23 percent for women. All in all, it seems like the estimates presented here "fit" within the literature.

CONCLUSIONS

The contribution of this chapter has been to extend in two directions the net impact estimates that have been generated through nonexperimental methods with administrative data. In two studies, the net earnings impacts were decomposed into employment, hours of work, and wage rate impacts. Secondly, the earnings impacts were combined with estimates of impacts on fringe benefits, tax payments, and income-conditioned transfers to conduct a benefit-cost analysis of workforce programs.

The policy implications of this work are several in number. First, the studies add to the inventory of work that demonstrates that useful evaluations of the federal job training programs can be done with administrative data. Second, the decomposition of net earnings impacts into employment, hours, and wage rates adds rich understanding to the variation in these impacts across programs. The rate of return analyses demonstrate that the public (i.e., taxpayers) and society as a whole can benefit financially from education and training investments, although the payoffs generally take more than 10 quarters to offset the costs.

Finally, the results for individual programs are illuminating. WIA services for adults seem to have a significant positive impact on employment, wage rates, and earnings. However, the analyses point out the large forgone earnings of dislocated workers that dampen their financial payoff to training. Policymakers may wish to consider stronger support mechanisms for these workers such as stipends during training.

Notes

The contractual support of and provision of administrative data by Washington, Virginia, and Indiana as well as the resources and support of the Upjohn Institute are gratefully acknowledged. Wei-Jang Huang provided invaluable research assistance. The usual caveat applies.

1. In the terminology of Imbens and Angrist (1994), the estimates that we have produced are local average treatment effects (LATE). If we had used entry date to define participation (and matched on it rather than exit date), then we would be estimating the average treatment effect (ATE). In general, the former are larger than the latter.
2. The Virginia study also used the wage record data to develop an outcome variable that was used to measure employer satisfaction.
3. The tables in this chapter present results for the entire population. In studies 3 and 4, we have estimated the net impacts separately by gender as well as for the whole population.
4. The results for Youth are mixed. The two studies in Washington State show positive and significant employment gain; but neither the Virginia nor Indiana studies have this result. In fact, the Virginia employment impact for Youth is negative and significant.
5. The exception to this is JTPA II-C (Youth). The net impact estimate of loss of TANF benefits is quite large for this population in Study 1, and this result "drives" the negative benefits.
6. Again, two of the returns are not calculable because costs are negative or zero.
7. Heinrich, Mueser, and Troske (2008) indicate that a difference-in-difference estimate for dislocated workers attenuates these impacts toward zero.

Appendix 12A

Methodology for Net Impact
Estimation and Cost-Benefit Analyses

The net impact evaluation problem may be stated as follows: Individual i, who has characteristics X_{it}, at time t, will be observed to have outcome(s) $Y_{it}(1)$ if he or she receives a "treatment," such as participating in the workforce development system and will be observed to have outcome(s) $Y_{it}(0)$ if he or she doesn't participate. The net impact of the treatment for individual i is $Y_{it}(1) - Y_{it}(0)$. But, of course, this difference is never observed because an individual cannot simultaneously receive and not receive the treatment.

The time subscript is dropped in the following discussion to simplify the notation without loss of generality. Let $W_i = 1$ if individual i receives the treatment, and $W_i = 0$ if i does not receive the treatment. Let T represent the data set with observations about individuals who receive the treatment for whom we have data, and let n_T represent the number of individuals with data in T. Let U represent the data set with observations about individuals who may be similar to individuals who received the treatment for whom we have data, and let n_U be its sample size. Let C be a subset of U that contains observations that "match" those in T, and let n_C be its sample size. Names that may be used for these three data sets are Treatment sample (T), Comparison sample universe (U), and Matched Comparison sample (C).

Receiving the treatment is assumed to be a random event—individuals happened to be in the right place at the right time to learn about the program, or the individuals may have experienced randomly the eligibility criteria for the program—so W_i is a stochastic outcome that can be represented as follows:

(12A.1) $W_i = g(X_i, e_i)$,

where e_i is a random variable that includes unobserved or unobservable characteristics about individual i as well as a purely random component.

An assumption made about $g(\bullet)$ is that $0 < \text{prob}(W_i = 1|X_i) < 1$. This is referred to as the "support" or "overlap" condition, and is necessary so that the outcome functions described below are defined for all X.[1]

In general, outcomes are also assumed to be stochastically generated. As individuals in the treatment group encounter the treatment, they gain certain skills and knowledge and encounter certain networks of individuals. Outcomes are assumed to be generated by the following mapping:

(12A.2) $Y_i(1) = f_1(X_i) + e_{1i}$

Individuals not in the treatment group progress through time and also achieve certain outcomes according to another stochastic process, as follows:

(12A.3) $Y_i(0) = f_0(X_i) + e_{0i}$

Let $f_k(X_i) = E(Y_i(k)|X_i)$, so e_{ki} are deviations from expected values that reflect unobserved or unobservable characteristics, for $k = 0,1$.

As mentioned, the problem is that $Y_i(1)$ and $Y_i(0)$ are never observed simultaneously. What is observed is the following:

(12A.4) $Y_i = (1 - W_i)Y_i(0) + W_iY_i(1)$

The expected value for the net impact of the treatment on the sample of individuals treated:

(12A.5) $E[Y_i(1) - Y_i(0)|X, W_i = 1] = E(\Delta Y|X, W = 1)$
$= E[Y(1)|X, W = 1] - E[Y(0)|X, W = 0] + E[Y(0)|X, W = 0]$
$- E[Y(0)|X, W = 1]$
$= \hat{f}_1(X) - \hat{f}_0(X) + \text{BIAS, where}$

$\hat{f}_k(X)$, $k = 1, 0$, are the outcome means for the treatment and comparison group samples, respectively, and BIAS represents the expected difference in the $Y(0)$ outcome between the comparison group (actually observed) and the treatment group (the counterfactual). The BIAS term may be called selection bias.

A key assumption that allows estimation of Equation (12A.5) is that $Y(0)$ $\perp W|X$. This orthogonality assumption states that given X, the outcome (absent the treatment), $Y(0)$, is random whether or not the individual is a participant. This is equivalent to the assumption that participation in the treatment can be explained by X up to a random error term. The assumption is called "unconfoundedness," "conditional independence," or "selection on observables." If the assumption holds, then the net impact is identified because BIAS goes to 0, or

(12A.6) $E[\Delta Y|X, W = 1] = \hat{f}_1(X) - \hat{f}_0(X)$.

In random assignment, the X and W are uncorrelated through experimental control, so the conditional independence assumption holds by design. In any other design, the conditional independence is an empirical question. Whether or not the data come from a random assignment experiment, however, because the orthogonality assumption holds only asymptotically (or for very large samples), in practice, it makes sense to regression-adjust Equation (12A.6).

Various estimation techniques have been suggested in the literature, but they may be boiled down to two possibilities: 1) use all of the U set, or 2) try to find observations in U that closely match observations in T. Note that identification of the treatment effect requires that none of the covariates X in the data sets are perfectly correlated with being in T or U. That is, given any observation X_i, the probability of being in T or in U is between 0 and 1. Techniques that use all of U are called full sample techniques.[2] Techniques that try to find matching observations will be called matching techniques. The studies reported here used the latter, although Hollenbeck (2004) tests the robustness of net impact estimates to a number of matching techniques.

The studies that are discussed here use a nearest-neighbor algorithm using propensity scores as the distance metric (see Dehejia and Wahba 1995). Treatment observations are matched to observations in the comparison sample universe with the closest propensity scores. The matching is done with replacement and on a one-to-one basis. Matching with replacement reduces the "distance" between the treatment and comparison group cases, but it may result in the use of multiple repetitions of observations, which may artificially dampen the standard error of the net impact estimator. Finally, a caliper is employed to ensure that the distance between the observations that are paired is less than some criterion distance.

For most of the programs analyzed (and identified in Table 12.1), we used the public labor exchange data (known as Job Service, Employment Service, or Wagner-Peyser data) as the Matched Sample universe (i.e., set U). This is tantamount to the assumption that were these workforce development programs unavailable, then the individuals who were served would have gone to the public labor exchange for services.[3]

The net impacts for the outcomes listed in tables were estimated by regression-adjusting levels or difference-in-differences. We generally relied on the difference-in-difference estimators except where stark changes in labor market experiences were likely to have occurred—for youth and for dislocated workers. The base period for difference-in-difference estimators was for quarters −6 to −3 before program registration. The timeline in Figure 12A.1 is intended to help explain the analysis periods. The timeline shows the registration and exit dates for a hypothetical individual of adult age who registered for WIA Title I-B in April 2000 (Q2 of 2000) and exited from services in November 2001(Q4 of 2001). The earnings profile shows that this person had average quarterly earnings of $2,500 (real) in the base period (1998:Q4–1999:Q3), $2,700 in the 3rd quarter after exit (2002:Q3); and $3,100 average quarterly

Figure 12A.1 Timeline and Earnings Profile for a Hypothetical WIA Title I-B Adult Client

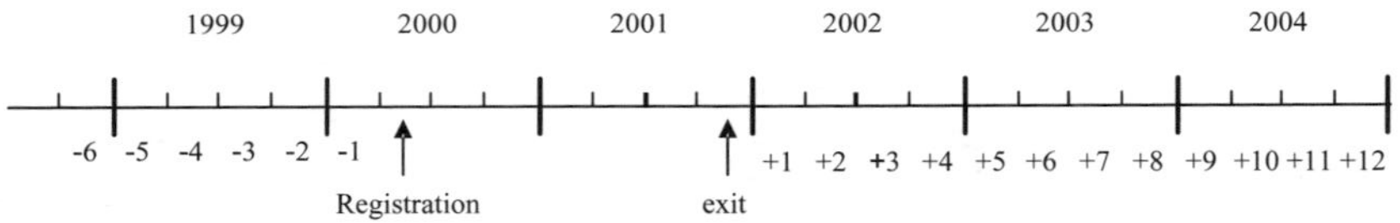

Timeline: 1999 2000 2001 2002 2003 2004

−6 −5 −4 −3 −2 −1 | +1 +2 +3 +4 +5 +6 +7 +8 +9 +10 +11 +12

Registration — exit — Training →

Earnings profile

Calendar quarter	98:Q1	98:Q2	98:Q3	98:Q4	99:Q1	99:Q2	99:Q3	99:Q4	00:Q1	00:Q2	00:Q3	00:Q4
Analysis quarter	−9	−8	−7	−6	−5	−4	−3	−2	−1	Training		
Real earnings ($)	2,300	1,500	0	1,000	2,800	3,000	3,200	3,200	1,600	0	0	1,200

Calendar quarter	01:Q1	01:Q2	01:Q3	01:Q4	02:Q1	02:Q2	02:Q3	02:Q4	03:Q1	03:Q2	03:Q3	03:Q4
Analysis quarter	Training				+1	+2	+3	+4	+5	+6	+7	+8
Real earnings ($)	2,000	0	0	1,500	2,500	2,700	2,700	2,700	2,900	0	1,600	2,900

Calendar quarter	04:Q1	04:Q2	04:Q3	04:Q4
Analysis quarter	+9	+10	+11	+12
Real earnings ($)	3,000	3,100	3,100	3,200

Outcome variables ($)

Earnings (+3)	2,700
Avg. earnings (9–12)	3,100
Base period earnings (−6 through −3)	2,500

earnings in the 9th–12th postexit quarters, which were 2004:Q1–2004:Q4. So in the regression adjustment of earnings levels, the dependent variables would have been $2,700 and $3,100 for the short-term and longer-term outcomes. In the regression adjustment of difference-in-differences, the dependent variables would have been $200 and $600, respectively.

COST-BENEFIT ANALYSES[4]

Earnings. Benefits and costs are projected for the "average" participant. Figure 12A.2 shows the earnings profiles for the average individual in the treatment group and in the comparison group. The hypothesis used to construct these profiles is that encountering a workforce development program enhances an individual's skills and productivity (thus increasing wage rates) and increases the likelihood of employment. Thus, after the training period, the treatment earnings profile is above the comparison earnings profile (both hourly wage and employment net impacts are positive). During the training period, the treatment earnings will be below the comparison earnings, on average. These are the forgone costs of training in the form of wages that are given up by the participant while he or she is receiving training.

**Figure 12A.2 Age-Earnings Profiles of Training Participants and
Comparison Group**

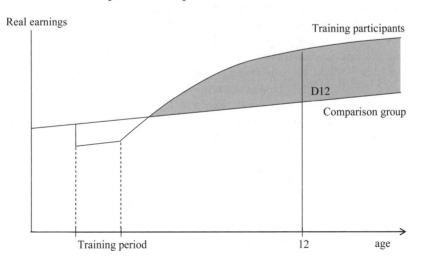

The theoretical lifetime earnings benefit is the shaded area in the graph. The average comparison group member's real earnings grow at some fairly constant rate (increase in productivity), and the average treatment group member's earnings eventually become higher after training and likely grow faster as they accumulate additional human capital in the form of work experience.

The problem that needs to be solved in estimating the benefits is how to compute the shaded area. In general, we have several quarters of outcome data, so we can get accurate estimates of the area up to the line denoted D12 (treatment minus comparison difference at the 12th quarter). Because the profiles represent the *average* individual, we use the *unconditional* net earnings impacts to calculate these benefits. (They automatically control for employment, hourly wage, and hours worked impacts.)

What is unknown (and unknowable) is the shape of the earnings profiles into the future after the D12 point. The profiles could continue to move apart from each other if the training participants continue to be more and more productive relative to the comparison group member, or the profiles eventually may converge over time if the training effect depreciates. Alternatively, the profiles may become parallel to reflect a scenario in which the training participants gain a permanent advantage, but then their productivity growth eventually matches the comparison group members. The typical approach is to extrapolate earnings into the future based on the observed time trend in the first 12 quarters after exit. Since the earnings benefits are received by the participants in future periods, they need to be discounted. The studies reported here used a 3 percent real discount rate.

Fringe benefits. With additional earnings, workers will also accrue additional fringe benefits in the form of paid leave, paid insurances, retirement/ savings plan contributions, and other noncash benefits. Two sources of data provided estimates of the ratio of fringe benefits (defined as paid leave plus paid insurances plus retirement plan contributions plus other) to gross wages and salaries (including supplemental pay such as overtime). The Bureau of Labor Statistics (2002), reports this ratio to be 23.3 percent for "All U.S." and 20.4 percent for the "West Census Region." The U.S. Chamber of Commerce (2001) reports a ratio of 24.3 percent for the Pacific region. Under the assumption that workforce development program participants are less likely to get fringe benefit coverage than the average worker, and to be conservative in our benefit estimation, we used the assumption that this ratio would be 20 percent (applied to the discounted annual earnings increments).

Tax payments. Higher earnings will lead to payment of increased payroll, sales/excise, local, state, and federal income taxes.[5] The increased taxes are a cost to participants and a benefit to the public. We used average (marginal) tax rates for each of the taxes and applied these rates to the annual earnings changes. For example, we used the current rate of 7.65 percent to estimate the future payroll tax liabilities. We relied on IRS data for the federal income tax rates that factor in earned income tax credits, and state sources provided average rates for the other types of taxes.

Unemployment compensation. Unemployment compensation benefits in the future may increase for participants if programs increase employment (and therefore the probability of receiving UI) or increase earnings (and therefore benefits) or they may decrease if programs decrease the likelihood of unemployment or decrease duration of unemployment spells. Increased UI benefits in the future would be a discounted benefit to participants and cost to the public. We used a similar empirical strategy as we did for lifetime earnings to interpolate and extrapolate these benefits. In particular, we estimated the unconditional UI benefit net impacts for the first 12 quarters after exit and used these estimates as the average impact for the program in those quarters. Then we used the estimate for the 12th quarter after exit to extrapolate for 28 more quarters (68 quarters for WIA Youth). In other words, we assumed that the UI benefit gain or loss would dampen to 0 after 10 years for the Adult and Dislocated Worker programs and after 20 years for the Youth program.

Income-conditioned transfers. The maintained hypothesis was that participation in the workforce development programs would decrease the probability of receiving TANF and Food Stamps, and the probability of enrolling in Medicaid. In addition, increased earnings may have resulted in reductions in benefit levels for TANF and Food Stamps. Finally, if individuals no longer receive TANF or Food Stamps, they would not receive any support services such as child care or other referrals.

For TANF/Food Stamps, we followed the same empirical strategy as we did for unemployment compensation. We estimated net impacts for unconditional TANF benefits and Food Stamp benefits for the 12 quarters after program exit cohort and extrapolated beyond that period using the estimate from quarter +12. We again assumed that on average, the program participants may receive these benefits (or lose these benefits) for up to 40 quarters (or 80 quarters for the youth program) even though TANF is time limited to 20 quarters. The reason for going beyond 20 quarters is that these are averages for the entire program group, and the dynamics of recipiency will be assumed to continue for up to 10 years.

The typical pattern for the workforce development programs is that in the short term, TANF benefits are decreased for participants who exit because, for the most part, employment rates increase—at least, some individuals leave the rolls. However, as time progresses, some workers begin to lose employment, or become single and have dependent children, and the group's TANF net impact benefits become positive, although of relatively small magnitude.

We followed a similar empirical strategy for Food Stamps as we did for TANF. We estimated net impacts for unconditional benefits for the 12 quarters after program exit and extrapolated beyond that period using the estimate from quarter +12. We again assumed that on average, the program participants may receive these benefits (or lose these benefits) for up to 40 quarters (or 80 quarters for the Youth program).

The states did not make actual benefit/usage information for Medicaid available, so we estimated net impacts of actually being enrolled in Medicaid. Our hypothesis was that training participants will tend to decrease their enrollment rates as they become better attached to the labor force over time and will thus lose eligibility. We converted Medicaid enrollment into financial terms by multiplying the average state share of Medicaid expenditures per quarter times the average number of household members per case. As with TANF and Food Stamps, this is a benefit to the participant and a cost to the public. To interpolate/extrapolate the net impact of a program on Medicaid eligibility, we either averaged or fit a linear equation time series of estimated enrollment net impacts.

Costs. Two types of costs were estimated for each of the programs. The first was forgone earnings, which would be reduced earnings while the participants were actually engaged in the training programs. The second type of cost was the actual direct costs of the training.

Forgone earnings represent the difference between what workforce development program participants would have earned if they had not participated in a program (which is unobservable) and what they earned while they did participate. The natural estimate for the former is the earnings of the matched comparison group members during the length of training. Specifically, we used Equation (12A.7) to estimate mechanistically the forgone earnings. Note that we did not discount forgone earnings, but did calculate them in real \$.

$$(12A.7) \quad Forgone_i = \left[0.5 \times \left(\hat{E}_{-1_i} + \overline{E}_{-1_i} \right) - \overline{E}_{0_i} \right] \times d_i \; ,$$

where $\overline{E}_{-1}, \overline{E}_0$ = average quarterly earnings (unconditional) for treatment group in quarter -1 and during training period, respectively.

$\hat{E}_1$ = average quarterly earnings in first postexit period for matched comparison group.

d = average training duration.

i = indexes program.

For the most part, the costs of providing services were supplied to us by the states. Staff members of the state agencies calculated these costs from administrative data on days in the program and daily cost information.

Appendix Notes

1. Note that Imbens (2004) shows that this condition can be slightly weakened to $\Pr(W_i = 1 | X_i) < 1$.
2. Some of these techniques trim or delete a few outlier observations from U but will still be referred to as full sample techniques.
3. For some of the programs other than the public job training programs focused on here, the public labor exchange was not an appropriate counterfactual, and alternative administrative data sources were used. These programs included secondary career and technical education, vocational rehabilitation, and blind and visually impaired services. For high school career and technical education, the matched comparison universe was all high school graduates in the state. For the other two programs, the matched comparison universe was composed of nonserved applicants.
4. This discussion will present general methodological issues. Readers can find the specific parameters or estimates that were used in the source reports.
5. Washington does not have local or state income taxes.

References

Bureau of Labor Statistics. 2002. "Employer Costs for Employee Compensation—March 2002." News release 02-346. Washington, DC: Bureau of Labor Statistics. http://www.bls.gov/opub/ted/2002/jul/wk3/art01.htm (accessed October 2, 2010).

Dehejia, Rajeev H., and Sadek Wahba. 1995. "Causal Effects in Nonexperimental Studies: Re-evaluating the Evaluation of Training Programs." Working paper. Cambridge, MA: Harvard University.

Government Accountability Office. 1996. *Job Training Partnership Act: Long-Term Earnings and Employment Outcomes*. Report HEHS-96-40. Washington, DC: U.S. Government Printing Office.

Heinrich, Carolyn J., Peter R. Mueser, and Kenneth R. Troske. 2008. *Workforce Investment Act Non-experimental Net Impact Evaluation*. Report to U.S. Department of Labor. Columbia, MD: IMPAQ International.

Hollenbeck, Kevin. 2004. "On the Use of Administrative Data for Workforce Development Program Evaluation." Paper presented at the U.S. Department of Labor, Employment and Training Administration's "2004 National

Workforce Investment Research" colloquium, held in Arlington, VA, May 24.

———. 2009. *Return on Investment Analyses of a Selected Set of Workforce System Programs in Indiana.* Kalamazoo, MI: W.E. Upjohn Institute for Employment Research.

Hollenbeck, Kevin M., and Wei-Jang Huang. 2003. *Net Impact and Benefit-Cost Estimates of the Workforce Development System in Washington State.* Technical Report No. TR03-018. Kalamazoo, MI: W.E. Upjohn Institute for Employment Research.

———. 2006. *Net Impact and Benefit-Cost Estimates of the Workforce Development System in Washington State.* Technical Report No. TR06-020. Kalamazoo, MI: W.E. Upjohn Institute for Employment Research.

———. 2008. *Workforce Program Performance Indicators for the Commonwealth of Virginia.* Technical Report No. 08-024. Kalamazoo, MI: W.E. Upjohn Institute for Employment Research.

Imbens, Guido W. 2004. "Nonparametric Estimation of Average Treatment Effects under Exogeneity: A Review." *Review of Economics and Statistics* 86(1): 4–29.

Imbens, Guido W., and Joshua D. Angrist. 1994. "Identification and Estimation of Local Average Treatment Effects." *Econometrica* 62(2): 467–475.

Mueser, Peter, Kenneth Troske, and Alexey Gorislavsky. 2007. "Using State Administrative Data to Measure Program Performance." *Review of Economics and Statistics* 89(4): 761–783.

U.S. Chamber of Commerce. 2001. *The 2001 Employment Benefits Study.* Washington, DC: U.S. Chamber of Commerce.

13
A Nonexperimental Evaluation
of WIA Programs

Carolyn J. Heinrich
LaFollette School of Public Affairs, University of Wisconsin

Peter R. Mueser
University of Missouri, IMPAQ International, LLC, and IZA

Kenneth R. Troske
University of Kentucky and IZA

Kyung-Seong Jeon
University of Missouri

Daver C. Kahvecioglu
IMPAQ International, LLC

The recent economic recession has highlighted and exacerbated difficulties faced by low-wage workers in recent decades. Perhaps most troubling is a significant and persistent rise in the rate of long-term unemployment—workers unemployed for more than six months. The 2009 American Recovery and Reinvestment Act includes an unprecedented level of funding for the public workforce development system and associated employment and training programs.[1] This injection of resources to aid unemployed and underemployed workers nearly doubled U.S. federal government funding for WIA programs—youth employment, adult job training, dislocated worker assistance, Job Corps, and other national activities—that had been steadily declining since the start of the WIA program in 2000 (Frank and Minoff 2005).

Since its inception, there has been no rigorous evaluation of the WIA programs that serve adults. In the face of this substantially expanded public investment in employment and training, we argue that rigorous evidence on the impact and effectiveness of WIA services is needed now to guide the use of these resources in generating the greatest potential benefit for workers and the highest possible return to taxpayer dollars.[2]

WIA is distinguished from its predecessor, JTPA, primarily by the introduction of a One-Stop service delivery system designed to improve coordination and integration of services, its use of ITAs in training services, and changes in governance structures at the state and local levels. Prior to the start of the recession in December 2007, WIA had reduced the share of low-income individuals served by one-third and decreased the length of time spent in training and the expenditures per trainee (Osterman 2007). Thus, important changes in both investments in and the implementation of public employment training programs have taken place under WIA, and yet surprisingly little is known about the impact of WIA and its components on labor market outcomes.

To date, evaluations of WIA have provided very limited information on program effectiveness.[3] This study employs nonexperimental matching methods to evaluate the WIA Adult and Dislocated Worker programs using data from 12 states that cover approximately 160,000 WIA participants and nearly 3 million comparison group members. Within each state, we compare WIA program participants with a matched comparison population of individuals who have not participated in the WIA program but who are observationally equivalent across a range of demographic characteristics, prior participation in employment programs, and labor market experiences. Comparison group members are drawn from those who have participated in the ES under Wagner-Peyser legislation or who have filed claims for UI benefits.

This study adds to an expanding literature that evaluates active labor market programs. In general, this literature is moderately supportive of the benefits of job training and related active labor market programs on participants. Card et al. (2009) observe that job training programs, especially longer-duration programs, tend to have very small or negative impacts on employment measures in periods of less than a year, presumably reflecting "lock-in" effects, but have positive effects in the second or third years (see also Dyke et al. [2006]; Hotz, Imbens, and Klerman [2006]). One useful benchmark is the random assignment evaluation of JTPA program participation in the late 1980s. Program enrollees experienced minimal incremental effects in the two quarters after random assignment (which took place at program entry), but the increment in quarterly earnings increased to $300–$350 (2006 $) by the tenth quarter (Orr et al. 1996, p. 107).

Our results indicate that the average participant in the WIA Adult program obtains a several-hundred-dollar increase in quarterly earnings. Adult program participants who obtain training have lower earnings in the months during training and the year after exit than those who do not receive training, but they catch up within 10 quarters, ultimately registering large gains. The marginal benefits of training exceed, on average, $400 in earnings each quarter three years after program entry. Dislocated workers experience several quarters for which earnings are depressed relative to comparison group workers after entering WIA, and although their earnings ultimately match or overtake the comparison group, the benefits they obtain are smaller than for those in the Adult program and in some cases are indistinguishable from zero.

OVERVIEW OF WIA ADULT AND DISLOCATED WORKER PROGRAMS

We evaluate two WIA programs: the Adult program, serving largely disadvantaged individuals, and the Dislocated Worker program, serving those who have lost jobs. Although the Adult program is designed largely for individuals who are unemployed, employed individuals are eligible to participate if participation allows them to achieve economic self-sufficiency. The target population for the Dislocated Worker program is workers facing layoffs and those eligible for unemployment insurance, although other individuals who have lost their jobs are eligible if staff decide they fall in several broad categories.[4] Participation in the WIA programs is voluntary, but access is restricted, as program staff must admit participants and authorize any services that are provided. The analyses here focus on individuals entering WIA in the period July 2003–June 2005 (program years 2003 and 2004), which allows sufficient time after the program's initial startup (July 2000 in most states), while providing an extended follow-up period.

Although legislative requirements establish a general programmatic structure, states and local areas have a great deal of latitude in implementing the WIA programs.[5] States have further specified rules, and, in keeping with the spirit of local control in WIA legislation, they have also left many decisions to the local agency, the WIB. Legislation does not define economic self-sufficiency, so whether an employed individual requires services is left largely to local discretion. In the first few years of WIA implementation, incentives to cream skim in admission to the program were documented by the GAO (2002), and the point at which individuals were formally registered in WIA differed substantially across sites.

For both the Adult and Dislocated Worker programs, WIA legislation specifies three levels of service. All participants who enter WIA receive core services, which include staff-assisted job search and placement, provision of labor market information, and basic counseling, corresponding closely to the staff-assisted services offered by state offices as part of the ES under Wagner-Peyser legislation. Once individuals receive core services, staff may recommend that they receive intensive services, which involve comprehensive assessment, more extensive counseling and career planning, and possibly short courses. Participants in intensive services may then be recommended to receive training services. Under WIA, most training is provided by separate organizations—including community colleges, proprietary schools, nonprofits servicing the disadvantaged, and others—through a voucher (the ITA).

Given that ES services are very similar to WIA core services, at least in terms of their basic structure, individuals needing such services who are not accepted into the WIA program are normally referred to ES—which is usually available at the same site. In some sites WIA enrolls only individuals who are authorized to receive intensive or training services. Despite the structure of the ITA as a voucher, WIA program staff retain power to determine who will receive the voucher and, in consequence, how it is used. Staff are generally required to assure that training prepares participants for jobs in high demand, although how this is implemented, including the extent of counselor involvement in the training decision, is highly variable.

Those locations that follow the spirit of the sequential service mandate might be expected to provide training primarily to individuals who had been unsuccessful in obtaining employment through less intensive services, causing negative selection into training. On the other hand, in most sites, as many as one-third of those who participate in WIA have a particular training goal prior to program entry (they are often referred to WIA by the training provider), and, in general, WIB staff make an effort to accommodate them. Finally, staff are under pressure to provide training to individuals whose employment outcomes will aid the performance measures, so insofar as counselors can identify those who will ultimately succeed in the labor market, we would expect positive selection.

In the period of our study, nationwide about one in five WIA participants received only core services, and about two in five were coded as receiving training services. Of those who received training, up to 10 percent received on-the-job training and another 5 percent received basic skills training. The remainder were coded as receiving occupational and other training, including an unknown amount of customized training for employers. About half of all training was funded by ITAs. Little is known about the character or intensity of the training offered, but approximately two-thirds of training recipients received some kind of credential. Between one-half and one-third of participants exited WIA in less than 26 weeks, whereas a similar proportion remained in the program for at least a year.[6] Both funding and maximum time limits for training activities varied dramatically across states and across WIBs within a state, as did expenditures per participant. The average state spent about $5,000 for each participant exiting the program; the lowest average expenditure was about $1,000 and the largest about $15,000 (USDOL/ETA 2009).

Although there is potential overlap between Adult and Dislocated Worker program participants, in practice they differ quite dramatically in terms average age, gender, race, and prior work experience. Given that the two programs serve very different functions, each is analyzed separately. The analysis presented here does not distinguish core and intensive levels of service.

STUDY SAMPLE, DATA, MEASURES, AND METHOD OF ANALYSIS

Study Sample

In December 2007, the USDOL issued a notice requesting that state workforce agencies provide access to administrative data for use in an evaluation of WIA activities funded under federal legislation. Agencies in all 50 states were contacted and efforts were made to negotiate agreements by which necessary data would be released to the researchers. Funds were made available to cover state expenses, and states were promised that individually identifiable state results would not be released. Ultimately, agreements were reached and necessary data were provided by 12 states: Connecticut, Indiana, Kentucky, Maryland, Missouri, Minnesota, Mississippi, Montana, New Mexico, Tennessee, Utah, and Wisconsin.[7]

As noted at the beginning of the chapter, we employ matching methods in which program participants are matched with individuals in a comparison group based on observed variables.[8] All analyses are based on state administrative data, with files identifying program participants and comparison group members, as well as employment data, drawn from each state. The comparison group is drawn from either UI claimants or from ES participants (i.e., individuals who register with the state's job exchange service and receive services under Wagner-Peyser legislation). Of the 12 states in our analysis, 9 have UI claimant comparison data, while three have comparison data from ES participants. Estimates of the incremental impact of training use a comparison group consisting of WIA participants who did not receive training services, i.e., of those receiving only core or intensive services.

Data Sources and Measures

The base data for the 12 states include annual WIASRD or closely related data files obtained from each state that provide information on all participants exiting the WIA program within a program year (July–June). For most states, the data files extend through June 2007 (program year 2006). These data also include an individual identifier to allow a match with other state data. The focus of the current analysis is on WIA participants who entered the WIA program in the period July 2003–June 2005.

Comparison group information derives from state administrative data for UI claims or ES participants. UI wage record data provide quarterly earnings for all employees in UI-covered firms within a state. Data extend through calendar year 2007, which, when matched with WIASRD information and information for individuals in the comparison groups, generate the study's primary outcome measures. These include earnings and employment for participants for up to 16 quarters following participation and for comparison group members in the same periods. These data also include earnings prior to WIA participation, facilitating the construction of employment histories for participants and comparison group members. All earnings have been adjusted for inflation to correspond with the first quarter of 2006.

It has long been recognized that controls for standard demographic characteristics such as gender, age, education, and race are important. In addition to these, we capture local labor market characteristics using aggregates of county of residence or service (or where county is not available, the local Workforce Investment Area), and the details of the labor market experiences of individuals in the period immediately prior to program participation.[9] Wage record data provide information on employment status at the time of initial program involvement and for prior years. Additional variables include controls for veteran status and prior earnings.

Analyses are performed separately by gender. Where possible, WIA participants who enter in a given quarter are also matched with individuals in the comparison sample who have contact with their respective programs in the same quarter, providing an exact match on quarter of entry.

Descriptive Statistics

Table 13A.1 in Appendix 13A provides sample sizes and means for WIA participants and the comparison group in the 12 states. A total of 95,580 unique individuals entered the WIA Adult program during the observation window. Since about 2 percent entered the program more than once, the total number of entries was 97,552. Similarly, 63,515 individuals entered the Dislocated Worker program, producing a total of 64,089 program entries.[10] Nearly 3 million unique individuals participate in comparison programs (UI claimants or ES participants) and are available to be matched to program participants, contributing approximately 6.2 million quarters of program activity.[11]

Individuals who participated in the WIA Adult program are more likely to be female and minority than individuals in the comparison sample; they are also appreciably younger. These differences reflect the fact that participants in the WIA Adult program tend to be economically disadvantaged, whereas participants in the comparison sample are individuals who have recently lost jobs. Therefore, individuals in the comparison sample have the characteristics of individuals with relatively strong labor market attachments—white, male, older workers with more education. Comparing participants in the WIA Dislocated Worker program with the comparison group, it is clear there are fewer differences—participants in the WIA Dislocated Worker program are more likely to be female and are slightly older, but differences are smaller. Participants in the WIA Adult program are less likely to have worked continuously in the six prior quarters and are much more likely to have not worked in any of the six quarters prior to entering the program; they also have much lower annual earnings in the two years prior to entering the program. In contrast, participants in the WIA Dislocated Worker program have similar labor market attachment and only slightly lower earnings than those in the comparison program.

Approximately 4–5 percent of WIA entrants had previously participated in WIA (either the Adult or Dislocated Worker program). About one-fifth of Adult program participants had prior comparison program experience, compared to over two-fifths of Dislocated Workers. About two-thirds of comparison program participants had participated in WIA in the prior two years.

Within each program, participants who receive training services are more likely to be female and much less likely to be black than participants who do not receive training services. Differences in education are very small. Based on prior earnings, those receiving training services appear to have had greater labor market success, but measures of employment imply only small differences in employment activity.

Notwithstanding these differences, there are important similarities in the patterns of earnings for treated and comparison cases. The earnings of the WIA participants display a decline in average earnings over the year or two prior to program entry, a pattern called the "Ashenfelter dip" (Ashenfelter 1978; Heckman and Smith 1999), reflecting the fact that individuals often enter such programs following a period of setbacks in employment. There is a similar decline preceding program participation for the comparison group, suggesting that there will be sufficient numbers of individuals to match with WIA participants on the basis of prior employment. Equally important, the common pattern suggests that there may be similarities in the individual employment environments faced by the comparison and treatment groups, suggesting that unmeasured factors may be similar as well.

Method of Analysis

We estimate the impact of participation in the WIA Adult or Dislocated Worker programs on outcomes for those who participate, that is, the effect of the treatment on the treated. We use propensity score matching, which, like other matching and related methods, assumes that the outcome that would occur in the absence of the treatment is conditionally independent of the treatment (Rosenbaum and Rubin 1983).

Control variables include calendar quarter of program entry, gender, age, years of educational attainment, race/ethnicity, disability status, veteran status (for males), local labor market, employment information based on wage record data over the two years prior to program entry (including employment transitions and earnings), industry of employment in the prior year, and program participation history up to four years prior to WIA entry (WIA; UI or ES).

Although the conditional independence assumption cannot be tested directly, we apply a reasonable specification test that examines prior earnings. If subsequent earnings in the absence of the treatment would have been the same for treated and comparison groups conditional on measured characteristics, we would expect prior earnings to be the same as well. Conversely, if differences in stable factors that influence earnings exist between the treatment and comparison group, we expect there to be differences in the conditional means. In practice, the test based on this comparison amounts to estimating the "effect" of program participation on prior earnings. If there is no significant effect, this suggests that there are no stable factors influencing income that differ for the treated and control group.

Where the specification test fails, individual fixed effects estimators provide an alternative approach to controlling for differences across individuals who participate in WIA.[12] So long as such differences have stable effects on earnings, this specification can eliminate bias. Despite the benefits of the difference-in-difference estimators, depending on the processes underlying earnings dynamics and program participation, estimates may have biases that are not present in cross-sectional matching. The difference-in-difference estimator needs to be understood as one of several estimates that make different assumptions.

The estimator of program impact that we use here is many-to-one caliper matching with replacement based on the propensity score. Matching is based on a constant radius expressed as the difference in the log-odds of the propensity score between treated and comparison cases. We report conditional standard errors based on methods recommended by Imbens and Wooldridge (2008) and Imbens (2008). The matching model specification was determined separately for each of the comparisons by gender within each of the 12 states.

RESULTS OF IMPACT ESTIMATION FOR ADULT PROGRAM

We obtain estimates of WIA program impacts on average inflation-adjusted earnings and employment in the 16 quarters following program start. After obtaining state-specific impact estimates, the mean across states is estimated by weighting the estimate for a given state by the number of participants who were matched in that state. The resulting weighted mean provides an estimate of the average impact for matched WIA participants who entered the program during the period considered. Associated with each state impact estimate is an estimated conditional standard error, which is combined across states in the conventional way to form the standard error for the weighted average. We focus on averages across participants in the 12 states to reduce sampling error—which is substantial—and average across idiosyncratic state differences.

Figures 13.1 and 13.2 provide estimates of the impacts of the WIA Adult program on earnings for women and men, respectively. The horizontal axis extends from 1 to 16, identifying the quarter following program entry. The vertical axis is in dollars, indicating the difference between average earnings in a quarter for the WIA Adult program participants and matched comparison program participants. Also on the graph are dashed lines that show the confidence interval for each estimate. The lower dashed line subtracts twice the conditional standard error from the estimate, and the upper dashed line adds twice the standard error.[13] Also presented in this figure are the estimates of "impact" on earnings 10 and 16 quarters prior to program entry, providing a specification test of the model.

The estimates reported in the figures imply that, for both genders, participants generally earn between $400 and $600 more per quarter than matched individuals in the comparison program over our follow-up period. For women, the impact estimate over most of the 16 quarters is between $500 and $600 per quarter, whereas for men there is a decline

Figure 13.1 Adult Program Treatment Effect on Quarterly Earnings for Females, WIA versus Comparison Group

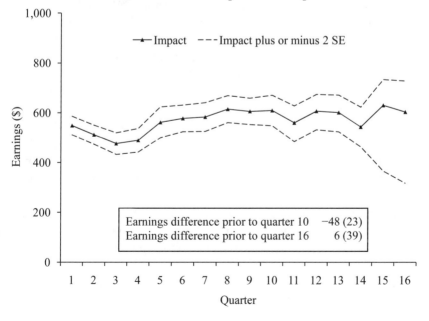

Figure 13.2 Adult Program Treatment Effect on Quarterly Earnings for Males, WIA versus Comparison Group

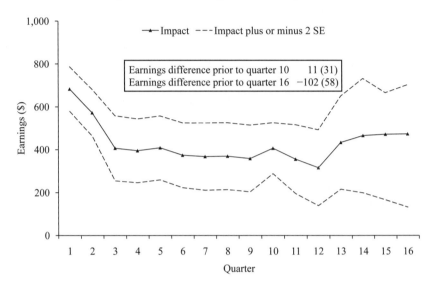

in the first three quarters, with the level settling in the range of $400. In percentage terms, the program increases earnings by about 30 percent for women after the second quarter and by about 15 percent for men.

We calculated analogous estimates for employment based on the same methods, using the proportion employed (identified as having received positive earnings in the quarter) as the dependent variable. The basic pattern of results was very similar to that for earnings. In particular, female participants' employment rate impact estimate was 13 percentage points in the first quarter after participation but declined to about 8 points within a year, and ultimately to about 6 points. Male impacts were one or two percentage points lower. The employment proportion is about 0.55 in the absence of the program, so employment increases by up to 15 percent.

As noted earlier, there are substantial differences in the proportion of individuals receiving training across the state programs, possibly contributing to differing patterns of effects for programs with different levels of training. First, long-run program impacts could be higher in states with more intensive services. Second, a large share of the value may well occur with a greater lag, since training benefits presumably accrue over a more extended period. We separately tabulated impact estimates for the seven states that provided training to more than half of their participants. In these states taken together, 68 percent of Adult program participants received training. The initial effects—during the first several quarters after program entry—in these seven states were very similar to the aggregate for all states. However, in contrast to the full sample, earnings were higher in subsequent quarters, providing at least weak evidence that high-training states produce benefits that endure longer.

Taken at face value, these results imply that the program has strong and substantial impacts with little or no lag. These could reflect aggressive actions by program staff to help workers obtain employment initially, with training assuring benefits that accrue over an extended period. Skeptics will argue, however, that the findings of such large initial impacts call into question the appropriateness of the comparison group and ultimately the validity of the results. With most training programs, participants are expected to obtain little benefit initially— possibly experiencing earnings reductions—as they engage in training activities that supplant employment that would otherwise occur. In these data, the mean time in the program is between two and three quarters, so we might expect that program participation would hinder participants' employment and earnings in the first few quarters.

In order for selection to cause these results, it must be the case that WIA participants have unmeasured attributes that make them more likely than those in the comparison program to obtain employment or higher earnings. Staff admission criteria or participant choice would need to select entrants who were appreciably more likely to obtain employment than other individuals with similar characteristics, employment, and program participation histories.

One test for selection is provided by analyses that predict prior earnings. Although controls are included for earnings in the eight quarters prior to entry, if there are stable factors that improve the employment prospects for treated cases relative to matched comparison cases, earlier earnings would be higher for the WIA cases. We calculate the difference in earnings between treated and comparison cases for measures applying to the 10th and 16th quarters prior to entry, presenting these estimates as inserts in the figures. These estimates show that earnings are *not* higher for WIA participants; in most cases, the differences are small (see Figures 13.1 and 13.2). The largest differences are for male WIA participants 16 quarters earlier, for which it appears that WIA participants had earnings about $100 *below* those of the comparison group. Although not quite statistically significant, the difference measures suggest a downward bias in program impact estimates; estimates from a difference-in-difference model would produce program impact estimates that were $100 greater. For males in the seven high-training states, earnings of program participants are $230 lower—again a difference that is not statistically significant. It is therefore clear that if selection is causing spurious positive impact estimates, selection is unlikely to be based on stable individual characteristics.

One alternative explanation would be that there are transient differences between WIA participants and others. The comparison group members receiving unemployment compensation may include a substantial portion of individuals who are not seeking employment. UI recipients classified as awaiting recall are not required to search for employment, and many others may have little interest in getting a job—despite formal requirements—until benefits are about to expire. According to this view, those obtaining UI benefits are in a phase where their short-term employment levels are expected to be depressed, reflecting the incentives created by UI benefits, which are contingent on remaining unemployed. WIA participants, in contrast, have chosen to select into a program with the purpose of improving their employment prospects.

If the bias is due to benefits provided by UI, it might be expected that such differences would be less important for the other comparison group, those seeking ES services. Although most UI claimants are required to register for ES services, those awaiting recall are exempt from this requirement, so the ES sample removes one group whose interest in employment may be modest. Since any individual seeking support for employment search can obtain ES services, this sample includes self-motivated job searchers.

We estimated Adult program impacts on earnings and employment for the three states where ES recipients form the comparison group. The most notable difference between these results and the full sample of states was that impacts in the first few quarters after entry were smaller, in the range of $200 for both men and women. There was a fairly steady growth in program impact up through the last quarters. These results support the view that the large impacts on earnings and employment in the quarters immediately after WIA entry could be at least partly due to differences between WIA participants and the UI claimant comparison group rather than to the effects of program participation. Of the nine states for which UI claimants are the comparison group, initial program impact in only two of them is as small as for the three states where ES is the comparison group.

We also undertook analyses that limited the treated group to those receiving UI benefits when they entered the WIA program. In these analyses, estimated effects were much smaller. Estimates were negative in the first 3–7 quarters after program entry, with quarterly estimates of impact after 10 quarters in the range of $200. Adult program participants who receive UI benefits at the point of entry account for less than 10 percent of entries during the period of our study. Although this is an important group, impacts in this group need not be representative of others in the program. These results suggest that impacts for Adult WIA participants receiving UI benefits are substantially smaller than for the full population of participants. In the discussion below of the Dislocated Worker program, we present evidence suggesting that the average impact in that program may be smaller than for the Adult program. This supports the view that the benefits of WIA for those who lose a "good" job may be smaller than for workers with generally poor work histories.

Impacts of Training

The heart of WIA services is the basic and vocational skills training provided to individuals. Although a variety of training opportunities are widely available outside of WIA, for many WIA Adult participants, the alternatives available are more costly. It is clear that acceptance into WIA alters the type and extent of training these individuals ultimately obtain.

Figures 13.3 and 13.4 present impact estimates of training based on analyses where the comparison group is Adult WIA participants not receiving training. Earnings impact estimates for females imply a $200 decrement in the first quarter after program entry, as would be expected if time in training limited initial employment options. Earnings catch up three or four quarters later, with a positive increment over $800 by the end of 10 quarters, implying an earnings increment of about 30 percent.

Figure 13.3 Adult Program Treatment Effect on Quarterly Earnings for Females, WIA Training versus Comparison Group

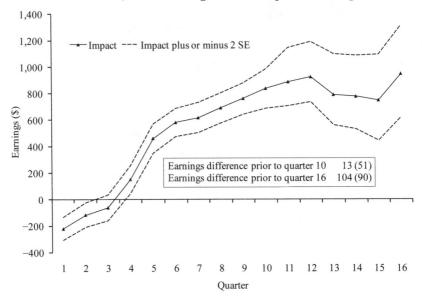

Figure 13.4 Adult Program Treatment Effect on Quarterly Earnings for Males, WIA Training versus Comparison Group

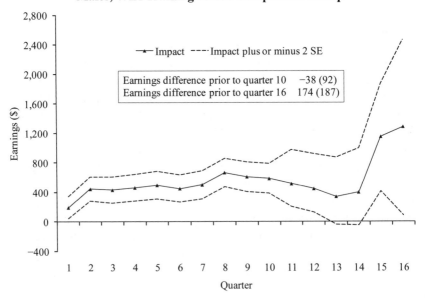

In contrast, males who receive training appear to experience positive initial impacts—in the range of $200 immediately after entry—with the increment remaining in the $500–$600 range, 10–20 percent of earnings for the next 10 quarters.[14]

The pattern for employment impacts is very similar. For women, initial employment is about five percentage points lower for those receiving training, and only catches up 4 quarters after entry. By the 10th quarter, the increment is in favor of training recipients by about 5 percentage points. For men, the increment is close to zero for 6 or 7 quarters after program entry, and the ultimate increment is slightly smaller than for women, in the range of three to four percentage points. The pattern of results does not vary substantially by whether states train a large share of their participants, nor are results substantially different for ES states.

Differences in patterns for men and women may partly reflect the types of training they receive. A study of exits for program year 2005 finds that, of males exiting from the WIA Adult program, 37 percent received on-the-job training, in contrast to 15 percent for females (Social Policy Research Associates 2007). Classroom training would be expected to reduce initial earnings and employment by more than on-the-job training and possibly provide greater earnings with a delay. In our sample of Adult program participants who obtain training, women average more than three months longer than men between entry and exit, consistent with the view that women are obtaining more intensive training.

A word of caution is in order in interpreting the impacts of training. One-third of women and nearly half of men receiving training were omitted from the analysis because it was not possible to match them with Adult program participants who did not receive training. There is no certainty that estimates of impact reported here apply for omitted individuals.

Summary of WIA Adult Program Impacts

Taken at face value, the results reported above imply large and immediate impacts on earnings and employment for individuals who participate in the WIA Adult program. Those who obtained training services have lower initial earnings, but they catch up to other WIA participants within ten quarters, ultimately registering large gains. Although there is evidence that estimates of effects in initial quarters following program entry may be biased, we do not believe a selection story can be constructed to explain away estimated effects for later quarters. In particular, growth in earnings for those receiving training would appear to reflect growth that has been widely observed in related programs.[15]

RESULTS OF IMPACT ESTIMATION FOR DISLOCATED WORKER PROGRAM

Figures 13.5 and 13.6 graph estimated program impacts on quarterly earnings for participants in all 12 states in the Dislocated Worker program. Participant earnings in the quarter following entry are about $200 below the comparison group, but relative earnings show an increasing trend over the 16 quarters of follow-up analysis. In the fifth or sixth quarter after program entry, participant earnings are equal to those of the comparison group. Ultimately, earnings grow to exceed those of comparison group workers by up to $400 per quarter. Despite the similarity in basic pattern, male earnings peak at around 10 quarters, whereas female earnings appear to grow until the end of the four-year window.

In separate analyses, we find that women's employment is initially approximately two percentage points below the comparison group, catches up within about three quarters, and is ultimately nearly eight percentage points above the comparison group. In contrast, for men, there is no initial employment difference, although the growth over time is smaller, with the positive increment after three years peaking at about six percentage points.

Dislocated Worker program participants are usually relatively high-wage individuals who are faced with permanent job loss. The initial negative impact estimates imply that their earnings are below unemployed workers with similar prior incomes and work histories. This is what would be expected if involvement in training activities precludes or reduces employment, inducing lock-in effects. Earnings growth observed over the three following years is consistent with the attainment of skills with training.

Figure 13.5 Dislocated Worker Program Treatment Effect on Quarterly Earnings for Females, WIA versus Comparison Group

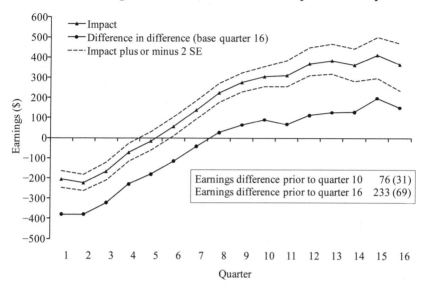

Figure 13.6 Dislocated Worker Program Treatment Effect on Quarterly Earnings for Males, WIA versus Comparison Group

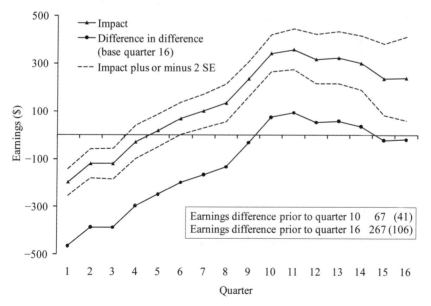

Such an interpretation is based on the assumption that dislocated workers are similar in unmeasured ways to the comparison group. Our specification test, based on predicting prior earnings, suggests this is not the case. The inserts in Figures 13.5 and 13.6 show that there are substantial differences between the participant and comparison groups 16 quarters earlier, with participant earnings more than $200 higher, and standard errors implying that these estimates are statistically significant. Prior employment levels are also several percentage points higher for program participants. That participants have higher prior earnings suggests the possibility that their higher earnings in later periods may not reflect program impact but rather unmeasured factors that become apparent in the three years after program entry.

Some indication of the possible extent of the bias is provided by difference-in-difference estimates that subtract the prior quarter 16 increment. These estimates are provided in Figures 13.5 and 13.6. As discussed above, this estimator provides a valid estimate of program impact if selection into the program is on the basis of stable characteristics that are not captured by variables that have been controlled. The difference-in-difference estimates imply that participants' earnings catch up to those of nonparticipants with a longer delay and that the ultimate impact on earnings is more modest. For women, earnings exceed those of nonparticipants only after eight quarters, and the positive increment is never over $200. These estimates imply that earnings are increased by between 2 and 5 percent. For men, the crossover point is between 9 and 10 quarters, and the increment is generally less than $100, increasing earnings by less than 2 percent.

Nearly a third of WIA Dislocated Worker participants in our sample were receiving UI benefits when they entered the program. Focusing on this subgroup—with both program participants and the comparison group limited to individuals receiving UI benefits in the nine states with the UI comparison group—allows us to control for possible incentive effects of UI receipt. Given that the Dislocated Worker program is largely targeted at individuals who have lost jobs, this subsample is quite similar to others in the program.

The results of this analysis show that the earnings of WIA participants receiving UI benefits do not catch up until 7 or 8 quarters after program entry. The initial negative effect is in the range of $700 for both men and women, and the maximum positive impact is also lower than the simple estimates reported in Figures 13.5 and 13.6, at about $200 for each, implying an average earnings increment of only 2–4 percent. As in the estimates reported above, the specification tests imply that program participants have higher prior earnings than matched comparison group members, so even these modest positive impacts may be spurious.

Impacts of Training

The incremental impact of training is based on a comparison of WIA Dislocated Worker participants who obtain training with those who do not. Initial earnings for those obtaining training are below those of other program participants for 8 quarters for women and for more than 10 quarters for men. Differences are $1,100 for females in quarters 2–4, implying a reduction in earnings of about a third, and $800 for males or about 20 percent of earnings. After quarter 10, earnings of those receiving training catch up with others, but they do not overtake them. Although the initial negative impact estimate is easily statistically significant, the confidence interval is large relative to estimated impacts after quarter 10. Confidence intervals include both –$200 and $200.

Of concern is the difference in earnings prior to entry into the program. For females, the individuals who select into training have lower earnings relative to other WIA participants in the sixteenth quarter prior to participation, suggesting that estimates of effects could be downwardly biased. This difference is not, however, statistically significant, so evidence of selection is inconclusive. Estimates for states offering high proportions of training are not substantively different. The pattern is similar when employment is taken as the dependent variable.

Taken at face value, point estimates suggest that WIA Dislocated Worker program participants who enter training experience large earnings losses relative to others in their first two years after program entry. Although consistent with a large training lock-in effect, these effects could be at least partly due to selection on short-term employment prospects, with those who land jobs leaving the program without obtaining training. Estimates of effects on earnings and employment three to four years after program entry—more than 18 months after program exit for most participants—show little evidence that training produces substantial benefits. These negative conclusions must be tempered, however, by the recognition that sampling error alone could obscure substantial impacts. It should also be noted that 28 percent of women receiving training were omitted from the analysis because no matching comparison case could be found; the analogous figure for men is 38 percent. Hence, the results may not be representative of the full population of those receiving training.

Summary of WIA Dislocated Worker Program Impacts

Dislocated workers are likely to face serious difficulties in obtaining reemployment, and the kinds of services WIA offers may require time to produce impacts. The pattern of results is consistent with these expectations. However, the extent of any benefits that accrue from participation is particularly hard to judge. Some specification tests suggest that our base results may be biased toward finding positive program impacts. Difference-in-difference estimates are smaller than the primary reported estimates. These estimates imply that program participants' earnings do not reach the level of earnings of comparable nonparticipants until more than two years after participation. Perhaps more important, the growth in earnings, relative to nonparticipants, slows at that point. As a result, these estimates imply that the gains from participation are very modest, even three to four years after entry.

Where employment is taken as the outcome of interest, estimates of program impact are more supportive of the program. Although the specification tests again suggest that there are unmeasured differences between the treated and matched comparison group, the difference-in-difference estimates of the program suggest at least a moderate positive impact.[16]

CONCLUSIONS AND IMPLICATIONS

The estimates of WIA program impact presented here are based on administrative data from 12 states, covering approximately 160,000 WIA participants and nearly 3 million comparison group members. Our focus on estimates that represent the average program impact across all states reduces sampling error substantially and averages across state-specific idiosyncratic variation. Table 13.1 presents information summarizing the implications of our findings. For each WIA program, we present annual earnings gains and the quarterly employment increment based on quarters 11–16. By focusing on these quarters, this measure captures the expected long-term benefits of training. If this measure is substantial, and the increment in earnings continues for even a few years, we argue below that the program will easily satisfy a benefit-cost standard.

Our best approximation of the WIA Adult program's impact is based on the estimates underlying Figures 13.1 and 13.2. We see that the average increment in annual earnings for women is nearly $2,400 per year, or 26 percent of average earnings for these women, and the increment for men is about $1,700, or 15 percent of average earnings. In a given quarter, program participation increases employment for women by about seven percentage points, and for men by about six percentage points. Since levels of employment are at base levels of 50–60 percent, this amounts to more than a 10 percent increase.

In the case of the Dislocated Worker program, we do not believe that the simple estimates are valid indicators of program impact because our specification tests suggest that participants are advantaged relative to the comparison group. In the face of this difference, Table 13.1 presents estimates based on a difference-in-difference structure. Increments in

Table 13.1 Summary Estimates of Program Impacts, Quarters 11–16

Program impact	Annualized earnings		Employment	
	$	%	Increment	%
Adult program ·				
Females	2,363*	26	0.067*	12
Males	1,676*	15	0.062*	12
Dislocated Worker program (difference-in-difference estimate)				
Females	523	3	0.051*	8
Males	138	1	0.041*	7

NOTE: *statistically significant at the 0.05 level. Annualized earnings impact estimates are based on quarters 11–16, with quarterly averages multiplied by 4. Employment refers to nonzero earnings in the quarter, with estimates averaged over quarters 11–16.

annual earnings are much smaller than for the Adult program, just over $500 for women, and less than $150 for men. Given that average earnings are appreciably higher for this group, these gains amount to less than 3 percent of earnings. Difference-in-difference estimates for the impact on employment imply four-to-five percentage point increments or about a 7–8 percent increase in employment proportions.

Do the net benefits we find satisfy a benefit-cost test? The costs associated with WIA participation are not available, nor are there accurate average costs for those entering the programs over a particular period, either for states or for the nation as a whole. However, it is possible to get some ballpark cost estimates. Published figures suggest that per capita direct costs of the Adult program (including ITA costs) aggregated for our 12 states are in the range of $2,400–$2,700 and Dislocated Worker costs are in the range $2,800–$3,200.[17] Because WIA provides some services that would be obtained elsewhere, it reduces expenses— either by the participant or others—that would otherwise be incurred, which tends to make social costs smaller than actual incurred costs. In their benefit-cost analyses of the JTPA program, Orr et al. (1996, pp. 97, 189, 269) estimate that such substitution is of importance, so social costs are less than half as large as the costs incurred due to the program. Some social costs, however, are omitted from our direct cost measures. When individuals receive certain WIA services, they may draw on other subsidies, such as when participants receive training at publicly subsidized community colleges. Orr et al. include such subsidies in the costs they use in their analysis, whereas the costs we cite above do not. Hence, our cost measures are subject to biases in both directions, and it would not be surprising if actual social costs differed by 30 or 40 percent.

Even given this uncertainty, the Adult program clearly satisfies a benefit-cost standard for both men and women if the earnings impacts continue for a period of just two or three years, which seems plausible. In contrast, using our best estimate of the impact on earnings for the Dislocated Worker program, in order for benefits for women to exceed costs, the improvement would need to be long lived, and estimated benefits for men could never cumulate to exceed costs at any reasonable interest rate. Estimates of employment impacts are, however, more supportive of the Dislocated Worker program. Judging the program in terms of its effects on the least successful workers, these are most likely to be individuals unable to obtain employment. If the program succeeds in increasing the number of individuals with jobs, it may be argued that those in need are clearly the gainers. Such a view may justify a program that fails a benefit-cost standard.

There are important policy implications of these results that go beyond a simple judgment of whether the program is effective. Program administrators typically look at the cross-sectional or "point-in-time" information that is available to them from performance management systems on a regular basis. They do not have at hand the data analysis tools to examine individual employment and earnings histories and trajectories for more than eight years (33 quarters that include up to 16 quarters of follow-up data) for both program participants and a comparison group, as in this study. The results of this evaluation show that program impacts typically "mature" over time, sometimes increasing in magnitude and sometimes diminishing. Insofar as this work underscores the fact that long-term impacts are of significance and that outcomes of interest may not be apparent for years, this may help to refocus training activities in beneficial directions.

Appendix 13A

Table 13A.1 Summary Statistics for WIA Participants and Comparison Group in 12 States

	WIA Adult			WIA Dislocated Worker			Comparison group
	Overall	No training	Training	Overall	No training	Training	
Sample size							
Unique individuals	95,580	68,255	27,325	63,515	43,513	20,002	2,929,496
WIA entries, or quarters of comparison program participation	97,552	69,712	27,840	64,089	43,894	20,195	6,161,510
Demographic	Mean	Mean	Mean	Mean	Mean	Mean	Mean
Male	0.420	0.445	0.356	0.482	0.494	0.456	0.585
Black	0.445	0.512	0.277	0.330	0.391	0.198	0.171
Hispanic	0.031	0.014	0.072	0.022	0.013	0.043	0.064
Age	32.70	32.91	32.16	40.24	40.14	40.46	39.59
Years of education	12.27	12.21	12.43	12.55	12.52	12.63	12.42
Employment							
Employment-employment	0.297	0.294	0.307	0.462	0.465	0.456	0.476
Employment-not employed	0.208	0.195	0.241	0.281	0.256	0.335	0.279
Not employed-employed	0.325	0.336	0.297	0.183	0.199	0.149	0.225
Not employed-not employed	0.168	0.175	0.151	0.070	0.078	0.053	0.040
Earnings second year prior	8,507	8,203	9,306	19,402	17,782	23,487	20,156
Earnings in prior year	8,149	8,050	8,398	20,499	19,450	22,779	21,584
Earnings following year	9,426	9,128	10,171	11,527	11,840	10,845	15,649
Earnings second year after	10,846	9,916	13,175	14,572	14,213	15,352	17,102

Program experience							
WIA in prior two years	0.052	0.058	0.035	0.041	0.044	0.034	0.020
Comparison program participation in prior two years	0.211	0.178	0.297	0.409	0.353	0.551	0.668

Notes

We wish to thank participants in seminars at the Australian National University, the Institute for the Study of Labor, Bonn (IZA), the Melbourne Institute for Applied Economic and Social Research, and participants in the Association for Public Policy Analysis and Management annual meetings, the Centre for European Economic Research (ZEW) workshop on policies against social exclusion, the European Association of Labor Economists annual meetings, the Institute for Poverty Summer Research Workshop (Wisconsin), and the Missouri Economic Conference, and in particular for comments by Jeffrey Smith, Burt Barnow, Marco Caliendo, Paul Decker, Andrew Leigh, Sheena McConnell, and Arne Uhlendorff. The analyses presented here include and follow from work undertaken for the USDOL and presented in "Workforce Investment Act Nonexperimental Net Impact Evaluation" (IMPAQ International, Final Report, December 2008, Department of Labor ETAOP 2009-10). The authors wish to acknowledge the central role in this project played by the staff at IMPAQ, including Nicholas Bill, Shirisha Busan, Goska Grodsky, Eileen Poe-Yamagata, and Ted Shen. Jacob Benus served as project director. Thanks are due to the many state agency staff who worked to provide data, to David Stevens, who facilitated provision of data for Maryland, and to SuZanne Troske, who supported data processing in Kentucky. Jonathan Simonetta oversaw the project for the USDOL. Notwithstanding the support provided by these individuals and the USDOL, the analysis and interpretation presented in the current paper are the sole responsibility of the authors. Please address correspondence to Peter Mueser, Department of Economics, University of Missouri, Columbia, MO 65211, mueserp@missouri.edu.

1. Recovery Act funding may only be used for authorized WIA and Wagner-Peyser Act activities and cannot be used to replace state or local funding currently dedicated to workforce development and summer jobs.

2. Source: http://www.recovery.gov/Transparency/agency/reporting/agency_reporting3 .aspx?agency_code=16&dt=02/12/2010 (accessed February 22, 2010).

3. Social Policy Research Associates (2004) and Rockefeller Institute of Government (2004) undertook process evaluations based on the first three years that the program was implemented but undertook no systematic study of participant outcomes (Barnow and King [2004] provide a summary of the Rockefeller study). Hollenbeck et al. (2005) examined outcomes in seven states for WIA participants who had completed the program during the period July 2000–June 2002, the first two years of implementation in most states. Given that over a third of participants require more than a year to complete the program, this sample would have been severely censored.

4. Eligibility criteria can be found at http://www.doleta.gov/programs/general_info .cfm (accessed August 2009).

5. For a discussion of actual implementation, see the Social Policy Research Associates study of WIA implementation (2004, sections VI and VII), and the Rockefeller

Institute of Government (2004; Barnow and King 2004). This section draws primarily from these reports.

6. These figures are based on participants exiting the program April 2004–March 2005 (Social Policy Research Associates 2006).

7. The primary contractor on the project was IMPAQ International, LLC, whose staff contacted all states and entered into agreements with nine of them. Three states provided data through the Administrative Data Research and Evaluation Project under separate contracts with the Department of Labor.

8. Further details on the methods of analysis can be found in Heinrich et al. (2010), which provides a full report of the results of this study. Additional information is available in Heinrich, Mueser, and Troske (2008).

9. Movements into and out of the labor force and between employment and unemployment in the 18 months prior to program participation are strongly associated with both program participation and expected labor market outcomes (Heckman, LaLonde, and Smith 1999; Heckman and Smith 1999).

10. Where an individual entered the program more than once during a quarter, this was coded as a single entry.

11. Comparison group individuals may contribute more than one unit as potential matches if they had contact with the program in multiple quarters.

12. Smith and Todd (2005) spell out the basic approach, which they describe as "difference-in-difference" matching. See also Mueser, Troske, and Gorislavsky (2007).

13. These correspond to the 95.5 percent confidence interval.

14. The very high estimates in quarters 15 and 16 should be discounted given the large standard errors.

15. In addition to the analyses presented above, we estimated impacts separately for various subgroups, focusing on those that are overrepresented among WIA participants or who face special challenges or barriers to working in the labor market, to wit, nonwhites, Hispanics, those under 26 years of age, those 50 or older, and veterans (males only). For the most part, estimated effects for these subgroups were similar to those for all WIA participants; there is no evidence of substantial differences in impact between these subgroups. Sampling error for many of these groups is large, however, implying modest statistical power of tests for subgroup differences.

16. In addition to analyses based on the full population of Dislocated Worker program participants, we estimated impacts separately for nonwhites, Hispanics, individuals under 26 years of age, those 50 or older, and male veterans. We found no evidence of important differences in program impacts for any of these subgroups. As in the case of subgroup analysis for the Adult program, sampling error is substantial, and there may be differences that are not statistically discernable.

17. These figures are based on taking total expenditures in the indicated programs for July 2003–June 2005 as detailed in USDOL/ETA (2009) divided by the number of reported exits during this period, or divided by the number of entries identified in our data. In the steady state, either of these correctly captures cost per participant.

References

Ashenfelter, Orley C. 1978. "Estimating the Effect of Training Programs on Earnings." *Review of Economics and Statistics* 60(1): 47–57.

Barnow, Burt, and Chris King. 2004. *The Changing Workforce Development Landscape: Report on the Operation of the Workforce Investment Act.* Washington, DC: U.S. Department of Labor.

Card, David, Jochen Kluve, and Andrea Weber. 2009. "Active Labor Market Policy Evaluations: A Meta-Analysis." IZA Discussion Paper No. 4002. Bonn, Germany: IZA.

Dyke, Andrew, Carolyn Heinrich, Peter R. Mueser, Kenneth R. Troske, and Kyung-Seong Jeon. 2006. "The Effects of Welfare-to-Work Program Activities on Labor Market Outcomes." *Journal of Labor Economics* 24(3): 567–608.

Frank, Abby, and Elisa Minoff. 2005. *Declining Share of Adults Receiving Training under WIA Are Low-Income or Disadvantaged.* Washington, DC: Center for Law and Social Policy.

Government Accountability Office (GAO). 2002. *Improvements Needed in Performance Measures to Provide a More Accurate Picture of WIA's Effectiveness.* GAO Report No. 02-275. Washington, DC: GAO.

Heckman, James J., Robert J. LaLonde, and Jeffrey A. Smith. 1999. "The Economics and Econometrics of Active Labor Market Programs." In *Handbook of Labor Economics*, Vol. 3, Orley Ashenfelter and David Card, eds. Amsterdam: North Holland, pp. 1865–2097.

Heckman, James J., and Jeffrey A. Smith. 1999. "The Pre-programme Earnings Dip and the Determinants of Participation in a Social Programme: Implications for Simple Programme Evaluation Strategies." *Economic Journal* 109(457): 313–348.

Heinrich, Carolyn J., Peter R. Mueser, and Kenneth R. Troske. 2008. *Workforce Investment Act Non-experimental Net Impact Evaluation.* Final report, ETAOP 2009-10. Washington, DC: U.S. Department of Labor, Employment and Training Administration. http://wdr.doleta.gov/research/keyword.cfm?fuseaction=dsp_resultDetails&pub_id=2419&mp=y (accessed August 25, 2010).

Heinrich, Carolyn J., Peter R. Mueser, Kenneth R. Troske, Kyung-Seong Jeon, and Daver C. Kahvecioglu. 2010. "New Estimates of Public Employment and Training Program Net Impacts: A Nonexperimental Evaluation of the Workforce Investment Act Program." University of Missouri Working Paper. Columbia, MO: University of Missouri.

Hollenbeck, Kevin Daniel Schroeder, Christopher King, and Wei-Jan Huang.

2005. "Net Impact Estimates for Services Provided through the Workforce Investment Act." Employment and Training Administration Occasional Paper ETAOP 2005-06. Washington, DC: U.S. Department of Labor, Employment and Training Administration.

Hotz, V. Joseph, Guido W. Imbens, and Jacob A. Klerman. 2006. "Evaluating the Differential Effects of Alternative Welfare-to-Work Training Components: A Reanalysis of the California GAIN Program." *Journal of Labor Economics* 24(3): 521–566.

Imbens, Guido W. 2008. "Estimating Variances for Estimators of Average Treatment Effects." Unpublished manuscript. Harvard University, Cambridge, MA, September.

Imbens, Guido W., and Jeffrey M. Wooldridge. 2008. "Recent Developments in the Econometrics of Program Evaluation." Institute for Research on Poverty Discussion Paper No. 1340-08. Madison, WI: University of Wisconsin.

Mueser, Peter R., Kenneth R. Troske, and Alexey Gorislavsky. 2007. "Using State Administrative Data to Measure Program Performance." *Review of Economics and Statistics* 89(4): 761–783.

Orr, Larry L., Howard S. Bloom, Stephen H. Bell, Fred Doolittle, Winston Lin, and George Cave. 1996. *Does Training for the Disadvantaged Work? Evidence from the National JTPA Study.* Washington, DC: Urban Institute Press.

Osterman, Paul. 2007. "Employment and Training Policies: New Directions for Less Skilled Adults." In *Reshaping the American Workforce in a Changing Economy*, Harry J. Holzer and Demetra S. Nightingale, eds. Washington, DC: Urban Instiute Press, pp. 119–154.

Rockefeller Institute of Government. 2004. "The Workforce Investment Act in Eight States: State Case Studies from a Network Evaluation." ETAOP 2004-02 and ETAOP 2004-03. Washington, DC: U.S. Department of Labor, Employment and Training Administration.

Rosenbaum, Paul R., and Donald B. Rubin. 1983. "The Central Role of the Propensity Score in Observational Studies for Causal Effects." *Biometrika* 70(1): 41–55.

Smith, Jeffrey A., and Petra E. Todd. 2005. "Does Matching Overcome LaLonde's Critique of Nonexperimental Estimators?" *Journal of Econometrics* 125(March–April): 305–353.

Social Policy Research Associates. 2004. *The Workforce Investment Act after Five Years: Results from the National Evaluation of the Implementation of WIA.* Oakland, CA: Social Policy Research Associates.

———. 2006. *2004 WIASRD Data Book.* Washington, DC: U.S. Department of Labor.

———. 2007. *PY 2005 WIASRD Data Book: Final.* Washington, DC: U.S. Department of Labor.

U.S. Department of Labor, Employment and Training Administration (USDOL/ETA). 2009. "WIA State Annual Reports & Summaries." PY2003 and PY2004. Washington, DC: U.S. Department of Labor, Employment and Training Administration. http://www.doleta.gov/performance/results/Reports.cfm?#wiastann (accessed August 2009).

Part 5

Future Evaluation Choices

14
Nonexperimental Impact Evaluations

Haeil Jung
Maureen A. Pirog
Indiana University

Job training for transitional workers and disadvantaged individuals is of keen interest for governments across the globe. Advancements in technology and globalized trade make some jobs obsolete or move them to lesser developed countries. Such structural transitions mean a sizable number of workers can lose their jobs. Also, inevitable business downturns lead to cyclical unemployment, which disproportionately affects disadvantaged workers with low human capital. In light of structural and cyclical changes in the labor markets, governments in industrialized nations have tried to support disadvantaged adults by retraining them. In the United States, training or retraining programs oftentimes have been accompanied by evaluations. This chapter briefly discusses what we have learned from these evaluations and then focuses on the related evaluation methods literature that informs how we can best design such evaluations in the future.

In the United States, there have been several major shifts in the goals, organization, groups targeted, and funding of employment and training programs. After the employment programs of the Great Depression, MDTA (1962–1972) was followed by CETA (1973–1982), JTPA (1982–1998), and eventually WIA (1998–present). CETA transformed a number of population-specific job training programs into block grants, which were then given to the states. This marked the first step in a devolutionary process that saw increased responsibility for job training delegated to states and localities. JTPA further devolved responsibility to the states. Later, WIA consolidated a number of USDOL job training programs and created One-Stop centers for job seekers negotiating their way through an otherwise bewildering system of federal job training programs. WIA includes all adults aged 18 and older, as well as dislocated workers and disadvantaged youth aged 14–21.

The early evaluations of MDTA were nonexperimental (Perry et al. 1975) and largely rudimentary (Barnow and Smith 2009). Similarly, the CETA evaluations were nonexperimental. These evaluations all relied on the CETA Longitudinal Manpower Survey, which combined random samples of CETA participants with comparison group data constructed from the Current Population Survey. Barnow's 1987 review of the CETA evaluations concludes that they relied on crude matching estimators, and lacked local labor market data and recent labor market and program participation histories. Even more sophisticated matching procedures have failed to consistently replicate experimental findings (Barnow and Smith 2009; Pirog et al. 2009), and the absence of data on local labor markets, work, and program participation choices has been important in arriving at unbiased treatment effects (Card and Sullivan 1988; Dolton et al. 2006; Heckman and Vytlacil 2007).

The widely varying findings from the CETA evaluations led to the USDOL decision to evaluate JTPA as a randomized experiment. Doolittle and Traeger (1990) describe the experiment which took place in 16 of over 600 local JTPA sites, while Bloom et al. (1997) and Orr et al. (1996) describe the experimental impact results. A variety of authors have synthesized numerous evaluations of employment and training programs (Friedlander, Greenberg, and Robins 1997; Greenberg, Michalopoulos, and Robins 2003; Heckman, LaLonde, and Smith 1999; LaLonde 1995). Overall, these authors report somewhat disappointing results. Impacts for adults are modest, with more positive effects reported for women than men and negligible impacts for out-of-school youth (Greenberg, Michalopoulos, and Robins 2003). The limited effectiveness of job training programs is hardly surprising when we consider participants' overwhelmingly low human capital levels and relatively small amount of job training investment.

Within the related literature on program evaluation methodologies, there has been a hot debate over the accuracy of these largely nonexperimental findings. Researchers interested in government programs across the board have been investigating whether and under what circumstances carefully executed nonexperimental methods can provide robust estimates of treatment effectiveness. In fact, the experimental JTPA study provided data for a variety of studies that constructed nonrandomized comparison groups and used various econometric corrections for self-selection bias to determine how effectively they work compared to the experimental results.

The approach of using experimental data to provide a benchmark against nonexperimental findings was used initially by LaLonde (1986) and Fraker and Maynard (1987). Both of these studies relied on data from the National Supported Work Demonstration. Other related studies of this type included Dehejia and Wahba (1999, 2002), Diaz and Handa (2006), Friedlander and Robins (1995), Heckman et al. (1996, 1998), Heckman and Hotz (1989), Heckman, Ichimura, and Todd (1997), Smith and Todd (2005), and Wilde and Hollister (2007).

LaLonde's 1986 study was particularly influential. He demonstrated that many self-selection correction procedures do not replicate estimated treatment effects in randomized experiments. In fact, nonexperimental methods were not robust to model specification changes in his study of the National Supported Work Demonstration, and the effectiveness of the program or estimated treatment effects were radically different from those determined experimentally. Later, Heckman, LaLonde, and Smith (1999) rebutted the LaLonde (1986) study in defense of nonexperimental methods, noting that each estimator is associated with testable assumptions and that by systematically testing them, the range of results resembles those originating from experimental methods.

The next section of this chapter provides a brief description of the types of parameters we may want to estimate in evaluating employment and training programs. After that we discuss conventional selection bias in studies of employment and training programs, followed by a discussion of pure selection bias and the robustness of different estimators that attempt to correct for self-section bias. The final section discusses what we have learned from previous studies.

FITTING THE METHODOLOGY TO THE POLICY QUESTION

When evaluating the impacts of any program, researchers should ask two questions. First, what policy question do we need to answer? Second, what research designs and econometric methods are best suited to answer the question? In employment and training programs, income (Y) is a typical outcome variable, although researchers have looked at a myriad of other possible outcomes, such as weeks worked, labor force attachment, and reliance on government cash assistance programs or poverty. Regardless of the outcome variable chosen (and for the purposes of this discussion, we focus on income), we need to establish a counterfactual. For example, we want to know the incomes of individuals given that they participated in a training program (Y_1) in order to compare it to the income of the same individuals without the benefit of the program (Y_0). In theory, a person can occupy either of these two potential states (treated or untreated), but in reality only one state is realized for a given individual. If people could occupy both states at the same time, then the problem of program evaluation would be easy and the treatment effect could be depicted as $\Delta = Y_1 - Y_0$. Four commonly discussed variants of treatment effects estimates are shown in Figure 14.1.

In practice, most randomized social experiments are designed to obtain intent to treat (ITT) estimates (Panel A of Figure 14.1). Eligible participants, frequently identified through administrative data, or those who have applied for services are randomly assigned to the treatment after which they comply with program requirements to some extent: some complete, others drop out, while still others are no-shows. When all individuals randomly assigned to treatment are compared to the randomized control group, the ITT estimates can be interpreted as the average impact over a sample of applicants, some of whom comply to some degree with the program. However, program administrators and supporters have often raised concerns with ITT estimates, arguing that they unfairly bias downward positive treatment effects by including the no-shows and even dropouts in the treatment group. After all, no-shows and dropouts either received no program services or only partial services. As such, no-shows and dropouts should not be expected to benefit either at all or fully from the program.

Largely in response to these concerns, experimenters created the treatment on the treated (TT) estimates. Individuals who started but dropped out at some point are typically, but not always, included with completers in these estimates. Viewed from this perspective, TT estimates are derivatives of ITT estimates—mechanical approximations with known properties and assumptions.

Figure 14.1 Variants of Treatment Effects

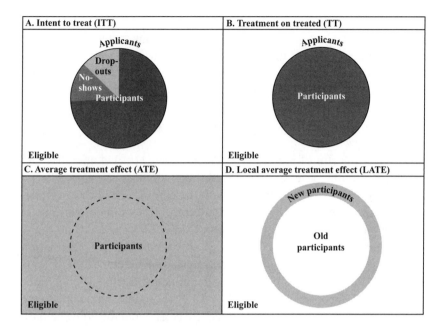

While most experimentors focus on ITT or TT estimation, it would be relatively straightforward to design a randomized experiment to estimate the impacts of program expansions (the local average treatment effect [LATE]). However, it is likely to be difficult to obtain good average treatment effects (ATE) estimates because randomly assigned individuals from an eligible population may well fail to comply with the treatment protocols. Moreover, unless treatment is mandated by court order or another mechanism, the usefulness of such estimates is rather limited. Each of these four types of estimators is discussed below.

ITT. This estimator is depicted in panel A of Figure 14.1. In this case,

$$\text{ITT} = E(Y_1 \mid D = 1, R = 1) - E(Y_0 \mid D = 1, R = 0),$$

including the no-shows and dropouts in the treatment group, where $D = 1$ if eligible individuals apply to the program and $D = 0$ if they do not, and $R = 1$ for the treatment group members and $R = 0$ for the controls. Under many circumstances this is an interesting and policy-relevant parameter that reflects how the availability of a program affects participant outcomes when participation in the program is incomplete.

TT. When we want to estimate the effect of a treatment like a job training program on actual participants, the parameter of interest is the effect of TT, depicted as follows:

$$TT = E(\Delta \mid D = 1, X) = E(Y_1 - Y_0 \mid D = 1, X),$$

where X is a vector of individual characteristics, $D = 1$ if an individual participates in the program, and $D = 0$ if they do not.

In our example, TT could compare the earnings of vocational program participants with what they would earn if they did not participate in the program. This is the information required for an "all or nothing" evaluation of a program and provides policymakers with information on whether or not the program generates positive outcomes. In panel B of Figure 14.1, the TT is depicted as the effect of treatment on participants. Social experiments randomly assigning eligible applicants to the treatment and control groups are generally considered the gold standard for obtaining ITT and TT estimates.[1]

ATE. This is the average impact that results from randomly assigning a person from the eligible population to a treatment. In panel C of Figure 14.1, the shaded rectangle constitutes the entire population for which the treatment effect is being estimated, regardless of whether or not they chose to participate in the program. The ATE is shown mathematically as

$$ATE = E(\Delta \mid X) = E(Y_1 - Y_0 \mid X).$$

Neither component of this mean has a sample analogue unless there is universal participation or nonparticipation in the program, or if participation is randomly determined and there is full compliance with the random assignment. As such, the ATE can be difficult, sometimes impossible, to compute. More importantly, however, this estimator is typically uninteresting to policymakers, who are typically loath to force randomly selected individuals to participate in programs.

LATE. This is the effect of treatment on persons who were induced to participate by an expansion or increased generosity of a program (see panel D of Figure 14.1). For example, LATE could measure the effect of a change in a policy (Z) of providing a new stipend or a more generous stipend to vocational program participants on those induced to attend the program because of the new policy. LATE is shown as follows:

$$\text{LATE} = E(Y_1 - Y_0 \mid D(z) = 1, D(z') = 0) = E(Y_1 - Y_0 \mid D(z) - D(z') = 1)$$

where $D(z)$ is the conditional random variable D, given $Z = z$, and where z' is distinct from z, so $z \neq z'$. Two assumptions are required to identify LATE. First, Z does not directly affect the outcome and program participation is correlated with Z controlling for other factors. This is a typical assumption for IV estimation. Second, there must be compliance with the policy change such that there are no individuals who refuse to participate if eligible and want to participate if not.[2]

Because it is defined by variation in an instrumental variable that is external to the outcome equation, different instruments define different parameters. When the instruments are indicator variables that denote different policy regimes, LATE has a natural interpretation as the response to policy changes for those who change participation status in response to the new policy. For any given instrument, LATE is defined on an unidentified hypothetical population—persons who would certainly change from 0 to 1 if Z is changed. For different values of Z and for different instruments, the LATE parameter changes, and the population for which it is defined changes. In other words, when we estimate the LATE parameter, we need to make sure who is possibly affected by the policy change from z' to z and how to interpret the estimated value in terms of relevant policy changes.

Most randomized experiments focus on estimating the ITT or TT in order to answer the policy question of how a program changes the outcomes of eligibles or eligible applicants and actual program participants compared to what they would have experienced if they had not participated. The ATE estimator is infrequently used largely because most researchers and policymakers are reluctant to force program participation. Finally, when programs became more generous or eligibility is expanded, the LATE estimator can be used to obtain the incremental effect of the policy change.

While random assignment studies are considered the gold standard for obtaining program impact estimates, the reality is that the vast majority of published evaluations are nonexperimental, with perhaps the exception of the randomized clinical trials in the medical literature (Pirog 2007). Thus, it is imperative to understand the issues relating to selection bias and the construction of a reasonable counterfactual. It is also important to follow closely the emerging literature on the non-experimental designs, estimators and statistical approaches that give rise to estimates of treatment effects that better approximate those that would be found using random assignment studies. These issues are discussed in the next three sections of this chapter.

CONVENTIONAL SELECTION BIAS AND LESSONS FOR PROGRAM DESIGNS AND DATA COLLECTION

Before addressing which econometric methods are relevant to answer the policy question, we want to discuss the selection bias that occurs when participation in job training programs is not randomized. Randomization should result in statistically equivalent groups of treatment and control group members in terms of both their observed *and* unobserved characteristics. This is not the case with nonexperimental studies, which often rely on propensity score matching, instrumental variable approaches, difference-in-difference techniques, and other statistical corrections to attempt to create a reasonable counterfactual or comparison group.

Early in the still ongoing debate on the relative merits of experimental versus nonexperimental evaluation, LaLonde (1986) pointed out that the use of nonrandomized comparison groups in evaluations can lead to substantial selection bias. Heckman et al. (1996, 1998) countered that LaLonde reached his conclusions incorrectly by constructing his comparison groups from noncomparable data sources. LaLonde's comparison groups were located in different labor markets from program participants, and their earnings were measured using different questionnaires. Heckman also noted that LaLonde lacked information on recent preprogram labor market outcomes, which are important predictors of participation in training. In sum, Heckman et al. (1998) concluded that simple parametric econometric models applied to bad data should not be expected to eliminate selection bias. In 1997, Heckman, Ichimura, and Todd (1997) showed how the bias found in estimates of treatment effectiveness can be decomposed into three sources. This analysis is still relevant for labor market researchers today who wish to construct a counterfactual or comparison group without the benefit of randomization.

The first source of bias that can occur when using a nonrandomized comparison group relates to differences in the values of the same observed characteristics in the treatment and comparison groups. This would occur, for example, if the treatment group included individuals aged 20–60 and the comparison group only included individuals aged 30–40.

When we have many observed characteristics, X's, they can be represented as $P(X)$, the propensity score, which is the probability of participation in a program based on a vector of observed individual characteristics. The second source of bias occurs when propensity scores obtained by matching on observable characteristics have different distributions over the same range.

The top panel of Figure 14.2 depicts a situation where both sources of bias are serious. In the top panel, the treatment and comparison groups have a modest overlap in their propensity scores, $P(X)$. In fact, no comparison group members are in the left tail of the distribution for the treatment group, and conversely, no treatment group members are in the right tail of the distribution for the comparison group. This difference reflects the first source of bias. In the top panel, you can also see that the distributions of propensity scores over the same range are different. This reflects the second source of bias. Both sources of bias are mitigated in the bottom panel of Figure 14.2.

The third source of bias in estimated treatment effects is from the pure self-selection on unobservables such as motivation. This would exist, for example, if the treatment group members of a job training program were highly motivated in contrast to comparison group members who lacked drive or motivation. This is the bias caused by the individuals' self-selection behavior based on information that researchers cannot observe and details of which are discussed later in the chapter.

Figure 14.2 Two Conventional Sources of Bias

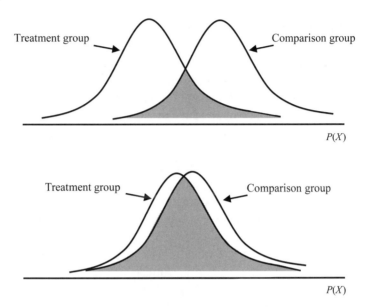

Propensity score matching can moderate bias from the first two sources of bias. Reweighting comparison group members so that the distribution of the comparison group's $P(X)$ more closely resembles that of the treatment group can further reduce bias from the second source. Because much of the bias attributed to selection by LaLonde (1986) was actually due to the first two sources described above, Heckman, LaLonde, and Smith (1999) continue to make arguments in favor of nonexperimental evaluations.

CONSTRUCTING A COUNTERFACTUAL

The characteristics of different types of comparison groups, including the randomized control group, are described below. The conclusion that the quality of data used to form a comparison group and the matching procedures utilized are keys to reducing the conventional bias is based on Heckman, Ichimura, and Todd (1997), who used data from a randomized control group, the no-shows from the treatment group, the eligible but nonparticipating group, and the Survey of Income and Program Participation (SIPP) in order to analyze the quality of the comparisons achieved.

Randomized Control Group as an Ideal Comparison Group

After applying to a program and being deemed eligible, individuals are randomly assigned to a control group. Data from the control and treatment groups should have nearly the same distribution of observed and unobserved characteristics. Because eligible applicants from the same local labor markets are randomly assigned to the treatment and control groups, and the same survey instruments were used with both groups, all three sources of bias should be controlled.

No-Shows from the Treatment Group as a Comparison Group

No-shows include individuals who are accepted to the program and randomized into the treatment group but who do not participate in the program. The simple mean difference between the treatment group and the no-show group without matching demonstrates that no-shows have similar characteristics as well as overlapping distributions of $P(X)$. The main source of bias is from selection on unobservables.

The Eligible but Nonparticipants (ENPs) as a Comparison Group

Individuals in the eligible but nonparticipating group are those who are located in the same labor market, and are eligible for the program but do not apply for the program. These individuals' information is collected by using the same questionnaire as for the treatment group. There were some clear differences in the characteristics and distribution of $P(X)$ between the ENPs and the treatment group members. By using propensity score matching and reweighting observations, it is possible to reduce the first two sources of bias as well as rigorously defined self-selection bias. While improvements in the estimated treatment effectiveness were obtained, the estimated treatment effect was still not equivalent to the TT estimate.

A Comparison Group from SIPP or Other Data Sources

To construct a comparison group, it is also possible to apply the eligibility criteria for a program to survey respondents in the SIPP or other large surveys. Two problems arise from using this approach. First, local labor market conditions are likely to be different for comparison and treatment group members when the comparison group members are selected from preexisting survey data. Second, data collected from the treatment and comparison groups are likely to come from different surveys or sources of measurement. In models comparing the treatment group with the SIPP comparison group, there was some discrepancy in observed characteristics and $P(X)$. They found that the first and second sources of bias were close to those found when using the ENPs for a comparison group. The discrepancies in the local labor markets and the questionnaires contributed to bias stemming from selection on unobservables; the third component of the selection bias is larger than that when they use ENPs.

Discussion

When we design training programs and collect information on participants to evaluate program effectiveness using nonexperimental methods, we need to consider how to develop comparison groups. Several factors are critical in reducing bias in our estimates of treatment effects: use the same questionnaire or data sources to obtain individual labor market outcomes and demographic information, draw individuals for the treatment and comparison groups from the same local labor markets, and use comparison group members whose observed characteristics largely overlap with those of the participants.

Restricting analyses to treatment and comparison group members with similar characteristics and using propensity score matching can reduce the first and second components of conventional bias, even though the characteristics of the parameter that we want to estimate can change. However, propensity score matching has its own limitations: it cannot control for self-selection on unobservables. Its uses and limitations are discussed with related empirical studies surveyed by Pirog et al. (2009). This study points out that matching is a nonparametric method that is flexible to any functional relationships between outcomes and programs. However, it needs a large sample size and is sensitive to various matching methods. There is no clear guidance for superior matching procedures.

SOURCES OF PURE SELF-SELECTION BIAS AND EMPIRICAL METHODS

Different Sources of Pure Self-Selection Bias

There are three reasons why individuals might self-select into an employment and training program:

1) they know they will earn higher incomes after participating in the program (heterogeneous response to the program in a random coefficient model);

2) individuals select into the program because their latent or forgone earnings are low at the time of program entrance (time constant individual heterogeneity in a fixed effect model); and

3) individuals' earnings are dependent on previous earnings that are low at the time of program entrance (autocorrelation between earnings in different time periods).

The first source of self-selection implies that individuals with higher returns from the program are more likely to participate in training programs. The second source of self-selection behavior implies that individuals with low opportunity costs or low earnings capacity are likely to participate in training programs. The third source of self-selection behavior implies that the low earnings capacity that encourages program participation at the time of participation is positively associated with earnings after program. Thus, the first source of self-selection results in overestimates of the effectiveness of employment and training programs while the second and third sources of self-selection result in underestimates. In the employment and training literature, it is understood that all three sources of bias contribute to the phenomenon known as "Ashenfelter's dip"; the fact that participants in employment and training programs often have earnings that are temporarily low at the time of program entry but that their earnings usually rebound (even in the absence of program participation) (Ashenfelter 1978).

Different empirical techniques appear to work better or worse depending on which sources of bias are operating. Theoretically, we expect that cross-sectional estimators provide consistent estimates only if there is no bias. Difference-in-differences estimators provide consistent estimates only if self-selection bias is coming from bias source 2. The AR (1) (autoregressive of order one) regression models provide consistent estimates only when self-selection bias is coming from bias source 3. The use of the instrumental variables method and the Heckman-selection correction provides consistent estimates only if bias sources 2 and 3 are present.[3] Thus, understanding which sources of bias we have in the program is critical in choosing which empirical method to use to best answer the policy question.

In simulations, cross-sectional estimation, difference-in-differences, and AR (1) regression estimation work relatively well when all three sources of bias are present, but it appears that they work well because the different biases offset one another (Heckman, LaLonde, and Smith 1999). Also, when bias source 1 is present, the estimation methods working for TT do not work for ATE. The authors argue that these parameters differ greatly because there is strong selection into the program by persons with high values of individual specific returns. However, they are not clear about how bias sources 1, 2, and 3 interact when different nonexperimental methods estimate ATE and TT. It seems that when all three bias sources are present, those three biases might offset one another. Difference-in-differences and AR (1) regression models also provide a similarly low bias in estimation. Finally, instrumental variables and the Heckman self-selection correction work best when bias sources 2 and 3 are present without bias source 1. However, when bias source 1 is present, IV and Heckman correction are the worst methods to use.

In sum, difference-in-differences and AR (1) regression estimators seem robust enough over different bias sources to estimate the TT. However, this does not mean that they are superior nonexperimental methods to others. In addition, it is not clear how offsetting of different bias sources works over different data and programs. Further research is needed.

NEW NONEXPERIMENTAL METHODS

Since the Heckman/LaLonde debate, a number of econometric methods have become more popular, and they relate directly to the issues of how best to estimate treatment effects for employment and training programs in the absence of random assignment. These additional methods include the difference-in-differences extension on matching, regression discontinuity design, and the marginal treatment effect (MTE) using local instrumental variables. Table 14.1 presents our summary of these methods as well as those for "kitchen sink" regression, propensity score matching, difference-in-differences, AR (1), and instrumental variables methods.

Difference-in-Differences Extension of Matching

As mentioned earlier, propensity score matching can be used to obtain impact estimates for treatment group members whose observable characteristics overlap with those of comparison group members. Of course, the impact estimates will only be valid for those individuals whose characteristics do overlap. Within the range of overlap of observables, the "comparable" comparison group can also be reweighted to better represent the distribution of observed treatment group characteristics, further reducing bias from different distributions of observables between treatment and comparison group members. Neither of these adjustments, however, controls for selection on unobservables.

Difference-in-differences extension of matching, introduced in Heckman, Ichimura, and Todd (1997), controls for some forms of selection on unobservables: it eliminates time-invariant sources of bias that may arise when program participants and nonparticipants are geographically mismatched or have differences in their survey questionnaire. Unlike traditional matching, this estimator requires the use of longitudinal data, which uses outcomes before and after intervention.

Regression Discontinuity Design

Regression discontinuity design became popular because it is easy to use and easy to present to a general audience. On the other hand, it

Table 14.1 Data, Methods, Self-Selection Behavior

Methods	Data	Consistency against self-selection on unobservables			Note
		$(1)^a$	$(2)^b$	$(3)^c$	
"Kitchen sink" regression estimator	Cross-sectional data Repeated cross-sectional data Panel data	No	No	No	Strict parametric assumption on a control function.
Propensity score matching	Cross-sectional data Repeated cross-sectional data Panel data (Large sample is required)	No	No	No	Flexible nonparametric method but large sample is required. Good at moderating the bias from the mismatched observed characteristics between the treatment and the comparison, and the bias from the mismatched distribution in the common values of observed characteristics.
Difference-in-differences	Panel data	No	Yes	No	Sensitive to choosing different time points before and after the treatment period.
AR (1) regression estimator	Panel data	No	No	Yes	It does not need to have outcome before the program; outcomes of two periods after the program is enough. AR (1) process assumption itself can be restrictive to represent the earnings dependency in practice.

Method	Data				Notes
Instrumental variable method	Cross-sectional data Repeated cross-sectional data Panel data	No	Yes	Yes	Hard to find a valid instrument variable.
Difference-in-differences extension of matching	Panel data	No	Yes	No	Flexible nonparametric method but large sample is required. Good at moderating the bias from the mismatched supports between the treatment and the comparison, and the bias from the mismatched distribution in the common support.
Regression discontinuity design	Cross-sectional data Repeated cross-sectional data Panel data	Yes	Yes	Yes	Hard to find a clear-cut participation rule and a large sample around the threshold; requires an assumption about the functional form of the dependence of the outcome on the assignment criterion variable.
Estimation using marginal treatment effect (MTE)	Cross-sectional data Repeated cross-sectional data Panel data	Yes	Yes	Yes	Hard-to-find valid and powerful instrumental variables that are needed to estimate a full schedule of marginal treatment effects.

[a] Individuals select into the program because they know they will earn higher returns from the program.
[b] Individuals select into the program because their latent or forgone earnings are low at the time of program entrance.
[c] Individuals' earnings are depending on previous earnings that are low at the time of program entrance.

requires a clear-cut participation rule and a large sample around the threshold. It also requires an assumption about the functional form of the dependence of the outcome on the assignment criterion variable. It is not easy to find data that satisfy such conditions (Pirog et al. 2009). Under the previous conditions, however, it works like random assignment. A recent study by Battistin and Rettore (2008) uses this method and discusses its weaknesses and strengths. They also warn that effects are obtained only for individuals around the threshold for participation. Thus, if there is a serious heterogeneous response across the population of interest, it is hard to generalize the estimates.

Estimation Using MTE

The MTE is the mean effect of treatment on those with a particular degree of intention to participate in the program. It can vary over different participation rates of participants and nonparticipants, and can be understood as a local average treatment effect using instrumental variables. Heckman and Vytlacil (2007) analyze how we can estimate different policy parameters as weighted averages of the MTE. It is attractive in the sense that we can estimate the different policy questions only using the MTE. However, it has its own limitation because the valid and powerful instrumental variables that are needed to estimate a full schedule of marginal treatment effects are often not available to researchers (Moffitt 2008).

DISCUSSION AND CONCLUSION

Because of recessions, technological advancements, global trade, and international migration of workers, job training programs in the United States have become more inclusive, pushing beyond their initial clientele of disadvantaged workers to additionally include more mainstream segments of the labor force. WIA clearly reflects this trend in training programs. Given the expanded scope of WIA, program evaluation has become more important and far more challenging given the highly heterogeneous nature of the target population.

This chapter summarizes the previous literature related to the methodology of evaluating training programs. We begin by noting that it is necessary to understand the policy question being posed so that the evaluation design can be tailored to answer that question. If policymakers are interested in ATEs for universal programs or LATEs that occur when program benefits or enticements are made more generous, then nonexperimental methods can be appropriate. After discussing the differences in the TT, ITT, ATE, and LATE parameters, the rest of the discussion focuses on the traditional question of program evaluation which requires estimation of the TT. This question is, how does the program change the outcomes of participants compared to what they would have experienced if they had not participated? The estimated treatment effect for program participants allows policymakers to answer whether or not a program should be retained.

Despite considerable debate in the literature, random assignment experiments are still considered the gold standard for such evaluations. If random assignment is not possible, we have learned that

- comparison groups should be drawn from the same local labor markets, and

- the same instrumentation should be used to collect data from the treatment and comparison groups.

Following these practices will reduce bias in estimated treatment effects. Unfortunately, this is not enough. To provide better nonexperimental estimates of treatment effects, the comparison group members should

- have observed characteristics that span the same range of values as members of the treatment group, and

- even if the observed characteristics span the same range, the distributions of these characteristics should also be the same.

Finding a comparison group that meets all of these criteria may well be onerous. For example, large, even very large, sample sizes are normally required if one uses propensity score matching to align the range and distributions of $P(X)$ that represents observed characteristics, X's, of the treatment and comparison groups.

Even if all of the above criteria can be met, it is also critically important to understand the sources of selection bias so that an econometric estimator can be used to correct for that particular type or combination of types of bias. Recall that there are three types of bias that typically arise in training programs:

1) self-selection by individuals who know they will earn higher incomes after participating in the program;

2) self-selection by individuals who enter a training program because their latent or forgone earnings are low at the time of program entrance; and

3) self-selection by individuals whose earnings are dependent on previous earnings that are low at the time of program entrance.

How to tease out the relative importance these sources of bias *a priori* is neither obvious nor easy. Nonetheless, it is clear that understanding how these sources of bias operate in any given evaluation of training programs is critical to choosing the most appropriate statistical methods.

Overall, we conclude that the choices made by evaluators regarding their data sources, the composition of their comparison groups, and the specification of their econometric models will have important impacts on the estimated effects of training. If a researcher cannot meet the conditions described above, estimated treatment effects from nonexperimental methods can give seriously misleading advice to policymakers. It has sometimes been argued that randomized experiments are impractical, take too long to implement, and are costly. However, the time and financial costs associated with collecting high-quality (usually longitudinal) data for nonexperiments will likely offset any extra time or financial costs of randomization. At the end of this exercise, we are forced to conclude that the logistical difficulties encountered in implementing a random assignment experiment must be weighed against the likelihood of giving bad advice to policymakers.

Notes

1. Social experiments assigning eligible applicants to the treatment and control groups to estimate the TT often have substitutes in the control group. Substitutes are individuals that have similar services from other programs even if they are assigned to the control group. When there are only no-shows, a Bloom-estimator is used to estimate the TT. When there are no-shows and substitutes, a Wald-estimator is used to estimate the TT. For further discussions of technical details and assumptions, refer to Bloom (1984) and Heckman et al. (1999, pp. 1903–1905).
2. There are four types of individuals in the program participation: 1) those who are induced to participate in the program if eligible, 2) those who will participate in the program whether or not they are eligible, 3) those who refuse to participate in the program whether or not they are eligible, 4) those who refuse to participate if eligible and want to participate if not. This second assumption for LATE eliminates the fourth type of individuals.
3. The Heckman-selection correction model is also restricted by the distribution assumption of unobservables.

References

Ashenfelter, Orley. 1978. "Estimating the Effect of Training Programs on Earnings." *Review of Economics and Statistics* 60(1): 47–57.

Barnow, Burt S. 1987. "The Impact of CETA Programs on Earnings: A Review of the Literature." *Journal of Human Resources* 22(2): 157–193.

Barnow, Burt S., and Jeffrey A. Smith. 2009. "What We Know about the Impacts of Workforce Investment Programs." In *Strategies for Improving the Economic Mobility of Workers: Bridging Research and Practice*, Maude Toussaint-Comeau and Bruce D. Meyer, eds. Kalamazoo, MI: Upjohn Institute for Employment Research, pp. 165–183.

Battistin, Erich, and Enrico Rettore. 2008. "Ineligibles and Eligible Non-participants as a Double Comparison Group in Regression-Discontinuity Designs." *Journal of Econometrics* 142(2): 715–730.

Bloom, Howard S. 1984. "Accounting for No-Shows in Experimental Evaluation Designs." *Evaluation Review* 8(2): 225–246.

Bloom, Howard S., Larry L. Orr, Stephen H. Bell, George Cave, Fred Doolittle, Winston Lin, and Johannes M. Bos. 1997. "The Benefits and Costs of JTPA Title II-A Programs: Key Findings from the National Job Training Partnership Act." *Journal of Human Resources* 32(3): 549–576.

Card, David, and Daniel Sullivan. 1988. "Measuring the Effect of Subsidized Training Programs on Movements In and Out of Employment." *Econometrica* 56(3): 497–530.

Dehejia, Rajeev H., and Sadek Wahba. 1999. "Causal Effects in Nonexperimental Studies: Reevaluating the Evaluation of Training Programs." *Journal of the American Statistical Association* 94(448): 1053–1062.

———. 2002. "Propensity Score-Matching Methods for Nonexperimental Causal Studies." *Review of Economics and Statistics.* 84(1): 151–161.

Diaz, Juan J., and Sudhanshu Handa. 2006. "An Assessment of Propensity Score Matching as a Nonexperimental Impact Estimator: Evidence from Mexico's PROGRESA Program" (Programa de Educacion, Salud y Alimentacion). *Journal of Human Resources* 41(2): 319–345.

Dolton, Peter, João Pedro Azevedo, and Jeffrey Smith. 2006. *The Economic Evaluation of the New Deal for Lone Parents.* Research Report No. 356. Leeds, West Yorkshire, England: UK Department for Work and Pensions.

Doolittle, Fred C., and Linda Traeger. 1990. *Implementing the National JTPA Study.* New York: Manpower Demonstration Research Corporation.

Fraker, Thomas, and Rebecca Maynard. 1987. "The Adequacy of Comparison Group Designs for Evaluations of Employment-Related Programs." *Journal of Human Resources* 22(2): 194–227.

Friedlander, Daniel, David H. Greenberg, and Philip K. Robins. 1997. "Evaluating Government Programs for the Economically Disadvantaged." *Journal of Economic Literature* 35: 1809–1855.

Friedlander, Daniel, and Philip K. Robins. 1995. Evaluating Program Evaluations: New Evidence on Commonly Used Nonexperimental Methods. *American Economic Review* 85: 923–937.

Greenberg, David H., Charles Michalopoulos, and Philip K. Robins. 2003. "A Meta-Analysis of Government-Sponsored Training Programs." *Industrial and Labor Relations Review* 57: 31–53.

Heckman, James J., and V. Joseph Hotz. 1989. "Choosing among Alternative Nonexperimental Methods for Estimating the Impact of Social Programs: The Case of Manpower Training." *Journal of the American Statistical Association* 84: 862–874.

Heckman, James J., Hidehiko Ichimura, Jeffrey Smith, and Petra E. Todd. 1996. "Sources of Selection Bias in Evaluating Social Programs: An Interpretation of Conventional Measures and Evidence on the Effectiveness of Matching as a Program Evaluation Method." *Proceedings of the National Academy of Sciences* 93(23): 13416–13420.

———. 1998. "Characterizing Selection Bias Using Experimental Data." *Econometrica* 66: 1017–1098.

Heckman, James J., Hidehiko Ichimura, and Petra E. Todd. 1997. "Matching as an Econometric Evaluation Estimator: Evidence from Evaluating a Job Training Program." *Review of Economic Studies* 64(4): 605–654.

Heckman, James J., Robert J. LaLonde, and Jeffrey Smith. 1999. "The Economics and Econometrics of Active Labor Market Policies." In *The Handbook of Labor Economics, Volume 3*, Orley Ashenfelter and David Card, eds. Amsterdam: Elsevier, pp. 1865–2097.

Heckman, James J., and Edward Vytlacil. 2007. "Econometric Evaluation of Social Programs, Part II." In *The Handbook of Econometrics, Volume 6B*, James J. Heckman and Edward E. Leamer, eds. Amsterdam: Elsevier, pp. 4875–5148.

LaLonde, Robert J. 1986. "Evaluating the Econometric Evaluations of Training Programs with Experimental Data." *American Economic Review* 76(4): 604–620.

———. 1995. "The Promise of Public Sector–Sponsored Training Programs." *Journal of Economic Perspectives* 9: 149–168.

Moffitt, Robert. 2008. "Estimating Marginal Treatment Effects in Heterogeneous Populations." Working paper. Baltimore, MD: Johns Hopkins University.

Orr, Larry L., Harold S. Bloom, Stephen H. Bell, Fred Doolittle, Winston Lin, and George Cave. 1996. *Does Training for the Disadvantaged Work? Evidence from the National JTPA Study.* Washington, DC: Urban Institute Press.

Pirog, Maureen A. 2007. "Trends in Public Program Evaluation in the US: Ramifications for Russia and China." *Chinese Public Affairs Quarterly* 3(1): 1–40.

Pirog, Maureen A., Anne L. Buffardi, Colleen K. Chrisinger, Pradeep Singh, and John Briney. 2009. "Are the Alternatives to Randomized Assignment Nearly as Good? Statistical Corrections to Non-randomized Evaluations." (A response to the Nathan-Hollister debate.) *Journal of Policy Analysis and Management*. 28(1): 169–172.

Perry, Charles, Bernard Anderson, Richard Rowan, and Herbert Northrup. 1975. *The Impact of Government Manpower Programs in General, and on Minorities and Women.* Philadelphia, PA: Industrial Research Unit, the Wharton School, University of Pennsylvania.

Smith, Jeffrey A., and Petra E. Todd. 2005. "Does Matching Overcome LaLonde's Critique of Nonexperimental Estimators?" *Journal of Econometrics* 125(1–2): 305–353.

Wilde, Elizabeth T., and Robinson Hollister. 2007. "How Close Is Close Enough? Evaluating Propensity Score Matching Using Data from a Class Size Reduction Experiment." *Journal of Policy Analysis and Management* 26(3): 455–477.

15
Designing Reliable
Impact Evaluations

Larry L. Orr
Johns Hopkins University

Stephen H. Bell
Abt Associates Inc.

Jacob A. Klerman
Abt Associates Inc.

This chapter reviews the U.S. experience in evaluation of job training programs over the past 40 years, examines why it is so difficult to reliably estimate the impacts of training programs with nonexperimental methods, and discusses ways to make experimental evaluations more feasible and cost-effective. We focus exclusively on *impact* evaluations, studies that seek to measure the contribution of a training program to improving worker outcomes *above and beyond what the same workers would have achieved without the training* (known as the counterfactual). Other types of workforce-focused evaluations—such as process studies of program implementation, or participation analyses that examine program targeting—while important, are not considered here.

A major distinction in our discussion is between experimental impact evaluation methods and nonexperimental impact evaluation methods. The experimental method randomly assigns eligible applicants for a training program to two groups, a treatment group that is allowed to enter the program and a control group that is not allowed to enter the program. Only by chance will subsequent outcomes of the two samples differ, unless the training improves treatment group outcomes. The difference in average outcomes between the treatment and control groups, tested for statistical significance (to rule out chance as the explanation of the observed difference) is the measure of program impact.

Nonexperimental impact evaluation methods also measure outcomes for a sample of training program participants, but—not having done random assignment—have no similar control group to compare to; instead, preprogram earnings of participants or earnings of some set of nonparticipants (called a comparison group) must be used as the counterfactual. The challenge is how to find a valid comparison group and then how to control for any remaining treatment group/comparison group background differences. The obvious approach is to select the comparison group from those who were eligible for the program but chose not to enroll. However, given that they chose not to enroll, they must be different from those who chose to enroll.

The alternative is to choose a comparison group from among those not eligible to enroll (e.g., from a different time period or a different geographic area, or not meeting one of the enrollment conditions). Again, whatever the condition is that makes the comparison group ineligible to enroll will also make them different from those who did enroll. Of course, a nonexperimental evaluation can and would control for observed differences between the treatment group and the comparison group, but nothing guarantees either that the only differences are in observed characteristics, or that the nature of the correction for those observed differences is correct. Thus, as we argue in detail below, those commissioning nonexperimental evaluations will always be left with the nagging concern that the nonexperimental methods chosen were not successful in producing accurate impact estimates.

A BRIEF OVERVIEW OF U.S. EVALUATIONS OF
TRAINING PROGRAM IMPACTS

Serious evaluation of government employment and training programs began in the United States in the 1960s, with nonexperimental impact analyses of programs funded by the Manpower Development and Training Act (MDTA). To estimate training impacts, analysts needed estimates of earnings with training and estimates of the counterfactual—what earnings would have been, for the same individuals, without training. Earnings with training were observed. The challenge was to estimate earnings without training. Some early MDTA studies took preprogram earnings for trainees as the benchmark. The impact of treatment could then be estimated as the change in earnings from before training to after training.[1] This approach clearly gave estimates of program impacts that were too large, and the reason was clear. People generally enter job training programs when they are at a low point in their labor market trajectory—e.g., when they are unemployed. As a result their earnings tended to rise, even quite substantially, even without training's assistance. The pre–post change measure credited this natural rebound to the employment and training intervention, giving the appearance of a program impact where there was none.

As it became clear that preprogram earnings were not a good counterfactual, MDTA analysts turned to comparison group strategies, in which training participants' counterfactual earnings were estimated using a sample of similar workers in a comparison group who did not enroll in training. As noted above, the measure of program impact was the difference in average outcomes between participant and comparison group members, usually adjusted for measured differences in background characteristics between the two populations.

In the 1970s, the USDOL sponsored a number of comparison group–based evaluations to measure the impacts of their training programs and demonstrations from that decade. Launched with high expectations, these efforts ended in disappointment. In many cases, the results were unclear or inconsistent; in others, they were overshadowed by controversy, often acrimonious, about the ability of the methods used to produce accurate results. The first of these efforts was a series of evaluations of the USDOL's major job training program for disadvantaged workers, CETA. The second was a set of over 400 demonstrations of employment and training programs for youth under the Youth Employment Demonstration Program Act (YEDPA). Most of these demonstrations involved nonexperimental evaluations.

More than a half dozen CETA evaluations produced widely divergent estimates of the impact of the program on participants' earnings, even though all the studies were based on essentially the same data (Barnow 1987). These differences in results were apparently due to differences in the assumptions underlying nonexperimental methods. And since those assumptions could not be tested or verified with data, there was no way to know which estimates were most reliable.[2] Moreover, when researchers applied the same set of nonexperimental methods to data drawn from a social experiment, where the experimental estimate provided an unbiased benchmark, the results were again widely dispersed and generally did not replicate the experimental findings (LaLonde 1986; Maynard and Fraker 1987; Heckman and Smith 1995). This experience led an expert panel convened to advise the USDOL on the evaluation of JTPA to recommend strongly that JTPA be evaluated with experimental methods (Stromsdorfer et al. 1985).

Similarly, when evaluations of YEDPA of the late 1970s were reviewed by a National Academy of Sciences committee, the committee concluded that "Despite the magnitude of the resources ostensibly devoted to the objectives of research and demonstration, there is little reliable information on the effectiveness of the programs in solving youth employment problems . . . It is evident that if random assignment had been consistently used, much more could have been learned" (Betsey, Hollister, and Pappageorgiou 1985, p. 22).

These recommendations led to the National JTPA Study, in which over 20,000 job training applicants in 16 local programs across the country, including both adults and youths, were randomly assigned either to go into the program or into a control group that was excluded from the program. The study had two major conclusions: 1) that the adult program components were cost-effective, and 2) that the youth programs had no discernable positive effects, and for some youths (those with arrest records) might have had a negative effect (Orr et al. 1995). When the study findings were released, Congress cut the youth program by 90 percent but maintained funding for the adult program.

Since the JTPA study, the USDOL has successfully used randomized designs for many of its other program evaluations and demonstration projects. For example, Job Corps, a residential training program for youth, was evaluated with an innovative design in which a national probability sample of sites was drawn and a small number of program applicants were randomly assigned to control status in each site (Schochet et al. 2008). The USDOL also followed up on the negative findings for youth in the JTPA evaluation by testing two approaches that had shown promise in previous evaluations—that of the Center for Employment Training (Miller et al. 2005) and the Quantum Opportunities Program (Schirm et al. 2006)—in an attempt to find more effective ways to serve disadvantaged youth. Because the studies had randomized designs, there was no disputing the findings when they showed both programs to be ineffective.

Reliance on experimental designs has continued at the USDOL up to the present. For example, a recent randomized study of Project GATE (Growing America through Entrepreneurship) measured the impact of providing microenterprise start-up services on participant employment and earnings (Benus et al. 2008). The USDOL's evaluation of Individual Training Accounts randomized consumers between three different voucher/counseling approaches (McConnell et al. 2006) to get unbiased measures of the *differential* effectiveness of the three strategies. A similar approach is being taken in the WIA impact evaluation, which will use random assignment to determine which consumers participate in which WIA program components (Mathematica Policy Research 2009). Another randomized study just under way at the USDOL, the Young Parents Demonstration, will have a true control group that receives no special services.[3]

THE CURRENT CONSENSUS

Frustration with the failure of nonexperimental methods to yield unequivocal estimates of program effects in cases such as CETA and YEDPA led to a consensus among evaluation specialists within the U.S. federal government that, where feasible, random assignment is the method of choice for evaluating public programs. Bell (2003) has argued that random assignment is almost always possible in federal workforce evaluations, even for mainline labor market interventions like local economic development assistance and UI benefits. This consensus among the technical experts has in turn led policymakers to accept experimental designs not only as scientifically accurate, but also as a way to avoid the methodological debates that often accompany the presentation of nonexperimental results, detracting from their credibility and deflecting the policy discussion from substance to method.

Experimental methods are also appealing to policymakers for their simplicity. In contrast to the statistical complexity of many nonexperimental methods, the experimental method is relatively simple and intuitively understandable. Even nontechnical policymakers can appreciate the logic of a contrast between two groups, one exposed to the program and the other not, but differing otherwise only by chance. This makes experimental studies more accessible and credible to laypeople in the policy process.

For these reasons, not only has the number of social experiments funded and conducted in the United States increased enormously over the last three decades, but on a number of occasions, random assignment evaluations have been mandated by Congress.[4] For example, the landmark welfare reform act passed in 1996 directed the Secretary of Health and Human Services to evaluate the programs funded under the act and "to the maximum extent feasible, use random assignment as an evaluation methodology."[5] Similarly, the Education Sciences Reform Act of 2002, which established the Institute of Education Sciences, defined "scientifically valid education evaluation" as evaluation that "employs experimental designs using random assignment, when feasible, and other research methodologies that allow for the strongest possible causal inferences when random assignment is not feasible . . . "[6] Congress has mandated random assignment evaluations of a number of specific programs in health, labor, housing, welfare, and education.

CHALLENGES TO THE CONSENSUS

One might ask, of course, whether nonexperimental evaluation methods have become more reliable in the 25 years since the publication of the National Academy of Sciences panel conclusions quoted above. There has, in fact, been a great deal of work on nonexperimental estimators during that period, and there is some evidence that they have gotten more reliable. Using the same dataset that LaLonde (1986) employed in his classic analysis of nonexperimental evaluations of CETA, Dehejia and Wahba (1999) show that the propensity score matching approach proposed by Rosenbaum and Rubin (1983) could replicate the experimental estimates with remarkable fidelity. And a recent meta-analysis by Greenberg et al. (2006) shows that, on average, 20 nonexperimental impact analyses of six job training programs yielded estimates that were quite similar to those obtained by nine randomized experiments.

After closer examination, however, these studies are less encouraging than they might originally seem. A reanalysis of the Dehejia-Wahba study by Smith and Todd (2005) found that the results were strongly sensitive to sample selection and specification of matching variables. In particular, although it was possible to find a nonexperimental approach that yielded estimates similar to the (known) experimental results, equally plausible approaches—in fact, only slight variations in the nonexperimental methods—yielded results different (sometimes very much so) from the experimental results. This is similar to the range of estimates from apparently reasonable nonexperimental methods which was noted by the National Academy of Sciences and others 25 years ago.

In Greenberg et al.'s meta-analysis, the nonexperimental studies reviewed evaluated different programs than the experimental studies examined.[7] The finding of no difference, on average, between experimental estimates for one set of programs and nonexperimental estimates for another set of programs does not address the key question—whether nonexperimental methods estimate the true impacts *for a given program*. Furthermore, Greenberg et al.'s study seems to confound period with method: all but one of the nonexperimental estimates are from before 1988, and all but two of the experimental estimates are from after 1988.

TESTS OF NONEXPERIMENTAL ESTIMATES AGAINST EXPERIMENTAL BENCHMARKS

A number of studies do compare experimental and nonexperimental impact estimates of job training impact for the same program, and they consistently find that nonexperimental estimates fail to replicate the experimental findings when taken one program at a time. Pirog et al. (2009), for example, examine 18 articles that explicitly compared propensity score matching (PSM), difference-in-differences (DD), or regression discontinuity design (RDD) estimates with estimates for the same program drawn from randomized experiments. Their summary assessment was that " . . . all [econometric corrections] are sensitive to the sampling frame and analytic model used . . . these corrections do not uniformly and consistently reproduce the experimental results; therefore, they cannot be relied upon to provide a satisfactory substitute for random assignment experiments" (p. 171).

Of particular relevance here is one of these studies, Glazerman et al. (2003), which examines 17 "within-study" comparisons of experimental and nonexperimental estimates of the impacts of training programs—i.e., studies that used both a randomized control group and a nonexperimental comparison group to estimate impacts for the same program. On the basis of their review, Glazerman et al. conclude that nonexperimental methods often produce estimates that differ from experimental findings by policy-relevant margins. The other paper that looks predominantly at nonexperimental validation studies for employment and training programs is Bloom et al. (2005). The bottom line of that assessment is that ". . . with respect to what methods could replace random assignment, we conclude that there are probably none that work well enough in a single replication, because the magnitude of [program group versus comparison group] mismatch bias for any given nonexperimental evaluation can be large" (p. 224).

WHY IT IS NOT WORKING (THE NONEXPERIMENTAL APPROACH)

The inconsistent performance of nonexperimental methods in evaluations of job training programs is not surprising. Job training programs are characterized by a selection process that is very difficult to replicate in choosing a nonexperimental comparison group. As noted earlier, the most common case is that individuals apply to training programs when they have lost their jobs. This means that, at the point of application, their earnings are atypically low. Even without any intervention, many of these individuals would become employed again and their earnings would rise. Figure 15.1 shows the path of monthly earnings from the National JTPA Study (Orr et al. 1995) over a 30-month period beginning 12 months before application to the program (month 0). As can be seen, average earnings of program applicants bottomed out in the month prior to application and then rose steadily for the next 18 months to a level roughly double the preprogram level. This is without any assistance from the JTPA program; the figure charts the progress of the control group sample. This exhibit illustrates the famous "preprogram dip" first noted by Ashenfelter (1978), and the natural recovery from the dip.[8]

It is the net addition to this upward trajectory caused by the program that an experiment measures, using as its benchmark a control group that experiences the same preprogram dip as the training group and then exhibits the recovery from that dip that the training group would have experienced in the absence of training. To yield a valid estimate of program impact, a nonexperimental method must be able to replicate—either through selection of the comparison group or through statistical adjustments—both the preprogram dip and the subsequent natural recovery of earnings. Many of the methods frequently used in nonexperimental evaluations are not well-suited to this task.

For example, immediate preprogram earnings (in, say, months −8 to −1) cannot be used as the basis of matching program participants to

Figure 15.1 Earnings Relative to Month of Program Entry, JTPA Control Group

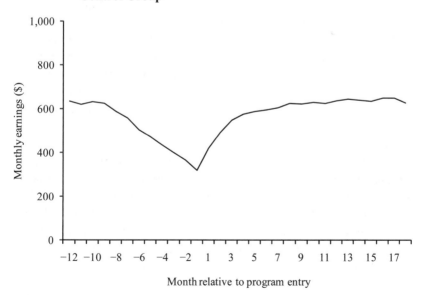

Month relative to program entry

a comparison group. Such an approach will almost certainly result in a comparison group with lower normal earnings than the participants, whose earnings are temporarily depressed. Comparison group earnings will stay down in the outcome period while participant earnings naturally rise even if the intervention has no effect. This will impart an upward bias on the participant minus comparison group impact estimates. Nor can participant/comparison group differences be removed through time-invariant covariates (e.g., education, demographics, etc.) in impact regressions or by methods that model time-invariant error terms. The mismatch between participants and comparison group members concerns the dynamics of earnings patterns over time. This essentially rules out both the use of propensity score matching on baseline characteristics and fixed effects estimators.

We want to be clear that our position is *not* that nonexperimental methods are never successful. Our position is simply that one cannot count on their success *a priori* and—in the absence of a randomized evaluation of the same program—cannot reliably tell *ex post* whether they have been successful. From over 40 years of experience with these methods, the American evaluation community has come to the conclusion that, if we are to base policy on evaluation results, the stakes are too high to accept this kind of risk and uncertainty. Until the evaluation community is convinced that some nonexperimental method can produce consistently reliable estimates of program impact in a given policy area, policymakers in that area will remain skeptical of all nonexperimental estimates. To date, whenever such estimators have been tested against an experimental benchmark they have been found wanting.

However, our critique suggests necessary critieria for a more reliable approach to designing nonexperimental methods to estimate training impacts: statistically control for (e.g., via regression, or better, propensity score matching) detailed patterns of pretraining employment and earnings when comparing participant and comparison group postprogram outcomes to obtain impact measures. The control variables used should include variables that measure the time pattern of earnings prior to job loss (this would have to be measured well before job loss) and the timing of job loss (i.e., binary employment indicators, perhaps by quarter). Recent work by Hollenbeck (2011) and Heinrich, Mueser, and Troske (2008) satisfies these necessary criteria.

Nevertheless, we suspect that these necessary criteria are not sufficient; i.e., that even these improved propensity score methods controlling for rich measures of recent employment and earnings will not replicate "gold standard" experimental results. These improved methods are simply not that different from the earlier approaches (e.g., Heckman, Ichimura, and Todd 1997; Bloom, Michalopoulos, and Hill 2005) that have failed replication. More precisely, we can sometimes find nonexperimental methods that pass a replication test, but this is not enough. To be useful, we need an algorithm—a rule specified before looking at the data—that identifies which estimate will be used; and it is that estimate that needs to pass replication, i.e., to provide an unbiased result just as does an experiment.

It is possible that the new results imply such an algorithm and that it would replicate the experimental results. But this has not been tested, and we are skeptical. We therefore urge the European Commission (EC) not to proceed with a purely nonexperimental approach until such an algorithm is proposed and shown to replicate multiple experimental results. Experiments take many years and they are expensive. Nevertheless, the alternative—making policy based on flawed nonexperimental methods—is much worse. The United States has gone down that path, spending billions of dollars on training programs which were later shown to have small or even negative impacts (e.g., JTPA; see Orr et al. 1995). Proceeding with unproven nonexperimental evaluation methods as a guide to policy is setting up the EC to repeat the United States' mistakes.

MAKING EXPERIMENTS MORE FEASIBLE AND AFFORDABLE

As a final point, we note that recent advances in experimental methods in the United States are making random assignment studies more feasible and affordable. Feasibility has been enhanced by a number of methodological developments, including:

- spreading the control group over many sites, so that very few individuals have to be turned away from program participation by the random assignment "lottery" in any location—a method used in the National Job Corps Study (Schochet et al. 2001);

- allowing program operators to increase the odds of assignment to the treatment group for preferred applicants (proposed for the Upward Bound evaluation; Olsen et al. 2007); and

- conducting "bump up" experiments in which *more* of the intervention is applied to the treatment group than in a normal program, rather than applying *less* than the customary amount to the control group (proposed for evaluating the impact of UI benefits; Bell [2003]).

Beyond these methodological advances, advances in data collection strategies can substantially lower costs and increase data quality. Early evaluations of training programs used survey data. However, survey data have several major disadvantages: high cost, leading to relatively small sample sizes; nonresponse bias due to imperfect survey tracking and refusals; large measurement error for contemporaneous outcomes (Duncan and Hill 1985; Bound and Krueger 1991; Bound et al. 1994); and limited retrospective histories due to the weakness of recall.

With the spread of computer technology in the administration of (near) universal public programs (e.g., social insurance programs), the role of surveys and thereby the cost of data collection for evaluations can decline sharply, while simultaneously increasing coverage, data quality, and earnings history. In most cases, intermediate and long-term follow-up can be left entirely to administrative data, such as UI quarterly wage data or Social Security Administration annual earnings records. Surveys need only be used for short-term follow-up to determine usage of "similar" training services outside the program being studied and to capture richer descriptors of the employment obtained by sample members.

Existing direct comparisons suggest that findings from survey and administrative data are often qualitatively similar. However, administrative data clearly underreport earnings, apparently omitting earnings from the informal sector (Kornfeld and Bloom 1999; Wallace and Haveman 2007). There is also some evidence of differential nonresponse between treatment and control groups in surveys (Schochet, Burghardt, and McConnell 2008). In light of these mixed indicators, reliance on administrative sources of earnings data is certainly appealing for reasons of economy. It is on the economy and efficiency front that the USDOL now looks to improve its use of experiments.[9] That random assignment studies provide the "gold standard" of scientific reliability has for now been firmly established as the main lesson of past and ongoing job training evaluations in the United States.

Notes

1. See Bell et al. (1995) for an in-depth history of U.S. training program evaluations and their impact estimation methodologies, from the MDTA era through the mid 1990s.
2. See Heckman and Hotz (1989) for a (much later) attempt to address this lack of ability to test implicit assumptions.
3. Personal correspondence with Young Parents Demonstration study leader Karin Martinson, October 28, 2009.
4. Greenberg and Shroder (2004) summarize more than 200 completed social experiments; many more have been finished (and others initiated) in the five years since.
5. Public Law 104-193, Sec. 413(b)(2).
6. Public Law 107-279, Sec. 102 (19)(D).
7. In the one case where both a nonexperimental and an experimental evaluation of the same program were included, Job Corps, the latter was conducted 18 years after the former.
8. For more recent analyses of the National JTPA Study data with respect to this issue, see Heckman and Smith (1999).
9. Discussions with ETA evaluation staff, October 29, 2009.

References

Ashenfelter, Orley. 1978. "Estimating the Effect of Training Programs on Earnings." *Review of Economics and Statistics* 60(1): 47–57.

Barnow, Burt S. 1987. "The Impact of CETA Programs on Earnings: A Review of the Literature." *Journal of Human Resources* 22(2): 157–193.

Bell, Stephen H. 2003. *Review of Alternative Methodologies for Employment and Training Program Evaluation.* Washington, DC: U.S. Department of Labor, Employment and Training Administration. http://wdr.doleta.gov/research/keyword.cfm?fuseaction=dsp_resultDetails&pub_id=2369&bas_option=Keywords&start=1&usrt=4&stype=basic&sv=1&criteria=Methodologies (accessed October 4, 2010).

Bell, Stephen H., Larry L. Orr, John D. Blomquist, and Glen G. Cain. 1995.

Program Applicants as a Comparison Group in Evaluating Training Programs. Kalamazoo, MI: W.E. Upjohn Institute for Employment Research.

Benus, Jacob, Sheena McConnell, Jeane Bellotti, Theodore Shen, Kenneth Forston, and Daver Kahvecioglu. 2008. *Growing America through Entrepreneurship: Findings from the Evaluation of Project GATE.* Report to the U.S. Department of Labor. Columbia, MD: IMPAQ International.

Betsey, Charles L., Robinson G. Hollister, and Mary R. Papageorgiou. 1985. *Youth Employment and Training Programs: The YEDPA Years.* Committee on Youth Employment Programs, Commission on Behavioral and Social Sciences and Education, National Research Council. Washington, DC: National Academies Press.

Bloom, Howard S., Charles Michalopoulos, and Carolyn J. Hill. 2005. "Using Experiments to Assess Nonexperimental Comparison-Group Methods for Measuring Program Effects." In *Learning More from Social Experiments: Evolving Analytic Approaches,* Howard S. Bloom, ed. New York: Russell Sage Foundation, pp. 173–235.

Bound, John, Charles Brown, Greg J. Duncan, and Willard L. Rodgers. 1994. "Evidence on the Validity of Cross-Sectional and Longitudinal Labor Market Data." *Journal of Labor Economics* 12(3): 345–368.

Bound, John, and Alan B. Krueger. 1991. "The Extent of Measurement Error in Longitudinal Data: Do Two Wrongs Make a Right?" *Journal of Labor Economics* 9(1): 1–24.

Dehejia, Rajeev H., and Sadek Wahba. 1999. "Causal Effects in Nonexperimental Studies: Re-evaluating the Evaluation of Training Programs." *Journal of the American Statistical Association* 94(448): 1053–1062.

Duncan, Greg J., and Daniel H. Hill. 1985. "An Investigation of the Extent and Consequences of Measurement Error in Labor-Economic Survey Data." *Journal of Labor Economics* 3(4): 508–532.

Glazerman, Steven, Dan M. Levy, and David Myers. 2003. "Nonexperimental versus Experimental Estimates of Earnings Impacts." *Annals of the American Academy of Political and Social Science* 589(September): 63–93.

Greenberg, David, Charles Michalopoulos, and Philip Robins. 2006. "Do Experimental and Nonexperimental Evaluations Give Different Answers about the Effectiveness of Government-Funded Training Programs?" *Journal of Policy Analysis and Management* 25(3): 523–552.

Greenberg, David, and Mark Shroder. 2004. *The Digest of Social Experiments.* 3rd ed. Washington, DC: The Urban Institute Press.

Heckman, James J., and Joseph Hotz. 1989. "Choosing among Alternative Nonexperimental Methods for Estimating the Impact of Social Programs: The Case of Manpower Training." *Journal of the American Statistical Association* 84(408): 862–880.

Heckman, James J., Hidehiko Ichimura, and Petra Todd. 1997. "Matching as an Econometric Evaluation Estimator: Evidence from Evaluating a Job Training Program." *Review of Economic Studies* 64(4): 605–654.

Heckman, James J., and Jeffrey Smith. 1995. "Assessing the Case for Social Experiments." *Journal of Economic Perspectives* 9(2): 85–110.

————. 1999. "The Pre-program Earnings Dip and the Determinants of Participation in a Social Program: Implications for Simple Program Evaluation Strategies." *Economic Journal* 109(457): 313–348.

Heinrich, Carolyn J., Peter R. Mueser, and Kenneth Troske. 2008. *Workforce Investment Act Non-experimental Net Impact Evaluation.* Final Report ETAOP 2009-10, prepared for the Department of Labor, Employment and Training Administration. Columbia, MD: IMPAQ International.

Hollenbeck, Kevin M. 2011. "Short-Term Net Impact Estimates and Rates of Return." In *The Workforce Investment Act: Implementation Experiences and Evaluation Findings,* Douglas J. Besharov and Phoebe H. Cottingham, eds. Kalamazoo, MI: W.E. Upjohn Institute for Employment Research, pp. 347–371.

Kornfeld, Robert, and Howard S. Bloom. 1999. "Measuring Program Impacts on Earnings and Employment: Do Unemployment Insurance Wage Reports from Employers Agree with Surveys of Individuals?" *Journal of Labor Economics* 17(1): 168–197.

LaLonde, Robert J. 1986. "Evaluating the Econometric Evaluations of Training Programs with Experimental Data." *American Economic Review* 76(4): 604–620.

Mathematica Policy Research, Inc. 2009. "National Evaluation of the Workforce Investment Act." Princeton, NJ: Mathematica Policy Research. http://www.mathematica-mpr.com/Labor/wia.asp (accessed July 9, 2010).

Maynard, Rebecca, and Thomas Fraker. 1987. "The Adequacy of Comparison Group Designs for Evaluations of Employment-Related Programs." *Journal of Human Resources* 22(2): 194–227.

McConnell, Sheena, Elizabeth Stuart, Kenneth Fortson, Paul Decker, Irma Perez-Johnson, Barbara Harris, and Jeffrey Salzman. 2006. *Managing Customers' Training Choices: Findings from the Individual Training Account Experiment.* Washington, DC: Mathematica Policy Research.

Miller, Cynthia, Johannes M. Bos, Kristin E. Porter, Fannie M. Tseng, and Yasuyo Abe. 2005. *The Challenge of Repeating Success in a Changing World: Final Report on the Center for Employment Training Replication Sites.* New York: MDRC.

Olsen, Robert, Stephen Bell, and Jeremy Luallen. 2007. "A Novel Design for Improving External Validity in Random Assignment Experiments." Paper presented at the Annual Conference of the Association for Public Policy Analysis and Management, held in Washington, DC, November 8–10.

Orr, Larry L., Howard S. Bloom, Stephen H. Bell, Fred Doolittle, Winston Lin, and George Cave. 1995. *Does Training for the Disadvantaged Work? Evidence from the National JTPA Study.* Washington, DC: Urban Institute Press.

Pirog, Maureen A., Anne L. Buffardi, Colleen K. Chrisinger, Pradeep Singh, and John Briney. 2009. "Are the Alternatives to Random Assignment Nearly as Good? Statistical Corrections to Nonrandomized Evaluations." *Journal of Policy Analysis and Management* 28(1): 169–172.

Rosenbaum Paul, and Donald B. Rubin. 1983. "The central role of propensity score in observational studies for causal effects." *Biometrika* 70(1): 41–55.

Schirm, Alan, Elizabeth Stuart, and A. McKie. 2006. *The Quantum Opportunity Program Demonstration: Final Impacts.* Washington, DC: Mathematica Policy Research.

Schochet, Peter Z., John Burghardt, and Steven Glazerman. 2001. *National Job Corps Study: The Impacts of Job Corps on Participants' Employment and Related Outcomes.* Princeton, NJ: Mathematica Policy Research.

Schochet, Peter Z., John Burghardt, and Sheena McConnell. 2008. "Does Job Corps Work? Impact Findings from the National Job Corps Study." *American Economic Review* 98(5): 1864–1886.

Smith, Jeffrey A., and Petra E. Todd. 2005. "Does Matching Overcome LaLonde's Critique of Nonexperimental Estimators?" *Journal of Econometrics* 125(1–2): 305–353.

Stromsdorfer, Ernst, Howard Bloom, Robert Boruch, Michael Borus, Judith Gueron, A. Gustman, Peter Rossi, Fritz Scheuren, M. Smith, and F. Stafford. 1985. *Recommendations of the Job Training Longitudinal Survey Research Advisory Panel.* Washington, DC: U.S. Department of Labor, Employment and Training Administration.

Wallace, Geoffrey, and Robert Haveman. 2007. "The Implications of Differences between Employer and Worker Employment/Earnings Reports for Policy Evaluation." *Journal of Policy Analysis and Management* 26(4): 737–753.

16
Neither Easy Nor Cheap

Sheena McConnell
Mathematica Policy Research

Peter Schochet
Mathematica Policy Research

Alberto Martini
Università del Piemonte Orientale

Title I of WIA is the largest source of federally funded employment services in the United States. Its purpose is to increase the employment, job retention, and earnings of its participants. WIA funds the Dislocated Workers, Adult, and Youth programs, as well as Job Corps—a primarily residential training program for disadvantaged youth—and specific programs for Native Americans, migrant and seasonal farm workers, and veterans. In fiscal year 2008, $4.5 billion was spent on WIA programs.

The European Social Fund (ESF) provides funding to promote employment in the 27 member states of the European Union (EU). Over the seven years of the current funding cycle (2007–2013), ESF will fund $114 billion in services, accounting for about 10 percent of the total EU budget. ESF has many important similarities to WIA. They are both large and decentralized. WIA allows state and local workforce investment areas to shape their programs. ESF funds are allocated to member states, which funnel the funds to one or more operational programs, which in turn have the ability to fund a wide variety of programs and services at the local level. A similar wide range of services are funded by both WIA and ESF, including counseling, job search assistance, basic education, vocational training, support services, retention services, and entrepreneurial assistance. Services under both WIA and ESF are provided by both government and nongovernment agencies, including small community-based organizations.

Given the considerable amount spent on employment services in both the United States and Europe, policymakers, participants, taxpayers, and program administrators on both continents want to know which services are effective. For more than three decades, the USDOL has invested heavily in conducting rigorous impact evaluations of its employment programs. In the past decade alone, it has funded experimental evaluations of Job Corps, approaches to administering training vouchers, entrepreneurial services, and prisoner reentry programs. (Benus et al. 2008, McConnell et al. 2006, and Schochet et al. 2008. The experimental evaluation of prisoner reentry programs is being conducted by Social Policy Research Associates and MDRC.) The USDOL has also funded nonexperimental evaluations of the WIA Adult and Dislocated worker programs and the Trade and Adjustment Assistance (TAA) program (Heinrich, Mueser, and Troske 2008). The nonexperimental evaluation of TAA is being conducted by Social Policy Research Associates and Mathematica Policy Research. Recently, the USDOL funded a nationally representative experimental evaluation of the WIA Adult and Dislocated Worker programs that is in its design phase.[1] Although the EU does sponsor evaluations of its operational programs, much less emphasis is placed on impact evaluations. And as noted by Greenberg and Shroder (2004), very few experimental evaluations have been conducted on employment programs outside the United States.

The purpose of this chapter is to inform EU officials about some of the lessons learned from conducting impact evaluations of employment programs in the United States. It begins by describing the role evaluations have played in decisions about employment policy and programs. It then discusses the three key main steps in any evaluation: 1) choosing the policy-relevant evaluation questions, 2) choosing the best design, and 3) collecting data. The chapter concludes with a summary of our recommendations.

EVALUATION CAN AFFECT POLICY AND PROGRAMMATIC DECISIONS

Information on the effectiveness of employment services is needed for three main reasons. First, because a considerable amount of government funds is invested in employment services, taxpayers need information on the investment's return. Second, most people in need of employment services are vulnerable and disadvantaged, so it is particularly important that the services offered to them are helpful. Third, a workforce with the skills required by employers is critical for the continued growth of the economy. As discussed below, evidence on service effectiveness has led the U.S. Congress to fund new programs, expand existing programs, and reduce funding for others. Evaluation findings have also been used by program administrators to improve programs.

An example of an evaluation that led to a new program is the New Jersey UI Reemployment Demonstration sponsored by the USDOL in the 1980s (Corson et al. 1989). The demonstration involved targeting UI recipients who were likely to have difficulty becoming employed and randomly assigning them to four groups: 1) a treatment group that received job search assistance, 2) a treatment group that received job search assistance and training or relocation assistance, 3) a treatment group that received job search assistance with a cash bonus for early reemployment, and 4) a control group that received no services or bonuses. The evaluation of the demonstration found that compared to the control, all three treatments led to increased earnings and employment and to benefits to society and claimants that outweighed their costs. As a result of this evaluation, in 1993 Congress required all states to establish a Worker Profiling and Reemployment Services (WPRS) system that identifies UI recipients who are likely to exhaust their benefits before they find employment and requires these UI recipients to receive reemployment services (Reich 1997).

Another example of the funding of a program based on research evidence occurred at about the same time. In the late 1980s, the USDOL funded the UI Self-Employment Demonstration in Massachusetts and Washington to help UI recipients start their own businesses by offering financial assistance and workshops on issues related to business start-up. The generally positive findings from an evaluation of these demonstrations (Benus et al. 1995) led to the 1993 legislation to establish the Self-Employment Assistance program for UI recipients.

Congress has also expanded funding for existing programs found to be effective. A nonexperimental evaluation of Job Corps conducted in the 1970s found that the program increased employment and earnings and was cost-effective for society and for the participants (Mallar et al. 1982). Following these findings, Congress increased funding for Job Corps.

While program designers and administrators nearly always ardently believe their programs are effective, rigorous evaluations have sometimes found that they are wrong. For example, an experimental evaluation of the youth program under JTPA found that overall the program had no significant impact on earnings for youth and may even have had negative impacts on male youth who had been arrested prior to random assignment (Bloom et al. 1997). The findings from this study led Congress to reduce funding for the JTPA youth program and subsequently require major changes in the youth program when JTPA was replaced with WIA.

Evaluation findings have also been used by program administrators to improve programs. The Job Corps program examined the services it provided Hispanic youth after the National Job Corps Study found that the program did not increase earnings for this population of youth (Schochet, Burghardt, and McConnell 2008). A study of different approaches to providing training vouchers, called individual training accounts, found that, contrary to the fears of program staff, the recipients of the vouchers made similar training and employment choices irrespective of whether they were required to be counseled by an employment counselor at the One-Stop Career Center (McConnell et al. 2006). This has direct implications for the administration of vouchers.

CAREFUL DEVELOPMENT OF EVALUATION QUESTIONS

The first step in any evaluation is to carefully specify what policymakers want to learn from the evaluation. Although most evaluations involve considerable exploratory analysis, an evaluation can usually only address a few questions rigorously. Hence, it is important to design the evaluation so that the questions it does ask are the ones that are most helpful to policymakers.

EVALUATING THE ENTIRE PROGRAM OR
PROGRAM COMPONENTS

In many cases, the most policy-relevant question is not whether an entire program is effective but rather which program components are effective. Evaluating an entire program is appropriate if policymakers are considering whether to fund the program or the program consists of only a few key components. Congress has asked for evaluations of entire programs, such as the Job Corps and JTPA programs. When the programs are large and comprised of many diverse components, such as WIA and ESF, policymakers are unlikely to stop funding the entire program, but they do want to know which components of the program are effective. In these cases, evaluating specific program components is more informative. For example, the USDOL's nonexperimental WIA evaluation did not attempt to evaluate the entire program but focused on evaluating just the Adult and Dislocated Worker programs, which are large but not the only programs funded by WIA (Heinrich, Mueser, and Troske 2008).

If individuals choose which service component to receive, care must be taken in interpreting impacts by program component. The impact estimates pertain only to the people who chose that component and not to all study participants. During the design phase of the National Job Corps Study, program administrators expressed interest in not only the effectiveness of the entire program but also in the effectiveness of the nonresidential component of the program. Most participating youth live at a Job Corps center, but some youth choose to live at home and commute to the center (and are referred to as nonresidents). The study found that both the residential and nonresidential components of Job Corps had positive impacts (Schochet and Burghardt 2007; Schochet, Burghardt, and McConnell 2008). However, as nonresidential and residential youth differ, it cannot be concluded that the nonresidential program is effective for those youth who chose the residential component.

DETERMINING FOR WHOM THE PROGRAM IS EFFECTIVE

Some programs and policies are effective for some people but not for others. In the design phase of the evaluation, policymakers should specify which target populations are of policy interest. The JTPA evaluation, for example, focused on four groups with different employment needs—adult women, adult men, young women, and young men. The National Job Corps Study estimated the impacts for youth in three different age groups—16–17, 18–19, and 20–24. The choice of estimating impacts for youth by age was motivated by conversations with Job Corps staff who viewed younger participants as much more difficult to serve than the older youth.

It is important to decide on the target populations that are of policy interest prior to conducting the evaluation for two reasons. First, the size of the target populations will affect the required sample size. Estimating impacts for subgroups requires a larger sample, and the required sample is larger the smaller the subgroup. Second, it avoids the temptation to estimate impacts for numerous subgroups and interpret any significant impact as a true program effect. If a large number of subgroup impacts are estimated, the estimate of the program impact for some subgroup is likely to be significantly positive by chance and may not reflect a true positive program impact (Schochet 2009a). Statistical adjustments can be made to account for estimating multiple subgroups, but these adjustments result in a loss of statistical power, with the loss increasing with the number of subgroups.

DETERMINING THE COUNTERFACTUAL

Perhaps the greatest challenge in designing evaluation questions is to determine the counterfactual—the scenario against which the intervention is tested. Evaluations in which the counterfactual is the absence of all employment services are rare or nonexistent. WIA is not the only source of employment services in the United States—people can receive training at a community college funded by a Pell grant, for example. Similarly, the ESF is not the only source of employment services in European countries. Hence, if people do not receive employment services from WIA or the ESF, they may receive services from other sources. In the National JTPA Study, for example, about 40 percent of the control group received some employment services not funded by JTPA (Bloom et al. 1997).

It may be that a counterfactual in which other employment services can be received is the more appropriate one. Such an evaluation provides policymakers information about the effectiveness of additional WIA funding in the real world, a world in which other services exist. The estimated impact of employment services in these cases is likely to be smaller because it is based on the impact of additional services, not the impact of receiving services versus no services. Hence the estimated impact of the JTPA services was not the impact of receiving the services versus no services, but the impact of more treatment group members receiving services. Correct interpretation of the impacts requires information about the receipt of services by both the treatment and control/comparison groups.

IMPACT EVALUATION DESIGN: CONSTRUCTING A COMPARISON GROUP

An ideal evaluation of employment services would compare the outcomes of people who receive the services with the outcomes of the same people who do not. As this is impossible, the challenge is to choose another set of people—a comparison group—who are as similar as possible to the people who receive the services. Under an experiment, this comparison group is determined randomly and is referred to as a control group. In nonexperimental evaluations, other approaches are used to construct a comparison group. Below, we describe the considerations in choosing an evaluation design.

EXPERIMENTS

Experiments involve randomly assigning individuals to two or more groups, with each group offered a different set of services. When implemented carefully, random assignment creates groups of individuals that, on average, have identical observable and nonobservable characteristics prior to the intervention, differing only in the program services they are offered. As a result, the great advantage of experimental designs is that differences in average outcomes between the groups can be causally attributed to the specific interventions under investigation. Under other designs, there is always a concern that the differences in outcomes are a result of differences in the underlying characteristics between the group receiving the intervention and the comparison group (or between the groups receiving different interventions).

The fundamental and unavoidable challenge of experiments is that they require that some people are offered more or different services than others. This may be politically challenging and often is resisted by program administrators. Yet, numerous social service experiments have been conducted successfully in the United States and developing countries.[2] To be successful, the evaluator needs to obtain political support for the study and minimize the burden on the program and study participants.

Experiments are often more acceptable politically and to program administrators when they are used to evaluate a demonstration or a pilot of an intervention rather than an existing program. In these cases, control group members receive the services they would in the absence of the experiment and treatment group members receive more services. The USDOL has supported numerous experimental evaluations of demonstrations, including the National Supported Work (NSW) Demonstration (Maynard et al. 1979), a series of UI job search assistance and bonus experiments (Corson et al. 1989, 1992; Spiegelman, O'Leary, and Kline 1992; Woodbury and Spiegelman 1987), the Individual Training Account Experiment (McConnell et al. 2006), and the recent evaluation of Project GATE (Growing America through Entrepreneurship) (Benus et al. 2008).

If the roll-out of new programs takes place over time, an experiment can be conducted if the order at which potential sites receive the program is determined randomly. In this case early implementation sites are the treatment sites and the later implementation sites are the control sites, at least until program implementation. This design requires a large number of sites to ensure enough statistical power due to the clustering of individuals within sites. While we do not know of an example of this design in evaluating employment service, it has been used extensively in education evaluations—schools have been randomly assigned to either receive funding for an intervention immediately or receive future funding for the intervention (see, for example, Glazerman et al. [2007]).

Evaluating existing programs experimentally is more difficult because the experiments lead to some people not participating or receiving fewer services than they would in the absence of the evaluation. The control group may also lead to empty slots at the program. The best conditions for an experiment occur when there is excess demand for the program. With a surplus of people wanting to participate in the program, the existence of a control group could affect who receives the intervention but not the number of people who received the intervention, and thus, the program would not suffer from empty slots. This was the case in an evaluation of Upward Bound, a program to assist disadvantaged youth to prepare for, enter, and succeed in college (Seftor et al. 2009). The program recruited enough students that the treatment group could fill all program slots and the control group was placed on a waiting list. If any openings in the program occurred, they were filled by selecting students randomly off the waiting list.

Experiments are also more acceptable when the research groups are offered different treatments, so that all study participants receive some services. In an evaluation of individual training accounts, people who were found eligible for the vouchers were assigned to three groups that varied in the extent to which counseling was required and the role the counselor played in setting the amount of the voucher (McConnell et al. 2006). No one was denied a voucher, and anyone could receive counseling by requesting it, even if they were in the group for which counseling was not mandatory.

Randomized encouragement is another experimental evaluation approach that does not involve denial of services. Under this design, both treatment and control group members can receive the intervention, but the treatment group is given additional encouragement to receive the intervention. This encouragement can take the form of information, financial, or other incentives, but the encouragement must not directly affect the outcomes of interest. While we know of no study of employment services that has used randomized encouragement, it has been used to evaluate the effectiveness of health interventions such as the influenza vaccine (Hirano et al. 2000).

Cooperation from program staff is a prerequisite for a careful implementation of an experiment, and so evaluators need to obtain support for the study from program staff at all levels, and then train and monitor them. Most program staff will support an evaluation if they understand that the findings will be used to inform the development of effective employment services. Staff must also understand the rationale behind an experiment and the drawbacks of alternative designs.

Evaluators should work with program staff to find ways to reduce the burden of the experiment to the program and participants. The Web-based random assignment systems used in recent experimental evaluations (such as the evaluation of a relationship-skills program, Building Strong Families) mean that program staff can learn the research assignment of a program applicant almost instantaneously rather than having to wait a few days before knowing the assignment. Another way to reduce the burden on program and participants is to have small control groups. The National Job Corps Study, for example, had control groups that were only 7 percent of all eligible Job Corps applicants (Schochet et al. 2008).

It can be challenging to estimate the impact of service components in an experiment because of a lack of information on which services the control group would receive. It is sometimes possible to ask program staff to predict prior to random assignment which services each sample member would receive if they were assigned to the treatment group. If the predictions are accurate, an estimate of the impact can be obtained by comparing the outcomes of those members of the treatment and control groups who are predicted to receive the services. This approach was used successfully in the National Job Corps Study to estimate the separate impacts of the residential and nonresidential services (Schochet et al. 2008).

A major drawback of experiments is that they cannot provide policymakers quick answers. The National Job Corps Study began in 1993; the last evaluation report was published over a decade later in 2006. It takes considerable time for an experiment to provide findings for three reasons. First, it takes some time to obtain political and program support for the evaluation. Second, it takes time for enough eligible people to request the services and be randomly assigned. Typical sample intake periods are one or two years. Third, as many programs are designed to have long-term effects, follow-up data collection needs to occur for a lengthy period after participants enter the program. The total follow-up period for the participants in the Job Corps Study was 48 months for survey data and 8–10 years for administrative data.

It is often said that experiments are more expensive than other evaluation designs (Levitan 1992). Some costs that are incurred for experiments but not nonexperimenal evaluations include recruiting sites, training staff, conducting random assignment, and monitoring. In practice, experiments can be very expensive—some have cost millions of dollars. However, it is not clear that this is because they are experiments or because experiments often involve surveys while many nonexperimental evaluations rely only on less costly administrative data. Yet, the type of data collected is unrelated to the design—experiments can be conducted with administrative data, and nonexperimental evaluations can include survey data collection. Rigorous nonexperimental evaluations require more detailed baseline data. More research is needed to compare the costs of experimental and nonexperimental designs, holding constant data collection costs.

NONEXPERIMENTAL DESIGNS

It is not always possible to conduct experiments. Experiments are typically not feasible for evaluating entitlement programs (because program services cannot be denied to eligible program applicants, thereby making it impossible to create control groups), and may not be appropriate for evaluating existing employment-related programs that are undersubscribed. It may also not be feasible to create control groups if there is no way of restricting program services (for example, reemployment services that are obtained by computer in one's home). Furthermore, experiments cannot be conducted using retrospective treatment samples (that is, past program participants who are identified using administrative program data) or treatment samples selected using secondary data (for example, using large national survey data). Finally, even if random assignment is feasible, program staff may refuse to participate in the experiment because of ethical concerns about restricting services to program applicants and the extra burden associated with implementing random assignment procedures (such as obtaining study consent forms, collecting additional customer information that is required for random assignment, notifying customers about random assignment results, and so on).

Consequently, researchers often use nonexperimental methods to estimate program impacts. In this section, we briefly discuss two key features of two nonexperimental methods that are becoming increasingly popular for evaluating employment and training programs: 1) regression discontinuity (RD) methods and 2) propensity score matching methods. We do not discuss pre–post designs where the outcomes of program participants are compared before and after program participation, because of obvious confounding factors that could bias the impact estimates (such as changes in economic conditions or participant's health status). In addition, we do not discuss instrumental variables methods, because it is often difficult to find defensible instruments that are strongly correlated with the decision to participate in an employment or training program, but that are uncorrelated with the disturbance terms that influence key postprogram outcomes (such as employment and earnings).[3] We conclude this section with a discussion of the available evidence on the validity of these methods.

REGRESSION DISCONTINUITY DESIGNS

RD designs are increasingly used by researchers to obtain unbiased estimates of intervention effects in the social policy area (see, for example, Cook [2008], Schochet [2009b], and Imbens and Lemieux [2008] for reviews). These designs are applicable when a continuous "scoring" rule is used to assign the program, policy, or other intervention to people or other study units (for example, One-Stop Career Centers). People or units with scores above a preset cutoff value are assigned to the treatment group and units with scores below the cutoff value are assigned to the comparison group, or vice versa. For example, Black,

Galdo, and Smith (2007) estimate the impacts of the WPRS system in the state of Kentucky using the rule that UI recipients are required to receive reemployment services if their model-based UI profiling scores are larger than a cutoff value. As another example, the effects of providing competitive grants to workforce investment areas for One-Stop Career Center innovations could be estimated using grant application scores and collecting data on a random sample of workers in both the winning and losing grantee sites.

Under an RD design, the effect of an intervention can be estimated as the difference in mean outcomes between treatment and comparison group units, adjusting statistically for the relationship between the outcomes and the variable used to assign people or other units to the intervention, typically referred to as the "forcing" variable. A regression line (or curve) is fit for the treatment group and similarly for the comparison group, and the difference in average outcomes between these lines at the cutoff value of the forcing variable is the estimate of the effect of the intervention; an impact occurs if there is a "discontinuity" between the two regression lines at the cutoff.

RD designs generate unbiased estimates of the effect of an intervention if the relationship between the outcome and forcing variable can be modeled correctly (using parametric, local linear, or other nonparametric methods, and using appropriate score bandwidths), and the forcing variable was not systematically manipulated to influence treatment assignments. Furthermore, the forcing variable must be reasonably continuous, and should not be binary (such as gender) or categorical with no natural ordering (like race). In addition, the cutoff value for the forcing variable must not be used to assign people or other units to interventions other than the one being tested. This requirement is necessary to ensure that the study can isolate the causal effects of the tested intervention from the effects of other interventions.

Well-planned RD designs can yield unbiased impact estimates, and may be easier to sell to program staff and participants than experimental designs because treatment assignments are determined by rules developed by program staff or policymakers rather than randomly. However, RD designs cannot necessarily be viewed as a substitute for experimental designs. Sample sizes typically need to be about three to four times larger under RD than experimental designs to achieve impact estimates with the same levels of precision (Schochet 2009b). The estimate of the impact under the RD design typically pertains to a narrower population (those with scores near the cutoff) than under an experimental design (those with a broader range of scores). Furthermore, the RD design requires critical modeling assumptions that are not required under the experimental design.

PROPENSITY SCORE MATCHING METHODS

Propensity score methods involve matching program participants to a comparison sample of people using available data on demographic characteristics, earnings histories, and local area characteristics. The best data source for selecting comparison samples will depend on the specific application and study research questions, but options often include administrative records (such as UI claims data), program data on ineligible program applicants or eligible applicants who decide not to participate in the studied program, program data for workers who are eligible for a related but less-intensive program to the one under investigation, and national surveys that cover the same time period as the treatment sample data and that include comparable matching variables. In all cases, the outcomes of the comparison group are intended to represent the outcomes of the treatment group had they not received the program services under investigation. The relevant counterfactual for the study, however, will often depend on the specific data source.

Under comparison-group designs, assumptions and statistical models must eliminate differences between the treatment and comparison group samples that could result from sources other than the intervention. If these efforts are successful, remaining differences can be attributed to the intervention, possibly with some measure of statistical confidence. However, if sources of unmeasured differences exist, this approach could produce impact estimates that suffer from sample selection biases.

Rosenbaum and Rubin (1983) developed a statistical procedure—propensity scoring—to select a matched comparison group. A propensity score is the probability that a worker with a given set of characteristics receives the treatment. Rosenbaum and Rubin proved the key result that individuals with the same propensity score will also have the same distribution of the matching variables.

Several methods can be used to perform the matching, such as nearest neighbor, caliper, or kernel methods. Smith and Todd (2005a) and Imbens and Wooldridge (2008) conclude that with sufficient sample overlap in the propensity scores and well-balanced matching variable distributions, impact estimates are relatively insensitive to the choice of matching methods. It is critical that the adequacy of the matching process be assessed, for example, by comparing the distribution of the matching variables and propensity scores of treatment and selected comparison group members within propensity score classes.

Several recent large-scale evaluations of employment and training programs have used propensity score matching methods that were structured to satisfy the conditions discussed above for obtaining credible impact estimates. For example, Heinrich, Mueser, and Troske (2008) estimate the impacts of WIA on the combined effects of core and intensive services relative to no WIA services and the incremental effect of WIA-funded training relative to WIA participants who did not receive training. The comparison group for their analysis was drawn from UI claimants or from ES participants in the 12 study states. The data used for propensity score matching were obtained from UI claims data, ES data, and WIA program data, and included employment histories, labor force status at the time of program entry, demographic characteristics (gender, age, race and ethnicity, education attained, veteran status, and welfare receipt), and local labor market characteristics.

As another example, a national evaluation of the TAA program is employing a propensity score matching design (Schochet 2005). The large TAA program provides training, extended UI benefits, and other employment-related services to workers who are displaced from their jobs due to trade-related reasons. A random assignment design was not feasible for the evaluation—because TAA services cannot be denied to eligible workers and so under program rules, it would not be possible to construct a control group. Furthermore, it was not feasible to randomly assign participants to different service groups, because TAA services are voluntary and are tailored to meet the needs of individual clients. Consequently, the evaluation is employing a comparison group design to obtain estimated impacts, where the comparison group was selected using UI claims data from the 26 study states, and using similar matching variables to those described above for the Heinrich, Mueser, and Troske study.

THE VALIDITY OF NONEXPERIMENTAL METHODS

There is a long-standing debate in the literature about whether social programs can be reliably evaluated using nonexperimental methods. To investigate their validity, data from experiments have been used to try to replicate the experimental estimates—the "gold-standard" estimates—using nonexperimental methods.

In an influential study, LaLonde (1986) finds that the impact results from the experimental NSW Demonstration could not be replicated using a comparison group design. He estimates program impacts using a number of standard nonexperimental evaluation econometric methods, including simple regression methods, difference-in-difference methods, instrumental variable procedures, and the two-step estimator of Heckman (1979), and finds that the alternative estimators produced very different impact results. Fraker and Maynard (1987) came to similarly pessimistic conclusions using a slightly different comparison sample. Similarly, Peikes, Moreno, and Orzol (2008) find that matching methods produced incorrect impact estimates when compared with a randomized design for the State Partnership Initiative employment promotion program.

Using the same data as LaLonde, however, Heckman and Hotz (1989) use a broader set of specification tests to help select among nonexperimental estimators, and find that their tests could exclude those estimators that produced impact results that differed from the experimental ones. A key specification test that they used was that a credible estimator should yield no differences between the treatment and comparison groups in their mean outcomes pertaining to the preintervention period.

In an influential study, Dehejia and Wahba (1999) reexamine LaLonde's data using propensity scoring to find matched comparison group members for the NSW treatment group; their resulting impact estimates were similar to the experimental ones. A key contribution of their study was the careful use of model specification tests that yielded treatment and comparison groups with similar distributions of the matching variables and propensity scores. Mueser, Troske, and Gorislavsky (2007) also conclude using JTPA data that matching methods may be effective in evaluating job training programs. Smith and Todd (2005a,b) caution, however, that the Dehejia and Wahba results are not robust to alternative analysis samples and matching variables included in their models.

Glazerman, Levy, and Myers (2003) survey 16 studies that each used nonexperimental methods to try to replicate impact findings from a social experiment. Their systematic review was intended to shed light on the conditions under which nonexperimental methods most closely approximate impact results from well-designed and well-executed experimental studies. They find that nonexperimental methods occasionally replicate the findings from experimental impact evaluations, but in ways that are not easy to predict. However, they identify several factors that lead to more successful replications. These factors, which are similar to the ones that Heckman, Ichimura, and Todd (1997, 1998) find in trying to replicate experimental results from the National JTPA Study, are as follows: the data should include a rich set of matching variables relevant to modeling the program participation decision, and in particular, preprogram earnings histories; the same data sources should be used for the treatment and comparison groups; and the treatment and comparison samples should be from the same geographic areas. Bloom, Michalopoulos, and Hill (2005) identify similar criteria for increasing the chances that nonexperimental methods can produce credible impact estimates.

Studies have shown that the RD approach has promise for evaluating employment and training programs when experimental methods are not viable. Cook, Shadish, and Wong (2008) provide empirical evidence that impact estimates based on RD designs can replicate experimental estimates in a range of settings. The advantage of the RD approach relative to the propensity score comparison group approach is that the selection rule for receiving the treatment is fully known under the RD approach and can be used to obtain unbiased estimates if the outcome-score relationship can be modeled correctly. In contrast, the propensity score approach assumes that the program participation decision can be adequately modeled using observable baseline data, which is typically very difficult to test, suggesting that one never knows for sure whether unobservable factors bias the impact findings.

COLLECTING THE NECESSARY DATA

Data on outcomes need to be collected for both the treatment and control/comparison groups. These data can be obtained from surveys or from administrative records. Much more complete and detailed information can be obtained from surveys than is typically available from administrative databases. Surveys can also collect details that may suggest a job's quality, such as the receipt of fringe benefits, union status, and wage rates. Data on criminal activity, substance abuse, and receipt of a wide range of services are often not available from sources other than surveys.

On the other hand, administrative data do not suffer from recall error or nonresponse bias. And because they are much cheaper than survey data to collect, they can provide data on many more study participants over a longer period of time. However, they are more limited in the variables they include and may miss some jobs. In the United States, state UI agencies collect quarterly earnings from all people covered by UI, and these data are often used to evaluate employment programs. These data, however, do not cover federal employment, jobs not covered by UI (such as self-employment or agricultural jobs), or any jobs that employees or employers do not want reported. Hotz and Scholz (2001) estimate that these data may understate employment by about 13 percent. In the United States, Social Security data are another potential source of administrative data on earnings, which are sometimes used in impact evaluations. These data do cover federal and self-employed workers and cover all states, but are annual rather than quarterly.

Baseline data—or data collected prior to the receipt of the intervention—are essential for implementing nonexperimental designs. For example, detailed data on the baseline characteristics of both participants and nonparticipants are required to construct a matched comparison group design. While baseline data are not essential for experiments, they are useful for ensuring that random assignment created research groups with similar baseline characteristics. Irrespective of the design, baseline data are also necessary for defining subgroups of interest, adjusting for baseline differences in the treatment and control/comparison groups due to sampling error, and testing and adjusting for survey nonresponse bias. Finally, baseline data on program participants are useful for describing those who receive the intervention.

Baseline data can be collected from administrative records, application forms, or surveys. In some studies, study-specific forms are administered to experiment participants, who typically need to be administered a consent form prior to random assignment. A form requesting additional baseline and contact information (to aid follow-up of the participant) can be administered at the same time.

Data on the receipt of services is needed to understand differences between the receipt of services by the treatment and control/comparison groups and hence the interventions and counterfactuals being tested. Program participants will likely vary in the intensity of the services received. And, as discussed above, study participants in both the treatment and control/comparison groups may also receive services from other programs.

The program is likely to be able to provide detailed and accurate data on service receipt among program participants. (Program administrators may need assistance in collecting these data.) However, these data are typically not available for the control/comparison group. Data on the service receipt of the control/comparison group are often unavailable from administrative records and hence need to be collected using a survey.

Correctly interpreting estimates of program effectiveness requires an understanding of the program as it is actually implemented, rather than how it is designed. This understanding requires an "implementation" or "process" analysis, which requires collecting detailed information on the program from program manuals, training materials, and budgets; interviewing both managers and frontline program staff; observing service provision; and talking with participants. If an impact is found, this information is important for replication. If no impact is found, or the impact is smaller than expected, this information will allow the evaluator to determine whether this was because the intervention was not implemented, because it was not implemented as designed, or because it was ineffective.

Finally, information on the cost of the program can be used to interpret the magnitude of a program impact and to inform others who may be considering replications of the program. A program may have positive impacts on earnings, but may not be cost-effective if its costs are high. Conversely, a low-cost intervention may be cost-effective even if it has modest impacts. With cost data, a benefit-cost analysis can be conducted that compares the cost of the intervention with the monetary value of the benefits of the employment services. The largest benefit of employment services is typically the increase in participants' earnings after they leave the program, which is already measured in dollars. Other potential benefits from participation in employment services, such as any reduction in public assistance use or crime, can be valued in dollars (see, for example, McConnell and Glazerman [2001]). In evaluations where it is difficult to place dollar values on program benefits (so that benefit-cost analyses are not possible), some researchers instead conduct cost-effectiveness studies where they compare the key impact estimates with the per-participant program costs. Benefits and costs are examined from different perspectives—usually society as a whole, taxpayers, the program's funder, and participants. Benefit-cost analysis is useful for comparing interventions to each other, and for identifying those interventions that improve participants' outcomes most efficiently.

RECOMMENDATIONS

First, we urge the EU to invest in data collection for evaluating program impacts. As well as collecting baseline and outcomes data, data should also be collected on costs, the implementation of the program, and the receipt of services by members of both treatment and control/comparison groups.

Second, we recommend that the EU consider conducting experiments. While not always possible, there are many situations in which they can be done and can yield rigorous findings. They need not be large or expensive.

Third, if experiments are not feasible, we recommend that rigorous nonexperimental methods be used, such as regression discontinuity or propensity score matching methods. However, it is critical that these methods be carefully selected and applied to ensure that potential sample selection biases can be overcome to yield credible impact estimates.

Finally, we recommend that the EU invest in conducting rigorous impact evaluation, whether experimental or not. The stakes for the taxpayers, the participants, and the health of the economy are too high for labor market policies not to be based on strong evidence.

Notes

1. The USDOL contracted with Mathematica Policy Research to conduct the WIA Adult and Dislocated Worker Program Evaluation.
2. The Poverty Action Lab at MIT (www.povertyactionlab.org/papers) has conducted numerous experiments in developing countries.
3. Instrumental variables methods are important in experiments when members of the treatment group do not receive the treatment or when control group members receive the intervention being tested (Heckman et al. 1998).

References

Benus, Jacob, Terry Johnson, Michelle Wood, Neelima Grover, and Theodore Shen. 1995. "Self-Employment Programs: A New Reemployment Strategy: Final Impact Analysis of the Washington and Massachusetts Self-Employment Demonstrations." Unemployment Insurance Occasional Paper No. 95-4. Washington, DC: U.S. Department of Labor.

Benus, Jacob, Sheena McConnell, Jeanne Bellotti, Theodore Shen, Kenneth Fortson, and Daver Kahvecioglu. 2008. *Growing America through Entrepreneurship: Findings from the Evaluation of Project GATE.* Washington, DC: U.S. Department of Labor, Employment and Training Administration.

Black, Dan, Jose Galdo, and Jeffrey Smith. 2007. "Evaluating the Worker Profiling and Reemployment Services System Using a Regression Discontinuity Design." *American Economic Review Papers and Proceedings* 97(2): 104–107.

Bloom, Howard S., Charles Michalopoulos, and Carolyn J. Hill. 2005. "Using Experiments to Assess Nonexperimental Comparison-Groups Methods for Measuring Program Effects." In *Learning More from Social Experiments: Evolving Analytic Approaches,* Howard S. Bloom ed. New York: Russell Sage, pp. 173–235.

Bloom, Howard S., Larry L. Orr, Stephen H. Bell, George Cave, Fred Doolittle, Winston Lin, and Johannes Bos. 1997. "The Benefits and Costs of JTPA Title II-A Programs: Key Findings from the National Job Training Partnership Act Study." *Journal of Human Resources* 32(3): 549–576.

Cook, T. 2008. "Waiting for Life to Arrive: A History of the Regression-Discontinuity Design in Psychology, Statistics, and Economics." *Journal of Econometrics* 142(2): 636–654.

Cook, T.D., W.R. Shadish, and V.C. Wong. 2008. "Three Conditions under Which Experiments and Observational Studies Produce Comparable Causal Estimates: New Findings from Within-Study Comparisons." *Journal of Policy Analysis and Management* 727(4): 724–750.

Corson, Walter, Paul Decker, Shari Dunstan, and Anne Gordon. 1989. *The New Jersey Unemployment Insurance Reemployment Demonstration Project*. Washington, DC: U.S. Department of Labor, Employment and Training Administration.

Corson, Walter, Paul Decker, Shari Dunstan, and Stuart Kerachsky. 1992. "Pennsylvania Reemployment Bonus Demonstration Project." Unemployment Insurance Occasional Paper No. 92-1. Washington, DC: U.S. Department of Labor.

Dehejia, Rajeev H., and Sadek Wahba. 1999. "Causal Effects in Nonexperimental Studies: Re-evaluating the Evaluation of Training Programs." *Journal of the American Statistical Association* 94(December): 1053–1062.

Fraker, Tom, and Rebecca Maynard. 1987. "The Adequacy of Comparison Group Designs for Evaluations of Employment-Related Programs." *Journal of Human Resources* 22(2): 194–227.

Glazerman, Steven, Dan M. Levy, and David Myers. 2003. "Nonexperimental versus Experimental Estimates of Earnings Impacts." *Annals of the American Academy of Political and Social Science* 589(1): 63–93.

Glazerman, Steven, Allison McKie, Nancy Carey, and Dominic Harris. 2007. *Evaluation of the Teacher Advancement Program (TAP) in the Chicago Public Schools: Study Design Report*. Chicago, IL: Joyce Foundation.

Greenberg, David H., and Mark Shroder. 2004. *The Digest of Social Experiments*. Washington, DC: Urban Institute Press.

Heckman, James J. 1979. "Sample Selection Bias as a Specification Error." *Econometrica* 47(1): 153–161.

Heckman, James J., and Joseph Hotz. 1989. "Choosing among Alternative Nonexperimental Methods for Estimating the Impact of Social Programs: The Case of Manpower Training." *Journal of the American Statistical Association* 84(408): 862–880.

Heckman, James J., Hidehiko Ichimura, Jeffrey A. Smith, and Petra E. Todd.

1998. "Characterizing Selection Bias Using Experimental Data." *Econometrica* 66(5): 1017–1098.

Heckman, James J., Hidehiko Ichimura, and Petra E. Todd. 1997. "Matching as an Econometric Evaluation Estimator: Evidence from Evaluating a Job Training Programme." *Review of Economic Studies* 64(4): 605–654.

———. 1998. "Matching as an Econometric Evaluation Estimator." *Review of Economic Studies* 65(2): 261–294.

Heinrich, Carolyn, Peter Mueser, and Kenneth Troske. 2008. *Workforce Investment Act Non-experimental Net Impact Evaluation.* Washington, DC: U.S. Department of Labor, Employment and Training Administration.

Hirano, Keisuke, Guido W. Imbens, Donald B. Rubin, and Xiao-Hua Zhou. 2000. "Assessing the Effect of an Influenza Vaccine in an Encouragement Design." *Biostatistics* 1(1): 69–88.

Hotz, V. Joseph, and John Scholz. 2001. "Measuring Employment and Income for Low-Income Populations with Administrative and Survey Data." In *Studies of Welfare Populations: Data and Research Issues,* Michele Ver Ploeg, Robert A. Moffitt, and Constance F. Citro, eds. Washington, DC: National Academies Press, pp. 275–315.

Imbens, G., and T. Lemieux. 2008. "Waiting for Life to Arrive: Regression Discontinuity Designs: A Guide to Practice." *Journal of Econometrics* 142(2): 615–635.

Imbens, Guido W., and Jeffrey M. Wooldridge. 2008. "Recent Developments in the Econometrics of Program Evaluation." Institute for Research on Poverty Discussion Paper No. 1340-08. Madison, WI: University of Wisconsin.

LaLonde, Robert J. 1986. "Evaluating the Econometric Evaluations of Employment and Training Programs with Experimental Data." *American Economic Review* 76(4): 604–620.

Levitan, Sar A. 1992. *Evaluation of Federal Social Programs: An Uncertain Impact.* Washington, DC: George Washington University, Center for Social Policy Studies.

Mallar, Charles, Stuart Kerachsky, Craig Thornton, and David Long. 1982. *Evaluation of the Economic Impact of the Job Corps Program.* Washington, DC: U.S. Department of Labor, Employment and Training Administration.

Maynard, Rebecca, Randall Brown, Jennifer Shore, Russell Jackson, Valerie Leach, and Judith Wooldridge. 1979. *Supported Work Demonstration: Effects during the First 18 Months after Enrollment.* Washington, DC: U.S. Department of Labor, Employment and Training Administration. http://www.eric.ed.gov/PDFS/ED197223.pdf (accessed October 13, 2010).

McConnell, Sheena, and Steven Glazerman. 2001. *National Job Corps Study: The Benefits and Costs of Job Corps.* Washington, DC: U.S. Department of Labor, Employment and Training Administration. http://wdr.doleta.gov/opr/fulltext/01-jcbenefit.pdf (accessed October 13, 2010).

McConnell, Sheena, Elizabeth Stuart, Kenneth Fortson, Paul Decker, Irma Perez-Johnson, Barbara Harris, and Jeffrey Salzman. 2006. *Managing Customers' Training Choices: Findings from the Individual Training Account Experiment.* Washington, DC: U.S. Department of Labor, Employment and Training Administration. http://www.mathematica-mpr.com/publications/PDFs/managecustappendices.pdf (accessed October 13, 2010).

Mueser, Peter R., Kenneth R. Troske, and Alexey Gorislavsky. 2007. "Using State Administrative Data to Measure Program Performance." *Review of Economics and Statistics* 89(4): 761–783.

Peikes, Deborah N., Lorenzo Moreno, and Sean Michael Orzol. 2008. "Propensity Score Matching: A Note of Caution for Evaluators of Social Programs." *American Statistician* 62(3): 222–231.

Reich, Robert B. 1997. *Locked in the Cabinet.* New York, NY: Vintage Books.

Rosenbaum, Paul R., and Donald B. Rubin. 1983. "The Central Role of the Propensity Score in Observational Studies for Causal Effects." *Biometrika* 70(1): 41–55.

Schirm, Allen, Elizabeth Stuart, and Allison McKie. 2006. *The Quantum Opportunity Demonstration: Final Impacts.* Washington, DC: U.S. Department of Labor, Employment and Training Administration.

Schochet, Peter Z. 2005 *Evaluation of the Trade Adjustment Assistance Program: Design Report.* Report submitted to the U.S. Department of Labor. Oakland, CA, and Princeton, NJ: Social Policy Research Associates and Mathematica Policy Research.

———. 2009a. "An Approach for Addressing the Multiple Testing Problem in Social Policy Impact Evaluations." *Evaluation Review* 33(6): 539–567.

———. 2009b. "Statistical Power for Regression Discontinuity Designs in Education Evaluations." *Journal of Educational and Behavioral Statistics* 34(2): 238–266.

Schochet, Peter Z., and John Burghardt. 2007. "Using Propensity Scoring to Estimate Program-Related Subgroup Impacts in Experimental Program Evaluations." *Evaluation Review* 31(2): 95–120.

Schochet, Peter Z., John Burghardt, and Sheena McConnell. 2008. "Does Job Corps Work? Impact Findings from the National Job Corps Study." *American Economic Review* 98(5): 1864–1886.

Seftor, Neil, Arif Mamun, and Allen Schirm. 2009. *The Impacts of Regular Upward Bound on Postsecondary Outcomes 7–9 Years after Scheduled High School Graduation.* Report prepared for the U.S. Department of Education, Policy and Program Studies Service. Washington, DC: Mathematica Policy Research, Inc.

Smith, Jeffrey A., and Petra E. Todd. 2005a. "Does Matching Overcome LaLonde's Critique of Nonexperimental Estimators?" *Journal of Econometrics* 125(1–2): 305–353.

———. 2005b. "Rejoinder." *Journal of Econometrics* 125(1–2): 365–375.

Spiegelman, Stephen A., Christopher O'Leary, and Kenneth Kline. 1992. "The Washington Reemployment Bonus Experiment." Unemployment Insurance Occasional Paper No. 92-6. Washington, DC: U.S. Department of Labor.

Woodbury, Stephen A., and Robert G. Spiegelman. 1987. "Bonuses to Workers and Employers to Reduce Unemployment: Randomized Trials in Illinois." *American Economic Review* 77(4): 513–530.

17
Improving Impact Evaluation in Europe

Jeffrey Smith
University of Michigan

This chapter briefly addresses three themes related to the evaluation of active labor market programs (ALMPs), drawing on evidence from the North American experience and contrasting it with current practice in Europe.[1] I begin by making the (measured) case for greater use of random assignment methods in Europe, including both familiar and, I suspect, less familiar, arguments. Second, I make the case for greater (which in many European countries means "any") use of serious cost-benefit analysis as a component of the evaluation of ALMPs. Third, I discuss the organization of the evaluation "industry" in North America and offer some suggestions about lessons it provides for the organization of evaluation in Europe.

The conference came at an opportune time given the explosion in nonexperimental evaluation work related to ALMPs in Europe. The papers by Kluve (2006) and Card, Kluve, and Weber (2009) describe and meta-analyze this work; see also Bergemann and van den Berg (forthcoming). The European Social Fund surely deserves praise for venturing across the pond in search of ways to improve the quality and quantity of this evaluation work (broadly conceived to include performance management). At the same time, I think it well worth noting that the United States and Canada have much to learn from the countries at the top of the European evaluation league tables as well. Lessons worth learning include both the general value of rich, well-maintained, and relatively accessible (to qualified researchers and with appropriate privacy protections) administrative data and the value of specific data elements such as caseworker ratings of the employability of the unemployed and detailed, complete data on educational qualifications. Though this view may generate some controversy, I read the recent nonexperimental evaluations of WIA by Heinrich et al. (2009) and Hollenbeck (2009) as indicating that existing U.S. administrative data systems do not quite have what it takes to provide compelling impact estimates. Perhaps this is not surprising given that the design of current U.S. administrative data systems did not include program evaluation as an objective. On another policy dimension, certain European countries have also done a good job of implementing, documenting, and studying regimes of sanctions for benefit recipients not sufficiently inspired by the "carrot" side of activation policies. Recent examples here include Arni, Lalive, and van Ours (2009), Boockmann, Thomsen, and Walter (2009), and Svarer (2007). The United States has sanctions in some programs, but to my knowledge, not much in the way of good data on them or—what follows immediately from the lack of good data—good studies. A related but different point concerns the sometime conflation in these sorts of discussions of U.S. policy with optimal policy. I make neither the claim that current U.S. policy is optimal in any meaningful sense for the current U.S. context or that all or even most of the good things about current U.S. evaluation policy can easily transfer to Europe. Nonetheless, I will argue for the view that some aspects of U.S. policy and practice suggest reforms worth considering in some (if not all) European countries.

The tremendous heterogeneity among European countries in the current state of research evaluating the performance of ALMPs and, more broadly, the heterogeneity in the relevant political and research institutions and in evaluation capacity also deserve note. Some European countries remain at the very beginning of the process of seriously evaluating their programs, while others have much to teach the North Americans. It nearly goes without saying that different aspects of the North American experience have relevance to different countries in Europe, depending on the current state of play in those countries.

Even on the topics directly covered in this chapter, much remains unsaid due to space limitations. In addition, I have not considered a variety of other topics closely related to the evaluation of ALMPs, such as recent developments in the literature regarding data and methods for nonexperimental evaluations (see, e.g., Dolton and Smith [2010]; Fredriksson and Johansson [2008]; Sianesi [2004]); performance management (see, e.g., Radin [2006]; Barnow and Smith [2004]; and Heckman, Heinrich, and Smith [2002]); statistical treatment rules (see, e.g., Smith and Staghøj [2009] and the references therein); and the broader issue of the role of caseworkers as gatekeepers, monitors, and information providers (see, e.g., Lechner and Smith [2007] and Buurman and Dur [2008]). These omissions reflect not lack of interest or importance but rather division of labor over time and among authors.[2]

EXPERIMENTATION

As a quick perusal of the *Digest of the Social Experiments* (Greenberg and Shroder 2004) makes clear, the United States has conducted the vast majority (indeed, all but a handful) of social experiments, most of them related to active labor market programs, primary and secondary education, and the criminal justice system.[3] The situation has not really changed since the publication of that volume. In the United States, experiments have provided evidence of great value for both policy and for our understanding of social interventions more broadly in areas as diverse as health insurance, electricity pricing, responses to domestic violence, educational interventions related to teachers, schools, and curricula, and of course, ALMPs. Widely hailed in the social science community (see, e.g., Burtless and Orr [1986] and Burtless [1995]), the key advantage of social experiments is that their simple design makes them easy to explain and hard to argue with. This gives them a policy-influencing power not enjoyed by even the cleanest nonexperimental designs.

In addition to these direct benefits, experiments have the under-appreciated benefit of providing high-quality data for other research purposes. In addition to the large literature that uses experimental impact estimates as a benchmark for the study of various combinations of nonexperimental estimators and data (see, e.g., LaLonde [1986], Fraker and Maynard [1987], Heckman and Hotz [1989], Friedlander and Robins [1995], Dehejia and Wahba [1999, 2002], and Smith and Todd [2005a,b]), experiments also have yielded a lot of substantive knowledge, particularly about low-income labor markets, and have provided a platform for methodological analyses of heterogeneous treatment effects that avoid the complications associated with first dealing with selection bias (see, e.g., Heckman, Smith, and Clements [1997], Bitler,

Gelbach, and Hoynes [2006], and Djebbari and Smith [2008]). Experimental data have even helped researchers to learn about structural models (in the sense that economists used that term), as in Todd and Wolpin (2006) and Lise, Seitz, and Smith (2004).

The literature documents a variety of limitations of experimental evaluations relative to nonexperimental evaluations. These limitations weigh against the advantages just discussed. At a most basic level, technological, political, and ethical concerns make it impossible to randomly assign some treatments of great interest, such as gender or family background. Except in unusual circumstances, such as the Progresa evaluation in Mexico, where random assignment took place at the level of relatively isolated villages, experimental evaluations capture only the partial equilibrium effects of policies (see Angelucci and di Giorgio [2009]). Depending on the placement of random assignment in the process of treatment receipt and on the availability of substitutes from other sources, both treatment group dropout and control group substitution often complicate the interpretation of the estimates from experimental evaluations of ALMPs (see the discussions in Heckman, Smith, and Taber [1998] and Heckman et al. [2000]).

The implementation of random assignment sometimes requires institutional changes that may compromise external validity. In the case of the National JTPA Study (NJS), the local sites in the experiment were concerned that the requirement of the design that they serve roughly the same number of participants while also filling a control group would mean digging deeper into the pool of potential participants. Depending on the nature of this pool and of the selection process, doing so could mean serving people with lower expected impacts. Some sites reacted to this by changing the nature of their selection process, e.g., reducing the number of visits to the center required to enroll, so as to reduce the extent of attrition during the process. Obviously, such changes compromise the external validity of the results. The scientific and political desirability of using volunteer sites also has implications for external validity. As documented in Doolittle and Traeger (1990), in the NJS, more than 200 of the (approximately) 600 local service delivery areas were contacted, and a substantial amount of money was spent on side payments in order to induce 16 sites to volunteer to participate, and even then at least one site left the experiment early. This issue often arises in evaluations of educational interventions conducted by the Institute of Education Sciences (IES) at the U.S. Department of Education as well. A related but different point is that heterogeneity in the size and organization of local sites may limit the set of sites at which it makes budgetary sense to do random assignment. The presence of random assignment may also alter the behavior of potential participants in ways that less salient and intrusive nonexperimental methods might not. For example, it might induce additional selection on risk aversion, or it might deter complementary investments. Such changes, sometimes dubbed "randomization bias" in the literature, are distinct from Hawthorne effects, which result from the mere fact of observation, and pose yet another threat to external validity. Heckman and Smith (1995) and Section 5 of Heckman, LaLonde, and Smith (1999) summarize these concerns about experiments.

In addition to these real issues, policymakers and program administrators sometimes offer ethical objections to random assignment. In my experience, these objections nearly always represent a cover for simply not wanting to know the answer. Experiments often provide compelling evidence that treatments do not work at all or do not work well enough to pass a cost-benefit test. Educational researchers have dubbed the What Works Clearinghouse, a formal compendium of quality-rated evidence on the impacts of educational treatments funded by the IES and operated by Mathematica Policy Research, the "Nothing Works Clearinghouse."[4] This usage illustrates the very real empirical pattern that many, maybe most, programs fail when subjected to serious evaluation. Programs that deliver ineffective treatments, and thus do not benefit their participants, still benefit important constituencies, such as the workers and agencies or firms that provide the treatments. Indeed, one sometimes suspects that it is these constituencies, and not the population served, who represent the real reason for the program's existence in the first place. These constituencies have an interest in the production of low-quality (and sometimes deliberately manipulated), nonexperimental evaluations and misleading performance measures in place of compelling experimental (or even nonexperimental) evidence.

One way to confront these specious ethical arguments is to point out what they miss, namely the problematic ethical position of forcing taxpayers to fund programs without any serious evidence that they pass cost-benefit tests when such evidence could easily be produced. Such "speaking truth to power" provides the warm glow of righteous satisfaction and carries some sway with stakeholders not completely in the service of their own narrow interests, but it does not always carry the day.

Variants of random assignment that do not require the complete denial of service to any potential clients constitute another response to the phony ethical arguments offered up against random assignment, as these arguments typically revolve around concerns about service denial. In contexts where some eligible individuals would not receive service anyway, advocates of serious evaluation can (and do) frame random assignment as an equitable way to allocate scarce resources. In contexts where resource constraints do not bind, variants of random assignment that do not assign anyone to a no-services control group can help to derail malicious objections.

The literature offers three variants of random assignment that (more or less) avoid a no-treatment control group. One rather obvious variant consists of random assignment with multiple treatment arms but no control arm. For example, in the WIA context one might randomly assign some clients to only core and intensive services, while excluding them from training services. Another variant consists of a randomized encouragement design, as in Hirano et al. (2000). Here eligible individuals get randomly assigned an incentive to participate. Thus, no one is excluded, but the incentive, when properly designed—learning about the impact of the incentive represents a side benefit of the design—induces exogenous variation in treatment status. The design identifies what the literature calls the local average treatment effect (LATE) rather than the average treatment effect on the treated. Put less technically, this design identifies the mean impact on those induced to participate by the incentive, but not the mean impact on all participants. Whether or not this parameter merits attention depends on the particular policy context. The final design consists of randomization at the margin, as in Black et al. (2003). This design does create a no-treatment control group, but only of individuals on the margin of participation. In the case of the Kentucky Worker Profiling and Reemployment Services System analyzed in Black et al. (2003), the margin consists of individuals whose predicted durations of benefit receipt put them in the last cell of treated individuals in a given local office in a given week. The state was willing to randomize these individuals but not those with long predicted spells. Like the randomized encouragement design, this design does not identify the average treatment effect on the treated, but it does identify the average impact of treatment for individuals at the margin of treatment. This parameter answers a different policy question of what the mean impact would be on individuals brought into the program by an increase in the number of slots. As with the randomized encouragement design, this parameter might have greater or lesser policy importance than the average treatment effect on the treated.

The push for random assignment evaluations of ALMPs (and other policies as well) ultimately has great value. For example, the zero (and sometimes negative) impact estimates for youth in the NJS led to large budget cuts in that program—cuts an order of magnitude larger than the cost of this (quite expensive) evaluation; see the discussion in Heckman and Krueger (2003). The experimental findings from the National Job Corps Study presented in Schochet, Burghardt, and McConnell (2008), which include positive impacts that fade out and so fail to pass a cost-benefit test given the high cost of the program, have led to some serious thinking about that popular and, prior to the evaluation, essentially untouchable program. Some of the IES experimental evaluation results, such as those for the Teach for America Program (Glazerman, Mayer, and Decker 2005), abstinence-only sex education programs (Trenholm et al. 2008), reading and mathematics software (Campuzano et al. 2009), and intensive teacher mentoring programs (Eisenberg et al. 2009), have had real impacts on expenditures and on the course of policy innovation and research. The Europeans can and should get in on this worthwhile game.

COST-BENEFIT ANALYSIS

Cost-benefit analysis combines impact estimates with information on program costs to produce a direct policy conclusion. In the case of impact estimates that capture the average effect of treatment on the treated, a comparison of the impacts with the average cost of the program provides a clear and direct message about the value of a program to the taxpayers who fund it. Historically, many U.S. evaluations have included at least rudimentary cost-benefit analyses. The cost-benefit analysis associated with the National Job Corps Study presented in

Schochet, Burghardt and McConnell (2006) represents a particularly fine example.

In contrast, one can look pretty hard and not find very many European ALMP evaluations that include serious cost-benefit analyses. Munch, Skipper, and Jespersen (2008) provide a notable Danish example, while Raaum, Torp, and Zhang (2002) do the same for Norway. Osikominu (2009) shows a more common situation, with only a very rudimentary comparison of costs and impacts. More generally, and despite these counterexamples, the modal European ALMP evaluation, at least in my experience, contains no cost-benefit analysis at all.

A number of reasons are given for the absence of cost-benefit analysis in European evaluations of ALMPs, the most common of which concerns the European focus on employment impacts, rather than earnings impacts, mainly for political reasons. This focus on employment has led to a lack of good administrative data on earnings in some countries, which makes cost-benefit analysis more challenging, as the researcher (or the literature more broadly) must come up with a compelling way to translate employment impacts into monetary units. In contrast, impacts on earnings, the most common case in North America, fit easily into a cost-benefit framework. Another reason sometimes given for the absence of cost-benefit analyses in Europe relates to the fact that the estimated employment impacts often turn out negative or zero or, in the bright and sunny cases, positive but small enough to make the negative result that would emerge from a serious cost-benefit analysis obvious in advance. This is the "why bother when the programs do not really work anyway" argument, and it has some sense to it.

The lack of good cost data also poses a barrier to serious cost-benefit analysis in many European contexts (and some North American ones as well). Ideally, one would have detailed data on both average and marginal costs for each service offered, broken down geographically in cases where costs varied substantially by, for example, location in a large city, a small city, or a rural area. Instead, researchers often have available little more than the program budget and the total number of persons served.

Both JTPA and WIA have attempted performance standards measures that included a cost component. These have faced real difficulties in assigning costs shared by JTPA or WIA and other programs, as when a variety of programs, often each having multiple funding sources, all share a common physical location as a One-Stop center. These common cost allocation issues (and others) are real and challenging, and carry over directly from performance measures to the problem of creating meaningful cost information for use in cost-benefit calculations. At the same time, private firms face similar difficulties and a large literature and equally large body of empirical practice in accounting lay out reasonable ways to deal with them.

In addition to its value at informing decisions about keeping or dropping programs, cost-benefit analysis has the further benefit of encouraging thinking about important aspects of program design and evaluation, and of public policy more generally. First, it encourages thinking about the outcomes an ALMP will affect. A focus on outcomes other than just earnings, in particular on crime, represents one of the notable aspects of the Job Corp cost-benefit analysis highlighted earlier. Not only do impacts on crime account for much of the gross impact of the program, particularly in the short term, their presence tells us a lot about how the program works, and suggests other possible treatments that might well pass a cost-benefit analysis.

Thinking about outcomes and about the behavioral theory that links treatments to outcomes also leads to a salutary focus on the possible general equilibrium effects (which include spillovers or displacement effects) of programs. Johnson (1980) and Calmfors (1994) are classic references; see Lise, Seitz, and Smith (2004) and the citations it contains for pointers to the more recent (and still much too small) literature. While difficult to estimate, they deserve a place in cost-benefit analyses, if only in the form of a sensitivity analysis using informal estimates drawn from the broader literature.

Thinking about cost-benefit analysis in a serious way also highlights the importance of learning about the duration of program impacts. Most evaluations of ALMPs provide only a year or two of follow-up. The available evidence on longer-term impacts suggests that sometimes impacts remain remarkably steady over time for years after an intervention, as in the National Supported Work Demonstration (Couch 1992) and the National JTPA Study (GAO 1996); other times they fade out, as in the National Job Corps Study (Schochet, Burghardt, and McConnell 2008) and the California GAIN program (Hotz, Imbens, and Klerman, 2006); and other times they appear only belatedly, as in the evaluation of German training programs by Lechner, Miquel, and Wunsch

(2004). The absence of both a clear general empirical pattern and compelling theory on when estimates should persist and when not suggests the value of more frequently undertaking long-term follow-up, so as to minimize the impact of extrapolation of the sort described in Heckman, LaLonde, and Smith (1999).

Finally, paying attention to cost-benefit analysis focuses policy and research attention on two important parameters: the discount rate and the marginal social cost of public funds or "excess burden." Having a well-justified social discount rate for use in government budgeting and investment decisions represents a basic task of public finance economists. As noted in Heckman, LaLonde, and Smith (1999), the discount rate employed to bring future net impacts (and costs, if applicable) forward in time to the present can affect the outcome of a cost-benefit analysis. Also important, and routinely ignored in North American cost-benefit analyses (including otherwise exemplary ones like that from the Job Corp evaluation), is the fact that a dollar of government budget for ALMPs costs society more than a dollar, both because the operation of the tax system directly consumes real resources (all those cheery Internal Revenue Service agents have to get paid) and because all developed countries rely on distortionary tax systems. While estimates of the marginal social cost of public funds vary widely in the literature even for specific countries, and we would expect them to vary across countries due to differences in tax systems and tax rates and other institutional features, the estimates never equal zero and often reach magnitudes that suggest the policy importance of incorporating this factor into cost-benefit analyses and thereby into decisions about program existence and funding (see, e.g., Auerbach and Hines [2002] for a survey).

In sum, cost-benefit analysis represents a useful tool, both in a direct sense via its role in clarifying and systematizing decisions about program existence, expansion, or contraction, and indirectly via its direction of policy and research attention to important, but often neglected, issues of program design and impact and of public finance more broadly.

ORGANIZING EVALUATION RESEARCH

Surprisingly little research seeks to document and explain differences in the quantity and quality of ALMP evaluation across countries. I am aware of Riddell (1991) and not much else. Given the heterogeneity in both quality and quantity obvious even to the most casual observer, this gap in the literature comes as a surprise. Filling the gap represents a worthy task for researchers. Because of this gap, my remarks here rely mainly on my own observations as a scholar studying evaluation methods, a provider of evaluation short courses to graduate students at various locations in Europe, a referee and editor handling academic evaluations, and an occasional evaluation consultant as well as on discussions with friends in the academic and policy worlds. The lack of quantitative evidence on national variation in quality and quantity necessitates the following caveat: I am well aware that low-quality research, such as PriceWaterhouseCoopers (2004, p. 15), with its smiley faces and confusion of outcome levels and impacts, or Gregory (2000), with its distinctive "sites of oppression matrix" evaluation tool, appear everywhere, including the United States and Canada, because of the universal demand for evaluation reports that promote the views of interested parties while providing an appearance of technical understanding and objectivity sufficient to fool the reading public.

I will argue that differences in the quality and quantity of evaluation research across countries result from much more than simply differences in the industrial organization of the evaluation industry, but those differences play a role and make a good place to start my discussion. The evaluation industry in the United States combines government, private for-profit firms, private nonprofit firms, and academia in remarkable and complex ways that differ across program types. For ALMPs, both nonprofit and for-profit firms, operating on contract to the USDOL, have undertaken many of the evaluations of large programs such as JTPA, WIA, the Job Corps, the Trade Adjustment Act, and so on. Additional evaluation work is performed by academics operating with research funding from places like the National Science Foundation or private foundations; this work often uses data from the original USDOL-funded evaluations, as with the long series of papers by Heckman and various coauthors using the data from the NJS; see Heckman et al. (1998) for an example. Other evaluation work, including process evaluation work, is also often contracted out to a somewhat wider set of firms than the small number of large firms (e.g., Abt, Mathematica, MDRC, etc.) with the capacity to undertake large evaluations. These firms compete in both the product market and the labor market; at least in regard to economists, they compete for the same newly minted doctorates as academic economics departments just outside the top 20. Some evaluation work is also done in-house at the USDOL, whose staff includes people trained in economics at the doctoral level. A similar pattern holds in the education world, though probably with more academic involvement in the actual performance of the evaluation work, as opposed to simply advising or undertaking secondary analyses using the data generated by evaluations conducted by others.

What makes the European evaluation market different from the North American ones? First, some European countries have an important player in their markets that is absent in the United States in the form of (mostly or entirely) government-supported research institutes devoted to labor market policy and evaluation that operate (more or less) at "arm's length" from the government itself. I have in mind here the IFAU in Sweden and the various institutes in Germany (e.g., the ZEW in Mannheim, the IZA in Bonn, the DIW in Berlin, and the RWI in Essen). My understanding is that these institutes both have base funding and do work on contract. They maintain a remarkable degree of independence, in the sense that they routinely report evaluation results indicating that ALMPs have zero or even negative impacts (and other more humorous but still somewhat embarrassing-to-the-government findings such as paternal leave being more common during hunting season and such like).

Neither the United States nor Canada has any direct analog to these institutes. The GAO does some work along the lines of process and implementation evaluation, but not much in the way of econometric impact evaluation.[5] The closest analogue in Canada, the Auditor General, is even less like the European Institutes. The U.S. Congressional Research Service largely confines itself to literature surveys. While I could imagine the Canadians setting up something like the IFAU, I find it hard to imagine the United States doing so, in part because it would present real competition to the various DC think tanks. These institutes represent a valuable component of the European scene, and countries that do not have them ought to reconsider.

Size represents a second important contrast between the evaluation market in the United States and that in Europe (and in Canada, for that matter). Size has two relevant dimensions here. The first is the simple magnitude of evaluation research going on. The United States spends quite a lot of money on evaluation in a number of policy areas, including for programs that it funds in developing countries. To the extent that evaluation firms, whether for-profit or not-for-profit, have economies of scale over some range, a larger market can support more firms and thus allow more competition between firms. The second dimension of size concerns the number of potential clients for evaluation research firms. My sense is that evaluation firms in the United States face many more potential clients both at the national level (where they might deal with the departments of labor, education, housing and urban development, health and human services, homeland security, transportation, agriculture, and so on, and in some cases even separate parts of particular departments), as well as the development banks, states and larger cities, and private foundations. This diversity of potential clients reduces the dependence of the firm on repeated interactions with a single client and thus, I think, reduces the potential costs associated with catering to the truth rather than to the client agency. Firms in smaller European countries with highly centralized governments and no private foundations may face a much, much smaller number of potential clients and thus face much stronger pressure to bend to the client's wishes of the moment.

One easy way to increase the size of the European evaluation market is for that market to become truly European rather than national. At present, I am aware of very little evaluation work that happens across boundaries in Europe. Transforming small national markets into a much larger European market would allow greater competition between providers and would give firms more freedom to avoid clients seeking a particular answer rather than necessarily the correct answer. I think entry by the major U.S. firms into the European market would aid in these developments. This has happened in a very limited way in the UK, with MDRC playing a role in the experimental evaluation of the Employment Retention and Advancement Demonstration (Miller et al. 2008). More activity on this front would, in my view, bring great benefits.[6]

In this context, the Association for Public Policy and Management (APPAM) is important because it fosters interactions between academics, government consumers and producers of evaluation research, evaluation firms, and policy people interested in the results of evaluations. Bringing these groups together, both via the annual meetings and via APPAM's publications and other activities, represents an important contribution not duplicated, to my knowledge, by any European organization. Efforts to replicate APPAM in Europe, with some linkages and occasional joint conferences as with the Society for Labor Economics in North America and its younger European compatriot the European Association of Labor Economists, would add value.

Finally, you have to want it. At a narrow level, this means having at least some people in government who care about evidence more than they care about the party line or about their narrow bureaucratic imperatives of budget increase and career advancement. It needs to encompass both the levels of administration that change at election time and those that do not. It also means that some people at both levels have to understand enough about evaluation to know what to ask for and to evaluate what gets produced in response. I think the U.S. practice of having serious academics spend brief stints in the national administration, say, as chief economist at the USDOL or on the Council of Economic Advisers, plays an important role in the (very much relative) success the United States has had on this dimension, and commend such institutions to European governments. The temporary nature of the appointments matters here precisely because you do not want the academics to assimilate into the bureaucratic culture. Rather, you want them to maintain their outsider perspective and their academic devotion to getting the right answer (helped along by the threat of ridicule from their university friends and colleagues if they sell out).

The George W. Bush administration provides a useful illustration here. At the Labor Department, evaluation research became a low priority during this administration. More broadly, the department had such a poor reputation in regard to its interest in evidence that it could not manage to fill the chief economist position with a serious academic economist (for eight years!). Contrast this to the distinguished list of chief economists under Clinton, which included Larry Katz and Alan Krueger. In contrast, less than one mile away, the U.S. Department of Education—in particular, the IES under Russ Whitehurst—made a serious run at transforming the entire field of educational policy evaluation through a program of experimental and high-quality nonexperimental evaluations, as well as the funding of a training grant program to create a generation of new, quantitative, serious education policy evaluators with disciplinary roots at least partially outside of traditional schools of education (see the discussion in IES [2008]). How do you create more places like IES? I must confess that I do not have a good answer here, but we should be thinking about it, because doing so has a very high payoff indeed.

More broadly, the demand for serious program evaluation has to come from somewhere. It can come from leaders within government. It can come from actors outside government, such as the media and public intellectuals. It can come from the general public. But it must come from somewhere. Casual empiricism suggests a link at the country level between the quality and quantity of evaluation and the imprint of neoclassical economics. Countries with long neoclassical traditions, including the UK, the Netherlands, and the Nordic countries, are pretty much the same as those with long traditions of serious research devoted to the evaluation of social programs. Looking within countries, Germany has gotten serious about empirical evaluation research only in the last 15 years or so, a time period that coincides with the triumph of neoclassical economics within academic economics in that country. This observed link between the demand for evaluation and neoclassical economics might reflect a causal relationship. Alternatively, both demand for serious policy evaluation and the dominance of neoclassical economics may reflect broader and deeper differences across countries in individualism, deference to authority, the importance of social class, average education, and so on. Regardless of whether the current relationship reflects causality or not, one might argue that increasing the number of individuals trained in economics, particularly a practical version of economics rather than just high theory or theoretical econometrics, at both the undergraduate and graduate levels might represent a long-term strategy for increasing the demand for quality policy evaluation, as well as the ability to supply it with domestic labor. Who knows, it might even improve European agricultural policy as well!

CONCLUDING REMARKS

This chapter has touched on three important areas where the European Social Fund can learn from the North American experience in evaluating ALMPs. I have argued that current European practice lies very far from the point where the marginal value of additional experimental evaluations would equal their marginal cost. I have also argued that Europe would benefit from much greater attention to careful cost-benefit analysis following evaluation. Such analyses would allow the evaluation results to provide more guidance to policy and, more broadly, would increase our understanding of how policy works and so aid in the design of future policies. Finally, I have argued that much room remains for improving the organization of evaluation in Europe. The European environment includes distinctive and valuable aspects not present in North America, but could usefully incorporate aspects of the North American experience as it seeks to improve the overall quality of European evaluations.

Notes

My thoughts on the issues discussed in this chapter have benefited from my interactions with a number of scholars over the years, including (but not limited to) Jim Heckman, Dan Black, Michael Lechner, Carolyn Heinrich, Burt Barnow, Lars Skipper, and Arthur Sweetman. I am very grateful for those interactions, and for comments from Jessica Goldberg, but, of course, retain all responsibility for the (occasionally provocative) views expressed here.

1. I use *North American* in the Canadian manner to mean the United States and Canada but not Mexico.
2. See Smith (2000, 2004) for broad nontechnical surveys of evaluation methodology. See Heckman, LaLonde, and Smith (1999), Imbens and Wooldridge (2009), and Blundell and Costa-Dias (2009) for somewhat more technical surveys. See Heckman and Abbring (2007) and Heckman and Vytlacil (2007a,b) for recent technical overviews.
3. I distinguish here between social experiments and both laboratory experiments under fully controlled conditions and the small-scale field experiments that have taken the development literature by storm over the last decade. For discussions and categorizations, see, e.g., Levitt and List (2009) and Banerjee and Duflo (2009).
4. The What Works Clearinghouse can be found at http://ies.ed.gov/ncee/wwc/.

5. For an exception, see GAO (1996), which presents long-term impact estimates for the JTPA experiment using administrative data.
6. This same point applies to Canada as well.

References

Angelucci, Manuela, and Giacomo di Giorgio. 2009. "Indirect Effects of an Aid Program: How Do Cash Transfers Affect Ineligibles' Consumption?" *American Economic Review* 99(1): 486–508.

Arni, Patrick, Rafael Lalive, and Jan van Ours. 2009. "How Effective Are Unemployment Benefit Sanctions? Looking Beyond Unemployment Exit." IZA Discussion Paper No. 4509. Bonn: IZA.

Auerbach, Alan, and James Hines. 2002. "Taxation and Economic Efficiency." In *Handbook of Public Finance, Volume 3*, Alan Auerbach and Martin Feldstein, eds. Amsterdam: North-Holland, pp. 1347–1421.

Banerjee, Abhijit, and Esther Duflo. 2009. "The Experimental Approach to Development Economics." *Annual Review of Economics* 1: 151–178.

Barnow, Burt, and Jeffrey Smith. 2004. "Performance Management of U.S. Job Training Programs: Lessons from the Job Training Partnership Act." *Public Finance and Management* 4(3): 247–287.

Bergemann, Annette, and Gerard van den Berg. 2008. "Active Labor Market Policy Effects for Women in Europe—A Survey." *Annales d'Economie et de Statistique* 91/92: 385–408.

Bitler, Marianne, Jonah Gelbach, and Hilary Hoynes. 2006. "What Mean Impacts Miss: Distributional Effects of Welfare Reform Experiments." *American Economic Review* 96(4): 988–1012.

Black, Dan, Jeffrey Smith, Mark Berger, and Brett Noel. 2003. "Is the Threat of Reemployment Services More Effective than the Services Themselves? Evidence from Random Assignment in the UI System." *American Economic Review* 93(4): 1313–1327.

Blundell, Richard, and Monica Costa-Dias. 2009. "Alternative Approaches to Evaluation in Empirical Microeconomics." *Journal of Human Resources* 44(3): 565–640.

Boockmann, Bernhard, Stephan Thomsen, and Thomas Walter. 2009. "Intensifying the Use of Benefit Sanctions—An Effective Tool to Shorten Welfare Receipt and Speed Up Transitions to Employment?" Unpublished manuscript. Universität Magdeburg, Magdeburg, Germany.

Burtless, Gary. 1995. "The Case for Randomized Field Trials in Economic and Policy Research." *Journal of Economic Perspectives* 9(2): 63–84.

Burtless, Gary, and Larry Orr. 1986. "Are Classical Experiments Needed for Manpower Policy?" *Journal of Human Resources* 21(4): 606–639.

Buurman, Margaretha, and Robert Dur. 2008. "Incentives and the Sorting of Altruistic Agents into Street-Level Bureaucracies." IZA Discussion Paper No. 3847. Bonn: IZA.

Calmfors, Lars. 1994. "Active Labour Market Policy and Unemployment: A Framework for the Analysis of Crucial Design Features." *OECD Economic Studies* 22: 7–47.

Campuzano, Larissa, Mark Dynarski, Roberto Agodini, and Kristina Rall. 2009. *Effectiveness of Reading and Mathematics Software Products Findings from Two Student Cohorts.* NCEE 2009-4041. Washington, DC: National Center for Education Evaluation and Regional Assistance, Institute of Education Sciences, U.S. Department of Education.

Card, David, Jochen Kluve, and Andrea Weber. 2009. "Active Labor Market Policy Evaluations: A Meta-Analysis." IZA Discussion Paper No. 4002. Bonn: IZA.

Couch, Kenneth. 1992. "New Evidence on the Long-Term Effects of Employment Training Programs." *Journal of Labor Economics* 10(4): 380–388.

Dehejia, Rajeev, and Sadek Wahba. 1999. "Causal Effects in Nonexperimental Studies: Reevaluating the Evaluation of Training Programs." *Journal of the American Statistical Association.* 94(448): 1053–1062.

———. 2002. "Propensity Score Matching Methods for Non-experimental Causal Studies." *Review of Economics and Statistics* 84(1): 151–161.

Djebbari, Habiba, and Jeffrey Smith. 2008. "Heterogeneous Program Impacts: Experimental Evidence from the PROGRESA Program." *Journal of Econometrics* 145(1–2): 64–80.

Dolton, Peter, and Jeffrey Smith. 2010. "The Econometric Evaluation of the New Deal for Lone Parents." Unpublished manuscript. University of Michigan, Ann Arbor.

Doolittle, Frederick, and Linda Traeger. 1990. *Implementing the National JTPA Study.* New York: Manpower Demonstration Research Corporation.

Eisenberg, Erik, Steven Glazerman, Martha Bleeker, Amy Johnson, Julieta Lugo-Gil, Mary Grider, and Sarah Dolfin. 2009. *Impacts of Comprehensive Teacher Induction: Results from the Second Year of a Randomized Controlled Study,* NCEE 2009-4072. Washington, DC: National Center for Education Evaluation and Regional Assistance, Institute of Education Sciences, U.S. Department of Education.

Fraker, Thomas, and Rebecca Maynard. 1987. "The Adequacy of Comparison Group Designs for Evaluation of Employment-Related Programs." *Journal of Human Resources* 22(2): 194–227.

Fredriksson, Peter, and Per Johansson. 2008. "Program Evaluation and Random Program Starts." *Journal of Business and Economic Statistics* 26(4): 435–445.

Friedlander, Daniel, and Philip Robins. 1995. "Evaluating Program Evaluations: New Evidence on Commonly Used Nonexperimental Methods." *American Economic Review* 85(4): 923–937.

Glazerman, Steven, Daniel Mayer, and Paul Decker. 2005. "Alternative Routes to Teaching: The Impacts of Teach for America on Student Achievement and Other Outcomes." *Journal of Policy Analysis and Management* 25(1): 75–96.

Government Accountability Office (GAO). 1996. *Job Training Partnership Act: Long-Term Earnings and Employment Outcomes*. Report HEHS-96-40. Washington, DC: U.S. Government Printing Office.

Greenberg, David, and Mark Shroder. 2004. *Digest of the Social Experiments*. 3rd ed. Washington, DC: Urban Institute Press.

Gregory, Amanda. 2000. "Problematizing Participation: A Critical Review of Approaches to Participation in Evaluation Theory." *Evaluation* 6(2): 179–199.

Heckman, James J., and Jaap Abbring. 2007. "Econometric Evaluation of Social Programs, Part III: Distributional Treatment Effects, Dynamic Treatment Effects, Dynamic Discrete Choice, and General Equilibrium Policy Evaluation." In *Handbook of Econometrics, Volume 6B*, James J. Heckman and Edward Leamer, eds. Amsterdam: Elsevier, pp. 5145–5303.

Heckman, James J., Carolyn Heinrich, and Jeffrey Smith. 2002. "The Performance of Performance Standards." *Journal of Human Resources* 37(4): 778–811.

Heckman, James J., Neil Hohmann, Jeffrey Smith, and Michael Khoo. 2000. "Substitution and Dropout Bias in Social Experiments: A Study of an Influential Social Experiment." *Quarterly Journal of Economics* 115(2): 651–694.

Heckman, James J., and V. Joseph Hotz. 1989. "Choosing among Alternative Methods of Estimating the Impact of Social Programs: The Case of Manpower Training." *Journal of the American Statistical Association* 84(408): 862–874.

Heckman, James J., Hidehiko Ichimura, Jeffrey Smith, and Petra Todd. 1998. "Characterizing Selection Bias Using Experimental Data." *Econometrica* 66(5): 1017–1098.

Heckman, James J., and Alan Krueger. 2003. *Inequality in America: What Role for Human Capital Policies*. Cambridge, MA: MIT Press.

Heckman, James J., and Jeffrey Smith. 1995. "Assessing the Case for Social Experiments." *Journal of Economic Perspectives* 9(2): 85–110.

Heckman, James J., Robert LaLonde, and Jeffrey Smith. 1999. "The Economics and Econometrics of Active Labor Market Programs." In *Handbook of Labor Economics, Volume 3A*, Orley Ashenfelter and David Card, eds. Amsterdam: North Holland, pp. 1865–2097.

Heckman, James J., Jeffrey Smith, and Nancy Clements. 1997. "Making the Most Out of Programme Evaluations and Social Experiments: Accounting for Heterogeneity in Programme Impacts." *Review of Economic Studies* 64(4): 487–535.

Heckman, James J., Jeffrey Smith, and Christopher Taber. 1998. "Accounting for Dropouts in Evaluations of Social Programs." *Review of Economics and Statistics* 80(1): 1–14.

Heckman, James J., and Edward Vytlacil. 2007a. "Econometric Evaluation of Social Programs, Part I: Causal Models, Structural Models and Econometric Policy Evaluation." In *Handbook of Econometrics, Volume 6B*, James J. Heckman and Edward Leamer, eds. Amsterdam: Elsevier, pp. 4779–4874.

———. 2007b. "Econometric Evaluation of Social Programs, Part II: Using the Marginal Treatment Effect to Organize Alternative Economic Estimators to Evaluate Social Programs and to Forecast Their Effects in New Environments." In *Handbook of Econometrics, Volume 6B*, James J. Heckman and Edward Leamer, eds. Amsterdam: Elsevier, pp. 4875–5144.

Heinrich, Carolyn, Peter Mueser, Kenneth Troske, Kyung-Seong Jeon, and Daver Kahvecioglu. 2009. "New Estimates of Public Employment and Training Program Net Impacts: A Nonexperimental Evaluation of the Workforce Investment Act Program." IZA Discussion Paper No. 4569. Bonn: IZA.

Hirano, Kei, Guido Imbens, Donald Rubin, and Xiao-Hua Zhou. 2000. "Assessing the Effect of an Influenza Vaccine in an Encouragement Design." *Biostatistics* 1: 69–88.

Hollenbeck, Kevin. 2009. "Workforce Investment Act (WIA) Net Impact Estimates and Rates of Return." Unpublished manuscript. W.E. Upjohn Institute for Employment Research, Kalamazoo, MI. See http://research.upjohn.org/confpapers/2/ (accessed April 7, 2011).

Hotz, V. Joseph, Guido Imbens, and Jacob Klerman. 2006. "Evaluating the Differential Effects of Alternative Welfare-to-Work Training Components: A Re-Analysis of the California GAIN Program." *Journal of Labor Economics* 24(3): 521–566.

Imbens, Guido, and Jeffrey Wooldridge. 2009. "Recent Developments in the Econometrics of Program Evaluation." *Journal of Economic Literature* 47(1): 5–86.

Institute of Education Sciences, U.S. Department of Education (IES). 2008. *Rigor and Relevance Redux: Director's Biennial Report to Congress.* IES 2009-6010. Washington, DC: IES.

Johnson, George. 1980. "The Theory of Labor Market Intervention." *Economica* 47(187): 309–329.

Kluve, Jochen. 2006. "The Effectiveness of European Active Labor Market Policies." IZA Discussion Paper No. 2018. Bonn: IZA.

LaLonde, Robert. 1986. "Evaluating the Econometric Evaluations of Training Programs with Experimental Data." *American Economic Review* 76(4): 604–620.

Lechner, Michael, Ruth Miquel, and Conny Wunsch. 2004. "Long-Run Effects of Public Sector Sponsored Training in West Germany." IZA Discussion Paper No. 1443. Bonn: IZA.

Lechner, Michael, and Jeffrey Smith. 2007. "What Is the Value Added by Caseworkers?" *Labour Economics* 14(2): 135–151.

Levitt, Steven, and John List. 2009. "Field Experiments in Economics: The Past, the Present, and the Future." *European Economic Review* 53(1): 1–18.

Lise, Jeremy, Shannon Seitz, and Jeffrey Smith. 2004. "Equilibrium Policy Experiments and the Evaluation of Social Programs." NBER Working Paper No. 10283. Cambridge, MA: NBER.

Miller, Cynthia, Helen Bewley, Verity Campbell-Barr, Richard Dorsett, Gayle Hamilton, Lesley Hoggart, Tatiana Homonoff, Alan Marsh, Kathryn Ray, James Riccio, and Sandra Vegeris. 2008. *Employment Retention and Advancement (ERA) Demonstration: Implementation and Second-Year Impacts for New Deal 25 Plus Customers in the UK*. New York: MDRC.

Munch, Jakob, Lars Skipper, and Svend Jespersen. 2008. "Costs and Benefits of Danish Active Labour Market Programmes." *Labour Economics* 15(5): 859–884.

Osikominu, Aderonke. 2009. "Quick Job Entry or Long-Term Human Capital Development? The Dynamic Effects of Alternative Training Schemes." Unpublished manuscript. Breisgau, Germany: Albert-Ludwigs Universität Freiburg.

PriceWaterhouseCoopers. 2004. *New Deal 25+ Evaluation Report No. 9*. London: Department for Employment and Learning. http://www.delni.gov.uk/new_deal25plus_final_report.pdf (accessed November 20, 2010).

Raaum, Oddbjørn, Hege Torp, and Tao Zhang. 2002. "Do Individual Programme Effects Exceed the Costs? Norwegian Evidence on Long Run Effects of Labour Market Training." Memorandum No. 15/2002. Oslo: Department of Economics, University of Oslo.

Radin, Beryl. 2006. *Challenging the Performance Movement: Accountability, Complexity and Democratic Values*. Washington, DC: Georgetown University Press.

Riddell, Craig. 1991. "Evaluation of Manpower and Training Programs: The North American Experience." In *The Evaluation of Manpower, Training and Social Programs: The State of a Complex Art*. Paris: OECD, pp. 43–72.

Schochet, Peter, John Burghardt, and Sheena McConnell. 2006. *National Job Corps Study and Longer-Term Follow-Up Study: Impact and Benefit-Cost Findings Using Survey and Summary Earnings Records Data, Final Report*. Washington, DC: Mathematica Policy Research.

———. 2008. "Does Job Corps Work? Impact Findings from the National Job Corps Study." *American Economic Review* 98(5): 1864–1886.

Sianesi, Barbara. 2004. "An Evaluation of the Swedish System of Active Labor Market Programs in the 1990s." *Review of Economics and Statistics* 86(1): 133–155.

Smith, Jeffrey. 2000. "A Critical Survey of Empirical Methods for Evaluating Employment and Training Programs." *Schweizerische Zeitschrift für Volkswirtschaft und Statistik* 136(3): 247–268.

———. 2004. "Evaluating Local Economic Development Policies: Theory and Practice." In *Evaluating Local Economic and Employment Development: How to Assess What Works among Programmes and Policies*, Alistair Nolan and Ging Wong, eds. Paris: OECD, pp. 287–332.

Smith, Jeffrey, and Jonas Staghøj. 2009. "Using Statistical Treatment Rules for Assignment of Participants in Labor Market Programs." Unpublished manuscript. University of Michigan, Ann Arbor.

Smith, Jeffrey, and Petra Todd. 2005a. "Does Matching Overcome LaLonde's Critique of Nonexperimental Methods?" *Journal of Econometrics* 125(1–2): 305–353.

———. 2005b. "Rejoinder." *Journal of Econometrics* 125(1–2): 365–375.

Svarer, Michael. 2007. "The Effect of Sanctions on the Job Finding Rate: Evidence from Denmark." IZA Discussion Paper No. 3015. Bonn: IZA.

Todd, Petra, and Kenneth Wolpin. 2006. "Assessing the Impact of a School Subsidy Program in Mexico: Using a Social Experiment to Validate a Dynamic Behavioral Model of Child Schooling and Fertility." *American Economic Review* 96(5): 1384–1417.

Trenholm, Christopher, Barbara Devaney, Kenneth Fortson, Melissa Clark, Lisa Quay, and Justin Wheeler. 2008. "Impacts of Abstinence Education on Teen Sexual Activity, Risk of Pregnancy, and Risk of Sexually Transmitted Diseases." *Journal of Policy Analysis and Management* 27(2): 255–276.

Authors

Burt S. Barnow is the Amsterdam Professor of Public Service and Economics at the Trachtenberg School of Public Policy and Public Administration at George Washington University.

Timothy J. Bartik is a senior economist at the W.E. Upjohn Institute for Employment Research.

Stephen H. Bell is an Abt Fellow and a principal associate/scientist in the Social and Economic Policy Division at Abt Associates Inc.

Douglas J. Besharov is a professor at the University of Maryland's School of Public Policy, where he teaches courses on poverty, welfare, children and families, policy analysis, program evaluation, and performance management, and he is director of the Welfare Reform Academy and the Center for International Policy Exchanges at the University of Maryland.

Dianne Blank is an assistant director in the Education, Workforce, and Income Security Team of the U.S. Government Accountability Office.

William S. Borden is director of Mathematica's Performance Management Group, which develops, tests, and implements high quality performance management systems.

Phoebe H. Cottingham recently retired from the position of commissioner of the National Center for Education Evaluation and Regional Assistance, within the U.S. Department of Education's Institute of Education Sciences.

Paul T. Decker is president and chief executive officer at Mathematica Policy Research.

Randall W. Eberts is president of the W.E. Upjohn Institute for Employment Research.

Cynthia M. Fagnoni recently retired as the managing director of the Education, Workforce, and Income Security Team of the U.S. Government Accountability Office.

Aaron Fichtner is assistant commissioner for Labor Planning and Analysis at the New Jersey Department of Labor and Workforce Development. When he wrote his chapter for this book, he was director of research and evaluation at the Heldrich Center for Workforce Development at Rutgers University.

Laura Heald is an assistant director in the Education, Workforce, and Income Security Team of the U.S. Government Accountability Office.

David Heaney is senior vice president of MAXIMUS, Inc., which provides consulting, program management, and business process outsourcing solutions to government.

Carolyn J. Heinrich teaches at and is the director of the University of Wisconsin-Madison's LaFollette School of Public Affairs; she is also an affiliated professor of economics and the Regina Loughlin Scholar.

Kevin Hollenbeck is a senior economist and the vice president of the W.E Upjohn Institute for Employment Research and is the director of Upjohn Institute Publications.

Wei-Jang Huang is a senior research analyst at the W.E. Upjohn Institute for Employment Research.

Kyung-Seong Jeon is a research associate in the Department of Economics at the University of Missouri-Columbia.

Haeil Jung is an assistant professor at Indiana University's School of Public and Environmental Affairs.

Daver C. Kahvecioglu is a research associate at IMPAQ International in Columbia, MD, and he specializes in labor and health economics.

Christopher King is director of and a senior research scientist at the Ray Marshall Center for the Study of Human Resources, and a lecturer at the University of Texas at Austin's Lyndon B. Johnson School of Public Affairs, where he currently holds the Mike Hogg Professorship in Urban Management.

Jacob A. Klerman is a principal associate in the Social and Economic Policy Division at Abt Associates Inc.

David A. Long works with Abt Associates Inc.

Alberto Martini is an associate professor of statistics and public policy evaluation at the Università del Piemonte Orientale.

Sheena McConnell is a senior fellow and associate director of research at Mathematica, specializing in policies to promote employment and strong families in disadvantaged populations.

Peter R. Mueser is a professor in the Department of Economics and in the Harry S. Truman School of Public Affairs at the University of Missouri–Columbia.

Larry L. Orr is currently an independent consultant and a member of the faculty of the Institute for Policy Studies at Johns Hopkins University. Formerly he was the chief economist and the vice president of Abt Associates Inc.

Maureen A. Pirog is the Rudy Professor of Public and Environmental Affairs at Indiana University and is the editor-in-chief of the *Journal of Policy Analysis and Management.*

Peter Schochet is a senior fellow and senior economist at Mathematica, specializing in experimental and nonexperimental evaluations of interventions in education, employment, and welfare.

Jeffrey Smith is a professor in the Department of Economics at the University of Michigan and a research associate at the National Bureau of Economic Research.

Kenneth R. Troske is the William B. Sturgill Professor of Economics, the Chair of the Economics Department, and the director of the Center for Business and Economic Research at the University of Kentucky.

Carl E. Van Horn is a professor at Rutgers's Edward J. Bloustein School of Planning and Public Policy and is the founding director of the Heldrich Center for Workforce Development.

Stephen A. Wandner is a visiting fellow at the Urban Institute and was formerly a senior economist at the U.S. Department of Labor.

Michael Wiseman is a research professor of public policy, public administration, and economics at the George Washington University and a visiting scholar in the Department of Agriculture's Economic Research Service.

Index

The italic letters *f*, *n*, and *t* following a page number indicate that the subject information of the heading is within a figure, note, or table, respectively, on that page. Double italics indicate multiple but consecutive elements.

About the Institute

The W.E. Upjohn Institute for Employment Research is a nonprofit research organization devoted to finding and promoting solutions to employment-related problems at the national, state, and local levels. It is an activity of the W.E. Upjohn Unemployment Trustee Corporation, which was established in 1932 to administer a fund set aside by Dr. W.E. Upjohn, founder of The Upjohn Company, to seek ways to counteract the loss of employment income during economic downturns.

The Institute is funded largely by income from the W.E. Upjohn Unemployment Trust, supplemented by outside grants, contracts, and sales of publications. Activities of the Institute comprise the following elements: 1) a research program conducted by a resident staff of professional social scientists; 2) a competitive grant program, which expands and complements the internal research program by providing financial support to researchers outside the Institute; 3) a publications program, which provides the major vehicle for disseminating the research of staff and grantees, as well as other selected works in the field; and 4) an Employment Management Services division, which manages most of the publicly funded employment and training programs in the local area.

The broad objectives of the Institute's research, grant, and publication programs are to 1) promote scholarship and experimentation on issues of public and private employment and unemployment policy, and 2) make knowledge and scholarship relevant and useful to policymakers in their pursuit of solutions to employment and unemployment problems.

Current areas of concentration for these programs include causes, consequences, and measures to alleviate unemployment; social insurance and income maintenance programs; compensation; workforce quality; work arrangements; family labor issues; labor-management relations; and regional economic development and local labor markets.